The
SANTA FE & TAOS
Book

A Complete Guide

Karen Klitgaard

THE
SANTA FE & TAOS
BOOK

A Complete Guide

FOURTH EDITION

SHARON NIEDERMAN
and
BRANDT MORGAN
with Keith Easthouse and Ramona Gault

Berkshire House Publishers
Lee, Massachusetts

On the cover and frontispiece:
Front Cover: *Cliffs and clouds, Echo Amphitheatre State Park, Abiquiu.* Photo © Robin Mitchell.
Frontispiece: *The Wheelwright Museum gift shop, known as the Case Trading Post, is packed floor to ceiling with the best in Navajo rugs, Pueblo pottery and silver and turquoise jewelry.* Photograph by Karen Klitgaard.
Back cover: *Mariachi Band,* photo © Robin Mitchell. *Palace of the Governors, downtown Santa Fe;* photo © Robin Mitchell. *Outdoor sculpture;* photo © Phil Lauro.

The Santa Fe & Taos Book: A Complete Guide
Copyright © 1991, 1994, 1996, 1998 by Berkshire House Publishers
Cover and interior photographs © 1991, 1994, 1996, 1998 by Murrae Haynes and other credited photographers.

Library of Congress Cataloging-in-Publication Data

Niederman, Sharon.

    The Santa Fe & Taos book : a complete guide / Sharon Niederman and Brandt Morgan, with Keith Easthouse and Ramona Gault. — 4th ed.
       p.   cm. — (Great destinations series)
    Rev. ed. of: The Santa Fe & Taos book / Brandt Morgan with Keith Easthouse and
       Ramona Gault. 3rd ed. c 1996.
    Includes bibliographical references and indexes.
    ISBN 0-936399-97-X
    1. Santa Fe. (N.M.)—Guidebooks. 2. Santa Fe Region (N.M.)—Guidebooks. 3. Taos (N.M.)—Guidebooks. 4. Taos Region (N.M.)—guidebooks. I. Morgan, Brandt. II. Morgan, Brandt. Santa Fe & Taos Book. III. Title. IV. Title: Santa Fe and Taos Book. V. Series.
F804.S23M67   1998
917.89'560453—dc21   97-43625
                                          CIP

ISBN 0-936399-97-X
ISSN 1056-7968 (Series)

Editor: Susan Minnich. Managing Editor: Philip Rich. Text design and typography: Dianne Pinkowitz. Cover design and typography: Jane McWhorter. Original text design for Great Destinations™ series: Janice Lindstrom.

Berkshire House books are available at substantial discounts for bulk purchases by corporations and other organizations for promotions and premiums. Special personalized editions can also be produced in large quantities. For more information, contact:

Berkshire House Publishers
480 Pleasant St., Suite 5, Lee, MA 01238
800-321-8526
E-mail: info@berkshirehouse.com
Website: www.berkshirehouse.com

Manufactured in the United States of America
First printing 1998
10 9 8 7 6 5 4 3 2 1

No complimentary meals or lodgings were accepted by the author and reviewers in gathering information for this work.

The GREAT DESTINATIONS™ Series

The Berkshire Book: A Complete Guide
The Santa Fe & Taos Book: A Complete Guide
The Napa & Sonoma Book: A Complete Guide
The Chesapeake Bay Book: A Complete Guide
The Coast of Maine Book: A Complete Guide
The Adirondack Book: A Complete Guide
The Aspen Book: A Complete Guide
The Charleston, Savannah & Coastal Islands Book: A Complete
     Guide
The Gulf Coast of Florida Book: A Complete Guide
The Central Coast of California Book: A Complete Guide
The Newport & Narragansett Bay Book: A Complete Guide
The Hamptons Book: A Complete Guide
Wineries of the Eastern States
The Texas Hill Country Book: A Complete Guide
The Nantucket Book: A Complete Guide

*The Great Destinations™ series features regions in the United States rich in natural
beauty and culture. Each Great Destinations™ guidebook reviews an extensive selection of lodgings, restaurants, cultural events, historic sites, shops, and recreational
opportunities, and outlines the region's natural and social history. Written by resident
authors, the guides are a resource for visitor and resident alike. The books feature maps,
photographs, directions to and around the region, lists of helpful phone numbers and
addresses, and indexes.*

Contents

CHAPTER ONE
The Dinosaurs to the Present
HISTORY
1

CHAPTER TWO
Getting Here, Getting Around
TRANSPORTATION
17

CHAPTER THREE
The Keys to Your Room
LODGING
29

CHAPTER FOUR
What to See, What to Do
CULTURE
70

CHAPTER FIVE
"God is everywhere, but His address is in Española"
SACRED SITES, ANCIENT RUINS, AND NATURAL WONDERS
126

CHAPTER SIX
Pleasing the Palate
RESTAURANTS AND FOOD PURVEYORS
136

CHAPTER SEVEN
For the Fun of It
RECREATION
192

CHAPTER EIGHT
Antique, Boutique and Unique
SHOPPING
228

CHAPTER NINE
Practical Matters
INFORMATION
256

Acknowledgments

For their help and generosity during the writing of this book, I would like to thank: Katherine Bomboy, Miriam Sagan, Carolyn Gilliland, Tom Sharpe, Curtis Bailey, Brandt Morgan, Cindy Bellinger, Jay Samuels, Melissa White and Charles Henry. I especially want to thank Brandt Morgan for bringing me in to the project, Charles Henry for his native's understanding of northern New Mexico and shared travel time, and Katherine Bomboy for impeccable editorial assistance. Many thanks to photographers Murrae Haynes and Karen Klitgaard and much appreciation to Berkshire House editors Philip Rich and Susan Minnich. And Patty Taylor and Christine Torres of the Taos County Chamber of Commerce made work a joy.

Sharon Niederman
Albuquerque, New Mexico
April, 1998

Introduction

While researching the *Transportation* chapter of this book, I called United Airlines to verify some flight information. "Hello," I said. "I'm interested in United Express flights from Denver to New Mexico." The person on the other end of the line came back immediately with, "I'll have to connect you with the international desk for that."

I make a point of this incident to emphasize what visitors may expect when they travel to New Mexico. In New Mexico, you remain a tourist in the United States. Experiences you encounter here may remind you more of a foreign country than the U.S.A. with which you are familiar. The vibrant mix of cultures, the variety of languages spoken and the respect for time-honored customs makes New Mexico an exciting place to be. However, the first-time visitor may be thrown off track by the unfamiliarity of a place thoroughly accustomed to doing things its own way. A happy and successful visit to New Mexico requires the appropriate attitude adjustment.

The back page item in *New Mexico Magazine* further illustrates this point. Titled "One of Our Fifty Is Missing," the monthly column reports first person accounts of amusing misunderstandings about passports, currency and water safety when people come to New Mexico.

This "foreignness" constitutes both the attraction and the challenge of visiting here. So it's best to arrive prepared for New Mexico's quirks. Here are a few pieces of honest advice from a twenty-year resident who has traveled down just about every back road in the state:

1. Always get precise directions before setting out. Travel with adequate maps. Once on the road, you will find a definite lack of signs, street names and markers. In addition, many streets are old and winding, not built for automobiles (this is one aspect of "Santa Fe charm") and travel along them can be disorienting. If you stop to ask directions, you may find they are skimpy and grudgingly given, or given with an assumption of familiarity you do not possess. Locals may be able to tell each other: "It's over there, just past the big cottonwood, turn right at the dip and look for the blue mailbox," while, after a half-dozen bumps in a dirt road, you may wonder exactly which "dip" was meant. The attitude is: you ought to know where you are going. To many locals, "tourist" is a four-letter word.

2. Always call in advance to be sure a restaurant or attraction is open. Although definite hours may be advertised, the reality is that hours of operation are often flexible.

3. Santa Fe and Taos remain extremely popular destinations. It is not unusual for favorite lodgings to be booked for the winter holiday season and Indian Market a year in advance; and, for many other wonderful B&Bs, six months in advance. The sooner you can make your travel plans, the more choices you will have, and the less compromise you will have to make.

4. Remember you are entering another time zone here. We're not just talking about "Mountain Time." "Mañana" does not mean "tomorrow." It may be translated as "not today." The room you booked was supposed to be ready at 2:00, yet when you arrive, you are told it will not be ready until 4:00. Or the tour you booked is canceled until next week. Patience, courtesy and flexibility are the best attitudes to maintain. I can absolutely guarantee you that big-city pressuring, threats to "talk to the manager" and so on will be counterproductive. New Mexico is not the place to throw your weight around. Any such display of self-importance will do nothing to improve the service you receive. It will only typecast you as an "outsider" and decrease the chances you will actually get what you want. Rushing is not efficient here. But you're on vacation anyway, right? So go with the flow. And carry a book with you for those times you may have to wait.

5. Be sure to take care of your health. You've probably heard it all before, but here goes: Allow a few days to adjust to the altitude, drink lots of water, wear sunscreen at all times of day, take a hat, dress in layers, give yourself lots of rest stops. The sun is very intense at this altitude, there's less oxygen and you may very well feel the effects. And whatever the season, it's best to be prepared for sudden changes in the weather.

6. In Santa Fe, especially at high season, you may encounter some treatment from restaurant, shop and hotel personnel that can only be termed rude. This, unfortunately, is as likely to occur at the high end as at the low. With high turnover and low wages, service people are often untrained and do not respond well to the pressures of a busy season. In my experience, outside of Santa Fe — in Taos or anywhere else in the state, for that matter — you will be far less likely to encounter this "bad attitude." Just be advised and either let it glide like water off a duck's back or take your business elsewhere. No need to take it personally or expect it to change.

7. You will find the most common question asked in New Mexico is: "Which is hotter, red or green?" Regardless of the answer you receive, if you are genuinely concerned it's best to ask for a small taste of each kind of chile before placing your order. It may take you a little while to become accustomed to the taste sensation of chile, but once you do, you will be addicted, eagerly anticipating your next bowl of red or green. And the touted health benefits of the chile are for real. Meanwhile, remember you can order any dish containing chile with the chile served on the side.

8. Even if you are not by nature a "shopper," you will undoubtedly find here things so special and unique that you will find yourself frequently reaching for your wallet. Art, jewelry, furniture, clothing, crafts — Northern New Mexico is a bazaar of the one-of-a-kind and the exquisitely hand-made. In Santa Fe, Spanish Market the last weekend in July, Indian Market held the weekend of August closest to the 19th of the month, and in the fall, the various artists' studio tours held in nearby villages of El Rito, Dixon and Galisteo offer especially appealing shopping opportunities. Be sure to factor shopping money into your vacation budget. And don't say we didn't warn you.

No one should spend a lifetime deprived of the state's unparalleled scenic beauty, from sweeping Ponderosa pine and aspen forests at 10,000 feet, to magical expanses of sagebrush mesas, to brilliant sunsets. Due to New Mexico's remoteness, nowhere else in the nation is the ancient history of so many people so well-preserved. Indeed, nowhere else in the country are these cultural traditions so alive. Then there's the wealth of arts activity. As well as the recreational possibilities.

It all adds up to the perfect vacation spot. While people speak of "off-season" and "on-season," I don't think there is any such thing as an "off-season" in New Mexico. Each time of year has its own magnificent beauty, whether on a peaceful desert hike on a dazzling summer morning or cuddling up in front of a sweet piñon fire after a winter afternoon walk through snowy Santa Fe. Personally, I like nothing better than an early November stroll through Taos when the cottonwoods are still golden and the scent of autumn is in the air. Whatever season you choose for your visit, New Mexico has the power to touch and satisfy your soul, and to give you experiences you will carry for a lifetime. The best plan is to visit during all seasons and choose your favorite time of year.

In New Mexico, be prepared to be surprised. The sweep of a red earth vista, the sight of a ten-foot stark white Penitente cross, the faded altar paintings of a centuries-old Spanish Colonial church, the drumbeats and jangling shells of hundreds of dancers at a Pueblo Corn Dance, the unexpected connection with a local grower at the Santa Fe Area Farmers' Market, the sight of more stars than you've ever seen in the clear night sky — any of thousands of moments have the power to move you deeply, and perhaps, to change your life in some way you could never have predicted.

In this fourth edition of *The Santa Fe & Taos Book*, we've included new restaurants and lodgings, some of which replace enterprises that have moved or gone out of business. We've also pored over each chapter, checking addresses and phone numbers and making sure all information is as current as possible. The result, we're convinced, offers you the most comprehensive, up-to-date and in-depth guide available to the area.

Through my experience as a travel and food writer here, I hope to inform you of a wide range of the best values, opportunities and experiences in lodging and cuisine. All the restaurants in these pages have been "taste-tested" and evaluated for price, service and atmosphere. Our cuisine is one of the great adventures available here, so enjoy the native foods unique to this place. Even if you feel like my Aunt Elaine, who visited last year and said she'd like to "try the Mexican food, so long as it isn't spicy," you can still find wonderful dining possibilities. Out of concern for the increasing public awareness of diet and nutrition, special attention has been paid to those establishments offering healthful dining selections.

Please use this book as your map through the most wonderful place on earth. It was compiled for you by a friend who has lived here many years and wouldn't live anywhere else. In New Mexico, the longer you stay, the deeper you get.

Once you visit, you may find, like so many, that a single vacation isn't enough. You must return, again and again, to learn more, see more, and delight more in this incredible place.

—Sharon Niederman

THE WAY THIS BOOK WORKS

This book is divided into nine chapters, each with its own introduction. If you are especially interested in one chapter or another, you can turn to it directly and begin reading without losing a sense of continuity. You can also take the book with you on your travels and skip around, reading about the places you visit as you go. Or you can read the entire book through from start to finish.

If you're interested in finding a place to eat or sleep, we suggest you first look over the restaurant and lodging charts in the *Appendix* (organized by area and price); then turn to the pages listed and read the specific entries for the places you're most interested in.

Entries within most of the chapters are arranged alphabetically under four different headings: "Santa Fe," "Near Santa Fe," "Taos" and "Near Taos." The first two headings refer to the area within the city or town limits. "Near Santa Fe" and "Near Taos" mean within a 30-mile radius of these two centers. (Look at the map on page 24; all points within the two circles are less than an hour — and frequently not more than a few minutes — from Santa Fe or Taos.) And for those "don't miss" places in parts beyond, we've included another category called "Outside the Area."

Some entries, most notably those in Chapter Three, *Lodging* and Chapter Six, *Restaurants*, include specific information organized for easy reference in blocks in the left-hand column. We've included a "Handicap Access" category for lodging and restaurants specifying "Full," "Partial" or "None." Full access includes such amenities as grab bars in restrooms, while partial access means the establishment has made at least some effort to accommodate the handicapped. All details given in the information blocks — as well as all phone numbers and addresses in other parts of the book — were checked as close to publication as possible. Even so, such details change with frustrating frequency. When in doubt, call ahead.

For the same reason, we've usually avoided listing specific prices, preferring instead to indicate a range of prices. Lodging price codes are based on a per-room rate, double occupancy, during high season (summer and ski months). Low-season rates are likely to be 20–40 percent less. Once again, it's always best to call ahead for specific rates and reservations.

Restaurant prices indicate the cost of an individual meal including appetizer, entree, dessert, tax and tip but not including alcoholic beverages.

Price Codes

	Lodging	Dining
Inexpensive	Up to $65	Up to $12
Moderate	$65 to $100	$12 to $25
Expensive	$100 to $150	$25 to $50
Very Expensive	Over $150	Over $50

Credit cards are abbreviated as follows:

AE—American Express
CB—Carte Blanche
D—Discover Card
DC—Diner's Club
MC—MasterCard
V—Visa

There is one telephone area code for all New Mexico: 505.

The best sources for year-round tourist information are the Santa Fe Convention and Visitors Bureau (505-984-6760 or 800-777-2489; Sweeney Center, 201 W. Marcy St., Santa Fe, NM 87501) and the Taos County Chamber of Commerce (505-758-3873 or 800-732-8267; P.O. Drawer I, Taos, NM 87571). For specific information on activities near Taos, contact the Angel Fire/Eagle Nest Chamber of Commerce (505-377-6661 or 800-446-8117; Angel Fire, NM 87710) or the Red River Chamber of Commerce (505-754-2366 or 800-348-6444; Red River, NM 87558).

TOWNS IN THE SANTA FE–TAOS AREA

Though we focus primarily on Santa Fe and Taos, many other towns in the area are worth a visit. Within the circle to the south of Santa Fe, for example, you'll find Golden and Madrid on the road known as the Turquoise Trail, and Galisteo and Lamy, all old towns that retain some of their Wild West and old New Mexico flavor. A few minutes to the north of Santa Fe, you'll find the picturesque little village of Tesuque, a favored suburb of Santa Fe with the Shidoni Gallery and the gathering spot of the Tesuque Village Market. To the west is Los Alamos, home of the Los Alamos National Laboratory and the birthplace of the atomic bomb.

Scattered up and down the Rio Grande are 11 different Indian pueblos — not towns but separate nations — all unique in their own ways, from ceremonies and dances to crafts and cooking. On the way to Taos via the Rio Grande on N.M. 68, you'll pass through the little farming and orchard villages of Velarde and Embudo, with the artists' community of Dixon and its La Chiripada Winery a quick side trip east. And if you take the High Road to Taos via N.M. 76 and N.M. 518, you'll cruise through more than a half dozen old villages where time virtually stands still — Chimayó — with its famous Santuario known for its healing "holy dirt," Truchas, Penasco, Vadito and others — that offer everything from wonderful crafts and galleries to venerable Spanish Colonial churches to looks at quieter times.

North of Taos are the old mining towns of Questa, Red River and Angel Fire, today all hubs of outdoor sports and backwoods places with wild and rustic flavors. West of Taos is Ojo Caliente, site of the famed mineral springs spa. And if you go as far west as Abiquiu, you'll find the home of artist Georgia O'Keeffe. One look at the landscape with its pink and red cliffs is enough to explain why she was so entranced with northern New Mexico and why her work seems so inspired. Another journey outside the area, this time 60 miles to the southeast via I-25, will take you to the busy metropolis of Albuquerque with its numerous historical and cultural attractions, including the new botanic gardens and biopark, the University of New Mexico and the Albuquerque Dukes baseball team.

The
SANTA FE & TAOS
Book

A Complete Guide

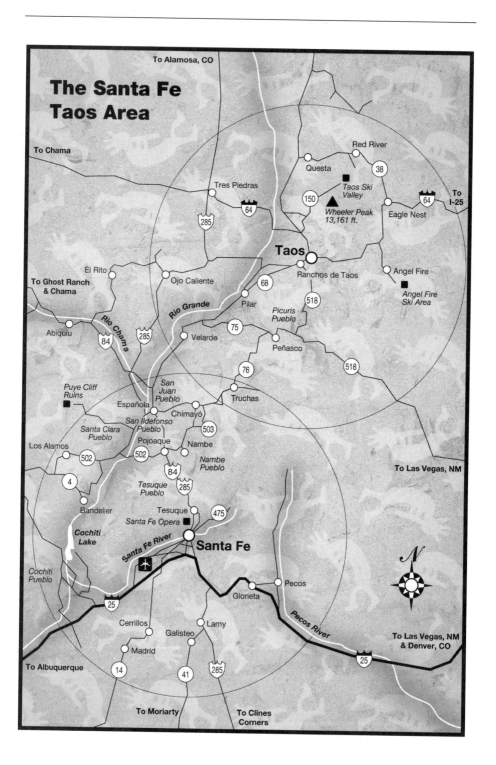

CHAPTER ONE

The Dinosaurs to the Present
HISTORY

> This was a land of vast spaces and long silences, a desert land of red bluffs and brilliant flowering cactus. The hot sun poured down. This land belonged to the very old Gods. They came on summer evenings, unseen, to rest their eyes and their hearts on the milky opal and smoky blue of the desert. For this was a land of enchantment, where Gods walked in the cool of the evening.
> —From *Land of Enchantment: Memoirs of Marian Russell Along the Old Santa Fe Trail*

The history of northern New Mexico is one of turbulent change. From the hot, crushing forces that originally shaped the land to the often violent social movements that molded its present-day mix of cultures, the area has been embroiled in flux since prehistoric times. The story of the Santa Fe–Taos area is one of an enchanting land and its varied peoples: of ancient hunter-gatherers and modern Pueblo Indians; of Spanish con-

Courtesy Pecos National Historical Park

Kiva and ruins of 18th-century church at Pecos National Monument.

quistadors and colonists; of American mountain men, French trappers, German merchants and adventurers of various origins; and more recently of artists, tourists, skiers and spiritual seekers.

New Mexico is a land that, through the centuries, has continually been "discovered" — first by wandering bands of indigenous people, then, five centuries ago, by the Spanish, and successively by 19th and 20th century pioneers determined to build a better life than the one they left behind. Each new group of "discoverers" attempted a new wave of colonization, claiming New Mexico's resources for itself.

The area's remoteness from major population centers, times of extreme weather conditions, scarce water and challenging terrain have proven both blessing and curse. Isolation protected and strengthened native cultures, while simultaneously it cut New Mexico off from innovation and economic growth. 1993 figures show New Mexico ranks as the 47th state in per capita income.

Many are surprised to learn that the myth of the "tri-cultural" state — Spanish, Indian and Anglo — is one that was coined early in the 20th century by Santa Fe town fathers seeking to encourage tourism. During the past decade, this myth has been called into question as greater understanding of the complex cultural mix of northern New Mexico's residents has been gained.

NATURAL HISTORY

If we could compress two billion years into a few minutes, we would see the New Mexico landscape being shaped and reshaped. The invasion and retreat of inland seas, the rise and fall of great mountain ranges, the shifting of subterranean plates, the cracking of mantle and crust; exploding volcanoes, seeping magma, shifting sands and continual erosion by wind and water — each of these forces has left its mark on the modern landscape.

More than 100 million years ago, great dinosaurs roamed the land, as evidenced by skeletons now on display at the Ghost Ranch Conference Center. At the same time, colorful sands and silts from the ancestral Rockies formed pink and red cliffs, and volcanoes spewed ash over the landscape. As the modern Rockies rose to the north, the dinosaurs mysteriously disappeared, giving way to the mammals.

To the east of Santa Fe–Taos, the Sangre de Cristo Mountains began to rise near the end of the Mesozoic. Later, about 30 million years ago, an upswelling in the earth's mantle created a pair of massive fault lines and the land between them caved in, resulting in the Rio Grande Rift, a trench up to five miles deep. It filled with debris, and water from the mountains created a long chain of basins. Finally, about 2.5 million years ago, the Rio Grande became a continuous river flowing 1,800 miles to the Gulf of Mexico. Thereafter, volcanic activity on the west side of the Rio Grande created basaltic mesas and broad volcanic tablelands, including the present-day Taos Plateau.

The Jemez (pronounced HAY-mess) Mountains west of Santa Fe are the remains of a composite volcano that geologists believe was once almost as high as Mount Everest. About a million years ago the volcano blew its top and caved in. The explosion, 600 times more powerful than the 1980 eruption of Mount Saint Helens, left a crater 15 miles wide and buried much of the land with ash up to 1,000 feet thick. Later some of that volcanic tuff became home to the Anasazi Indians, whose cave dwellings still pepper the bases of canyon walls at Bandelier National Monument.

The Rio Grande Gorge near Taos.

Murrae Haynes

During the recent Ice Ages, lava seeped in the foothills and glaciers scoured the mountains. Heavy snows and rains formed lakes and created wide, sloping foothills. As the weather warmed, these areas sprouted new vegetation, from scrub brush and small pines in the lowlands to lush aspens and evergreens in the mountains.

Such was the landscape discovered by the first human inhabitants of the Santa Fe–Taos area some 12,000 years ago. Today it is essentially the same: the wide, fertile Rio Grande Valley flanked by spectacular sets of mountains. To the east lies the Sangre de Cristo range, a modern ski paradise that stretches north to the Colorado Rockies, while to the west lie the volcanic Jemez.

From north of Taos, the Rio Grande rushes through a 50-mile stretch of basalt, the gorge providing excellent year-round fishing and summer thrills and chills for whitewater enthusiasts. Likewise the Chama River, flowing north of the Jemez into the Rio Grande, offers some of the most spectacular wild and scenic excursions in the state. Flowing south through the fertile farms and orchards of Velarde, the Rio Grande eventually meanders through the ancient Pueblo lands north of Santa Fe and the hills and valleys to the west.

Elevations in the area range from under 6,000 feet in the valley to 13,161 feet at the top of Wheeler Peak, the highest point in the state. The air is clear and dry, with sunny skies 300 days of the year. A 14-inch average annual rainfall leaves a desert-like setting in the lowlands, while winter storms dump up to 320 inches of snow a year on lush mountain areas such as the popular Taos Ski Valley.

These factors make for a diversity of life zones and an especially rich flora and fauna. Santa Fe and Taos have wonderful shade trees, the most prominent being the giant willow and cottonwoods that grace municipal plazas and downtowns. Juniper and piñon pines dominate the dry, lower elevations, giving way to scrub oak and thicker forests of ponderosa pine; and finally to high alpine forests with a spectacular mix of fir, aspen and spruce. Spring and summer wildflowers, especially in the mountains, make a colorful spectrum, from Indian paintbrush and woodland pinedrops to buttercups and alpine daisies.

Northern New Mexico is a haven for animals large and small. The *arroyos* (dry gullies or washes) and foothills are dominated by mice, prairie dogs, jackrabbits and cottontails, and by the coyotes and bobcats that feed on them. Muskrat and beaver thrive in some rivers and streams, and signs of river otter can be found on secluded parts of the Rio Grande. Some sure-footed bighorn sheep still roam parts of the Sangre de Cristo, while pronghorn antelope are common on the plains. The mountains are home not only to snowshoe hares and various species of squirrels, but to herds of mule deer and elk and a fair number of black bears. And mountain lions are sighted in these parts.

Birds fill every available avian niche, from seed-eating finches and bug-eating swallows to breathtakingly beautiful bluebirds and a variety of large, winged predators. Eagles and hawks soar above canyons, while quail, doves and roadrunners (the state bird) skitter through the brush below. Lowland wet and marshy areas play host to myriad ducks, geese and shorebirds, while the mountains are home to a wide range of species.

SOCIAL HISTORY

EARLY HUMAN INHABITANTS

The first human inhabitants of the Santa Fe–Taos area were Stone Age hunters who followed herds of giant bison and mammoth more than 12,000 years ago. As the centuries passed, they became less nomadic, gathering fruits, nuts and greens in the lowlands, hunting deer and elk in the mountains and trapping small game. By around 5,500 B.C., these hunter-gatherers were living seasonally in what is today the Santa Fe–Taos area, mostly in caves and other natural shelters. Soon afterward, they began to plant corn and other crops and to make baskets. Eventually they constructed circular pithouses, which centuries later gave way to above-ground dwellings of stone and adobe. Around 200 B.C. they began making pottery.

From A.D. 900–1300, great Anasazi complexes (*Anasazi* is a Navajo word meaning "ancient strangers") flourished at Chaco Canyon and Mesa Verde to the west and north. These centers were marked by extensive roadways and huge, multi-tiered complexes of stone. The people performed sophisticated ceremonies, irrigated extensive farmlands and accurately predicted the movements of the sun and moon. Another group of Anasazi developed a similar complex in Frijoles (Free-HOL-ace) Canyon about 30 miles northwest of Santa Fe, in what is now Bandelier National Monument. However, by A.D. 1300 most of these great centers had been abandoned. It is widely believed that the "ancient ones" were some of the ancestors of present-day Pueblo people.

Sometime during the era of the Anasazi, a number of stone and adobe villages sprang up in the Santa Fe area. The largest of these, called Ogapoge or

Kuapoge ("Dancing Ground of the Sun"), once occupied part of Santa Fe. Scores of other small settlements, including the beginnings of present-day Taos Pueblo and other pueblos north of Santa Fe, were built along the Rio Grande.

Ogapoge and other settlements around Santa Fe were abandoned around 1425, during the worst drought in a thousand years. Others remained and continued to flourish, including Pecos Pueblo to the southeast and the present-day pueblos of Tesuque, Pojoaque, Nambe, San Ildefonso, Santa Clara, San Juan, Jemez, Picuris and Taos to the north. When the first Spaniards arrived in New Mexico, the Pueblo Indians (*pueblo* is Spanish for "village") were well established in some 150 adobe villages, large and small, scattered along the Rio Grande and its tributaries.

Ancient rock art near Galisteo.

Courtesy Museum of New Mexico

Before the arrival of the Spaniards, the Pueblos lived a life of ceremony in accord with the seasonal cycles of hunting and planting. They cultivated corn, beans and squash and gathered greens, berries, fruits and seeds. They hunted myriad species of wild game, from prairie dogs, rabbits and turkeys to deer, elk and antelope. They made clay pottery; wove baskets and mats from corn, cattail and yucca leaves; and fashioned blankets from feathers and animal hides. Although they traveled exclusively on foot, they not only maintained close ties with each other, but also had trade links with the Plains Indians, the Pacific Coast Indians and tribes in Mexico.

The ancient Pueblos, like their modern counterparts, spoke a number of different languages. They continually honored the Great Spirit and the forces of nature. Underground they built circular chambers called *kivas*, adaptations of their ancestral pithouses that served as centers for prayer and teaching. They also developed elaborate ceremonial dances that expressed their sense of oneness with nature. With the exception of raids from neighboring Plains tribes, their lives were generally tranquil until the arrival of the Spaniards from Mexico.

THE SPANISH INFLUENCE

One of the first Spaniards to come to New Mexico, then known as New Spain, was Fray Marcos de Niza, a Franciscan friar who arrived in 1539 after hearing fabulous accounts of the Seven Cities of Cibola, supposedly made of gold. De Niza never visited these cities himself, but he embellished the stories he heard. His own overblown reports of riches spurred a massive expedition in 1540, in which Francisco Vasquez de Coronado rode north from Mexico City with 300 soldiers. Cibola turned out to be nothing more than the little pueblo of Zuni, which Coronado and his men conquered and subjugated. Other pueblos to the north were similarly invaded, yet neither Coronado nor those who followed him could find any gold. Thereafter, Spain turned its focus toward colonization.

The first official colonizer of the area was Juan de Oñate. In 1598, with 129 soldier-colonists and their families, 10 Franciscan friars and thousands of cattle, sheep, horses and mules, he set out to establish the first permanent Spanish settlement in New Mexico. Many of the horses escaped, eventually providing the Plains Indians and the rest of North America with a new form of transportation.

Oñate chose a spot across the Rio Grande from San Juan Pueblo, about 25 miles north of present-day Santa Fe. The settlement, called San Gabriel, was beset with problems from the beginning. Some settlers were apparently still under the illusion that they would find easy riches. Others balked at the hard labor and difficult living conditions, still others at the difficulty of converting the Indians to Catholicism. By 1600, almost half the settlers had given up and gone back to Mexico. A few years later, referring to the fantastic stories of riches and abundance in the area, the viceroy of New Spain wrote to the king from Mexico City, "I cannot help but inform your majesty that this conquest is becoming a fairy tale. . . . If those who write the reports imagine that they are believed by those who read them, they are greatly mistaken. Less substance is being revealed every day."

Many Spaniards thought the most reasonable alternative was to leave New Mexico altogether. However, after long debate, they decided to stay, partly to maintain their claim to the huge territory west of the Mississippi but primarily because the friars were so reluctant to abandon the Indians to paganism. A new governor, Pedro de Peralta, was appointed and sent to New Mexico to found a permanent settlement. He chose a spot south of San Gabriel that offered more water and better protection. The result was La Villa de Santa Fe — the City of Holy Faith. (In 1823 St. Francis became its patron saint; hence its current name, the Royal City of the Holy Faith of Saint Francis of Assisi.) In 1610, a decade before the arrival of the Pilgrims at Plymouth Rock, the Spanish settlers laid out their new plaza and began building the Palace of the Governors, today the oldest continuously occupied public building in the United States. That same year, supplies began moving northward to Santa Fe along the newly opened Camino Real ("Royal Road") from Chihuahua, Mexico.

Over the years, the settler-soldiers built adobe houses and dug a network of *acequias,* or irrigation ditches, to divert water from the Santa Fe River. They cultivated fields of beans, squash, corn and wheat with hand-held plows and wooden hoes. Accompanied by Franciscan friars, they ranged far and wide, subjugating the pueblos, building churches and trying to convert the Indians to Catholicism. By 1625 the Spaniards had built some 50 churches in the Rio Grande Valley with forced Indian labor, and more than half of the original pueblos had disappeared.

One that continued to thrive was Taos Pueblo, about 70 miles north of Santa Fe. (*Taos* is the Spanish version of a Tiwa phrase meaning "Place of the Red Willows.") The first Spanish settlers moved there with Fray Pedro de Miranda in 1617. They settled near Taos Pueblo, even moving within its walls during the 1760s for protection against the Comanches.

The Indians objected to Spanish encroachment. All through the Rio Grande Valley, Pueblo spiritual and political leaders were routinely treated harshly, while others were forced to build churches, work in the fields and weave garments for export to Mexico. Conflicts between Spanish civil and religious authorities fueled the discontent. Over a 75-year period, the Indians attempted a number of revolts, most of them stemming from attempts to outlaw their religious ceremonies. None were successful. Rebellions at Taos and Jemez Pueblos in the 1630s resulted in the deaths of several priests and were met with even more repression from the Spaniards. While some governors allowed the Indians to continue their dances, most supported the Franciscans in their attempts to stamp out all remnants of Pueblo ceremony.

One of the most brutal of these attempts came in 1675, when Governor Juan Francisco de Trevino charged 47 Pueblo religious leaders with sorcery and witchcraft and sentenced them to death or slavery. A San Juan leader named Popé, who was frequently flogged because of his religious influence, secretly vowed revenge. For several years he hid at Taos Pueblo, quietly plotting and sending out runners to orchestrate a revolt of all the pueblos.

The revolt took place on August 10, 1680. At the break of day, Indians in pueblos from Taos in the north to Acoma in the south to Hopi in the west suddenly turned on the Spaniards, killing men, women, children and priests and setting the mission churches ablaze. In Santa Fe, about 1,000 settlers holed up in the Palace of the Governors. When Governor Otermín learned of the widespread devastation, he and the others loaded their belongings onto mules and wagons and abandoned Santa Fe on August 21.

The refugees eventually made their way to El Paso del Norte, the site of present-day Juarez, Mexico, where they lived in exile for the next 12 years. Meanwhile, the Indians took over the Palace of the Governors at Santa Fe. In spite of several Spanish attempts at reconquest, they lived largely unhindered there until 1692.

Even so, the Spaniards had left deep and indelible marks on Pueblo society — and even on the rebels themselves. After 70 years, Catholicism was almost as alive as Pueblo ceremonialism, and most of the Indians spoke Spanish as well as their own native languages. Moreover, like their Spanish predecessors, Popé and other Indian leaders now ruled with an iron hand, demanding tributes and trying to stamp out forcibly all remnants of Spanish influence. Crop failures and attacks by the Apaches and Navajos eroded the Pueblo resolve, and by the time the new territorial governor returned in September 1692, the Indians seemed ready to submit once more.

That governor was Don Diego de Vargas, a man as bold and fearless as he was vain and arrogant. With only 40 soldiers he confronted the fortified pueblo that had once been the Palace of the Governors. To allay the Indians' fears, he entered the palace completely unarmed. Reassured that they would be pardoned and protected from marauding Plains Indians, the Pueblos agreed to Spanish rule.

Spanish Colonial document signed by Don Diego de Vargas, 1696.

Courtesy Museum of New Mexico

Unfortunately, Vargas's reconquest was only briefly bloodless. When he returned the following December with more soldiers and colonists, he was met with defiance and hostility. After many days of suffering in the cold and snow, the Spaniards stormed the palace, killing 81 Indians in the process. In subsequent years, Vargas met similar resistance; once, his soldiers even rode north to raid Taos Pueblo after its leaders refused to supply the starving settlers with grain. Only in 1696, after a number of bloody battles, another Taos revolt and the deaths of many Pueblo leaders, did the new governor finally succeed in establishing a new Spanish reign.

With the exception of repeated Comanche raids on Taos, the 1700s were relatively peaceful, a time of festivity, drama and art. In the fall of 1712, the colonists celebrated the first annual Fiesta de Santa Fe, a holiday commemorating Vargas's "bloodless" reconquest of New Mexico and his return of La Conquistadora, the small statue of the Virgin Mary that the colonists believed protected them when they fled Santa Fe for Mexico. Frequent dances, musicals and comedies celebrated the Spanish heritage. Silversmithing, goldsmithing, woodworking and weaving flourished among the Spaniards while the Pueblos supplied the colonists with cookware and crockery of all kinds.

San Miguel bulto *by Raphael Aragon, circa 1825.*

Michael O'Shaughnessy

Meanwhile, as the *acequias* irrigated the land, farms and orchards around Santa Fe and Taos sprouted fields of wheat, corn, beans and a variety of fruits and vegetables. Gambling and smoking were popular among men and women alike, and cock fights were frequently held on the plazas in the afternoons. By the time of the American Revolution (which some wealthy Santa Feans helped finance), more than 100 colonial families were living in the Santa Fe area. Horses, cattle and sheep, first brought into the New World by the Spaniards, had proliferated, and annual fairs at Pecos and Taos provided major trade opportunities between the Spanish, the Pueblos and the Plains Indians.

After the reconquest, the Indians were no longer treated as slaves, and church and *kiva* coexisted side by side. By mid-century, Franciscan friars, frustrated over their failure to stamp out native ceremonies after eight generations, were replaced by secular priests. The new priests seemed satisfied as long as the Indians professed to be Catholic. Some of the Indians still worked as indentured servants, and many were abused.

On the other hand, fundamental changes took place after the reconquest that contributed to lasting respect and cooperation between Hispanics and Pueblos. One, they often banded together to fight their common enemies, usually the raiding Plains tribes. (On one occasion, the Villasur Expedition of 1720, Spaniards and Pueblos fought side-by-side against French and Pawnees who were encroaching on their eastern territory.) Two, the Pueblos incorporated Catholicism and certain Hispanic ceremonies (the Matachines dances, for example) into their own native traditions. More fundamental still, they intermarried; today the great majority of Pueblo people are of mixed blood, and many have Hispanic surnames.

Segesser hide painting depicting Spaniards (wearing broad-brimmed hats) and Pueblo Indians (with hair tied behind) fighting French and Pawnees in present-day Nebraska, 1720.

Courtesy Museum of New Mexico

ARRIVAL OF THE ANGLOS

Though the Spanish government forbade foreigners inside New Mexico, a few mountain men and explorers sneaked into the Santa Fe–Taos area in the early 1800s. One of these was Zebulon Pike, who was arrested by the Spaniards in 1807 while on a mission to explore the area west of the Louisiana Purchase. As Pike was escorted into Santa Fe under armed guard, he made the following observations of the capital city:

> *Its appearance from a distance struck my mind with the same effect as a fleet of the flat-bottomed boats which are seen in the spring and fall seasons descending the Ohio River. There are two churches, the magnificience of whose steeples form a striking contrast to the miserable appearance of the houses.*
> —from *The Journals of Zebulon Montgomery Pike,*
> *With Letters and Related Documents* University of Oklahoma Press, 1966

After his release from prison in Chihuahua, Pike published his journals, which attracted more American adventurers to the area.

Gradually, especially during the Napoleonic Wars, Spain loosened its grip on its colonies and Mexico drifted farther from the king. In 1821 Mexican independence was celebrated in Santa Fe with "universal carousing and revelry," according to American observer Thomas James. The great event brought many more Anglos, as mountain men filtered in from the Rockies to hunt and trap around Taos, and New Mexico was finally opened up to foreign trade.

That same year, trader William Becknell drove a heavy-laden wagon over Raton Pass, making Santa Fe the western terminus of the Santa Fe Trail from Independence, Missouri, some 800 miles to the east. Now an unstoppable stream of Americans began rushing into and through the area. Stretching across the prairies like great billowing armadas, covered wagons initially took almost a month to get to Santa Fe. They carted tremendous amounts of merchandise —

including textiles, tools, shoes, flour, whiskey, hardware, medicines, musical instruments, ammunition and even heavy machinery. Some merchants sold their goods in Santa Fe or Taos; others pushed on to Mexico over the Camino Real.

One of the most famous of those who stayed was Indian fighter and federal agent Kit Carson, who once observed, "No man who has seen the women, heard the bells or smelled the piñon smoke of Taos will ever be able to leave." True to his word, Carson lived in Taos for 42 years, and many merchants, traders and mountain men followed suit.

During the 1820s, the increasing number of Americans in New Mexico and Texas became a major threat to the Mexican government. Mexico itself was struggling with severe instability at this time, and it both neglected and over-taxed its northern colony. Colonial anger over these policies came to a head in 1837 when a group of northern New Mexicans formed a mob, decapitating Governor Albino Perez and killing 17 of his officers. The rebellion was put down by former Governor Manuel Armijo, who was returned to office.

Courtesy Museum of New Mexico

Banquet at Fort Marcy Headquarters Building, Santa Fe, 1887.

Armijo served New Mexico well, often bending the law to meet the real needs of the people. However, it soon became obvious that the United States was eyeing the area for westward expansion. In 1846, President James K. Polk declared war on Mexico and sent a contingent of 1,600 soldiers along with General Stephen Watts Kearny to take over Santa Fe and all of New Mexico. The takeover was bloodless. The few Spanish who resisted were put in jail, and Taos merchant Charles Bent was appointed the new governor.

Bent's tenure was short. In January of the following year, a large group of irate Taoseños, including enraged Hispanics and Indians fearful of losing their land, broke into Bent's house, killed and scalped him and then went looking for other Anglos. As the revolt spread, a contingent of U.S. troops under Colonel Sterling Price rode from Santa Fe to Taos, where the rebels had taken cover in the mission church at the west end of the pueblo. The soldiers destroyed the church with cannonballs, and the rebels were hanged after a brief trial. Today Bent's house is a museum (see Chapter Four, *Culture*), and the remains of the mission church still stand as a grim reminder of the violence that undergirds today's multicultural New Mexico.

Mexico reluctantly signed the Treaty of Guadalupe Hidalgo with the United States, giving up its claim to New Mexico, Texas, Arizona and California in 1848. Two years later, New Mexico officially became a United States territory, inspiring an even bigger rush of soldiers, traders and pioneers from the east. Women first came to New Mexico with their soldier and trader husbands or as missionaries, and also as health-seekers and seekers of personal and artistic freedom not available to them in the east.

From the outset, the Americans had troubles with raiding Apaches and Navajos. A group of powerful citizens known as the Santa Fe Ring was instrumental in the takeover of New Mexicans' property during the late nineteenth and early twentieth century. The American government reneged on its promise to give the Pueblos full citizenship; instead, through the removal of Indian children from their homes and their forced education in government-run Indian Schools, it greatly suppressed Pueblo religion and culture. Though New Mexico became the nation's 47th state in 1912, Indians were not recognized as U.S. citizens until 1924 and were not allowed to vote until 1948. Newly arrived Santa Fe and Taos artists and writers, such as Mabel Dodge Luhan and Mary Austin, who made northern New Mexico their adopted home, were instrumental in winning Indian rights and in cultural preservation.

One of the men who fought vigorously for the rights of poor Hispanics was Father Antonio José Martinez, head of the parish at Taos during the 1830s–1850s. Martinez not only openly opposed the mandatory church tithe but fought Anglo land takeovers and championed Hispanic folk traditions. In these and other activities, Martinez defied the authority of Bishop Jean Baptiste Lamy (subject of Willa Cather's classic novel *Death Comes for the Archbishop*). Though Martinez was excommunicated in 1857, he continued to lead his people spiritually and politically until his death 10 years later. Lamy, though no champion of the poor, made major contributions to education and architecture, overseeing the construction of such lasting landmarks as Santa Fe's Romanesque Cathedral of St. Francis, reminiscent of the churches of his childhood France, and the nearby Gothic-style Loretto Chapel.

During the Civil War, Santa Fe fell briefly into the hands of Confederate troops when General Henry H. Sibley marched into New Mexico from Texas on

Photo by Ben Wittick. Courtesy School of American Research Collection, Museum of New Mexico

The Glorieta battlefield in June, 1880.

March 10, 1862. Two weeks later, Sibley was defeated at the Battle of Glorieta Pass, about 20 miles east of Santa Fe. After the Civil War, railroads took the place of the Santa Fe Trail, reaching Santa Fe and Taos around 1880. Over the next several decades, the iron horse brought hordes of farmers, gold diggers, outlaws, businessmen, health seekers and tourists to the Land of Enchantment.

Between 1880 and the turn of the century, the Anglo population of New Mexico quadrupled, from fewer than 10,000 to almost 40,000. One of the first Anglos to popularize the area's attractions was Governor Lew Wallace, who in 1878 finished his famous novel *Ben Hur* while occupying the Palace of the Governors. "What perfection of air and sunlight!" Wallace wrote to his wife Susan after arriving in Santa Fe. "And what a landscape I discovered to show you when you come — a picture to make the fame of an artist, could he only paint it on canvas as it is." Wallace also made the statement, found hanging today on the walls of many state offices: "Every calculation based on experience elsewhere fails in New Mexico."

THE ARTIST'S ERA

The man usually given credit for igniting the art boom was Joseph Henry Sharp, who in 1883 spent the summer painting in Taos. He was followed by Bert Phillips, Ernest Blumenschein and Irving Couse, and a few years later these four founded the Taos Society of Artists. By the 1890s, Anglo artists were displaying their works at the Palace of the Governors, a part of which was dedicated as the Museum of Fine Arts in 1917.

Other artists and writers quickly filtered into the Santa Fe–Taos area. During the 1920s, the Santa Fe Art Colony was founded by Will Shuster and four others, who became known to some as Los Cinco Pintores ("the five painters") and to others as "the five nuts in adobe huts." Soon the area also boasted the likes of Mabel Dodge Luhan, Georgia O'Keeffe, Willa Cather, Mary Austin and D.H. Lawrence. Lawrence spent only a few seasons in Taos but was deeply moved, especially by Pueblo life. Among his posthumous papers is the following passage:

You can feel it, the atmosphere of it, around the pueblos. Not, of course, when the place is crowded with sightseers and motor-cars. But go to Taos Pueblo on some brilliant snowy morning and see the white figure on the roof; or come riding through at dusk on some windy evening, when the black skirts of the silent women blow around the wide boots, and you will feel the old, old root of human consciousness still reaching down to depths we know nothing of.

Other events during the '20s and '30s contributed to Santa Fe's reputation as a center for the arts. Dr. Edgar Lee Hewitt, director of the Museum of New Mexico, and other Anglos organized the first Indian Market in 1922, which continues to be held annually on the third weekend of each August. Three years later, Mary Austin and others founded the Spanish Colonial Arts Society to encourage a revival of Hispanic folk art. The annual Spanish Market is held on the last weekend of July. In 1926, Will Shuster created Zozobra, an effigy of "Old Man Gloom" that each year since has been set ablaze to touch off the annual Fiesta de Santa Fe. At the same time, Indian potters such as Maria Martinez of San Ildefonso began to achieve popularity. The Santa Fe Concert Series was founded in 1936, followed by the opening of the Wheelwright Museum of the American Indian, founded by Bostonian Mary Cabot Wheelwright and Navajo medicine man Hosteen Klah. It was also during the '30s that the dedicated Dorothy Dunn began nurturing a new generation of artistic talent at the Santa Fe Indian School.

World War II brought more changes to the area. One of the most profound was the 1943 purchase of the Los Alamos Ranch School for Boys and its conversion into Los Alamos National Laboratory, birthplace of the atomic bomb. Since the war, the lab has been a focal point for defense research, from hydrogen bombs to Star Wars technology.

A lesser known fact is that during the war there was a Japanese detention camp in Santa Fe. Surrounded by barbed wire and located in the Casa Solana area, the camp imprisoned more than 4,500 Japanese-American men from the East and West Coasts who, by virtue of their origins, were considered to be "dangerous enemy aliens."

After the war, Santa Fe and Taos were again "discovered." As artists and tourists continued to arrive, the first galleries began to sprout in Santa Fe and Taos. During the latter half of the 1950s, the newly opened Taos Ski Valley spurred tourism in the area, as did the Santa Fe Opera and the Museum of International Folk Art.

At the same time, Santa Fe–Taos became known as a spiritual power center, attracting individuals and groups that have promoted everything from Oriental philosophies and healing to American Indian and New Age thought. During the '60s and '70s Indians and Hispanic farmers accommodated thousands of hippies and experimenters in alternative living. Today both Santa Fe and Taos have large alternative healing communities offering everything from massage and acupuncture to herbology, ayurveda and past-life regression. In recent years, the area has also attracted the film industry, and numerous well-known movie stars have taken up at least part-time residence here. Star-spotting has become a popular spectator sport around Santa Fe.

Expensive homes dot the hillsides around Santa Fe.

Murrae Haynes

Since the war, the population of Santa Fe has more than tripled, from about 20,000 to about 65,000, and there is no end of growth in sight. Many newcomers are quite affluent, as evidenced by the fact that the average Santa Fe home price in 1997 rose to more than $205,000. In 1990, Santa Fe's population was approximately 50 percent Anglo, 46 percent Hispanic, and 4 percent Native American and other races.

Though Taos still remains a town of about 4,000, its population rose nearly 20 percent during the last census period, and it swells markedly during the ski and summer tourist seasons. Moreover, tourism revenues in Taos have been increasing almost 8 percent a year for the last nine years. At the 1990 census, the population of Taos was about 65 percent Hispanic, 28 percent Anglo and 7 percent Native American and other races.

In recent years, the Santa Fe–Taos boom has been stimulated by aggressive nationwide promotion, including countless newspaper and magazine articles extolling the virtues of the land, the arts, and the varied people and their high level of cultural integrity. In 1992, the readers of *Condé Nast Traveler* magazine declared Santa Fe the world's number one tourist destination; by 1997, the city ranked number three, right after San Francisco and New Orleans. Along with that acclaim came a wave of development that has filled the hills with condos and housing complexes, glutted both towns with cars, gas stations and convenience stores, and set into motion serious concern and continuous political debate over water use, pollution, overcrowding and cultural integrity. Resentments continue to surface over the rights of "newcomers" versus "natives" and "outsiders" versus "real New Mexicans" as old-timers continue to be displaced from their traditional way of life by those with the cash to purchase the ancient "charm."

While tourists marvel over the astounding mix of history, culture and art that comes alive in these two bustling centers, longtime locals mourn the passing of small-town feelings and quiet traditions. In the midst of the boom, citizens and governments alike explore ways of limiting growth, protecting the fragile desert environment, providing more affordable housing, and creating tax breaks to prevent further displacement of native residents.

Whatever the future holds for the Santa Fe–Taos area, it will be shaped by a combination of factors, including the national economy, the availability of water and the will of the people. If present trends are any indication, though, it will continue not only as a fascinating and fun-filled tourist center but as an ongoing stage for the interactions of the many diverse cultures that have shared in the area's rich and turbulent past.

CHAPTER TWO
Getting Here, Getting Around
TRANSPORTATION

New Mexico stagecoach, ca. 1895.

Santa Fe and Taos are beautiful auto destinations — which is a good thing, because neither is directly accessible by train or by major commercial airliners. The nearest train station is in the hamlet of Lamy, 18 miles southeast of Santa Fe. A shuttle service coordinates its runs with the arrival of trains, so this is one relatively easy way to reach Santa Fe without a car. Another is Greyhound, which provides bus service to Santa Fe from almost anywhere in the country. A third way is to fly directly into Santa Fe's modest airport, either by private plane or via Mesa Airlines, a small commercial carrier that flies from Denver and may be accessed by calling United Airlines. The majority of visitors, however, simply drive straight from their homes or fly into Albuquerque and rent a car.

By whatever means you arrive, once you're here it's nice to have a car, as towns in New Mexico tend to be many miles apart. Also, driving northern New Mexico's back roads through centuries-old Hispanic villages, Indian pueblos, and magnificent desert and mountain scenery is an experience you won't forget. You'll be happiest if you pace your own tour through this part of the world.

For your convenience, a host of details about Santa Fe–Taos transportation follows.

GETTING TO SANTA FE AND TAOS

BY CAR

From Albuquerque: The quickest route to Santa Fe is I-25 north (65 miles). A more scenic route is I-40 east to Cedar Crest, then north along N.M. 14, known as the Turquoise Trail because it meanders through several old mining villages: Golden, the site of the first gold rush west of the Mississippi; Madrid, a coal town turned arts-and-crafts center and well worth a stop; and Cerrillos, a once-bustling mining camp that is now a sleepy town with plenty of Old West character. Whichever way you go, if you're used to fog or smog at home, you'll be struck by the crystal-clear air and the expansive views.

The most direct way to get to Taos from Santa Fe is to take U.S. 84/285 north to Española, then N.M. 68 up the Rio Grande, a 70-mile drive. This is scenic all the way, but the last part, through the Rio Grande Gorge and up onto the expansive Taos Plateau, is particularly magnificent. Two of the greatest views in the world are available on this route: the sweep of piñon-studded desert as you crest Opera Hill north of Santa Fe and the unforgettable sweep of the Taos Plateau as you approach Taos driving out of the gorge. Also a beautiful drive, but at least an hour longer, is the ancient High Road to Taos, which winds its way along the Sangre de Cristo range, passing through old Hispanic villages, including Truchas, the setting for Robert Redford's film, *The Milagro Beanfield War.* Don't miss the church in the village of Las Trampas, a masterpiece of Spanish Colonial architecture built in 1763. To absorb the true flavor of old northern New Mexico, a tour of the High Road is a must. To follow this route, take N.M. 76 east out of Española to Peñasco, go east for a few miles on N.M. 75, then north on N.M. 518. This highway eventually hooks up with N.M. 68, the main route to Taos. An alternate High Road route is to take N.M. 503 east from Pojoaque, connecting with N.M. 76 in Chimayó. Taos is 70 miles from Santa Fe and 135 miles from Albuquerque. The best way to go would be to take the Gorge road one way and the High Road the other.

From Los Angeles: This is a two-day drive at minimum. Flagstaff is a good halfway point. The quickest and easiest route is to take I-15 northeast to Barstow, then I-40 east all the way to Albuquerque, where you'll take I-25 north to Santa Fe. Distance to Santa Fe: 850 miles.

From Dallas: Another long haul. Take I-20 west through Fort Worth, then go northwest on U.S. 84 through Lubbock, Clovis and Fort Sumner to Santa Rosa, where you'll take I-40 to Clines Corners. Then go north on U.S. 285 to I-25 and south on I-25 to Santa Fe. Distance: 718 miles.

From Phoenix: Take I-17 to Flagstaff, then proceed as in directions for I-40 travel to Albuquerque. Distance 525 miles.

From Tucson: Take I-10 east to Las Cruces, then I-25 north up the Rio Grande Valley to Santa Fe. Distance: 636 miles.

From Denver: A beautiful drive along Colorado's rugged Front Range. It's simple, too: just go south on I-25; after 386 miles you'll be in Santa Fe.

From Salt Lake City: There is no direct route from Salt Lake to Santa Fe. One option is to take I-15 south to I-70, then I-70 east through the heart of the Rockies to Denver, then I-25 south to Santa Fe for a journey of 879 miles. A shorter and more scenic route, albeit more complicated, is to cut through the southeastern corner of Utah (magnificent canyons) and the southwestern edge of Colorado (equally magnificent mountains) before entering northern New Mexico. Or drive a little farther south into northeastern Arizona and see the Navajo and Hopi Indian reservations. There are any number of interesting ways to go; consult a map to help you choose.

From Las Vegas: Take U.S. 95 to Hoover Dam, U.S. 93 to I-40, then proceed according to I-40 travel directions to Albuquerque and I-25 north to Santa Fe. Distance: 625 miles.

BY BUS

Greyhound Lines, Inc. (800-231-2222) serves Santa Fe and Taos from outside the state. To go to Taos by bus, you must first stop in Santa Fe no matter where you're coming from, so the information below is for service to Santa Fe unless otherwise specified. (For bus service between Santa Fe and Taos, see "Getting Around Santa Fe and Taos" later in this chapter.)

From Albuquerque (1.5 hours to Santa Fe, 2.75 hours to Taos): *Greyhound* (505-243-4435; 300 2nd St. S.W.) runs four buses daily to Santa Fe. The 1996 one-way fare was $11.55, round-trip $22.05 The *Shuttlejack* (505-982-4311) runs 11

Shuttlejack at Santa Fe's Hotel Loretto.

Murrae Haynes

SANTA FE–TAOS ACCESS

The chart below will tell you about how long a drive it is from the following cities to Santa Fe. Times do not include stops and are calculated to the nearest hour at the posted speed limit. Allow more time for bad weather.

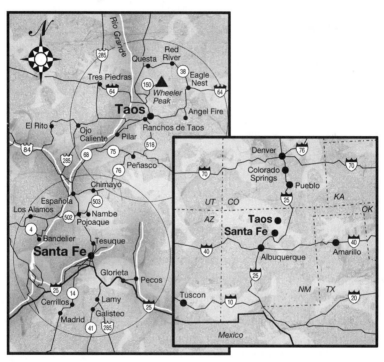

CITY	TIME	MILES
Albuquerque	1 hr.	59
Amarillo	7 hrs.	348
Cheyenne	9 hrs.	481
Dallas	13 hrs.	718
Denver	7 hrs.	385
El Paso	6 hrs.	330
Flagstaff	7 hrs.	375
Houston	17 hrs.	959
Las Vegas, Nev.	12 hrs.	625
Los Angeles	15 hrs.	850
Oklahoma City	10 hrs.	607
Phoenix	10 hrs.	525
Reno	21 hrs.	1,078
Salt Lake City	14 hrs.	680
San Antonio	16 hrs.	952
Wichita	13 hrs.	754

Taos is 70 miles north of Santa Fe, about a 1 1/2-hour drive in good weather. The two circles on this map indicate points within a 30-mile radius of Santa Fe and Taos. These circles delineate the areas referred to in the text as "Near Santa Fe" and "Near Taos." All points within the circles are less than an hour's drive from either center.

departures daily each way between 6:45 a.m. and 10:45 p.m. from the Albuquerque International Airport for Santa Fe. Drop-off spots in Santa Fe are at the Hotel Loretto and the Eldorado Hotel, both only a few blocks from the downtown plaza. You can make arrangements for other drop-off locations if you contact the shuttle service 24 hours in advance. The 1997 one-way fare was $20 for adults. *Faust's Transportation Service* (505-758-3410) provides one bus at 1 p.m. each day, to the major hotels in Taos from the Albuquerque airport. The cost of a one-way ticket in 1997 was $35. *Pride of Taos* (505-758-8340) makes the run between the Albuquerque airport and Taos twice a day, at noon and 5 p.m., once a day during the summer, and from Dec. 15 through March at noon, 2:45 p.m. and 5 p.m. The one-way ticket price in 1997 was $35; $40 to the Taos Ski Valley.

From Los Angeles (20 hours): *Greyhound Lines* (213-629-8400) has four buses departing daily for Santa Fe from the downtown station at 1716 E. 7th St. The 1997 one-way fare was $109 one-way, $218 round-trip.

From Dallas (19 hours): *Greyhound Lines* (214-655-7082) runs four buses daily to Santa Fe from its station at 205 S. Lamar. The 1997 one-way fare was $105, round-trip $112.

From Phoenix (12 hours): *Greyhound Lines* buses (602-389-4200) leave three times a day for Santa Fe from the station at 2115 E. Buckeye Rd. The 1997 one-way fare was $68 round-trip fare was $136.

From Tucson (13 hours): *Greyhound Lines* (520-792-3475) provides four buses daily to Santa Fe from its station at 2 S. 4th Ave. The 1997 one-way fare was $85, round-trip $170.

From El Paso (8 hours): *Greyhound Lines* (915-542-1355) has three buses leaving for Santa Fe every day from its station at 200 W. San Antonio. A one-way ticket in 1997 cost $50, round-trip $100.

From Denver (9 hours): *Greyhound Lines* (303-293-6555) runs four buses daily to Santa Fe from its station at 1055 19th St. One-way ticket prices in 1996 were $59, round-trip $118.

From Salt Lake City (20 hours): One *Greyhound Lines* (801-355-9579) bus leaves daily for Santa Fe from the station at 160 W. S. Temple. One-way tickets in 1997 cost $99, round-trip $198.

From Las Vegas (16 hours): *Greyhound Lines* (702-384-9561) runs two buses a day to Santa Fe from its station at 200 South Main St. In 1997, one-way tickets cost $89, round-trip $178.

BY TRAIN

Getting to Santa Fe and Taos by train can be fun and relaxing. The train station servicing the area is in the little village of Lamy, 18 miles southeast of

Santa Fe. The *Lamy Shuttle* (505-982-8829) times its runs to meet the two trains — one east-bound and one west-bound — that pass through Lamy daily. The 1997 cost was $14 for adults, $7 for children 12 and under. It's a good idea to call the shuttle service a day ahead of time to reserve a spot, as the van holds just 15 people. Another way to get into town is to call a cab. *Capital City Cab Co.* (505-438-0000) is the only taxi service in Santa Fe. The 1997 fare from Lamy to the plaza was approximately $40.

Santa Fe cannot be reached by passenger train from either Dallas or Denver, but you can take the *Amtrak* train (800-872-7245) from Los Angeles, Chicago or New York:

From Los Angeles: Amtrak has a train leaving downtown L.A. each evening and arriving in Lamy the following afternoon. This is a popular mode of travel, so make reservations early. Round-trip rates in 1997 ranged from $108 to $200 for coach. Sleepers, depending on time of year, cost $144–$360 one-way.

From Chicago: Amtrak also runs a daily train from Chicago. It takes approximately 22 hours. The 1997 fares ranged from $198–$382 in coach. Sleepers are $176 to $460.

From New York: The train ride from New York takes two days. Fares in 1997 ranged from $258–$570 in coach; $398–$1003 for sleepers.

BY PLANE

If you're like most people, you'll get to Santa Fe and Taos by flying into the Albuquerque airport. As you disembark and head for the baggage-claim area, take note of the Southwestern decor, the pastel colors, the outstanding

Small craft at the Santa Fe Airport carry passengers in and out of town.

Murrae Haynes

regional artwork on the walls and the huge cast-metal sculpture of a soaring Indian clutching an eagle. The airport commissioned works by 93 major New Mexico artists, including 30 Native Americans. If you have doubts about New Mexico's reputation as a land apart, they'll begin to evaporate in this airport. Thanks to a multi-million-dollar renovation and expansion in the late 1980s, it's one of the most attractive in the country.

It's possible to bypass Albuquerque altogether and fly directly into Santa Fe or Taos. One option is to charter a prop plane from your home base. Another is to fly in on **United Express** (800-241-6522), the only commercial carrier serving Santa Fe (there is no commercial service to Taos). The only flights are out of Denver, four times daily. The 1997 fare, depending on how far in advance you make reservations, was $152 to $239 one way, and $157 to $478 round trip.

GETTING AROUND SANTA FE AND TAOS

G iven the relatively long distances between towns in the Santa Fe–Taos region, the best way to see the area is by car. However, there are other options.

BY BUS

Santa Fe Trails (505-438-1464) is Santa Fe's first and only widespread public transportation system. Operations began in 1993, and the attractive tan buses provide service along 11 different routes covering most parts of the city. Descriptions of the routes and schedules can be picked up at City Hall (200 Lincoln Ave, two blocks north of the plaza), the Public Library (145 Washington Ave., one block north of the plaza) and at most supermarkets. The buses run from 6:40 a.m. to 9:50 p.m. on weekdays and from 8 a.m. to 8 p.m. on Saturdays. There is no bus service on Sundays. Fares are 50 cents for adults and a quarter for seniors and kids under 18. Day passes are a dollar for unlimited mileage. Monthly fares that allow for unlimited rides cost $10 for adults and $5 for seniors and children ages 6–18.

Chile Line (505-751-7786) provides public bus transportation in Taos daily, except Sunday, between 7 a.m. and 9 p.m. The buses stop every 45 minutes along Paseo, between Ranchos de Taos and Taos Pueblo. Fares are 50 cents one way; a dollar gives you unlimited rides for a day. Weekly and monthly passes are available. Pick up schedules at hotels and motels and at Town Hall, 400 Camino de la Placita.

Greyhound Lines runs two buses from Santa Fe to Taos daily and two from Taos to Santa Fe. For the latest departure times, call 505-758-1144 (Taos) or 505-471-0008 (Santa Fe). The 1997 ticket price was $16.80 one way, and $31.92 round trip. The Greyhound station in Santa Fe is located at 858 St. Michael's Drive,

---

Ski and Opera Specials

For skiers who would prefer not to deal with icy roads after a hard day on the slopes, there's hotel-to-slopes transportation available in Santa Fe and Taos. The *Shuttlejack* (505-982-4311) will pick you up at the Eldorado Hotel, 309 W. San Francisco St. at 7 a.m., ferry you up to the Santa Fe Ski Basin in time to catch first powder and bring you back into town after the lifts have closed for $10 (1997 rate). *Pride of Taos* (505-758-8340) does two runs up to the Taos Ski Valley and two runs back into town for the same 1997 rate. It will pick you up and drop you off at virtually any hotel or motel in Taos; just call ahead.

Opera-goers can have their transportation needs taken care of as well. *Shuttlejack* (505-982-4311) provides transport from the Eldorado Hotel to the Santa Fe Opera about seven miles north of town. Boarding is at 8 p.m. Reservations are necessary 24 hours in advance. And, they'll even pick you up after you've had dinner at a local restaurant, providing the establishment is easily accessible. The 1997 fare was $10 round trip. *Custom Tours by Clarice* (505-438-7116) will also take you out to the opera — for $15 (1997 round-trip price), with gourmet chocolates and monogrammed umbrellas. To go in style, try their White Glove Champagne Shuttle, which will pick you up two hours prior to a performance, wine and dine you in the gardens of a private Santa Fe home, provide an informative lecture, and then whisk you to your seat just in time for the show. Seating is very limited, so make reservations well in advance. In 1997, prices were $50 per person.

---

three miles from the city center. The Greyhound station in Taos is located at 1353 S. Santa Fe Dr., about two miles south of the plaza.

Faust's Transportation (505-758-3410) operates one bus daily from Santa Fe to Taos at 2 p.m. and one each day from Taos to Santa Fe at 7:30 a.m. They'll pick you up or drop you off at almost any motel or hotel in Taos. The pickup and drop-off spot in Santa Fe is the Inn at Loretto, two blocks south of the plaza. The 1997 rates were $25 one way, $45 round trip.

Pride of Taos (505-758-8340) provides bus service to Santa Fe once daily during the summer and three to four times daily during the winter. The 1997 rates were $20 one way, $40 round-trip. They'll go right to your hotel door in Taos, but their only "station" in Santa Fe is the Hilton Hotel, three blocks west of the plaza.

BY PLANE

The quickest way between Santa Fe and Taos, of course, is by air. It's also a great way to get a sense for the lay of the land. The following charter airplane operations offer direct flights as well as sightseeing tours from Santa Fe and Taos:

Air Taos	505-758-9501
Air West Aviation	505-471-4500

Southwest Safaris   505-988-4246 or 800-842-4246
Zia Aviation   505-471-2700

The average 1997 rate for a single-engine plane (a pilot with three passengers) between Santa Fe and Taos was $160. The average rate for a twin-engine plane (pilot plus five) was $250. The rates for sightseeing tours ranged from $110 to $400 an hour, depending on the size of the plane and the number of passengers.

BY TAXI OR LIMOUSINE

Want to be chauffeured around the Land of Enchantment in a full-service limousine replete with wet bar, TV and VCR? Or maybe you just need a good old-fashioned taxi to get you from point A to point B as quickly as possible. Here some options. (In the list below, (L) indicates limousine, (T) indicates taxi).

Santa Fe

Capital City Cab Co.   505-438-0000 (T)
Limotion Limousine Service   505-471-1265 (L)

Taos

Faust's Transportation Service   505-758-3410 (T)

BY RENTED CAR

Perhaps the simplest thing to do if you arrive by air is to rent a car at the Albuquerque airport. Virtually all the major car rental agencies are based there:

Avis	800-831-2847
Budget	800-527-0700
Dollar	800-800-4000
Hertz	800-654-3131
National	800-227-7368

Once you're in Santa Fe and Taos, you can also rent a car from one of the following companies:

Santa Fe

Avis (505-982-4361; 311 Old Santa Fe Trail at Garrett's Desert Inn, two blocks south of the plaza).
Budget (505-984-8028; 1946 Cerrillos Rd.).
Hertz (505-982-1844; 100 Sandoval St. at the Hilton).

Taos
Dollar Rent a Car (800-800-4000 at Taos Municipal Airport).
Payless Car Rental (505-737-0514 at Taos Municipal Airport).

Most rental cars come equipped with air conditioning for summer weather and all-terrain tires for icy conditions in wintertime. Virtually all of the agencies listed above also rent a limited number of four-wheel-drive trucks or jeeps for bumpy dirt roads. Ski racks can also be requested, usually at a small additional cost.

BY BICYCLE

Northern New Mexico, with its abundant open space and miles of dirt roads, is prime mountain-biking territory. While the area is also first-rate for strenuous road biking, it's next to impossible to rent racing bikes. In 1996, mountain bike rentals varied widely — from $10 a day to $200 a week with credit card as deposit. For further information, see "Bicycling" in Chapter Seven, *Recreation*.

ON FOOT

Perhaps the best way to see Santa Fe and Taos is on foot. Good walking maps can be found at the ***Santa Fe Convention and Visitors Bureau*** (505-984-6760 or 800-777-2489; 201 W. Marcy St., in the Sweeney Center). Santa Fe information is available on the web at http://www.nets.com/Santafe or e-mail at santafe@nets.com. Also try the ***Santa Fe County Chamber of Commerce*** (505-983-7317; 510 N. Guadalupe St., north of DeVargas Mall). In Taos, the ***Taos County Chamber of Commerce*** (505-758-3873 or 800-732-8267; 1139 Paseo del Pueblo Sur) is most helpful. Contact the Taos website at http.//taoswebb.com/nmusa/TAOS or e-mail at taos@taoswebb.com. There are also hundreds of miles of superb hiking trails in the Santa Fe National Forest and the Carson National Forest outside Taos. For further information on walking, see "Hiking and Climbing" in Chapter Seven, *Recreation*; "Tour Companies" in Chapter Nine, *Information*; or consult Elaine Pinkerton's book, *Santa Fe On Foot*.

NEIGHBORS ALL AROUND

Near Santa Fe and Taos are ten Indian pueblos (see "Pueblos" in Chapter Four, *Culture*); three ancient Indian ruin sites; and at least a score of old Hispanic villages, all in a marvelous desert-mountain setting that offers endless recreational opportunities. Listed below are some of the things to do and places to see within the area.

Two Suggested Strolls

Santa Fe

For a 30–45 minute walking tour of Santa Fe, we suggest starting on the plaza, perhaps right at the monument that stands in the middle of the old square. Take time to look at the blend of the old and new, the Spanish and Territorial architecture that coexists with gleaming art galleries and boutiques. Then head east for a block, stopping in at Sena Plaza on Palace Avenue, a hidden courtyard filled with shops. Turn south on Cathedral Place past tree-filled Cathedral Park, and pay a visit to the magnificent St. Francis Cathedral. Then go west on San Francisco Street back toward the plaza and peek in at the historic La Fonda Hotel, located at the end of the Old Santa Fe Trail. Stroll south along this famous commerce route and you'll soon come to lovely Loretto Chapel with its marvelous spiral staircase. Continue south across the Santa Fe River until you come to San Miguel Mission, the oldest church in America, dating from the early 1600s. Another block south is the state capitol building, also known as the Roundhouse (see "Architecture" in Chapter Four, *Culture*). A major renovation was completed in 1992.

Taos

For a similarly pleasant tour of Taos, start at the Kit Carson Museum half a block north of the plaza. The museum gives a fine sense of the region's history. Then walk toward the plaza. Just before you get there, turn north on N.M. 68, Taos's main street. A short stroll away is the historic Taos Inn, a popular gathering place for Taoseños. After you've poked your head in or sat for a bit, cross N.M. 68 and amble down Bent Street. It's filled with art galleries and all sorts of interesting shops. Then make your way to the plaza and go to the Hotel La Fonda, where you can see artwork by D.H. Lawrence. From the plaza, go west one short block and turn south on Placitas Rd. Follow Placitas until you come to Ledoux Street, then turn west again. Here is the former home of Ernest Blumenschein, one of the founding members of the Taos art colony. A beautiful example of Southwestern architecture, it looks just like it did in Blumenschein's day, and the famous artist's private collection is open for public viewing.

NEAR SANTA FE

Santa Fe is flanked by two mountain ranges, the Sangre de Cristo to the east and the Jemez to the west. Both offer hiking, cross-country skiing, downhill skiing, fishing, car camping and backcountry camping — all less than an hour's drive. There are a number of Indian pueblos to visit, as well as three major Indian ruins: Pecos National Historical Park (28 miles east of Santa Fe), Bandelier National Monument (45 miles west of Santa Fe), and Puye Cliffs (45 miles northwest of Santa Fe). For a taste of the rich cultural traditions of rural Hispanic New Mexico, you can do no better than to visit the old village of Chimayó (25 miles north of Santa Fe on the High Road to Taos), known for its historic church and its tradition of fine Spanish weaving. If you have a hankering for the Old West, check out the old mining towns of Cerrillos and Madrid (20 to 25 miles southwest of Santa Fe).

NEAR TAOS

Taos is surrounded by natural and human-made marvels. Ojo Caliente hot springs, a curative bathing spot for ancient Indians, and today a delightful spa offering mud baths, salt glows and massage, in addition to four kinds of mineral waters, lies some 30 miles to the west. About 30 miles south of Taos is Las Trampas Church, which dates from the early 1800s, and Picuris Pueblo, the only pueblo in the mountains (the rest are in the Rio Grande Valley or on the Taos Plateau). Less than an hour's drive north from Taos, you'll find the Taos and Red River ski areas. Deep in the Sangre de Cristo Mountains, 30 miles to the northeast, shimmers Eagle Nest Lake, a prime fishing and boating spot, and Angel Fire Ski Resort, along the "Enchanted Circle." To the west of Taos, the Rio Grande cuts a dramatic gash in the Taos Plateau known as the Rio Grande Gorge, a playground for boating and fishing enthusiasts.

OUTSIDE THE AREA

A little outside the area to the west on U.S. 84 sits the Hispanic village of Abiquiu, where artist Georgia O'Keeffe lived. You'll see why when you get a look at the landscape with its spectacularly colored cliffs and mesas. A few miles up the road, you'll come to spacious Abiquiu Lake and the Ghost Ranch Living Museum. The nearby Chama River, a federal Wild and Scenic River, flows through some of the most gorgeous desert scenery on the planet. Farther north, you can take a trip on the Cumbres and Toltec scenic railroad, an old-fashioned, smoke-belching clunker that runs between Chama and Antonito in southern Colorado. Snaking back and forth along the border through the San Juan Mountains, it's a wonderful way to see spectacular mountain scenery from the comfort of a railroad car. Beyond the Sangre de Cristo to the east, at the edge of the Great Plains, stands historic Cimarron, one of the major way-stations along the Santa Fe Trail. A few hours' drive outside the area to the west and north will take you to Chaco Canyon and Mesa Verde, two of the most spectacular Anasazi sites.

CHAPTER THREE
The Keys to Your Room
LODGING

Courtesy Museum of New Mexico.

The Old Exchange Hotel on E. San Francisco St. in Santa Fe, ca. 1866. Sketch by Theodore R. Davis.

There was a time when the only roadside lodge in all northern New Mexico was located at the end of the Santa Fe Trail, on the site now occupied by *La Fonda Hotel*. In the late 19th century, the railroad brought more visitors and the number of lodging establishments increased accordingly. But the lodging boom didn't really get going until the motorcar appeared on the scene in the 1920s and '30s. Many of Santa Fe and Taos's oldest hotels date from that era. The *Taos Inn,* dating from 1936, was and still is a gathering place for visitors and Taoseños of all stripes. Santa Fe's *De Vargas Hotel*, built in 1924 and now known as the *Hotel St. Francis,* was a popular hangout for state and local politicians.

The 1980s brought an explosion of bed-and-breakfast inns, many of them restored adobe and Victorian residences from 100 to 200 years old, and in some cases even older. The ***Preston House,*** on Santa Fe's east side, dates from 1886 and is possibly the only Queen Anne Victorian in the world with a Spanish tin roof. Nearby is ***La Posada,*** a hotel-and-*casita* complex that includes the Staab House, a 19th-century Victorian reputed to have a ghost roaming its corridors. And up in Taos is the luxurious ***Casa Europa,*** which occupies a restored adobe farmhouse so old no one is sure when it was first built, complete with "the oldest door" in Taos.

In addition to the B&Bs and the old-time hotels, there are a large number of roadside motels built in the 1940s and '50s. The bulk of them do not offer luxurious accommodations, but they do provide nostalgia, often with reasonable rates. Finally, there are the newer hotels, built at the height of Santa Fe's popularity, like the ***Eldorado*** and the ***Inn of the Anasazi,*** offering the height of luxury, and the fashionable ***Hotel Santa Fe,*** partly owned by the Picuris Pueblo of northern New Mexico. If you prefer a recognizable chain motel, you now have an abundance of choices in both Taos and Santa Fe. Both cities offer accommodations to suit every taste and pocketbook.

In this chapter, we describe and review some 100 lodging establishments in Santa Fe, Taos and surrounding communities. This list covers the spectrum, from low- to high-budget options. In evaluating them, we've considered numerous factors, including history, architecture, friendliness, convenience, service and atmosphere.

SANTA FE–TAOS LODGING NOTES

RATES

Traveling through northern New Mexico, you may encounter a somewhat confusing and inconsistent array of "off-season" and "on-season" definitions. In Santa Fe, many lodging establishments have summer and winter rates, summer being more expensive because it's the high season. Taos gets a bigger ski crowd than Santa Fe, and its high season is less well defined; consequently, many Taos lodges have one set of rates that applies throughout the year, but sometimes summer brings lower rates. Some places raise their regular rates at Christmas and New Year holiday time. If you are planning such a holiday visit, or are arriving for Indian Market in August and want your choice of accommodations, it is best to make reservations a year in advance. Off-season rates in both Santa Fe and Taos may range from 10 to 30 percent lower. If you are planning a stay of at least a week or more, or if you are traveling during a quiet time, such as October–November or March–May, it pays to ask about off-season rates, even if the establishment has no declared policy.

Price codes in this chapter are based on a per-room rate, double occupancy during the high season.

Lodging Price Codes

Inexpensive	Up to $65
Moderate	$65 to $100
Expensive	$100 to $150
Very Expensive	Over $150

These rates do not include required room taxes or service charges that may be added to your bill.

Credit Cards

AE — American Express
CB — Carte Blanche
D — Discover
DC — Diner's Club
MC — MasterCard
V — Visa

MINIMUM STAY

Many higher-priced lodgings in Santa Fe and Taos, including the B&Bs, require a minimum stay of two or three nights on high-season weekends and busy holidays. During such times, your best bet for a single night's stay are motels.

DEPOSIT/CANCELLATION

To reserve a room in Santa Fe or Taos, you generally must make a deposit to cover the first night, although more is sometimes required — particularly if you're going to be staying for several nights. If you have to cancel a reservation, you'll usually get your deposit back provided you cancel ten days to two weeks prior to your arrival. Be sure to check the particular cancellation policy of your lodging, as these regulations vary widely. Some establishments refund the deposit minus a 10–15-percent service fee, a few will refund only if your room gets rented, and many don't give refunds at all for cancellations at peak times (such as Indian Market weekend and during the Christmas holiday). If you cancel only a few days before your expected arrival, you're most likely to lose your deposit, although sometimes it may be applied to a future stay. During the high season, the demand for lodging often exceeds the supply, so plan well in advance — at least three to six months ahead for the most popular lodgings — so you will not be disappointed. Be warned: the popularity of this destination does not leave room for spontaneity in travel planning.

HANDICAPPED ACCESS

The information blocks for each lodging list handicapped access in one of three categories: *none, partial* or number of rooms with *full access*. Full access includes wide doors, grab bars and other special amenities. Partial access means that there has been some effort made to accommodate the handicapped (usually ramps and access to common areas) and that one or more rooms are at least accessible by wheelchair.

OTHER OPTIONS

For information on all kinds of camping, from tents to RVs, see "Camping" in Chapter Seven, *Recreation*. If you plan on camping with an RV, be sure to make reservations well in advance of your visit. If you plan on tent camping, most of the public campgrounds in the national forests and state parks are available on a first-come, first-served basis, although a few can be reserved.

INFORMATION

For last-minute or emergency lodging arrangements in the Santa Fe and Taos area, here are some numbers to phone.

Marisha's Magic Carpet: The Ultimate Concierge: 800-211-8267.
New Mexico Reservations: 800-473-1000.
Northern New Mexico Reservations: 800-672-7991.
Santa Fe Central Reservations: 800-982-7669.
Santa Fe Detours: 800-338-6877.
Ski Central Reservations – Taos: 800-238-2829.
Taos Accommodations Unlimited: 800-548-2146.
Taos Bed & Breakfast Association: 800-876-7857.
Taos Central Reservations: 800-821-2437.

CONDOMINIUMS AND SHORT-TERM RENTALS

Tired of the tourist scene? Want to live in Santa Fe and Taos like a native, in a real home or apartment or at least a condominium compound? You've got plenty to choose from. They're usually rented on a weekly or monthly basis, although some rent for single nights. In the case of condominiums, you have the option to buy your own home-away-from-home in the Land of Enchantment. Rental prices vary widely. Weekly rates can run from several hundred to a few thousand dollars. Maid service is often, but not always, provided. Here is a partial list of condominium complexes and other short-term rental possibilities, as well as some property-management firms that can mail you current listings in the Santa Fe and Taos areas. (Under the Taos listings, *TSV* stands for Taos Ski Valley.)

Santa Fe

Arius Compound	505-982-2621
Fort Marcy Compound Condominiums	505-982-6636
Frontier Property Management	505-984-2192
Las Brisas Condominiums	505-982-5795
Manzano House	505-983-2054
Zona Rosa	505-988-4455 or 800-955-4455

Taos

Kandahar Condominiums (TSV)	505-776-2226 or 800-756-2226
Powderhorn Condominiums (TSV)	505-776-2341
Sierra del Sol Condominiums (TSV)	505-776-2981 or 800-523-3954
Sonterra Condominiums	505-758-7989
Taos Lodging Vacation Rentals	505-751-1771 or 800-954-8267

LODGING IN SANTA FE

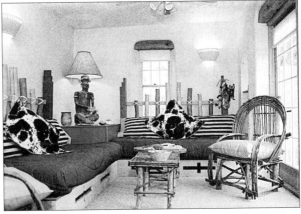

The Adobe Abode, a contemporary Southwestern B&B.

Courtesy the Adobe Abode

ADOBE ABODE
Owner: Pat Harbour.
505-983-3133.
202 Chapelle, Santa Fe, NM 87501.

This small, unpretentious B&B is a wonderful jumble of architectural styles, works of art and knickknacks. Owner Pat Harbour, a casual and friendly woman who lives on the premises, is a col-

4 blocks W. of plaza.
Price: Expensive.
Credit Cards: D, MC, V.
Handicap Access: 1 full.

lector of the unique, including a hand-carved Philippine planter's chair, a 100-year-old French armoire, Balinese antique dolls, a shadow puppet from Java and 19th-century wooden ship moldings from Vermont. There are six units, three in the main house, and three in a walled courtyard compound. The rooms combine New Mexican, Victorian and Art Deco furnishings. The two newer rooms are quite spacious, with 12-foot ceilings, *vigas,* brick floors, patios and fireplaces. This inn specializes in hearty breakfasts. It's located in a quiet residential area a short, lovely walk from downtown and has received raves from many national publications.

ALEXANDER'S INN
Owner: Carolyn Lee.
505-986-1431.
529 E. Palace Ave., Santa Fe, NM 87501.
5 blocks E. of plaza.
Price: Moderate–Expensive.
Credit Cards: D, MC, V.
Handicap Access: None.

Located in a wooded residential area, this lovely Victorian B&B is within easy walking distance of the plaza and Canyon Road. Originally built in 1903, windows and skylights have been added to make it sunnier, but it still retains a delightful charm of its own. If you like antiques, four-poster beds, stained-glass, and the scents of lilac and lavender, you'll love this place. The ample Continental breakfast includes homemade muffins and granola, and fresh fruit. In winter, breakfast is served in the cozy kitchen warmed by a roaring wood stove. An all-day tea service (also included in the room rate) offers cheese and freshly-baked cookies, which you may want to enjoy on the front porch swing. There are 16 rooms, two with shared baths. The outdoor hot tub is available for guests, as are mountain bikes and guest privileges at a nearby spa.

CASA DE LA CUMA
Owners: Donna and Arthur Bailey.
505-983-1717 or 888-366-1717.
105 Paseo de la Cuma, Santa Fe, NM 87501.
4 blocks N. of plaza.
Price: Moderate–Expensive.
Credit Cards: MC, V.
Handicap Access: Partial.

Informal and unpretentious, this B&B features three attractive Southwestern-style rooms, an outdoor hot tub, a common patio and a storage area for bicycles (the proprietors know the local cycling routes). Continental breakfasts feature strong coffee, fresh fruit and homemade breads. If you walk up the road, you'll find a hill leading to a large cross, a Santa Fe landmark known as the Cross of the Martyrs. The climb will give you a superlative view of Santa Fe.

COTTONWOOD COURT
Owner: Sam Bhakta.
505-982-5571.
1742 Cerrillos Rd., Santa Fe, NM 87501.

Here's an old, classic roadside motel with 15 rooms. It's a little shabby but has two big advantages: it's cheap and it's near the east end of Cerrillos Road, not far from downtown. Keep in

Price: Inexpensive.
Credit Cards: AE, D, MC, V.
Handicap Access: None.

mind that it is located directly on one of the busiest streets in town. For those counting their pennies, this might be a worthwhile place to stop; on the other hand, a bit of research might yield a better value for a few more dollars.

DANCING GROUND OF THE SUN
Innkeeper: Connie Wristen.
505-986-9797 or
  800-645-5673.
711 Paseo de Peralta, Santa
  Fe, NM 87501.
3 blocks E. of plaza.
Price: Expensive.
Credit Cards: MC, V.
Handicap Access: 1 full.

From the outside, this B&B looks like a tiny apartment or condominium complex. But walk into any of the five spacious *casitas*, each with evocative names like "Buffalo Dancer" and "Spirit Dancer," and you'll enter a delightfully different world. They're all distinctive and offer a great sense of privacy. *Nichos, vigas*, Indian drums, locally-made furniture, hand-painted tiling, alcoves and archways abound. Most units have fireplaces, a couple have their own washers and dryers and all have their own kitchens. There is a delightful courtyard with fountain. This place sings of being lovingly cared for, as is evident from the surroundings and the exceptional welcoming friendliness of the innkeeper.

DOS CASAS VIEJAS
Innkeepers: Susan and
  Michael Strijek.
505-983-1636.
610 Agua Fria St., Santa Fe,
  NM 87501.
5 blocks W. of plaza.
Price: Very Expensive.
Credit Cards: AE, MC, V.
Handicap Access: 1 full.

This elegant jewel lies behind an electronically controlled gate in a Santa Fe barrio. The innkeepers advertise "total privacy," and indeed the inn has the feel of a place apart, living up to its moniker as "a luxury bed & breakfast compound." The common area glows with color; one has a sense of well-being just from walking in the door. Tables and chairs made of native willow twigs, gleaming Saltillo tile floors, dark *vigas*, African art and exquisite terra-cotta plastered walls make this inn distinctive. Its eight units are arrayed in three buildings; two are adobe and date from the 1860s — two-foot-thick walls attest to their age. Each suite has a separate entrance, a private patio and a fireplace. There's a 40-foot lap pool. Breakfast includes fresh-baked muffins, fruit, juice and coffee.

DUNSHEE'S
Owner: Susan Dunshee.
505-982-0988.
986 Acequia Madre, Santa
  Fe, NM 87501.
10 blocks SE of plaza.
Price: Expensive.

Tucked into Santa Fe's historic and picturesque east side, this romantic B&B is located on the town's most beautiful, winding old street. It features two units: one, a spacious suite done up tastefully with all the usual New Mexico touches: *kiva* fireplace, *viga* ceilings, folk art, Mexican tile bath;

Credit Cards: MC, V.
Handicap Access: None.

the other a two-bedroom adobe *casita*. In warm weather, there's a sheltered, flower-filled patio for relaxing. Best of all, perhaps, is the hostess, a gracious artist who can clue you in on the local arts scene — this B&B is only a short hop away from the gallery district of Canyon Road and Camino del Monte Sol. Be sure to get specific directions before you arrive, because this place is really tucked away!

EL FAROLITO
Owner: Walt Wyss.
505-988-1631 or
   888-634-8782.
514 Galisteo St., Santa Fe,
   NM 87501.
5 blocks S. of plaza.
Price: Expensive.
Credit Cards: AE, D, MC, V.
Handicap Access: None.

This B&B offers seven renovated adobe *casitas*, some with private courtyards, all with fireplaces. The establishment has a few unusual touches like cedar ceilings and varnished plaster walls for an antique, rough-hewn look. The rooms also include some of the more typical features of Southwestern style: flagstone floors, Mexican hide chairs, *trasteros*, Spanish-style beds, exposed *vigas* and skylights.

El Paradero features charming sunlit rooms.

Murrae Haynes

EL PARADERO
Owners: Thom Allen and
   Ouida MacGregor.
505-988-1177.
220 W. Manhattan Ave.,
   Santa Fe, NM 87501.
5 blocks S. of plaza.
Price: Moderate.
Credit Cards: None.
Handicap Access: Limited.

This family-owned-and-operated B&B, one of the oldest in town, has an informal air to it. The front part of the building was a Spanish farmhouse in the early 1800s. Later additions, both Territorial and Victorian, give the inn a rambling character. It's full of nooks, crannies, private alcoves and hideaways to curl up with a book, talk or unwind. The 14 rooms are charming, sunlit and accented with handwoven textiles and folk art. The mood here is delightfully unpretentious, and it is apparent the owners take pride in the hospitality they offer. The location, just off the Guadalupe Street shopping area and ten minutes' walking distance from the plaza, is most convenient. A major plus is the substantial delicious breakfast prepared daily by the proprietor.

EL REY INN
Owner: Terrell White.
505-982-1931 or
800-521-1349.
1862 Cerrillos Rd., Santa Fe,
NM 87505.
Price: Moderate.
Credit Cards: AE, CB, D,
DC, MC, V.
Handicap Access: 4 full.

This is easily the best motel in Santa Fe and quite possibly the city's best lodging bargain. Built in 1935, it is a classic roadside motel, so well maintained that it looks like it was built yesterday, offering both nostalgia and updated comfort. Many of the 87 rooms have flagstone floors, exposed *vigas*, Indian rugs, carved furniture and ornate tinwork. Nine have wood-burning fireplaces; 11 others have gas log fireplaces in operation year-round. A large central courtyard is graced with a fountain and several large cottonwoods, creating a special world reminiscent of Mexico. Beautiful tile paintings both inside and out give the motel a Spanish flavor. A unit of passive-solar rooms overlooks a heated pool, and an indoor hot tub sits nearby. The outdoor hot tub and indoor sauna are recent additions. This is one of the most in-demand lodgings in Santa Fe, so book early.

Leslie Tallant

The Eldorado Hotel in Santa Fe.

ELDORADO HOTEL
Guest Service Director:
Debra Dayton.
505-988-4455 or
800-955-4455.
309 W. San Francisco St.,
Santa Fe, NM 87501.

If any hotel in Santa Fe has an air of big-city luxury, it's the Eldorado. Spacious and imposing, this 1997 Five Star Diamond winner has its own underground parking lot, valet service, two restaurants, several retail shops, live music every night, butler service and the largest banquet halls in the

3 blocks W. of plaza.
Price: Very Expensive.
Credit Cards: AE, CB, D,
  DC, MC, V.
Handicap Access: 4 full.

city. Built in the '80s, the five-story, 291 room hotel has a monolithic appearance that initially seemed out of scale for Santa Fe, yet it is actually about the same height as the much older La Fonda Hotel. The Eldorado also has a couple of oddities for a hotel its size: a tiny swimming pool and no lobby. The views from the top floor are magnificent; they will cost $350–$400 a night. Shopping, ski, romance and "bargain" packages are available.

FOUR KACHINAS INN &
BED & BREAKFAST
Innkeepers: John Daw and
  Andrew Beckerman.
505-982-2550 or
  800-397-2564.
512 Webber Street, Santa Fe,
  NM 87501.
5 blocks S. of plaza.
Price: Moderate.
Credit Cards: D, MC, V.
Handicap Access: 1 full.

Located in a quiet residential area, this B&B features three lower-level guest rooms with private garden patios and an upstairs room with a spectacular view of the Sangre de Cristo Mountains. An adobe *casita* with a wood-burning stove serves as a common area. Breakfast is brought to your room. Don't miss John Daw's homemade pastries, made fresh daily. He took *Best of Show* at the 1997 Santa Fe County Fair for his pannetone. Two additional guest rooms have been added in the historic brick cottage, originally built by one of the stonemasons Archbishop Lamy brought from Italy to build St. Francis Cathedral.

GARRETT'S DESERT INN
General Manager: Sharon
  Garrett.
505-982-1851 or
  800-537-8483.
311 Old Santa Fe Trail,
  Santa Fe, NM 87501.
1.5 blocks S. of plaza.
Price: Moderate.
Credit Cards: AE, D, DC,
  MC, V.
Handicap Access: None.

Nothing fancy here. Just a standard, light, very conveniently-located motel — which is probably the reason the 82 rooms are a bit overpriced. If you want to be less than two blocks from the plaza and avoid the hassle of driving and parking, this is as good a bargain as it gets. And how much time do you spend in your room, anyway? Cerrillos Road motels provide similar accommodations at slightly more reasonable rates, but it's nice to be downtown.

GRANT CORNER INN
Owners: Louise Stewart
  and Martin Walter.
505-983-6678.
122 Grant Ave., Santa Fe,
  NM 87501.
2.5 blocks W. of plaza.
Price: Expensive.
Credit Cards: MC, V.
Handicap Access: 1 full.

The delightful Grant Corner Inn feels so much like New England that you half expect to see the Atlantic out the window. A graceful 1905 Colonial manor house, it's fronted by a white picket fence, flower gardens and a gazebo, and some of the rooms have front porches. The interior features tieback curtains, wallpaper, old black-and-white family photographs, ceiling fans, brass and four-poster beds. The superb breakfasts include such dishes as blue corn blueberry pancakes, New Mexican soufflé, fresh fruit frappes, and herb skillet potatoes. Tea and lemonade are available through the day. The 10 guest rooms are quaint, several rather small, two with shared baths. There are also two rooms in a nearby condominium. The plaza is minutes away, and the innkeeper is an especially gracious host. Open at this location for 17 years, this is one of the town's most venerable B&B's.

HOTEL PLAZA REAL
Manager: Jim Bagby.
505-988-4900 or
  800-279-7325.
125 Washington Ave., Santa
  Fe, NM 87501.
1 block N. of plaza.
Price: Very Expensive.
Credit Cards: AE, CB, D,
  DC, MC, V.
Handicap Access: 1 full.

Located on a long, narrow property a block from the plaza, this contemporary Territorial-style hotel manages to house 56 rooms (41 with fireplaces), an attractive lobby and an intimate bar. Most of the rooms look out onto a brick courtyard that lend a New Orleans-style stateliness to the hotel. Massive wooden beams, hand-carved *trasteros* and Indian pottery remind you that this is the Southwest, however, as do a number of fine landscape paintings. Delicate wrought-iron chandeliers and small iron light fixtures adorn the hallways. Be forewarned: the management style is rather highhanded. If you don't mind — or if you prefer — the snob treatment, this is your kind of place.

HOTEL SANTA FE
Manager: Paul Margetson.
505-982-1200 or
  800-825-9876.
1501 Paseo de Peralta,
  Santa Fe, NM 87501.
6 blocks S. of plaza.
Price: Very Expensive.
Credit Cards: AE, CB, D,
  DC, MC, V.
Handicap Access: 4 full.

This three-story hotel at the southern entrance to Santa Fe's downtown area is the result of a partnership between the Picuris Pueblo and a group of Santa Fe developers. Its terraced, pueblo-style architecture gives the facade a pleasingly varied appearance. Its smallish 131 rooms are attractively furnished in contemporary Southwestern style and equipped with modern conveniences. The lobby, a matrix of wooden beams and columns, serves as a dining room during the daily breakfast buffet and as a lounge in the afternoons and evenings. Laundry facilities are available, as well as free shuttle service to the plaza (ten minutes away on foot). Emphasizing its Native American aspect, the hotel offers guests cultural experiences such as story telling and special packages for those interested in exploring these traditions.

HOTEL ST. FRANCIS
Owners: Goodwin and
  Patty Taylor.
505-983-5700 or
  800-529-5700.

Between the world wars, the De Vargas Hotel was one of Santa Fe's grand hotels and a popular gathering place. Its glory had all but vanished by the early 1980s when a group of local investors

210 Don Gaspar Ave., Santa Fe, NM 87501.
1.5 blocks S. of plaza.
Price: Expensive–Very Expensive.
Credit Cards: AE, CB, D, DC, MC, V, Japanese Credit Bureau.
Handicap Access: 1 full.

decided to restore its old romantic grace. A $6-million renovation job and a new name have not destroyed the hotel's Roaring '20s charm. The atmosphere evokes a faraway time and place and is a favorite with European travelers; the concierge is fluent in seven languages. Art Deco lamps, potted plants, original works by the Cinco Pintores (founding members of Santa Fe's art colony) and high-backed chairs adorn the most attractive hotel lobby in Santa Fe. The 83 rooms feature high ceilings, casement windows, brass and iron beds, porcelain pedestal sinks and period pieces of cherry wood and marble. A bar and a restaurant branch off from the lobby, where afternoon tea is served daily. Tea at the St. Francis is a very special Santa Fe custom.

HOTEL LORETTO
General Manager: Janine Shelton.
505-988-5531 or 800-727-5531.
211 Old Santa Fe Trail, Santa Fe, NM 87501.
2 blocks S. of plaza.
Price: Very Expensive.
Credit Cards: AE, D, DC, MC, V.
Handicap Access: 2 full.

Built in 1975 on the site of Loretto Academy, a reputedly-haunted girls' school founded in the 19th century, this inn's terraced architecture is modeled after Taos Pueblo. The building, with 141 guest rooms, is an impressive site, especially at Christmas-time when it's decked out with hundreds of electric *farolitos*. Rooms start at $290 a night and go up from there. It includes a swimming pool, a bar with live entertainment, a restaurant and a number of retail businesses, and you can walk to the Loretto Chapel to see the "Miraculous Staircase." The hallways are adorned with Indian-style murals, and the rooms, while of standard design, are attractive. Some of the Southwestern furnishings are made by local craftsmen. This is a busy, popular place.

The Inn of the Anasazi, one of Santa Fe's more recent examples of Pueblo Revival style.

Murrae Haynes

INN OF THE ANASAZI
Manager: Jeff Mahan.
505-988-3030 or
 800-688-8100.
113 Washington Ave., Santa
 Fe, NM 87501.
0.5 blocks N. of plaza.
Price: Very Expensive.
Credit Cards: AE, CB, D,
 DC, MC, V.
Handicap Access: 1 full.

This relatively new 59-room hotel is about as close to the plaza as you can get without being on it. It is done in classic Pueblo Revival style, with *viga*-and-*latilla* ceilings throughout, stone floors and walls and a beautiful flagstone waterfall on the second floor. The local artwork reflects New Mexico's three major ethnic groups, as does the cuisine in the hotel's restaurant. If you like to stay physically fit, the staff will bring an exercise bike to your room or rent you a mountain bike for touring. The austerely-elegant hotel also maintains a small library. An underground wine cellar with a capacity of 12 guests is available for dinner. Offering the best sense of peace and privacy money can buy, this small luxury hotel reigns as Santa Fe's most chic address for visitors. Convenient on-site services are available for business travelers.

**INN OF THE ANIMAL
 TRACKS**
Owners: Myrna and Allan
 Wheeler.
505-988-1546.
707 Paseo de Peralta, Santa
 Fe, NM 87501.
3 blocks E. of plaza.
Price: Moderate–Expensive.
Credit Cards: AE, MC, V.
Handicap Access: 1 full.

Cozy and whimsical, this small inn, which bills itself as a "grown-up fantasy" has a delightful personality. Each of its five cheerful rooms with full bath is named and decorated after an animal: "Sign of the Soaring Eagle," for example, is light and airy with six large windows and lots of feathers on the walls. The owners chose this motif out of their belief that "animals can be our teachers in the ways of harmony." This century-old house was formerly a private home, and it retains that sense of warm domesticity. A central living room is filled with big pillows, soft chairs, a fireplace and probably the biggest teddy bear in Santa Fe. Breakfasts are sumptuous, with homemade pastries, breads, fresh fruit and a different egg dish every day. Afternoon tea offers a delicious array of goodies, both sweet and savory. The innkeeper invites you to ask about low-season rates.

**INN OF THE
 GOVERNORS**
Manager: Charlotte Sliva.
505-982-4333 or
 800-234-4534.
234 Don Gaspar, Santa Fe,
 NM 87501.
2 blocks S. of plaza.
Price: Very Expensive.
Credit Cards: AE, DC, MC,
 V.
Handicap Access: 1 full.

Enclosed patios, carved *vigas* and deep red doors set this inn apart from standard motels. Many of the 100 rooms, located in three buildings, have wood-burning *kiva* fireplaces, most have stocked mini-refrigerators, and there's complimentary coffee, newspapers, and a restaurant on the premises. There's also a year-round heated outdoor pool in this efficiently-run lodging. The rooms facing south on Alameda St., a popular cruising drag for teenagers, used to be a tad noisy on weekend nights, but more stringent police controls have quieted the kids down. This site is considered one of the best examples of Territorial architecture in downtown Santa Fe. You are invited to ask about discounts.

Inn on the Alameda is a perfect small hotel in the heart of Santa Fe.

Murrae Haynes

INN ON THE ALAMEDA
General Manager: Elizabeth
  Coleman.
505-984-2121 or
  800-289-2122.
303 E. Alameda, Santa Fe,
  NM 87501.
3 blocks E. of plaza.
Price: Very Expensive.
Credit Cards: AE, D, DC,
  MC, V.
Handicap Access: 3 full.

Within easy walking distance of the plaza and Canyon Road, this 67-room inn across the street from the Santa Fe River has two hot tubs, an exercise room, a full-service bar, a comfortable sitting room and a conference room. The decor is a tasteful mix of Southwestern style and modern convenience. With private patios and a daily breakfast feast, this inn makes a good choice for the guest who prefers the casual elegance and custom service of a smaller inn. And pets are welcome!

INN ON THE PASEO
Owners: Mick and Nancy
  Arseneault.
505-984-8200 or
  800-457-9045.
630 Paseo de Peralta, Santa
  Fe, NM 87501.
3 blocks N.E. of plaza.
Price: Expensive.
Credit Cards: All.
Handicap Access: 1 full.

Part of this inn is a three-story A-frame, a rarity in this land of low-lying adobe. On either side of this structure are two recently renovated brick homes. One of the more luxurious rooms (there are 19 in all) is the honeymoon suite, which has a floor all to itself and its own hot tub. Another has a wonderful brick fireplace and a classic French armoire. The rooms take their names from the quilts of the owner's collection. Guests may enjoy afternoon snacks on the large sunporch, or before a fire in the reading room. The inn faces a busy street, so it's not as quiet as it could be.

LA FONDA HOTEL

Manager: James Bradbury.
505-982-5511 or
   800-523-5002.
100 E. San Francisco St.,
   Santa Fe, NM 87501.
On the plaza.
Price: Very Expensive.
Credit Cards: AE, CB, D,
   DC, MC, V.
Handicap Access: 2 full.

For almost all of Santa Fe's nearly 400-year history, there has been an inn of some sort on the southeast corner of the plaza. Throughout much of the 19th century, the U.S. Hotel stood there, and its location at the end of the Santa Fe Trail made it a major destination for trappers, traders, merchants, soldiers, gamblers, politicians and others. Kit Carson and a brigade of Confederate soldiers stayed there, and Billy the Kid did a stint as a dishwasher. By the 1920s, the old hotel, which had become a boarding house, was torn down. Within a few years a new hotel, La Fonda (*fonda* means "inn") rose in its place.

Today the hotel is locally owned, and the days when it was *the* hotel in Santa Fe are long gone. But it is still the only hotel on the plaza, and no other can match its storied past. The lobby, though a bit dark and musty, still has the feel of a crossroads, and the rooms exude old Spanish charm. Even if you don't stay here, pay a visit to the rooftop lounge for a marvelous view of the city, or sip a margarita in the historic bar, its dark wood and tile redolent with Santa Fe of yesteryear, and enjoy live music nightly. There's also a restaurant (See "La Plazuela" in Chapter Six, *Restaurants*), the delightful French Pastry Shop, a swimming pool, hot tubs and a massage therapist. La Fonda now features 14 totally "non-toxic" suites for environmentally-sensitive guests, and it offers *bizcochitos* (cookies) and milk for kids at night. Without a doubt, La Fonda embodies the heart and essence of Santa Fe.

LA POSADA DE SANTA FE

Manager: Merry Stephen.
505-986-0000 or
   800-727-5276.
330 E. Palace Ave., Santa Fe,
   NM 87501.
5 blocks E. of plaza.
Price: Very Expensive.
Credit Cards: AE, MC, V.
Handicap Access: 4 full.

A 19th-century mansion reputed to be haunted, a complex of Pueblo-style *casitas*, and six acres covered with huge cottonwoods and fruit trees are just some of the hallmarks of this unusual inn. The central building is known as the Staab House, after 19th-century German immigrant Abraham Staab. The three-story brick residence was a classic of its time and the original interior remains intact. On its main level is a restaurant and a Victorian lounge, a popular watering hole where you can rub elbows with local Santa Feans. Upstairs are five turn-of-the-century rooms, including Room 256, where the ghost of Julia Staab is alleged to reside. The majority of guests stay in the *casitas*, where the decor is classic New Mexican: adobe fireplaces, flagstone floors, archways, hand-painted tiles, stained-glass windows, Indian rugs, exposed *vigas*, and skylights. La Posada has a good-sized swimming pool and a lovely courtyard for drinking and dining in nice weather.

PECOS TRAIL INN
Managers: Edward and
  Barbara Lozano.
505-982-1943.
2239 Old Pecos Trail, Santa
  Fe, NM 87505.
Price: Moderate.
Credit Cards: MC, V.
Handicap Access: 1 full.

This is the first motel you run across if you're coming into Santa Fe from the east, located at the convergence of two Old West trails — Old Santa Fe Trail and Old Pecos Trail. The quite modern lodging is relatively inexpensive by Santa Fe standards and has a good-sized swimming pool, a hot tub and a festive restaurant. It has a pleasant, family-welcoming attitude, with a park, walking trails and a children's playground. Add easy access to town (only a few minutes' drive), half-price breakfasts at the restaurant on the premises and $2.50 fee to visit the nearby health spa, and this becomes an even more attractive place to stay. Modern comfort, airiness and cleanliness supersede "old Santa Fe charm" here. Kitchenettes are available. All in all, a good value. (See Peppers Restaurant & Cantina in Chapter Six, *Restaurants*).

PRESTON HOUSE
Owner-Manager: Signe
  Bergman.
505-982-3465.
106 Faithway St., Santa Fe,
  NM 87501.
5 blocks E. of plaza.
Price: Moderate–Expensive.
Credit Cards: AE, MC, V.
Handicap Access: Partial.

The Preston House may be the only Queen Anne Victorian in the world with a Spanish tin roof. Eight of the 15 rooms are located in the main house, built in 1886. Stained glass, heavy furniture, brass beds, frilly curtains, high ceilings and ornate woodwork abound. There are two lovely cottages in the backyard. A decanter of sherry and a bowl of fresh fruit await every occupant. Every need of guests is beautifully catered to. Other pluses include an on-call masseuse and a splendid quiet location on a cul-de-sac five minutes from the plaza.

Private courtyards and thick adobe walls are characteristic of Pueblo Bonito.

Leslie Tallant

PUEBLO BONITO
Owners: Herb and Amy
 Behm.
505-984-8001 or
 800-461-4599.
138 W. Manhattan Ave.,
 Santa Fe, NM 87501.
3 blocks S. of plaza.
Price: Moderate.
Credit Cards: AE, D, MC, V.
Handicap Access: 1 full.

Of all the B&Bs that popped up in Santa Fe in the 1980s, this one has some of the most charming and distinctive guest rooms, each of the eighteen named for an area Indian tribe. The look is rustic and colorful Southwestern, with wood floors, three-foot-thick adobe walls, small corner fireplaces, Indian rugs, Mexican pottery and Spanish carvings of saints, called *bultos*. The grounds are graced by private courtyards, narrow brick paths, adobe archways and huge shade trees. Although near a busy street, this inn is secluded while still convenient to shopping, restaurants and cultural activities.

**RADISSON HOTEL
 SANTA FE**
Manager: Jim Bagby.
505-982-5591 or
 800-333-3333.
750 N. St. Francis Dr., Santa
 Fe, NM 87501.
Price: Expensive
Credit Cards: AB, CB, D,
 DC, MC, V.
Handicap Access: 2 full.

Located on a hillside on the north edge of town, this 160-room hotel has magnificent views of the city and the Sangre de Cristo range. But it has a generic feel that its contemporary Southwestern decor does not try to hide. It's also pricey. On the upside, the pool area is pleasant, there's an outdoor hot tub, guests have free access to Santa Fe Spa (right next door), the Santa Fe Salsa Co. is a nice place to have a drink, and the hotel's nightclub features the unforgettable flamenco of Maria Benitez.

SANTA FE MOTEL
Manager: Martha Valdez.
505-982-1039 or
 800-999-1039.
510 Cerrillos Road, Santa
 Fe, NM 87501.
5 blocks S. of plaza.
Price: Moderate.
Credit Cards: AE, MC, V.
Handicap Access: None.

If you're looking for an attractive, affordable motel in a downtown location, this is the place. It's set just far enough off a busy road to have an air of seclusion. In addition to typical motel rooms, it includes eight adobe *casitas* with patio entrances. Across the street there's also a two-bedroom adobe with fireplace, and kitchenettes are available. Many will find this an excellent value, a reasonable way to stay in comfort without breaking the bank. During high season, complimentary Continental breakfast is included.

**SANTA FE
 INTERNATIONAL
 YOUTH HOSTEL**
Owner: Preston Ellsworth.
505-988-1153.
1412 Cerrillos Rd., Santa Fe,
 NM 87501.

For the most affordable — but not the most private — lodging in Santa Fe, between $25–$33 a night, you can't beat this place. In typical hostel style, men and women stay in separate, dorm-style rooms, and the kitchen is available for a dollar a day. It's pretty spartan and there aren't many extras (no

Price: Inexpensive.
Credit Cards: None.
Handicap Access: Partial.

TV, no pinball, just a radio), but for little more than a song you've got a safe, warm place to stay and a great, convenient base of operation. Like most hostels in the world-wide circuit, this is an excellent place for networking and information-gathering.

SILVER SADDLE MOTEL
Manager: Penelope Aley.
505-471-7663.
2810 Cerrillos Rd., Santa Fe, NM 87505.
Price: Inexpensive.
Credit Cards: D, MC, V.
Handicap Access: One full.

Clean and affordable, this motel has 25 rooms, ten with kitchenettes. Despite the nostalgia pitch, you can't get much more basic than this place. A Southwestern furniture and import outlet is located next door. Noise from Cerrillos Road is offset by the convenience to the shopping experience of Jackalope.

STAGE COACH MOTOR INN
Owner: Scott Diez
505-471-0707.
3360 Cerrillos Rd., Santa Fe, NM 87505.
Price: Inexpensive.
Credit Cards: AE, MC, V.
Handicap Access: None.

As you might expect from the name, this 14-room motel has a Western flavor. However, on the upper end of inexpensive, it's still a little pricey for what you get — especially considering that it's a 10-minute drive from the plaza.

TERRITORIAL INN
Owner: Lela McFerrin.
505-989-7737.
215 Washington Ave., Santa Fe, NM 87501.
2 blocks N.E. of plaza.
Price: Moderate–Expensive.
Credit Cards: AE, D, MC, V.
Handicap Access: 1 partial.

The Territorial Inn is the last of the grand turn-of-the-century homes that once stood on tree-lined Washington Avenue, just north of the plaza. The house incorporates some elements of Pueblo Revival style but remains essentially a fine example of Territorial architecture enhanced by a well-kept lawn, a rose garden and several large cottonwoods.

Inside, heavy print curtains, Victorian antiques and ceiling fans blend seamlessly with skylights, archways and enclosed patios. There are ten rooms: eight have private baths and two have fireplaces. A Continental breakfast comes with the room, as does afternoon wine and cheese, plus brandy and cookies in the evening. The outdoor patio is a wonderful place to be in nice weather, and a gazebo-enclosed hot tub is relaxing at any time of the year. The air of dignified intimacy, providing a respite from busy days of shopping and sight-seeing, the helpfulness of the host and the lavish care apparent in the details add up to a superlative choice for a stay.

THUNDERBIRD INN
Manager: Vinu Bhakta.

This is an old-fashioned roadside motel, the kind where you park right outside your room.

505-983-4397.
1821 Cerrillos Rd., Santa Fe,
NM 87501.
Price: Inexpensive.
Credit Cards: AE, D, MC, V.
Handicap Access: None.

It appears to be a nostalgic relic from the days when Cerrillos Road was a quiet thoroughfare instead of the many-mile-long strip mall it's become. It's been around a long time and looks a trifle run down, but the rooms are clean, it has a pool, morning coffee is complimentary, and the price is right. On weekends and holidays, rates may vary from those stated, so be sure to ask ahead to avoid any unpleasant surprises.

WATER STREET INN
Owner: Tom Getgood.
505-984-1193.
427 W. Water St., Santa Fe,
NM 87501.
4 blocks W. of plaza.
Price: Expensive.
Credit Cards: AE, MC, V.
Handicap Access: 1 full.

This handsomely restored adobe B&B has an air of romantic intimacy. It is also well located on a hidden side street within strolling distance of downtown. The 12 rooms are spacious, with brick floors, beam ceilings and four-poster beds, and a hot tub is available. Most have fireplaces, some have private patios with fountains, and one has an antique wood-burning stove. Sunset views from the upstairs balcony are splendid, and hot hors d'oeuvres are served with New Mexican wines at cocktail hour. When it comes to B&B's, God is in the details, and the details are beautifully attended to here. For luxury and convenience to launch a perfect stay, you could not go wrong here.

LODGING NEAR SANTA FE

BISHOP'S LODGE
Manager: Lore Thorpe.
505-983-6377 or
 800-732-2240.
P.O. Box 2367, Santa Fe,
NM 87504.
Bishop's Lodge Rd., 3 miles
N. of Santa Fe.
Price: Very Expensive.
Credit Cards: AE, D, DC,
MC, V.
Handicap Access: 6 full.

Bishop Jean Baptiste Lamy chose this magnificent spot in the foothills of the Sangre de Cristo range for his retirement and getaway home and garden some 100 years ago. Back then the old adobe was a small ranch that had been planted with fruit trees by Franciscan fathers in the early 17th century. After Lamy died, the property was briefly owned by publisher Joseph Pulitzer, who constructed two summer homes. In 1918, James Thorpe, a Denver mining magnate, bought the property and turned it into a resort. His family owns it to this day.

The lodge is activity- and family-oriented. Horseback riding, tennis, swimming, trap and skeet shooting, and fishing are all available in season on its more than 1,000 acres. The rooms have plenty of New Mexican flavor, and the restaurant offers a very good Sunday brunch. Best of all, there's still an air of serenity here, and Lamy's private chapel stands untouched.

Leslie Tallant

The Bishop's Lodge, former home of Archbishop Jean Baptiste Lamy.

CASA ESCONDIDA
Owner: Irenka Taurek.
Manager: Matthew Higgi.
505-351-4805 or
    800-643-7201.
P.O. Box 142, Chimayó, NM
    87522.
28 m. N. of Santa Fe.
Price: Expensive.
Credit Cards: AE, MC, V.
Handicap Access: None.

The beautiful simplicity of northern New Mexico awaits the visitor at the secluded seven-room Casa Escondida, or "Hidden House." Built in the Spanish Colonial adobe style typical of this region, and situated on six beautiful acres, this is the perfect place to rest deeply, to go for long, undisturbed country walks, and to enjoy the pleasures of the brilliant light, the scent of piñon fire, and the profound sense of history and the sacredness of the land that characterize northern New Mexico. It's a three mile hike to an ancient Anasazi Indian ruin. Lovingly decorated in the American Arts & Crafts style, this inn wraps you in its sense of tradition. Breakfast is served on the enclosed patio and terrace, and a large hot tub is tucked into a stand of trees.

THE GALISTEO INN
Owners: Joanna and Wayne
    Aarniokoski.
505-466-4000.
HC-75, Box 4, Galisteo, NM
    87540.
Off N.M. 41, 23 miles. SE of
    Santa Fe.
Price: Expensive.

About half an hour south of Santa Fe, Galisteo was founded as a Spanish colonial outpost in 1614 following the massacre of hundreds of Indians. Today this funky, dusty village is a mecca for artists, writers, healers and the like, but its Spanish character remains predominant. No other place in northern New Mexico feels as timeless as Galisteo, and few can match its expansive, windswept setting.

Credit Cards: D, MC, V.
Handicap Access: 1 full.

The Galisteo Inn, an exquisite restored 250-year-old adobe hacienda with 12 guest rooms, is located in the heart of the village on eight acres with giant cottonwoods. The grounds are gorgeous, and the interior is luxurious, with polished wood floors, a sparkling blue swimming pool and an expensive restaurant. There's also a dry sauna, a bubbling Jacuzzi, soothing massage, exhilarating horseback rides and mountain bikes. Stay here and you will enjoy a guest ranch experience you will never forget.

Hacienda Rancho de Chimayó.

Murrae Haynes

HACIENDA RANCHO DE CHIMAYÓ
Owner: Florence Jaramillo.
505-351-2222.
Box 11, Chimayó, NM 87522.
N.M. 520, 25 miles N. of Santa Fe.
Closed: Early Jan.
Price: Moderate.
Credit Cards: AE, MC, V.
Handicap Access: None.

This charming place is located in the heart of the ancient village of Chimayó, known for its historic church and its tradition of fine Spanish weaving. The inn was converted from a 19th-century rural hacienda in 1984. The plasterless, straw-streaked adobe walls are adorned with red chile *ristras*, and the enclosed courtyard is bursting with fruit trees. Seven guest rooms, predominantly Spanish in appearance, but with an air of the Victorian, feature dark massive *vigas* and heavy, hand-woven curtains, the work of a local artisan. Antiques, wallpaper and high ceilings give the rooms an almost American Colonial touch. Some have private balconies, and one has a fireplace. The hacienda is directly across the street from the acclaimed Restaurante Rancho de Chimayó (see Chapter Six, *Restaurants*), also owned by Florence Jaramillo and her family.

LA POSADA DE CHIMAYÓ
Owner: Susan Farrington.
505-351-4605.
P.O. Box 463, Chimayó, NM 87522.
Off N.M. 76, 30 miles N. of Santa Fe.
Price: Moderate.
Credit Cards: None.
Handicap Access: None.

Hidden on a twisting dirt road in Chimayó, this place is a little-known gem. There are two guest suites with *kiva* fireplaces in a solar-heated traditional adobe. The style is Southwestern rustic, with brick floors, Mexican leather chairs, handwoven bedspreads, colorful tilework and rough-hewn *vigas*. Paintings by local artists add a note of civility. Hearty breakfasts are served. A climb to the top of a nearby hill provides a spectacular view. Weekly rates are available.

RANCHO ARRIBA
Owner: Curtiss Frank.
505-689-2374.
P.O. Box 338, Truchas, NM 87578.
40 miles N. of Santa Fe.
Price: Inexpensive.
Credit Cards: MC, V.
Handicap Access: None.

You won't find a setting much more spectacular than this. Located on the Truchas plateau above 8,000 feet, this hacienda-style adobe B&B sits at the foot of the southern Rockies with amazing views. A mile to the west is the centuries-old Hispanic village of Truchas, one of the more picturesque of northern New Mexico's mountain communities.

The inn caters to hunters. The four guest rooms are fairly small, none have private bathrooms, but all are authentically decorated in Spanish Colonial style. The inn, also a small working farm and ranch, is organized around a central courtyard big enough to qualify as a plaza. Breakfasts are served in a cozy common area with fireplace and *viga*-and-*latilla* ceilings. Frank knows the mountains well and can recommend hikes. In winter, he can be persuaded to take guests on horse-drawn sleigh rides. A visit at that time of year should not be attempted unless you have a four-wheel drive vehicle or tire chains.

RANCHO ENCANTADO
Owner: Michael Cerletti.
505-982-3537 or
    800-722-9339.
Rte. 4, Box 57-C, Santa Fe, NM 87501.
Off N.M. 592 in Tesuque, 8 miles. N. of Santa Fe.
Price: Very Expensive.
Credit Cards: AE, D, DC, MC, V.
Handicap Access: 1 full.

Fifteen minutes north of Santa Fe, this Southwestern-style ranch-inn is the best lodge around for viewing New Mexico's stunning sunsets. The expansive, enchanted setting is sprawled over 168 acres, offering horseback riding, tennis courts, swimming pool and hot tub, as well as a fine restaurant and a full-service bar. You'll find great hiking trails in the foothills of the Sangre de Cristos.

The rooms in the main building have an Old West flavor, while those in the low-lying *casitas* nearby are decorated in traditional New Mexican style, with *kiva* fireplaces, exposed *vigas*, brick

Leslie Tallant

Rancho Encantado has hosted the likes of Robert Redford, Princess Caroline and the Dalai Lama.

floors, Indian rugs and hand-painted tiles. A cluster of nearby condominiums lacks the intimacy and charm of the older rooms. The "Betty Egan Bed & Breakfast Inn," located north of the main building, is comprised of four units done in contemporary Southwestern style.

RANCHO MANZANA
Owners: Jody and Chuck
  Apple.
505-351-2227 or
  888-505-2227.
HCR 64, Box 18, Chimayó,
  NM 87522.
24 miles NE of Santa Fe.
Price: Moderate.
Credit Cards: MC, V.
Handicap Access: None.

Set on four lush acres, this establishment is a working farm; highlights include an adobe with 29-inch thick walls from the 1700s, fruit orchards, fields of New Mexico chile, lavender that blooms in June and September, and an age-old *acequia*. The full gourmet breakfasts can be enjoyed under a grape arbor in warm weather. An outdoor fire-pit made of river rock and flagstone inlaid with mosaic is a splendid place for a barbecue, and a bubbling hot tub offers a relaxing spot to contemplate Chimayó's starry sky. There are two guest rooms downstairs in the ancient adobe. It's possible for one party with as many as six people to rent out the entire lower level. A new garden cottage with two-room guest suite overlooking the lavender fields is available. Not only is there a hot tub, but a pond (for dipping) graces the grounds as well. Rancho Manzana is known locally as the spot for many special events.

THE TRIANGLE INN SANTA FE
Owners: Karan Ford, Sarah Hryniewicz.
505-455-3375.
P.O. Box 3235, Santa Fe, NM 87501.
U.S. 84/285, 10 miles N. of Santa Fe in Cuyamungue.
Price: Inexpensive–Expensive.
Credit Cards: MC, V.
Handicap Access: 1 full.

This renovated inn, with nine adobe *casitas* clustered around an inner courtyard, is charmingly rustic. The *casitas* sleep from two to four people and five come with fireplaces, color televisions, VCRs, CD and radio players and kitchenettes. Four have private courtyards. A Continental breakfast is included with the room price. A hot tub and barbecue pit are on the premises. There are splendid views of eroded red mesas against the blue Sangre de Cristos. The inn caters mainly to the gay and lesbian community, but welcomes others.

LODGING IN TAOS

ADOBE WALL MOTEL
Managers: Ted and Donna Motsinger.
505-758-3972.
227 E. Kit Carson Rd., Taos, NM 87571.
3.5 blocks E. of plaza.
Price: Inexpensive.
Credit Cards: AE, MC, V.
Handicap Access: None.

Since the turn of the century, travelers have stopped here, first in tents and wagons, and later in Model T's. Here's an old-fashioned roadside motel with 20 clean, standard motel rooms surrounded by several tall cottonwoods. *Kiva* fireplaces are available in many rooms. In summer, the shady courtyard and sculpture garden make a pleasant stopping place. Complimentary coffee, tea and cocoa are available in the refreshment room. It's just five minutes' walking distance from the plaza. Weekly rates are available.

ALMA DEL MONTE–SPIRIT OF THE MOUNTAIN
Owner: Suzanne S. Head.
505-776-2721 or 800-273-7203.
P.O. Box 1434, Taos, NM 87571.
Price: Very Expensive.
Credit Cards: CB, D, DC, MC, V.
Handicap Access: Partial.

If Martha Stewart came to Taos, she'd very likely choose to stay in this meticulously appointed and run inn. Custom built as a luxury inn according to the owner's superb taste, this exquisite hacienda with five guest rooms is surrounded by spectacular panoramic views. Guests can relax in the antique-filled living room, luxuriate in a private whirlpool, snuggle into down comforters and pillows or swing in courtyard hammocks. Rooms are furnished in a stunning combination of antique and Southwest style, each with its own *kiva* fireplace. Located on Hondo Seco Road, midway between the plaza and Taos Ski Valley, this place has the feeling of a true getaway. If money is no object, and you have ability to appreciate the host's unsurpassed pampering and attention to every detail of your stay, as well as her lavish breakfasts and snacks, this could be the place for you.

Murrae Haynes

The Brooks Street Inn: specializing in attention to detail.

BROOKS STREET INN
Owner: Carol Frank.
505-758-1489 or
  800-758-1489.
119 Brooks St., Box 4954,
  Taos, NM 87571.
3.5 blocks N.E. of plaza.
Price: Moderate.
Credit Cards: AE, MC, V.
Handicap Access: None.

Built in the '50s as a residence, this B&B is not a particularly remarkable structure, nor is there anything unusual in its quiet residential setting. Instead, the secret to its success is attention to detail: bowls of freshly cut flowers; Western and Native American artifacts; fine Southwestern art adorning the six guest rooms and the large common area; the cozy reading alcove in the Aspen room; the two-person hammock out back; the marvelous garden. A full-service espresso bar is in operation at breakfast. The fact that it's within easy walking distance of numerous art galleries and shops and a short drive away from Taos Pueblo is just icing on the cake.

CASA BENAVIDES
Owners: Tom and Barbara
  McCarthy.
505-758-1772.
137 Kit Carson Rd., Taos,
  NM 87571.
1 block E. of plaza.
Price: Expensive.
Credit Cards: AE, MC, V.
Handicap Access: 1 full.

Airy, light and colorful, this sprawling B&B boasts 31 guest rooms in six different buildings on five downtown acres. Five of the buildings are traditional Southwestern adobe and one is a Western Victorian home. The rooms are spacious and modern with all the usual Southwestern accents: Navajo rugs, flagstone floors, ceiling fans, skylights, Indian pottery and *kiva* fireplaces. There are even a few surprises, including deerskin drums and an authentic Indian tomahawk. Owners Tom and Barbara McCarthy are native Taoseños who've headed a number of different retail businesses in town. If you want to know where the shopping bargains are, you can't do better than to consult them. Return for an afternoon break to the aroma of freshly baked cookies. The big breakfasts include homemade tortillas and waffles, Mexican eggs and homemade muffins.

Courtesy Casa de las Chimeneas

Casa de las Chimeneas, a hacienda-like B&B.

CASA DE LAS CHIMENEAS

Owner: Susan Vernon.
505-758-4777.
405 Cordoba Rd., Box 5303, Taos, NM 87571.
1 block E. of N.M. 68., two blocks from the plaza.
Price: Very Expensive.
Credit Cards: AE, MC, V.
Handicap Access: 1 partial.

Screened from the surrounding residential neighborhood by a high adobe wall and shaded by giant cottonwoods and willows, this hacienda-like inn offers six guest rooms, each with fireplace, that look out onto a spacious lawn and a brilliantly colored flower garden. Two new rooms feature vaulted ceilings, skylights and jetted tubs. Potted plants, hand-carved wooden columns, dark brown *vigas*, skylights, flagstone floors and regional works of art make it an example of New Mexico style at its most refined. Breakfast, which has been featured in *Bon Appétit* and *Gourmet*, is different every day but usually includes a fruit frappe, a fruit dish, stratas, huevos rancheros or blue corn pancakes. A variety of cakes, cookies and tarts are served in the afternoon, along with homemade stews and soups. Not to worry! The new fitness/workout room is truly state of the art.

CASA EUROPA INN & GALLERY

Owners: Rudi and Marcia Zwicker.
505-758-9798 or 888-758-9798.
840 Upper Ranchitos Rd., Taos, NM 87571.
1.7 miles W. of N.M. 68. (1.3 m. from plaza).
Price: Moderate–Expensive.
Credit Cards: MC, V.
Handicap Access: None.

It's hard to say what's better at Casa Europa: the inn itself (a 200-year-old restored adobe ranch house), the delectable food or owners Rudi and Marcia Zwicker. Rudi was trained in Nuremberg, Germany, and the Zwickers previously ran a highly successful restaurant. Breakfasts are superb, and afternoon tea includes an array of decadent cakes, tortes, fresh fruit tarts, eclairs and cream puffs.

There are six guest rooms. One of the loveliest, the French Room, has a marvelous 1860s French brass bed, 100-year-old hand-hewn wood floors, a marble bath and a triangular blue mirror. This inn has everything—even "the oldest door" in Taos. The Spa Room has its own full-sized whirlpool, while the Taos Mountain Room has a picture-perfect view of Taos Mountain. Outside, a recently built hot tub bubbles invitingly in an enclosed courtyard. There's also a sauna on the premises. The site possesses an air of country spaciousness. This has to be a top choice for a Taos visit.

COTTONWOOD INN
Owners: Bill and Kit Owen.
505-776-5826 or
    800-324-7120.
HCR 74, Box 24609, El
    Prado, NM 87529.
Credit Cards: CB, D, DC,
    MC, V.
Price: Expensive.
Handicap Access. One full.

Located en route to Taos Ski Valley, Cottonwood Inn is the brainchild of two delightful and charming California refugees who are very much in love with their recently renovated classic Pueblo estate, formerly the residence of flamboyant local artist Wolfgang Pogzeba. With *kiva* fireplaces, balconies, *viga* ceilings, Jacuzzis, wet bars and skylights in most rooms, all guests need do is kick back and enjoy the spectacular views and fabulous breakfasts. Winters bring the warmth of a roaring fire while summer is the time to enjoy the lovely gardens. You may feel as though a magic carpet has landed you in a bygone era of gracious living, "before the invention of the wristwatch."

EL MONTE LODGE
Owners: George and Pat
    Schumacher.
505-758-3171 or
    800-828-TAOS.
317 Kit Carson Rd., Taos,
    NM 87571.
4 blocks E. of the plaza.
Credit cards: D, DC, MC, V.
Price: Moderate.
Handicap Access. None.

The big cottonwoods in the courtyard, the picnic tables and outdoor barbecues, as well as the reasonable prices, make this 1932 vintage motel a great choice for families. The 13 units of "individual adobes" have *kiva* fireplace and four have kitchens. You can snuggle up by the fire and fall in love with Taos as easily here as anyplace else.

EL RINCON
Owners: Nina Meyers and
    Paul Castillo.
505-758-4874.
114 Kit Carson Rd., Taos,
    NM 87571.
0.5 block E. of plaza.
Price: Moderate.
Credit Cards: AE, D, MC, V.
Handicap Access: 1 full.

If you want to be surrounded by colorful folk art and have the plaza right out your front door, this 200 year-old inn is the place for you. These walls contain enough history and stories to keep you intrigued during your entire visit. The 12 guest rooms in this centrally located inn are all dazzlingly different — decorated with a collection of angels from around the world, or filled with authentic Indian artifacts nestled in *nichos*, or displaying a Franklin stove, claw-foot tub, blacksmith's tools and Winchester rifle. One features hand-carved teak woodwork, Afghani rugs, a Kuwaiti chest, and

El Rincon B&B is loaded with Taos charm.

Karen Klitgaard

a Balinese fertility goddess suspended over the queen-size bed. Much of this amazing array comes from a trading post on the property. Located in three different buildings (including an adobe compound with its own courtyard), five of the rooms have their own whirlpools and ten have fireplaces.

FECHIN INN
General Manager: Joy Barr.
227 Paseo del Pueblo Norte,
   Taos, NM 87571.
505-751-1000 or
   800-811-2933.
3 blocks from plaza.
Price: Expensive.
Credit Cards: D, DC, MC, V.
Handicap Access: 1 full.

It's something of a surprise to come upon the Fechin Inn, located in the heart of town alongside Kit Carson Park, directly behind the historic home of Russian artist Nicolai Fechin, now a museum. Designed to reflect his art, the interiors, handcarved woodwork and Fechin's prints set a tone for luxury that is almost more Santa Fe than Taos in feel. Offering 85 rooms and suites, an open-air hot tub, a six-acre parklike setting and exercise and massage rooms, this is the place for those who want all rough edges smoothed; and those who prefer a bigger city-type accommodation than the customary intimacy offered at most Taos lodgings. Pets are welcome, and a Continental breakfast is available for an extra charge.

HACIENDA DEL SOL
Owner: Dennis Sheehan.
505-758-0287.
109 Mabel Dodge Lane,
   Taos, NM 87571.
Price: Expensive.
Credit Cards: AE, MC, V.
Handicap Access: 2 full.

Shaded by giant trees, this B&B was chosen by *U.S.A. Today Weekend* as one of America's ten most romantic inns. Five of the nine guest rooms are located in the main house, a beautiful 180-year-old adobe; three are in an adobe *casita*; the other one is attached to the owners' residence. Brick floors, Saltillo tiles and hardwood floors are found in the main building, as are pueblo-style archways, *viga*-and-*latilla* ceilings, *bancos*, *nichos* and stained-glass windows. One room has its own steam bath, while the honeymoon suite has a double-size black Jacuzzi with a skylight for stargazing. The level of comfort provided by the hosts is superlative. (They will gladly pack you a lunch when you set off for your day's adventures.) You could easily wake up here from a restful night on the most comfortable bed in the world, look out at Taos Mountain and weep for joy, have a vision and decide to move to Taos! Another place to put at the top of your list when shopping for accommodations.

Art gallery at the Kachina Lodge.

Murrae Haynes

KACHINA LODGE
Manager: Dean Koop.
505-758-2275 or
800-KACHINA.
413 N. Pueblo Rd., Box NN,
Taos, NM 87571.
4 blocks N. of plaza.
Price: Moderate–Expensive.
Credit Cards: AE, CB, D,
DC, MC, V.
Handicap Access: Seven.

Just north of the city center, this Best Western is a classic roadside motel straight out of the 1950s. Don't miss the circular Kiva Coffee Shop, dominated by a bizarre, hand-carved totem pole. All 118 guest rooms look out onto a spacious courtyard with a broad lawn, tall pine trees and a large outdoor heated swimming pool. The grounds have a country club feel. The Indian decor here is laid on a bit thick, and there are even Indian dances on summer nights, but that's how they did things 40 years ago. What makes this place is that it evokes nostalgia without really trying, right down to the Naugahyde chairs in the Kachina Cabaret.

LA POSADA DE TAOS
Owners: Bill Swan and
Nancy Brooks-Swan.
505-758-8164 or
800-645-4803.

Opened in 1982, this B&B has an air of romantic seclusion, perhaps because it's located at the end of a quiet dirt road that may take a bit of patience to find. Or maybe it's the honeymoon suite

309 Juanita Lane, Taos, NM
　87571.
2.5 blocks W. of plaza.
Price: Moderate.
Credit Cards: None.
Handicap Access: Limited.

with a skylight directly over the bed. Whatever it is, this is an especially wonderful place to stay. The house, built by a founding member of the Taos Society of Artists, is replete with *kiva* fireplaces and private patios. The owners have installed their personal antique collection from England, making the six-room inn a distinctive blend of Southwest style and English country. The two styles make an amazingly harmonious blend. You won't find a better mix of relaxation, romance, convenience and congeniality. The owners pride themselves on the stimulating conversations held around the breakfast table among guests.

LAUGHING HORSE INN
Owner: Bob Bodenhamer.
505-758-8350 or
　800-776-0161.
729 Paseo del Pueblo Norte,
　P.O. Box 4889, Taos, NM
　87571.
On N.M. 68, 0.5 mi. N. of
　plaza.
Price: Inexpensive.
Credit Cards: AE, D, MC, V.
Handicap Access: None.

You've never stayed *anywhere* like this. The inn describes itself as "a European-style hotel in a Southwestern setting," but that doesn't even come close. It's more like a blend of '60s funk, '90s technology and old, old Hispanic. Call it unorthodox — and a lot of fun. Located right off Taos's main drag on the banks of the Rio Pueblo, this ramshackle old adobe was at one time home to Spud Johnson, buddy of D.H. Lawrence and quintessential Taos character in the '20s.

The oldest part of the inn, originally built in 1887, is a labyrinth of dark, heavily atmospheric rooms, including a kitchen with a cracked mud floor. Attached to it is an enclosed passive-solar wing filled with light. The 12 guest quarters vary in size, style and options. Bathrooms are mostly shared. A separate guesthouse may hold a group of six, the spacious penthouse sleeps seven, while many of the older rooms can barely handle two. Some rooms have fireplaces, one has its own sauna, a few have futons. The inn also has an extensive music and video library and provides mountain bikes free of charge. A hot tub froths and foams under the New Mexico sky. If you have a spirit of adventure and the desire to feel like a kid on the top bunk again, you'll enjoy climbing the ladder to the loft bed in one of the tiny rooms to play music from a variety of tape cassettes or borrow one of the 500 videotapes to view in your bedside VCR. Breakfast is available for a modest extra charge. Pets welcome.

**MABEL DODGE LUHAN
　HOUSE**
Manager: Maria Fortin.
505-751-9686 or
　800-846-2235.
240 Morada Lane, Taos, NM
　87571.

Set on five acres at the edge of a vast open tract of Indian land, this rambling three-story, 22-room adobe hacienda is part of Taos history. This is primarily because of Mabel Dodge Luhan, the famous patroness of the arts who arrived in New Mexico in 1918. She came at the urging of her hus-

1 mile N. of U.S. 64.
Price: Moderate.
Credit Cards: MC, V.
Handicap Access: None.

band at the time, artist Maurice Sterne, who was in Taos to paint Indians. Sterne eventually left, but Mabel stayed, married a Taos Pueblo Indian named Tony Luhan, and bought and renovated this 200-year-old structure. It quickly came to be known as the Big House.

From the 1920s through the '40s, the Big House was visited by a procession of artistic and literary figures, including D.H. Lawrence, Georgia O'Keeffe, Carl Jung, Aldous Huxley and Willa Cather. After Mabel died in 1962, the property was bought by actor-producer Dennis Hopper, who lived in it during the filming of *Easy Rider*. In 1977, it was bought by a group of academics as a center for seminars and study groups. It became a B&B in the early '80s, although workshops are still held here, as are guided tours every Sunday, Monday and Friday. If it sounds like peace and quiet are in short supply, keep in mind that this is a very big house and that care is taken not to disturb guests.

The house is filled with *viga-and-latilla* ceilings, arched Pueblo-style doorways, fireplaces and dark hardwood floors. Mabel's Bedroom Suite still contains her original bed; Tony's Bedroom opens out onto a sleeping porch; and the Solarium, accessible only by a steep, narrow staircase, is literally a room of glass (Mabel sunbathed in the nude here). There are nine rooms in the main house, a cottage for two, and a new guest house containing eight Southwestern-style rooms. Breakfast, included in the room rates, is served in the spacious dining room.

Tranquility and natural beauty await guests at the Old Taos Guesthouse.

Karen Klitgaard

OLD TAOS GUESTHOUSE
Owners: Tim and Leslie Reeves.
505-758-5448 or 800-758-5448.

Nestled amid a stately grove of trees in a rural area just east of Taos, this 150-year-old adobe hacienda has plenty of rural Spanish charm — not to mention wonderful views of the nearby Sangre de Cristo range and the Taos Plateau, and a nature

1028 Witt Rd., Taos, NM
87571.
1.8 miles E. of plaza.
Price: Moderate.
Credit Cards: MC, V.
Handicap Access: None.

trail of its own, and a traditional *acequia* (ditch). Its nine guest rooms, with hand-made aspen furniture and all sorts of thoughtful little touches, look out onto a lovely courtyard, and the century-old central living area (where breakfast, described as "on the healthy side of Continental" is served) is classically Southwestern in design and decor with a red oak floor. Owners Tim and Leslie Reeves, hosts exceptionally gifted in their ability to make you feel at home, are outdoor enthusiasts who can discuss in detail what the Taos area has to offer, from downhill skiing to hot-springs bathing. They profess to "cater to a blue jeans crowd," and delight in helping you find the hike perfectly suited to you. You will not find a warmer accommodation in all of Northern New Mexico, nor a better value.

ORINDA
Owners: Cary and George
Pratt.
505-758-8581 or
800-847-1837.
P.O. Box, 4451, Taos, NM
87571.
461 Orinda Lane, 0.5 mi.
N.W. of plaza.
Price: Moderate–Expensive.
Credit Cards: AE, D, MC, V.
Handicap Access: None.

This tiny B&B combines closeness to the plaza with sweeping views of mountain and plateau. The three guest rooms, each with separate entrance, are all part of one adobe home. Breakfast is served in a large sun room adorned with a collection of fine photos and Southwestern art. In warm weather, you can unwind on an expansive lawn under towering cottonwoods. When the mercury drops, you can pull down a book from the inn's extensive library and draw close to a fireplace.

THE RUBY SLIPPER
Owners: Diane Fichtelberg
and Beth Goldman.
505-758-0613.
416 La Lomita, P.O. Box
2069, Taos, NM 87571.
About 1 mile S.W. of plaza.
Price: Moderate.
Credit Cards: AE, D, DC,
MC, V.
Handicap Access: 1 full.

The Ruby Slipper is named for the magical slippers that transported Dorothy from the Land of Oz back home to Kansas. The seven guest rooms are named after Oz characters, by owners who agree, "There's no place like home." If you're getting the idea that this is a B&B with a bit of whimsy, you're on the right track. The rooms have some unusual touches, like an aqua-colored tile floor (with radiant heat, most appreciated in winter), but the decor is mostly standard Southwestern. Breakfasts are composed around whole and natural foods, and the innkeepers pride themselves on providing both privacy and personal attention to assist you in finding just the right hike or the right restaurant for your taste. Close to town, eco-friendly, casual, tucked away in a country-like setting, this makes for a most comfortable stay.

**SAGEBRUSH INN AND
CONFERENCE
CENTER**
Manager: Louise Blair.
505-758-2254 or
  800-428-3626.
1508 Paseo del Pueblo Sur.
P.O. Box 557, Taos, NM
  87571.
N.M. 68, 2 mi. S. of plaza.
Price: Expensive.
Credit Cards: AE, D, DC,
  MC, V.
Handicap Access: 2 full.

Opened in 1929 to cater to the trade between New York and Arizona, the Sagebrush Inn is one of Taos's oldest hotels. It's also one of the town's hottest night spots, with live music and dancing nightly. Built in Pueblo Mission style, the inn is a sprawling structure with 100 rooms, two restaurants, a bar, a swimming pool, two whirlpools. The decor, both Indian and Spanish, includes a fabulous collection of paintings by Southwestern masters and Navajo rugs. The rooms have a heavy, dark feel to them. You may want to stay in the third floor room where Georgia O'Keeffe painted. A newer addition, the Sagebrush Village, offers alternative family lodging, including spacious suites with fireplaces

that sleep up to six people. A complimentary breakfast is included in the rate. Ski packages with reduced rates on room and lift tickets are available.

SUN GOD LODGE
General Manager: Jim
  Francisco.
505-758-3162.
#5513 NDCBU, Taos, NM
  87571.
N.M. 68, 1 mile S. of plaza.
Price: Inexpensive–
  Moderate.
Credit Cards: AE, D, MC, V.
Handicap Access: 1 full.

A cute roadside motel done in pueblo style, it's been at this location since 1958. The rooms are quiet, attractive and exceptionally well-kept, airy and bright, with handmade Taos-style furniture. The rates may be bargain-level, but the Southwest style does not feel at all cut-rate. A recent expansion has brought the total number of rooms to 55. Most are organized around a parking lot and a grassy area with trees, and all are of standard motel design. Some have kitchenettes. This place bills itself as "the best value in Taos," and that claim could well be the truth.

TAOS INN
Owner: Carolyn Haddock.
505-758-2233 or
  800-826-7466.
125 Paseo del Pueblo Norte,
  Taos, NM 87571.
0.25 block N. of plaza.
Price: Expensive.
Credit Cards: MC, V.
Handicap Access: 1 full.

If immersion in the colorful atmosphere of New Mexican arts, crafts, history and legend is your cup of tea — or tequila — you can do no better than to stay at the Taos Inn. You would join a guest register that includes the like of Greta Garbo, Thornton Wilder and D.H. Lawrence. It has National Landmark status and was thoroughly restored and modernized in the early 1980s. Sometimes called "the community living room," the lobby is both an art gallery and a people-watcher's paradise.

Each of the 37 guest rooms at the inn is graced with a distinct personality. Most rooms have pueblo fireplaces, Taos-style antique furniture, bathrooms

Karen Klitgaard

The walls of the historic Taos Inn are steeped in legend and lore.

with Mexican tile, handwoven Indian bedspreads — even cable TV. Squeaky, old-time wooden floorboards can be heard under the new wall-to-wall carpeting. Several rooms open onto a balcony overlooking the lobby, while several more open onto a quiet courtyard in the rear. A swimming pool is open in warm weather; and for weary skiers, a Jacuzzi bubbles invitingly in the plant-filled greenhouse.

THE WILLOWS INN
Owners: Doug and Janet Camp.
505-758-2558.
Box 6560 NDCBU, Taos, NM 87571.
412 Kit Carson at Dolan.
Price: Moderate.
Credit Cards: MC, V.
Handicap Access: Limited.

A tiny green sign inlaid on a large adobe wall marks this B&B. Behind that wall you'll see a spacious lawn, lily pond and several graceful willow trees leaning over a stately two-story adobe. (They are the two largest willows in the United States.) The former home of a well-known local painter, E. Martin Hennings, one of the original members of the Taos Society of Artists, it has been a lodge since 1990. The double adobe construction, rare in this century, is one of the reasons the property is listed on National and State Historic Registries. The five guest rooms each have their own themes, each with *kiva* fireplace. It is also possible to stay in Hennings' high-ceilinged studio, deservedly titled the inn's "honeymoon suite." Breakfasts are hearty and different every day. The artwork throughout the inn is exquisite, and the hosts are absolutely wonderful people. An irresistible place to stay.

LODGING NEAR TAOS

THE ABOMINABLE SNOWMANSION

Manager: David Sharpe.
505-776-8298.
P.O. Box 3271, Taos, NM 87571.
Off N.M. 150, halfway to Taos Ski Valley in Arroyo Seco.
Price: Inexpensive.
Credit Cards: D, MC, V.
Handicap Access: Partial.

Located in the old Hispanic village of Arroyo Seco, the Abominable Snowmansion wins, hands down, the contest for the best-named ski lodge in the Taos area. It's also tops when it comes to informality, fun and affordability. The Snowmansion is a youth hostel in the summer and a budget B&B in the winter. Though the Snowmansion attracts mainly young people, old-timers are more than welcome. Most of the quarters are dormitory-style with bunk beds, and the sexes are segregated. There are four private rooms for couples. All-you-can-eat breakfasts are straightforward: eggs, bacon and pancakes. The common area is a social hub, containing pinball games, a pool table, piano and a fireplace. This lodging makes a ski vacation affordable for just about anyone. This place is very clean, well-run and quite comfortable, for a hostel. In warmer weather, it is possible to pitch your tent or rent a teepee. Group rates are available.

ALPINE LODGE

Owners: Jerry and Verna Henson.
505-754-2952 or 800-252-2333.
P.O. Box 67, Red River, NM 87558.
At the ski area.
Price: Inexpensive–Moderate.
Credit Cards: AE, D, MC, V.
Handicap Access: Three full.

On the banks of the Red River within easy walking distance of the Red River ski area, Alpine Lodge was run by native German Ilse Woerndle and her family for over 30 years. The current owners, who took over in 1991, have spruced up some of the 45 rooms but have basically taken the attitude, "If it ain't broke, don't fix it." Charmingly Bavarian, this cozy inn includes a restaurant and a bar with live music. Very clean and comfortable, with a hot tub, this is an excellent choice for a ski vacation.

ANGEL FIRE RESORT

Manager: Peter Gutman.
505-377-6401 or 800-633-7463.
Drawer B, Angel Fire, NM 87710.
At the ski area.
Price: Expensive.
Credit Cards: AE, D, DC, MC, V.
Handicap Access: 2 full.

With 157 rooms, Angel Fire Resort is by far the biggest lodging establishment in Angel Fire. The decor is contemporary Southwestern, and the ski area is right outside the window. The inn has two restaurants, a lounge and an indoor pool and hot tub.

ARROWHEAD LODGE
Owners: Ron and Paula
  Compton.
505-754-2255 or
  800-299-6547.
P.O. Box 261, Red River,
  NM 87558.
Closed: End of ski season to
  mid-May.
Price: Moderate.
Credit Cards: AE, D, MC, V.
Handicap Access: None.

This quiet, no-frills lodge is located on a side street off Red River's main drag, within easy reach of the ski area. There are 19 units, some with fireplaces, some with kitchenettes. In warm weather, a sundeck, barbecue pit and several picnic tables are available for your use.

AUSTING HAUS HOTEL
Owner: Paul Austing.
505-776-2649 or
  800-748-2932.
P.O. Box 8, Taos Ski Valley,
  NM 87525.
Off N.M. 150, 1.5 miles W.
  of Taos Ski Valley.
Price: Moderate–Expensive.
Credit Cards: AE, CB, D,
  MC, V.
Handicap Access: 2 full.

Over 70,000 board feet of timber with 3,000 interlocking joints were used in the construction of this hotel, making it the largest timber-frame building in the United States. An impressive feat, but this Alpine-style lodge is missing that intangible thing called character. Continental breakfast is included, and there is a restaurant on the premises, serving dinner throughout the ski season in the "glass dining room." Pets are allowed in the private chalets, and ski packages are available. The hotel caters to groups and families.

THE BAVARIAN
Owner: Thomas Schulze.
505-751-6661 or
  505-770-0450.
PO Box 653, Taos Ski Valley,
  NM 87525.
Price: Very Expensive.
Credit Cards: AE, D, DC,
  MC, V.
Handicap Access. None.

Completed in 1996, this is the last word in ski lodging, conceived, as the genial young German owner says, "as a private high Alpine retreat for a few precious guests. . ." The mid-mountain log-mansion is perched at 10,200 feet in the Wheeler Wilderness Area, and is surrounded by mountain peaks. Modeled on high Alpine guest houses of Austria and Bavaria, the Bavarian invites you to ski to its exquisite restaurant. Or, you may be driven up from the lower Ski Valley. The luxurious guest suites feature marble-tiled bathrooms, Bavarian antiques and hand-carved and painted appointments.

CASA RINCONADA DEL RIO
Owner: JoAnne Gladin de
  la Fuente.
505-579-4466.
Box 10-A, Taos Highway
  68, Rinconada, NM
  87531.

Set in the ancient farming village of Rinconada, this reasonably priced B&B borders a fruit orchard and is literally a stone's throw from the Rio Grande. There are two units, one in a small adobe that can accommodate up to five people, the other in a separate building that can hold six. These are not luxurious accommodations, but they have all

N.M. 68, 20 mi. S. of Taos.
Price: Moderate.
Credit Cards: None.
Handicap Access. None.

you need: full kitchen, full bath, TV, air conditioning, wood-burning stove, even a small exercise room. The owner lives on the premises and will provide you with a Continental breakfast including homemade bread. A lovely time to visit Casa Rinconada is in the spring, when the fruit trees are in full blossom. Harvest time in early fall is even better: the trees produce so much fruit that you're welcome to help yourself. Rates are flexible according to length of stay. A home away from home.

Courtesy of the Dobson House

Dobson House offers solar comfort on the edge of the Taos Gorge.

DOBSON HOUSE.
Owners: Joan and John
  Dobson.
505-776-5738.
P.O. Box 1584, El Prado,
  NM 87529.
13 miles north of Taos.

If you think you are ready for the visit of a lifetime, you ought to consider staying at the spectacular new Dobson House. Built on the principles of the famous Taos eco-friendly "Earthships", the totally solar-powered Dobson House is a magnificent modern adobe castle located at 7,000 feet on a

Price: Moderate.
Credit Cards: None. Cash,
  personal checks and
  traveler's checks only.
Handicap Access: None.

100-foot hill, on 25 acres beside the Rio Grande Gorge. From the enormous circular, glassed-in great room, you can watch hawks and ravens soar past. And the suites are the ultimate in comfort and eco-sensitivity. The Dobson house is filled with beautiful tile-work and stunning art; the spectacular stairway alone is worth the visit. But that doesn't begin to compare with the Dobson's excellent hospitality and lovely meals. Since you are in a rather isolated location (it's best not to arrive after dark — not much of a dirt road in, and the trip can be confusing the first time), you may request dinner be prepared for you. You will be in walking distance of the Manby Hot Springs. On request, Paradise Balloons will take off from the Dobson's hill. This is one of those rare places that must be experienced to be believed. Children under 14 are not accepted.

HOTEL ST. BERNARD
Owner: Jean Mayer.
505-776-2251.
PO Box 88, Taos Ski Valley,
  NM 87525.
Closed: Non-ski season.
Price: Moderate (weekly ski
  packages).
Credit Cards: None.
Handicap Access: None.

Jean Mayer, owner of Hotel St. Bernard (named for the patron saint of skiers), is also technical director of the Taos Ski Valley Ski School. Most guests accepted at the hotel are those on the ski school's seven-day plan; exceptions are made for nightly stays at beginning and end of ski season. The package includes three meals a day, including seven-course gourmet dinners prepared by French chefs. The hotel's 28 rooms are located in three buildings and include attractive A-frame units with sun decks at the bottom of the slopes. The ski season is usually booked by July, so plan ahead. The hotel's staff is exceptionally professional and helpful, and the bar is a well-known après-ski spot. A top choice for anyone serious about skiing and having a good time.

**THE INN AT
  SNAKEDANCE**
Owner: Mary Madden.
505-776-2277.
P.O. Box 89, Taos Ski Valley,
  NM 87525.
Closed: End of ski season to
  June 15; Oct. 15 to
  beginning of ski season.
Price: Very Expensive.
Credit Cards: MC, V.
Handicap Access: 3 full.

This on-slope establishment, at the former site of the Hondo Lodge, now named for the first ski run at Taos, brings some first-rate lodging to Taos Ski Valley. The look is a blend of Alpine and Southwestern, with exposed pine beams, a huge stone fireplace, locally carved wood furniture, a glass-walled bar, a sun deck that's ideal for barbecuing, live entertainment, a hot tub, sauna and exercise room. There are 60 rooms, including 34 equipped with fireplaces. Weekly ski packages (in conjunction with the Taos Ski School's Ski Better Week) including lodging, meals and ski passes are available but not required. The Taos Ski School has a rep-

The Inn at Snakedance, an Alpine touch at Taos Ski Valley.

Sandra Lee Tatum

utation as the nation's best. The restaurant offers fine dining, and the staff is most eager to please. Summer rates are a real bargain, with fishing, riding, hiking, mountain biking and wildflowers offering their attractions.

THE LITTLE TREE B&B
Owners: Charles and Kay Giddens.
505-776-8467 or 800-334-8467.
PO Drawer II, Taos, NM 87571.
County Rd. B143, 10 miles N.E. of Taos.
Price: Moderate.
Credit Cards: AE, D, MC, V.
Handicap Access: Partial.

Located about halfway between Taos and Taos Ski Valley, this charming Pueblo-style adobe B&B looks like it's been part of the landscape for decades. In fact, it was built in the early 1990s. "We wanted to make it look old," says one of the owners, Charles Giddens, a retired lawyer from Dallas. Four guest rooms, arranged around a courtyard bursting with flowers in springtime, are named for four species of small trees native to the Taos region: piñon, juniper, aspen and spruce. Each room has its own private entrance, two have *kiva*-style wood-burning fireplaces, and two have glazed adobe mud floors. There are three cats on the premises, so if you're allergic to felines, this is probably not the place for you. The owner's favorite season is fall, but this is a favorite of cross-country skiers.

MOORE REST INN
Manager: Owen Smith.
505-377-6813.

This modest, well-maintained 31-room motel on the shore of Eagle Nest Lake isn't fancy, but it is functional and does offer nice views of Eagle Nest

Box 138, Eagle Nest, NM
  87718.
U.S. 64, 30 mi. E. of Taos.
Price: Inexpensive.
Credit Cards: AE, D, MC, V.
Handicap Access: 1 full.

Lake. A kitchen is available, as is a recreation room with fireplace. Owen Smith, the manager, has fishing tales to share and pointers for those who want to try their luck in the lake.

OJO CALIENTE MINERAL SPRINGS

Manager: Cassandra
  Ortega.
505-583-2233.
P.O. Box 68, Ojo Caliente,
  NM 87549.
U.S. 285, 35 miles S.W. of
  Taos.
Price: Inexpensive–
  Moderate.
Credit Cards: AE, D, MC, V.
Handicap Access: 1 full.

In the 1500s, Spanish explorer Cabeza de Vaca chanced upon these desert hot springs, a favorite bathing spot of local Indians, and described them as "wonderful waters bursting out of a mountain." (See "Spas and Hot Springs" in Chapter Seven, *Recreation.*) Locals have come to "take the waters," for half a century, and the place still retains the air of an old-fashioned sanitorium. Today they are the focus of this no-frills, 36-room resort located next to the springs. The resort offers special rates for overnight stays with soak and breakfast. You may stay in the funky, somewhat drafty old lodge or rent a private cottage. Campsites are available, and a restaurant featuring healthful offerings is located in the lodge. While locals bemoan the higher rates and modernization, Ojo Caliente caters increasingly to the more affluent tourist trade. Still, many New Mexicans advise their guests that this is a "must-do."

SALSA DEL SALTO

Owners: Dadou Mayer and
  Mary Hockett.
505-776-2422 or
  800-530-3097.
P.O. Box 1468, El Prado,
  NM 87529.
N.M. 150, 10 miles W. of
  Taos Ski Valley.
Price: Expensive.
Credit Cards: AE, MC, V.
Handicap Access: None.

Salsa del Salto has the best of two worlds. Located at the dramatic junction of the Sangre de Cristo range and the Taos Plateau, it offers easy access to the mountains and expansive views of the desert. The inn itself, designed by award-winning architect Antoine Predock, is light, airy and contemporary. Its ten guest rooms are accented in Southwestern style, the central area is divided by a massive stone fireplace, and green tennis courts and a sparkling blue pool beckon outside. Dadou Mayer, one of the owners, is an amateur ski racer and an accomplished chef, while his partner, Mary Hockett, is an experienced equestrian and a top-notch baker. The inn's omelettes have been featured in *Gourmet* magazine.

TAOS MOUNTAIN LODGE

Manager: Margaret Weber.
505-776-2229 or
  800-530-8098.

Located on a south-facing mountainside, Taos Mountain Lodge has ten condominiums, split-level A-frame suites that can hold from four to six people. Eight have fireplaces. The suites are equip-

P.O. Box 698, Taos Ski
  Valley, NM 87525.
N.M. 150, Taos Ski Valley.
Closed: End of ski season to
  mid-May.
Price: Expensive.
Credit Cards: AE, D, MC, V.
Handicap Access: Partial.

ped with satellite television sets and kitchens. All
the rooms are done in tasteful, if typical, Southwestern decor. Indoor and outdoor whirlpools can
relieve your aches, and there is a steamroom. Outdoor gas grills are available. Completely surrounded by National Forest, the owner claims this
is the "most beautiful spot on the mountain." You
can have serenity plus a seven minute trip to the
lift!

THUNDERBIRD LODGE
Owners: Elisabeth and Tom
  Brownell.
505-776-2280 or
  800-776-2279.
P.O. Box 87, Taos Ski Valley,
  NM 87525.
Closed: Non-ski season.
Price: Moderate.
Credit Cards: MC, V.
Handicap Access: None.

The Thunderbird is in the heart of Taos Ski Valley, within easy walking distance of the slopes.
Preference is given to guests on seven-day ski week
packages, which include lifts, meals and ski
lessons. The lodge will take guests not on the package, but they must stay a minimum of two nights.

The guest rooms are small, but the beds are excellent and each room has a humidifier. The rustic
Thunderbird has a lot to offer: saunas and whirlpools, professional massage therapists, a fine
restaurant specializing in European and Southwestern cuisine, a lively bar, a massive stone fireplace,
and live C&W or jazz seven nights a week. There's
even regular wine and beer tasting.

CHAPTER FOUR
What to See, What to Do
CULTURE

Band concert under Palace of the Governors portal, ca. 1915.

The renowned enchantment of the Santa Fe–Taos area has simple origins: the place is powerfully unlike any other in the world. With the exception of nature itself, nothing is more enchanting here than the interweaving of the area's three primary cultures: Indian, Spanish and Anglo. The result is more like a three-layer cake than the proverbial American melting pot. Each layer is made with different ingredients and recipes, and each has its own distinct flavor. The Indian and Spanish recipes in particular have been a long time in the making. Native Americans were building complex communities across the Southwest when Europe was in the Dark Ages, and Santa Fe was founded more than a decade before the Pilgrims set foot on Plymouth Rock.

Partly because of its ancient roots, many visitors are drawn to the art of the area's Indian and Hispanic peoples — art that grew out of what Taos photographer Bill Davis calls "the mixture of the divine and the human in the landscape." The Pueblo Indians see no distinction between physical and spiritual landscape. The land is home to the spirits, and the Pueblos read the earth as Europeans read their Bibles: mountains, rivers and mesas all contain stories about historical events and how to survive on the land. Dances are offered as prayers for the well-being of the people. Likewise, the creation of objects such as pottery, jewelry and baskets are acts guided by spirit.

Many Indian artists acknowledge spirit as the source of their talents. "Clay is very special," says Santa Clara potter Ray Tafoya. "It's giving us life. We can't use it out of disrespect." Even artists who produce highly individualistic work operate from the matrix of their own tribal cultures, building and adapting it to new needs and purposes.

For Hispanics, spirituality is not so much imbued in the land as it is an inseparable part of the identity brought from Spain. Through the many generations they have lived in New Mexico, long isolated from their original Spanish culture, the land has been the mother who sustained them. The art of Hispanic people springs from an everyday life permeated with Catholic faith. The statue of San Ysidro carried to the fields each spring to ensure a good planting and the *retablos* (paintings on wood slabs) of Our Lady of Guadalupe touched each morning with a whispered prayer are art that is both loved and used. Likewise, the murals of the Virgin that grace many adobe homes, the pageantry of fiestas, the village parades on saints' days — even the meticulously accessorized "lowrider" automobiles — are forms of art found in everyday life.

The Santa Fe–Taos area provides fertile ground for art rooted in Europe. In the early part of the 20th century, Santa Fe and Taos were home to Eastern artists who established Southwestern "Sohos" of their day. Their breathtaking landscape paintings hang in area galleries and museums (See "Traditional Art" under "Galleries" in Chapter Eight, *Shopping*). These painters — men like Josef Bakos, Nicolai Fechin, Ernest Blumenschein and Randall Davey — inspired generations of successors who continue to explore the landscape and the unusual clarity of light. And the work of Georgia O'Keeffe — now recognized in Santa Fe in a "museum of her own" — conveys the magic of the place in color and light, as it continues to inspire visitors to come and seek that magic for themselves. Europe also has provided Santa Fe–Taos with magnificent opera and chamber music, both of which thrive in the clear desert air.

ARCHITECTURE

Adobe architecture, as much as the landscape itself, gives New Mexico a distinctive identity. In a nation where many places look the same, the Santa

Fe–Taos area still holds precariously to its identity. It's not that architecture here doesn't change — it certainly does — but the thread of continuity has spun itself through hundreds of years and through the evolutions of three strikingly different cultures.

For a look at the old adobe architecture, stroll around the Santa Fe Plaza, along E. De Vargas St. and up Canyon Rd. Or explore Taos Plaza and its intriguing side streets. The soft, rounded adobe structures appear to have grown right out of the earth. Modern flourishes notwithstanding, these buildings are the architectural descendants of mud-and-stick dwellings built thousands of years ago by the first Indian inhabitants of the Southwest.

As the centuries passed, these people adapted their techniques and materials. For example, mud walls were built up a handful at a time, a technique called "puddling." Or they were laid with "bricks" of mud cut from stream banks. Ruins like those at Chaco Canyon and Bandelier National Monument reveal sophisticated use of natural sandstone and other rock for the construction of four- and five-story apartment-type buildings. The stone walls were mortared with mud.

When Spanish settlers arrived in the early 1600s, the Pueblo Indians quickly adopted the newcomers' adobe brick-making techniques. The Spaniards' knowledge of adobe construction can be traced back to the Middle East and Mesopotamia, as can their use of the *horno* (OR-no), a beehive-shaped outdoor oven originally acquired from the Moors.

To get a feel for the city's early adobe residences, visit the so-called Oldest House in the U.S.A. at 215 E. De Vargas St. in Santa Fe. The cavelike interior features a corner fireplace of Spanish origin. The oldest parts of the walls are of puddled adobe. Contrast this humble home with the modern, five-story Eldorado Hotel at 309 W. San Francisco St. to see how flexible the idea of mud construction can be. The Eldorado is a recent expression of the Santa Fe style, or Spanish-Pueblo Revival style, which has been in vogue since the 1920s. The Eldorado, however, like most newer buildings in Santa Fe, is not real adobe; it simply wears an adobe-style stucco veneer.

In some ways, the transition from the "Oldest House" to the Eldorado has been a natural process of cultural and technological change. However, it was also a calculated effort by a small group of influential Santa Feans to save the city's architectural heritage from the forces of "progress."

Before the railroad arrived in 1880, the Spanish-Pueblo style of architecture prevailed; most houses were built as square, one-story adobe structures around a central patio. Protruding *vigas* formed the roofs, which were topped with rows of smaller poles and earth. The largest structures were adobe churches, built in Spanish Mission style. But soon the "Anglicization" of New Mexico threatened this unique form of architecture. In the 19th century, Anglo traders and others from the East often described area dwellings as unsightly and criticized the poverty and "backwardness" of Hispanic residents. As a result of these Anglo cultural biases, many natives as well as newcomers began a push to tear down the old and replace it with a hodgepodge of styles imported from the East Coast and the Midwest.

These "progressive" Santa Feans were especially proud of their new state capitol. Dedicated in 1900, with a rotunda and an Ionic-columned portico, it was a fine example of the classical style then in vogue in the United States — and it was totally out of place in New Mexico. This structure was completely redesigned in the 1950s to make it consistent with Spanish-Pueblo Revival style.

The movement to remake Santa Fe into an imitation of Midwestern and Eastern cities would have succeeded had it not inspired a powerful countermovement. A group of Anglo artists, archaeologists and others, alarmed by the loss of the city's architectural heritage, dedicated themselves to preserving older Spanish structures and to searching for a new regional building style. This group staged an exhibition in 1912 to awaken interest in preserving the "Old Santa Fe" and in promoting Santa Fe as the "unrivaled tourist center of the Southwest." It was this second goal that eventually won over the city's business community. For the first time, people began to realize that in order to attract tourists Santa Fe must remain unique.

Success did not come overnight. One of the key battles took place over the Palace of the Governors, three years before the exhibition. "Progressives" wanted to demolish this symbol of New Mexico's Hispanic past and put up a proper "American" courthouse. But in 1909 the "conservatives" — Hewitt and his group — persuaded the legislature to preserve the Palace as a historical museum. In the restoration that followed, the building's Territorial-style *portal* and brick coping were replaced with a Spanish-Pueblo *portal* and *vigas*. These renovations were intended to evoke the building's early history, and they helped establish the newly emerging "Santa Fe style."

The Museum of Fine Arts across from the palace, designed by Isaac Hamilton Rapp, was another milestone that helped to firmly establish the "new-old"

Santa Fe style architecture began with the Museum of Fine Arts.

Corrie Photography

style Hewitt and others wanted to achieve. Building the structure of brick rather than adobe, Rapp nevertheless incorporated many elements of Hispanic Mission churches for the museum design. Though the Museum of Fine Arts was built in 1916–17, its evocative design makes it appear far older.

Two commercial buildings designed by Rapp to boost the Santa Fe style can still be seen: the Gross, Kelly & Co. Almacen, a warehouse near the railroad tracks on Guadalupe St., and La Fonda, off the southeast corner of the plaza. The warehouse, though in poor condition, still clearly displays its Spanish-style towers, *portal, vigas* and *canales*.

As a result of accolades for the museum and the palace, the city adopted the Santa Fe style (called Spanish-Pueblo Revival), which was carried on by enthusiasts like Meem and writer Oliver La Farge. Meem, who like many in his day sought New Mexico's climate as a cure for tuberculosis, stayed in Santa Fe to become the most eloquent architect of Santa Fe style. One of the most memorable of his dozens of buildings is the Cristo Rey Church. (See "Historic Buildings and Sites" in this chapter.) This massive structure, built in 1940 with 150,000 adobe bricks, bespeaks the architect's love for New Mexico's early Mission churches.

The look of Santa Fe's downtown plaza also owes much to Meem, who remodeled several Victorian or commercial buildings there, among them the former Woolworth building, the Franklin store, the Renehan building, the old Masonic Lodge, and the original and present buildings of the First National Bank. In 1966, he also designed the *portals* that run along three sides of the plaza.

Soft lines of classic adobe walls grace Santa Fe's streets.

Karen Klitgaard

In 1957, after six years of study, the city council adopted the Historic Zoning Ordinance and established Santa Fe's Historic District, which roughly encompasses the downtown area and Canyon Road. The ordinance gave an official stamp to two architectural styles: Spanish-Pueblo Revival and Territorial. The first, a modern version of the Santa Fe style, is characterized by massive walls, rounded parapets and hand-hewn woodwork. Territorial is recognized by brick coping atop adobe walls, milled woodwork and decorative pediments on doors and windows. A number of fine Victorian buildings from New Mexico's territorial days still survive in Santa Fe (for example, the First Ward School at 400 Canyon Rd.); however, that style was deemed politically incorrect in 1957 and remains so today.

Anglicization came somewhat later to Taos, which lost many of its original buildings to "progress" in the 1920s and '30s. In 1984, the Taos Town Council approved a Historic Design Review ordinance that included many elements borrowed from Santa Fe's ordinance. The Historic District includes the plaza and several clusters of buildings within Taos's three square miles.

Though Spanish-Pueblo Revival style borrows some important features from Pueblo architecture, such as rounded contours, large blank surfaces and stepped-back levels, the philosophy and purposes of the two styles are quite different. To feel the difference, visit the older sections of some of the pueblos. (see "Pueblos" in this chapter).

To the Pueblo Indians, "home" means much more than a building where one eats and sleeps. It begins at the center point of the pueblo and extends outward to encompass the fields beyond the village, the river, the foothills — even the mountains where the secret shrines lie. If an adobe wall cracks and threatens to destroy a house, the owner may decide to allow the house to "go back to the earth" and build a new one. The event is not a disaster, only part of nature's process.

This fact is beautifully expressed by Santa Clara Pueblo native and architectural consultant Rina Swentzell. Reflecting on the old Pueblo world, she writes, "Landscaping, or the beautification of outdoor spaces, was a foreign concept. The natural environment was primary, and the human structures were made to fit into the hills and around boulders or trees. In that setting, planting pretty flowers that need watering was ridiculous. Decoration for decoration's sake was unnecessary." In that Pueblo world, she concludes, "All of life, including walls, rocks and people, were part of an exquisite, flowing unity."

CINEMA

Santa Fe

CINEMATHEQUE

Besides producing a full range of arts programs, the Plan B for Evolving Arts (505-982-1338; 1050 Old Pecos Trail) — formerly the Center for Contemporary Arts of Santa Fe — offers foreign and U.S. art films, including the best foreign and U.S. oldies. Ethnographic films and video art presentations by independent artists are especially popular. Each March, Plan B sponsors the Film Expo, a cinema festival that features premieres of new independent films. To get on the mailing list, write Plan B, P.O. Box 148, Santa Fe, NM 87504.

JEAN COCTEAU CINEMA AND COFFEE HOUSE

This Art Deco-style theater (505-988-2711; 418 Montezuma St.) screens specialized films and selected commercial films. You can buy popcorn and soda and head straight into the intimate theater, or linger at a table for two in the coffee house.

COMMERCIAL MOVIE HOUSES

Santa Fe's commercial movie houses include *United Artists North* (505-471-3377) and *South* (505-471-6066), both at Villa Linda Mall at Rodeo and Cerrillos Rds.; *The De Vargas 6* (505-988-2775) in De Vargas Center Mall, St. Francis Dr. and Paseo de Peralta; the *Lensic* (505-982-0301) at 211 W. San Francisco St.; the *Grand Illusion* (505-471-8935) at St. Michael's Dr. and Llano St.

Taos

The *Trans-Lux Storyteller* (505-758-9715) near the Holiday Inn on Paseo del Pueblo Sur screens commercial and offbeat films. The *Taos Community Auditorium* (505-758-4677), a half block north of the plaza on Paseo del Pueblo Norte, occasionally offers films; call for a schedule.

DANCE

Santa Fe

BALLET DE SANTA FE

A ballet school and youth company which performs the highly popular *Nutcracker* each December with guest artists. The school's summer dance program culminates with a performance of contemporary works. For information, call 505-471-7035, or write Ballet de Santa Fe, 1121 Calle La Resolana, Santa Fe, NM 87501.

MARIA BENITEZ SPANISH DANCE COMPANY

Flamenco, that fiery Spanish dance, was born centuries ago in southern Spain's Andalusia, where Moorish, Byzantine and Hebraic influences meshed with Christian. Few who have seen New Mexican Maria Benitez per-

Maria Benitez performing.

Lois Greenfield

form this highly stylized yet passionate dance can forget her powerful, concentrated energy. Her group performs each summer July through Labor Day in Santa Fe at the Picacho Plaza Hotel (505-982-5591; 750 N. St. Francis Dr., Santa Fe, NM 87501). Write the hotel or call the box office (505-982-1237) for a schedule. Magnificent. Do not miss.

SANTA FE DANCE FOUNDATION

This professional dance school offers year-round classes for children and adults. Ask about their summer workshops. For more information call 505-983-5591 or write *SFDF*, 1504 Cerrillos Rd., Santa Fe, NM 87501.

GALLERIES

Most galleries in the Santa Fe–Taos area are retail establishments (for listings, see Chapter Eight, *Shopping*). The following exhibition spaces present art in an educational context.

Santa Fe

Site Santa Fe (505-989-1199) 1606 Paseo de Peralta, Santa Fe, NM 87501. A contemporary arts organization, offering exhibits, lectures, poetry readings, music series and workshops, established in 1995. Biennial exhibits feature cutting edge art by renowned artists in a wide variety of media. Headliners from the contemporary art world exhibit here.

Plan B Evolving Arts (formerly the Center for Contemporary Arts) (505-982-1338; 1050 Old Pecos Trail) promotes artwork that reflects our times and world culture. Exhibits primarily feature progressive contemporary art by local and emerging artists. Prepare to have your preconceptions shaken by installations and multimedia works. Call or write for a schedule.

Several other educational Santa Fe galleries are well worth a visit. The ***Governor's Gallery*** in the Roundhouse (505-827-3000; State Capitol) presents excellent changing exhibits by New Mexico artists. The ***Fine Arts Gallery*** at the College of Santa Fe (505-473-6555; 1600 St. Michael's Dr., Southwest Annex Bldg.) mounts major exhibitions on various contemporary themes several times a year. ***St. John's College Art Gallery*** (505-982-3691; 1160 Camino Cruz Blanca) also presents several exhibitions during the school year.

Near Santa Fe

The Fuller Lodge Art Center (505-662-9331; 2132 Central, Los Alamos, NM 87544) emphasizes the work of northern New Mexican artists and craftspeople. The center takes up one wing of the famous lodge, once the dining and recreation hall for Los Alamos Ranch School. In 1943, the federal government took over the school for the Manhattan Project, which created the atomic bomb. An impressive log building designed by John Gaw Meem (see "Architecture" in this chapter), it is now a National Historic Landmark.

Taos

The Stables Art Gallery, owned and operated by the ***Taos Art Association***, a non-profit arts organization for performing and visual art (505-758-2036; 133 Paseo del Pueblo Norte), is a principal exhibitor of contemporary art in the Taos area. The center offers a broad range of work by nationally and regionally recognized artists. Annual exhibitions include *The Best of Taos, Taos Impressionists* and *Non-Representational Art of Taos.*

HISTORIC BUILDINGS AND SITES

Santa Fe

CANYON ROAD

One of Santa Fe's oldest and most colorful streets, Canyon Road was originally an Indian trail through the mountains to Pecos Pueblo (see "Pecos National Historical Site" in Chapter Five, *Sacred Sites*). In the 1920s, it was adopted by artists from the East Coast. Now the narrow, winding street has become home to dozens of galleries and boutiques and several fine restaurants.

A stroll along Canyon Road is a must for visitors. Enter off Paseo de Peralta, just south of E. Alameda about six blocks southeast of the plaza. Take time to view the old adobe buildings, constructed in typical Spanish Colonial style with walls that begin at the edge of the street. Their plain exteriors can fool you; a compound may surround a lovely patio or garden. These historic structures are not open to the public, but you can still enjoy them from the street.

Take note of 18th-century *El Zaguan* (545 Canyon Rd.), which is now a private apartment complex and the site of the Historic Santa Fe Foundation. The beautiful garden was originally planted by famed archaeologist Adolph Bandelier, who once lived there, and contains chestnut trees he planted and peonies he imported from China.

The *Olive Rush Studio* (630 Canyon Rd.) was the residence of one of the city's outstanding artists during the early decades of the century. She bequeathed her property to the Santa Fe Society of Friends (Quakers), who use it as their meeting place.

The *Borrego House* (724 Canyon Rd.) is now a restaurant. Some sections of the house were built in 1753, and additions in the Territorial style were made in the 19th century.

Cristo Rey Church.

Murrae Haynes

CRISTO REY CHURCH
505-983-8528.
1120 Canyon Rd., Santa Fe, NM 87501.
Intersection of Canyon Rd. & Camino Cabra.
Open: Daily, 7–5
Call one month ahead to arrange tours.
Donations appreciated.

An outstanding example of Spanish Colonial Mission architecture, Cristo Rey Church was designed by Santa Fe architect John Gaw Meem and built to commemorate the 400th anniversary of Coronado's arrival in the Southwest. One of the largest modern adobe structures in existence, it was constructed with bricks made from the earth on which it stands.

The church contains a magnificent stone *reredo*, or altar screen, that was carved by craftsmen from Mexico in 1760, using stone quarried in the Jacona region north of Santa Fe. It depicts God the Father, Our Lady of Valvanera, Santiago, St. Joseph, St. John Nepomuk, St. Ignatius, Loyola, St. Francis of Solano and Our Lady of Light. Visitors should keep in mind that such events as weddings or funerals might be scheduled during their visits.

CROSS OF THE MARTYRS WALKWAY
Enter on Paseo de Peralta, between Otero St. & Hillside Ave.
Always open.

Only a five-minute walk from the plaza, this historic spot boasts the best view of downtown. A brick walkway winds up a small hill, and plaques posted along the way summarize highlights of Santa Fe's prehistory and history. At the top, you can gaze across the entire city and beyond The white metal cross at the summit is a memorial to the 21 Franciscan monks killed in the Pueblo Revolt of 1680 (see Chapter One, *History*).

Murrae Haynes

Miraculous staircase, Loretto Chapel.

LORETTO CHAPEL MUSEUM
505-984-7971.
207 Old Santa Fe Trail, Santa Fe, NM 87501.
Open: Summer 8–6, winter 9:30–4:30; closed Christmas.
Fee (1998): $2; under 7 free.
Gift shop.

Loretto Chapel was built at the same time as St. Francis Cathedral (see below) for the Sisters of Loretto, the first nuns to come to New Mexico. The Chapel of Our Lady of Light, as it was called then, was begun in 1873 and was designed along the same lines as Sainte Chappelle in Paris, France. Stones for the chapel came from the same quarry as that for St. Francis Cathedral, and the same French architects and French and Italian stonemasons worked on the two structures.

The architects were a father and son named Mouly. The son was killed before the chapel was completed, and he left no plans for a stairway to the choir loft. Indeed, there wasn't enough space left for a conventional staircase. The story goes that the sisters prayed for help to St. Joseph, patron saint of carpenters. In due time, an unknown carpenter arrived and proceeded to build an amazing circular staircase — a structure lacking both nails and visible means of support. He departed without leaving his name or asking for pay.

PALACE OF THE GOVERNORS

(See "Museums" in this chapter.)

THE PLAZA
Center of town.
Always open.

Four hundred years of history speak from the Santa Fe Plaza. Originally the plaza was a rectangle, laid out according to plans specified by Spain's King Philip II in 1610. For much of its history, it consisted mainly of packed earth. Though it has been dusty, it has never been dull. Countless celebrations both religious and secular have been held here. This is also the spot where Hispanic residents used to conduct Saturday night promenades, complete with strolling musicians.

Today, cruising "low-riders" and teenage "plaza rats" still keep the plaza hopping on pleasant summer evenings. The music still rings out, too — especially during the city's free summer concerts. Hardly anyone would think of holding a demonstration or vigil anywhere but the plaza, and it's still one of the best people-watching spots in the city.

RANDALL DAVEY AUDUBON CENTER
505-983-4609.
P.O. Box 9314, Santa Fe, NM 87504.
End of Upper Canyon Rd.
Open: Summer 9–5 for garden and trails; winter hours may vary—call ahead; summer house tours Mon. 1–4.
Fee (1998): $3 for house tours; $1 donation requested for trails.
Gift shop and bookstore.

One of the few historic homes in Santa Fe open to the public, the Randall Davey Center is a state office, an environmental education center and *National Audubon Society* wildlife refuge. Set on 135 acres at the mouth of the Santa Fe River Canyon, the home of musician and artist Randall Davey is listed in national, state and city registers of historical and cultural buildings. What is now the house was the original mill; the *acequia* behind it served both as irrigation ditch and millrace. The house features massive beamed ceilings and 16-inch-thick stone walls covered by plaster.

Randall Davey moved to Santa Fe in 1920. His innovative works are exhibited throughout the house and his adjacent studio. The center is also a good introduction to local flora and fauna. Trails wind through natural vegetation of piñon, juniper and ponderosa pine and there is a large meadow. The area is rich in bird life and home to black bear, mountain lion, bobcat, coyote, raccoon and mule deer. The center offers an extensive schedule of bird walks, natural history workshops and school programs and an eight-week summer program for children.

SAN MIGUEL CHAPEL
505-983-3974.
401 Old Santa Fe Trail,
   Santa Fe, NM 87501.
Open: Summer 9–4:30,
   winter 10–4, Sun.
   2:30–4:30 all year; Sun.
   Mass 5 p.m.
Admission: $1; children
   under 6 free.
Gift shop.

The oldest church in the United States, San Miguel is estimated to have been built around 1610. It seems likely that the original walls and adobe altar were built by Tlaxcalan Indians brought from Mexico by the Spaniards.

During the Pueblo Revolt of 1680 (see Chapter One, *History*), Indian attackers burned the chapel roof. The Spaniards returned in 1692 and put on a new roof so the chapel could be used until the parish church was rebuilt. More renovations were made around 1710. Early in the 19th century, the chapel was remodeled with an unconventional three-tiered tower that toppled in 1872. A new tower and stone buttresses supporting the front were added in 1887. In 1955, the interior was restored to its Spanish Colonial appearance and the present tower constructed.

The chapel contains several magnificent oil paintings (restored in the 1950s) that are believed to date back to around 1725. Colonial buffalo hide paintings of the Crucifixion and of the Good Shepherd hang on the walls. Displays show pottery shards and other archaeological findings dating back to A.D. 1300.

**SANTUARIO DE
   GUADALUPE**
505-988-2027.
100 S. Guadalupe St., Santa
   Fe, NM 87501.
Open: May–Oct., Mon.–Sat.
   9–4; Nov.–April,
   Mon.–Fri. 9–4; closed
   Sun.
Donations accepted.
Gift shop.

The Santuario is a longtime Santa Fe landmark and a performing arts center. It was built by Franciscan missionaries between 1776 and 1796 with adobe walls three to five feet thick. It is the oldest shrine in the United States dedicated to the Queen of the Americas, Our Lady of Guadalupe, who revealed herself in a vision to Indian convert Juan Diego in Mexico in 1531. Across the altar hangs a breathtaking painting of Our Lady of Guadalupe, the work of Jose de Alzibar, one of Mexico's finest Colonial painters.

The Santuario has survived several architectural metamorphoses; in the 1880s it even suffered a New England-style steeple! Work done in 1976 restored it to what is believed to be its original appearance. It is operated by the Guadalupe Historic Foundation.

**ST. FRANCIS CATHE-
   DRAL**
505-982-5619.
131 Cathedral Pl., Santa Fe,
   NM 87501.
East end of San Francisco
   St.
Open: Daily 6–6; use side
   doors. Mass Mon.–Sat. at

This is one of Santa Fe's most spectacular structures — and also one of its most incongruous. Built in French-Romanesque style, it was the inspiration of Frenchman Jean Baptiste Lamy, Santa Fe's first archbishop. The cornerstone of the cathedral was laid in 1869, and construction proceeded with stone quarried in an area south of Santa Fe.

Murrae Haynes

Archbishop Lamy's St. Francis Cathedral, dedicated in 1886.

7 a.m., 5:15 p.m.; Sun. 8 &
10 a.m., noon, 7 p.m.
Donations accepted.

St. Francis Cathedral was dedicated in 1886 but was never fully completed. Its stained-glass windows, including the rose window in front and the lateral nave windows, were brought from France and installed in 1884. The bronze doors of the cathedral, installed for its rededication in 1986, contain 16 panels depicting scenes in the history of the Catholic Church in Santa Fe. Also worth viewing is the *reredo* carved for the 100th anniversary celebration in 1986.

La Conquistadora Chapel, an adobe structure on the northeast side of the cathedral, was built in the 1600s to honor a statue of the Virgin Mary brought to Santa Fe in 1626. Originally called the Lady of the Rosary, the statue was renamed Our Lady of the Conquest in 1692, when the Spaniards reentered the city 12 years after the Pueblo Revolt. It is probably the oldest representation of the Virgin Mary in the United States. La Conquistadora leaves her chapel each

June for a processional to commemorate Don Diego de Vargas's return to the city.

Note: Visitors not attending Mass may slip into the cathedral quietly at other times, using the side doors and taking care not to disturb those at prayer.

SENA PLAZA
125-137 E. Palace Ave.
Enter on Palace Ave., just E. of plaza.
Always open.

A separate world that resonates with the flavor of Colonial Santa Fe, Sena Plaza is reached by an adobe passage from busy Palace Ave. In the 19th century, the most gracious homes were built as compounds with rooms surrounding a central *placita,* or courtyard. In the 1860s, Major Jose D. Sena built just such a home a block from the downtown plaza — and kept adding rooms as more children were born. Now Sena Plaza houses private shops and a restaurant. Here you can stroll around and imagine the old days as you listen to the fountain, watch the birds, and enjoy the flowers and greenery. The patio garden, where you can order a drink or lunch from *La Casa Sena* (see Chapter Six, *Restaurants*), remains one of downtown Santa Fe's most enjoyable spots for relaxing and socializing.

Near Santa Fe

BANDELIER NATIONAL MONUMENT
SAN JOSE CHURCH
No phone.
In Las Trampas, on N.M. 76 about 40 miles N.E. of Santa Fe.
Open: Daily in summer 8–5.
Donations accepted.

This structure, built between 1760 and 1780, is frequently described as the most beautiful Spanish Colonial church in New Mexico. The village of Las Trampas was established in 1751 by 12 Santa Fe families led by Juan de Arguello, who had received a land grant from Governor Tomas Velez Capuchin. In the summer, the church is usually open from 8 a.m. to 5 p.m.; in the winter, you'll probably find it locked. Ask at one of the nearby gift shops for the person who keeps the key.

In Taos

ERNEST L. BLUMEN-SCHEIN HOME
505-758-0505.
222 Ledoux St., just S. of plaza.
Open: Year-round 9–5 except Christmas, New Year's, Thanksgiving. Winter 11–4.
Fee (1998): $4 adults, $3 seniors, $2 under 16; family rate available.
Gift shop.

Ernest and Mary Greene Blumenschein were among the founders of the famous Taos art colony around 1915. Their home, a 1797 Spanish Colonial adobe, is open for tours and exhibits of area artists' work. The house appears much as it did in the Blumenscheins' day: original adobe plaster inside and out, traditional Taos furniture, European antiques and artwork from around the world.

Courtesy Ernest L. Blumenschein House

Ernest L. Blumenschein at work, ca. 1920.

FECHIN MUSEUM
505-758-1710.
227 Paseo del Pueblo Norte.
2 blocks N. of plaza on N.
  Pueblo Rd.
Open: Summer Wed.–Sun.
  10–5. Winter Wed.–Sun.
  10–2. Call about exhibitions.
Fee (1998): $4.

This distinguished adobe home was designed in the Russian style by renowned artist Nicolai Fechin, a Russian emigrant. Built from 1927–33, the house features hand-carved Russian folk art wood-work. The home and studio are operated as a cultural center, with tours available. Exhibitions throughout the year feature Fechin's artwork, his collections of Oriental and Russian art, as well as art from other countries.

GOVERNOR BENT
  HOUSE
505-758-2376.
117-A Bent St., 1 block N. of
  plaza.
Open: Daily 10–5, except
  Christmas, New Year's,
  Easter.

Charles Bent, a prominent citizen of Taos, owned wagon trains on the Santa Fe Trail and trading posts in Taos and Santa Fe. However, the peculiar politics of New Mexico proved to be his undoing. After the 1846 American invasion, he was appointed the first U.S. governor of the territory; he awoke in his home on the morning of Jan. 19, 1847, to find an angry mob of Hispanics and Indians breaking down

Fee (1996): Adults $1, 15 and under 50 cents, under 8 free.
Gift shop and gallery.

the doors. When Bent asked what they wanted, the response was: "We want your head, gringo!" Bent's family was allowed to leave, but he was killed and scalped. The old adobe house, which contains historic artifacts, is on the National Register of Historic Places. (See also Chapter One, *History*.)

KIT CARSON HOME
505-758-0505, 505-758-4741.
113 E. Kit Carson Rd.
0.5 block E. of plaza.
Open: Summer 8-5. Winter 9-5. Closed Christmas, New Year's, Thanksgiving.
Fee (1998): $5 adults, $2.50 under 16, families $10
Gift shop.

Kit Carson was the consummate mountain man, scout and soldier. He was also a family man. In 1843, he married Josefa Jaramillo, and the couple raised a large family in this 12-room adobe. Kit and Josefa both died in 1868, a month apart. Three rooms of the house are furnished as they might have been during the quarter century the Carsons lived there. Other rooms are filled with exhibits on Taos's colorful frontier history.

Karen Klitgaard

Taos' Martinez Hacienda offers an intimate view of Spanish Colonial history.

MARTINEZ HACIENDA
505-758-0505, 505-758-1000.
2 miles S. of plaza on N.M. 240 (Ranchitos Rd.) or 4 miles W. of Ranchos de Taos on N.M. 240.

This 19th century hacienda features thick adobe walls and a windowless exterior, with twenty-one rooms enclosing two central *placitas*. This fortress-like building was designed to keep out Comanche and Apache raiders. Livestock were dri-

Open: Summer 9–5. Winter 10–4 except Thanksgiving, Christmas, New Year's.
Fee (1998): $5 adults, $2.50 under 16, families $10.
Gift shop.

ven through the gates and into the *placitas* when raiders threatened.

This is perhaps the only hacienda in the Southwest that has been restored to its original condition. Rooms are furnished in Colonial style, reflecting a time when goods were either made by local artisans or hauled by ox cart from Mexico City. Exhibits tell the story of trade on the Camino Real and of the Spanish Colonial culture of New Mexico. Demonstrations of contemporary and traditional crafts are presented on a regular basis.

Near Taos

Murrae Haynes

St. Francisco de Asis, Ranchos de Taos, is the most photographed and painted church in America.

SAN FRANCISCO DE ASIS CHURCH
505-758-2754.
Ranchos de Taos, about 4 miles S. of Taos on N.M. 68.

The most frequently painted and photographed church in the United States was built sometime between 1776 and 1813 and was in use by Franciscans in 1815. Viewed from the west, its massive, windowless adobe walls change appearance hourly

Open: Year-round
    Mon.–Sat. 9–4; Mass
    Sat. 6 p.m., Sun. 7 a.m.
    (Spanish), 9 a.m., 11:30
    a.m.
Fee (1998): $2.
Gift shop next door.

as the light changes, posing an irresistible challenge to artists. Visitors are also intrigued by artwork inside the building, including Henri Ault's *The Shadow of the Cross.* ($2; closed at noon; closed on Sun.)

**FORT BURGWIN
    RESEARCH CENTER**
505-758-8322.
P.O. Box 314, Ranchos de
    Taos, NM 87557.
About 8 miles S.E. of Taos
    on N.M. 518.
Open: June–Aug.
Fee: Varies with class.

Set in a small valley on a tributary of the Rio Grande, Fort Burgwin was a U.S. cavalry fort in the 1850s. Now it's an archaeological research and training center for Southern Methodist University based in Dallas, Texas. During the summer, Fort Burgwin offers cultural programs and a lecture series that emphasizes archaeology. Call or write for current listings.

LIBRARIES

If you want to delve a little more into Southwestern lore, several libraries in Santa Fe and Taos can help you scratch the information itch.

Santa Fe

The *Santa Fe Public Library* (505-984-6780; 145 Washington Ave.) is notable for its attractive Santa Fe style architecture and Southwestern furnishings. The Southwest Room contains a moderately large collection of works on the Southwest.

The *Museum of New Mexico* research libraries, open to researchers, are part of each of the four Santa Fe museums. (Be sure to call ahead.) The *History Library* (505-827-6470) at the Palace of the Governors houses more than 12,000 volumes on regional history, as well as a vast repository of original documents and maps. Its Photo Archive section (505-827-6472) contains more than 340,000 historical images; prints are available for purchase or rental. The *Museum of Fine Arts Library* (505-827-4453) contains about 5,000 volumes emphasizing New Mexican and Southwestern art. The *Museum of International Folk Art Library* (505-827-6350) has more than 10,000 volumes on folk art topics. The *Laboratory of Anthropology* (505-827-6344), next to the Museum of Indian Arts and Culture, contains volumes on Southwest anthropology and archaeology.

In Taos

The *Taos Public Library* (505-758-3063; 238 Ledoux St.) is housed in a beautiful new building. The 30,000-volume collection is strong in Southwestern literature and history.

MUSEUMS

The state of New Mexico operates four museum facilities in Santa Fe under the aegis of the *Museum of New Mexico*. In 1998, a three-day pass to all four museums cost $10. If you see all four, you will have given yourself an exciting introduction to New Mexico arts, culture and history. The museums include the *Palace of the Governors* and the *Museum of Fine Arts*, both on the plaza, and the *Museum of Indian Arts and Culture* and the *Museum of International Folk Art*, both on Camino Lejo, about a five-minute drive southeast of downtown. For information about the individual museums, see below.

Santa Fe

The new Georgia O'Keeffe Museum is worth a trip to Santa Fe.

Murrae Haynes

GEORGIA O'KEEFFE MUSEUM
505-995-0785.
217 Johnson St., Santa Fe, NM 87501.
Four blocks west of the plaza.
Open: Tues.–Sun. 10–5; 10–8 Fri. Closed Mon., New Year's Day, Easter, Thanksgiving, Christmas.
Fee (1998): $5 per day; $10 four-day pass to all branches of the Museum of New Mexico, Fri. eve. 5–8 free.

"In New Mexico, half your work is done for you," Georgia O'Keeffe is reputed to have said. Certainly the pull of the land here was enough to draw her away from her New York artist's life to the isolated village of Abiquiu, the region of Ghost Ranch's marvelous red rocks. Here she found the light and the subject matter that built a career acclaimed as that of "the most singularly original American artist before World War II."

The discerning iconoclast O'Keeffe herself would probably have approved this classically simple, brand-new, adobe-colored, elegantly lit museum that houses her inspired work. Visitors can take in the span of the pioneering modernist's work — from early figurative watercolors, to her paintings of New York in the first decades of the century, to her celebrations of New Mexico in the enormous flowers, the crosses, the clouds, the walls, and the studies of rocks, sky and bone. Nowhere else does such a concentration of her magic exist. Absolutely stunning, worth the trip to Santa Fe.

Provocative contemporary sculpture is on view in the Allen Houser Sculpture Garden of the Institute of American Indian Arts Museum.

Murrae Haynes

INSTITUTE OF AMERICAN INDIAN ARTS MUSEUM
505-988-6211.
108 Cathedral Pl., Santa Fe, NM 87501.
Across from St. Francis Cathedral.
Open: Mon.–Sat. 10–5; Sun. noon–5.
Fee (1998): $4 adult, $2 seniors and students with ID; children under 16 free.
Gift shop.

Founded during the John F. Kennedy administration, the Institute of American Indian Arts (IAIA) proved to be a highly successful experiment of the federal government in art education for Indians. Some of the best-known names in Indian art — Allan Houser, Fritz Scholder, the late T.C. Cannon and others — were teachers or students there. Now operating independently, the IAIA offers an associate of fine arts degree. The newly opened museum houses the nation's largest collection of contemporary Indian art and demonstrates the vitality and innovation of Indian artists. Don't miss the Performance Gallery and the Allan Houser Sculpture Park.

MUSEUM OF FINE ARTS
505-827-4468 or 505-827-6463 for 24-hour information.
107 W. Palace Ave., Santa Fe, NM 87501.
On the plaza.
Open: Tues.–Sun. 10–5 except Thanksgiving,

The Museum of Fine Arts, a unit of the Museum of New Mexico, anchors the northwest corner of the plaza with its 1917 Spanish-Pueblo building designed by Isaac Hamilton Rapp. The mission-style structure houses more than 8,000 works of art, including paintings, prints, drawings, photographs and sculptures. The collection emphasizes 20th-century American art, particularly Southwestern.

Christmas, New Year's, Easter.

Fee (1998): $10 adults for 4-day pass to all 4 state museums; under 17 free, Fri. evenings free.

Gift shop.

Among its highlights are Georgia O'Keeffe's *Red Hills and Pedernal*, Marsden Hartley's *El Santo*, Robert Henri's *Dieguito, San Ildefonso Drummer*, Bert Phillips's *Musicians of the Baile*, Jesus Morales's *Mountain Fountain*, Laura Gilpin's *O'Keeffe's Studio* and John Marin's *Ranchos Church*.

On permanent exhibition are works by early 20th-century New Mexico artists such as Jozef Bakos, Gustave Baumann, and William Penhallow Henderson. Also look for changing exhibitions of traditional and contemporary art assembled from the permanent collection or loaned by other institutions. The *Alcove Show*, which changes several times a year, features exciting contemporary work by area artists.

MUSEUM OF INDIAN ARTS AND CULTURE

505-827-6344 or 505-827-6463 for 24-hr. information.

710 Camino Lejo, Santa Fe, NM 87501.

Open: Tues.–Sun. 10–5 except Thanksgiving, Christmas, New Year's, Easter.

Fee (1998): $10 adults for 4-day pass to all 4 state museums; under 17 free.

Gift shop.

This newest state museum brings together the past and present of Southwest Indian culture. It houses an extraordinary collection of more than 50,000 Native American arts and crafts objects gathered over 61 years by the adjacent *Laboratory of Anthropology* (505-827-6344). Included in the collection are basketry, pottery, textiles, jewelry, clothing and other items. Artifacts are rotated on exhibit, emphasizing the Navajo, Apache and Pueblo peoples.

The continuing exhibit, "From This Earth: Pottery of the Southwest," covers archaeological, historic and contemporary Southwestern Indian pottery, with many beautiful ceramics and new videos. Artist demonstrations of everything from pottery making to basket weaving are offered frequently during the summer. The continuing exhibit "Natural Belongings: Classic art Traditions from the Southwest" includes baskets, textiles and jewelry.

MUSEUM OF INTERNA- TIONAL FOLK ART

505-827-6350 or 505-827-6463 for 24-hr. information.

706 Camino Lejo, Santa Fe, NM 87501.

Open: Tues.–Sun. 10–5 except Thanksgiving, Christmas, Easter, New Year's & Mon. in Jan. & Feb.

You'll never see art like this unless you travel to six continents and cover 100 countries. This amazing collection of folk art — the world's largest — was founded in 1953 by Florence Dibell Bartlett. According to a museum publication, Bartlett believed that the art produced by craftspeople, not highbrow artists, would unite the different cultures of the world. Judge for yourself as you wander among traditional clothing and textiles, masks, folk toys, miniatures and items of everyday use. The

All ages revel in the extensive collections at Santa Fe's Museum of International Folk Art.

Karen Klitgaard

Fee (1998): $10 adults for 4-day pass to all 4 state museums; under 17 free.

collection numbers more than 125,000 pieces, including 106,000 from the Girard Foundation Collection, which the museum received in 1976.

Among the highlights are Mexican masks and costumes, Turkish folk art and textiles from India. Children are delighted by the miniature Mexican village scenes consisting of colorful and imaginative clay figurines. Traveling exhibits and those curated by the museum staff are presented year-round.

The *Hispanic Heritage Wing,* opened in 1989, must also be described in superlatives. With about 5,000 artifacts dating from the late 1600s to the present, it's the largest collection of Spanish Colonial and Hispanic folk art in the United States. It emphasizes northern New Mexico but includes folk art from the Spanish Colonial Empire around the world — including religious folk art, textiles, tinwork, utilitarian implements, gold and silver jewelry, and furniture. Truly a must-see.

PALACE OF THE GOVERNORS
505-827-6474 or
505-827-6463 for 24-hr. information.
914 Palace Ave., Santa Fe, NM 87501.
On the plaza.
Open: Tues.–Sun. 10–5 except Thanksgiving, Easter, Christmas, New Year's.

In 1610, a decade before the Pilgrims landed at Plymouth Rock, the Palace of the Governors was built by Spanish settlers who established Santa Fe, making it the oldest continually-occupied public building in the U.S. The palace has served as a seat of government for Spain, Mexico, the Confederacy and the United States. Between 1680 and 1692 it was home to the Pueblo Indians, who remodeled and used it after driving the Spaniards out of New Mexico. It became a museum in 1911. (See also "Architecture" in this chapter.)

Fee (1996): $10 adults for 4-day pass to all 4 state museums; under 17 free. Gift shop.

Today the Palace of the Governors houses the Museum of New Mexico's collection of more than 17,000 historical objects. The collection comprises artifacts from the Spanish Colonial period, the Mexican-American War, the American expansion along the Santa Fe Trail, the transition from Mexican to U.S. control and the 20th century. Permanent exhibits illustrate the state's multicultural heritage, and special exhibits focus on aspects of history such as traditional celebrations and the Civil War.

One of the "exhibits" is the *Portal Program,* where New Mexico Indian vendors sell hand-crafted jewelry and other items under the Palace *portal.* Since Native Americans have been trading in this spot for centuries, they are considered a "living historical exhibit." Only New Mexico Indians may sell here, and all work must be certified to be made by the vendor or his or her immediate family. If you're interested in authentic Indian work, this is a good place to make purchases.

Within the palace compound is the *Palace Press,* which produces limited editions of works related to the Southwest, using historic hand-operated printing and binding equipment.

Amusement and learning go hand in hand at the Santa Fe Children's Museum.

Corrie Photography

SANTA FE CHILDREN'S MUSEUM
505-989-8359.
1050 Old Pecos Trail, Santa Fe, NM 87501.
Open: Year-round, Thurs.–Sat 10–5, Sun. noon–5; also Wed. 10–5 from June 1 to Labor Day.

This child-friendly museum is a place where youngsters are *encouraged* to touch, move, create, make noise and play. It is filled with hands-on exhibits like "Make and Take," a wooden "house" where children can create collages with recyclable foam, spools, rubber, etc. In other action exhibits, children can do experiments in the arts, humanities, science and technology. The museum also sponsors

Fee (1998): $3.00 adult,
$2.00 under 12; first Sun.
of month free.

ongoing family programs, workshops, demonstrations and performances.

SCHOOL OF AMERICAN
RESEARCH
505-954-7205.
P.O. Box 2188, Santa Fe,
NM 87504.
660 Garcia St., Santa Fe,
NM 87501.
Open: Year round; public
tours Fri. 2–3:30; reserva-
tions required.
Suggested donation: $15.

A nonprofit center for anthropological research,
the School of American Research (SAR) has a
10,000 piece collection of historic Southwestern
Native American art. Its strongest areas are Pueblo
pottery, Navajo and Pueblo textiles and 20th-cen-
tury Indian paintings. Volunteer docents give regular guided tours of the Indian Arts Research Center
of the SAR, but tours must be arranged in advance.
SAR also offers a wide variety of books and other
literature for sale, most having to do with anthropology and culture.

WHEELWRIGHT
MUSEUM OF THE
AMERICAN INDIAN
505-982-4636.
P.O. Box 5153, Santa Fe,
NM 87502.
704 Camino Lejo.
Open: Mon.–Sat. 10–5, Sun.
1–5 except Thanksgiving,
Christmas, New Year's.
Donations welcome.
Gift shop.

Here's a story only the West could produce:
Mary Cabot Wheelwright, a wealthy New
England heiress, scholar and world traveler, went
by horseback to the Navajo Reservation in 1921, at
age 40. There she met Hosteen Klah, a powerful
Navajo singer and healer. He spoke no English, and
she spoke no Navajo, but somehow they developed
a rapport. She wanted to know more about his religion, and he revealed that he was ready to pass on
some of his knowledge to people who could write it
down. Both feared that the traditional Navajo way
of life was about to be lost to "progress."

Mary Cabot Wheelwright and Hosteen Klah spent years in research together
on the vast Navajo Reservation. In 1927, they founded the *Museum of Navajo
Ceremonial Art* in Santa Fe to house all the sacred materials they had collected.

As it turned out, Navajo culture proved much more resilient than these two
had predicted. Even today, the Navajo ceremonial system remains very much
alive. In acknowledgment of that fact, the museum returned much of the sacred
material to the Navajo Nation in the 1970s, and its name was changed to the
Wheelwright Museum of the American Indian to express the institution's interest in all American Indian cultures.

The Wheelwright's collection is strong in Navajo weavings, including tapes-
tries of sand-painting designs made by Hosteen Klah himself; Southwestern
jewelry, basketry and pottery; cradleboards from throughout the United States;
and contemporary Indian art.

Don't miss the *Case Trading Post*. Modeled after Southwestern trading posts
of the early 1900s, the Case is stuffed with top-quality Indian artwork in a range
of prices, from Navajo weavings and Hopi baskets to old pawn jewelry and

Pueblo pottery. There's also contemporary sculpture, books on Indians and many tapes of Indian music.

Near Santa Fe

> If you are a scientist . . . you believe that it is good to find out how the world works . . . to turn over to mankind at large the greatest possible power to control the world and to deal with it according to its lights and values.
>
> – *J. Robert Oppenheimer,*
> *Manhattan Project Director of Research*

BRADBURY SCIENCE MUSEUM
505-667-4444.
15th & Central , Los Alamos, NM 87545.
35 miles N.W. of Santa Fe via U.S. 285 N. & N.M. 502 W.
Open: Tues.–Fri. 9–5, Sat.–Mon. 1–5 except major national holidays.
Admission: Free.

Photographs and documents give you a glimpse of the unfolding of "Project Y," the World War II code name for the laboratory that developed the first atomic bomb. But there's more: An impressive display of Los Alamos National Laboratory's weapons research program includes an actual rack for underground nuclear testing and presents an overview of the U.S. nuclear arsenal. You can also view a model of an accelerator and exhibits on the latest research in solar, geothermal, laser and magnetic fusion energy. Hands-on exhibits allow you to peer through microscopes, align lasers and talk to computers.

Films from the laboratory, screened in a small theater, include features on computer graphics, geothermal energy and the history of the Manhattan Project, the creation of the first atomic bomb. A very well-done museum.

LOS ALAMOS HISTORICAL MUSEUM
505-662-6272.
P.O. Box 43, Los Alamos, NM 87544.
1921 Juniper, adjacent to Fuller Lodge.
35 miles N.W. of Santa Fe via U.S. 285 N. & N.M. 502 W.
Open: Winter, Mon.–Sat. 10–4, Sun. 1–4; summer, Mon.–Sat. 9:30–4:30, Sun. 11–5.

This museum is housed in a log-and-stone building that was originally part of the Los Alamos Ranch School. The museum covers a million years, beginning when the Jemez volcano blew its top and created the Pajarito Plateau. Exhibits include artifacts of the first known residents, farmers and hunters who lived here about A.D. 1100. Another exhibit, Life in the Secret City, reveals the story of Los Alamos during World War II, when it was closed to outsiders as the best scientific minds in the nation rushed to make the bomb.

On the museum grounds are the remains of a Tewa Indian settlement of the 1300s. For a small fee

Admission: Free.
Bookstore.

the museum provides a 12-page booklet for a self-guided walking tour of Los Alamos. Guided tours are available by prior arrangement. There's also a book shop with more than 600 Southwest titles.

**OLD COAL MINE
MUSEUM**
505-473-0743.
Madrid, about 25 miles S.
of Santa Fe on N.M. 14,
next to Mine Shaft
Tavern.
Open: Daily 9:30–5,
weather permitting
summer. Winter 10:30–5.
Fee: (1998): $3 adults, $1
under 12; group rates.

The village of Madrid was a thriving coal mining town until 1956, when its main client, Los Alamos, switched fuel sources. Madrid quickly became a ghost town full of decaying little Victorian-style wooden houses. About 20 years ago, artists and entrepreneurs began moving back. At this wonderful, funky museum, you can see a fully restored 1906 Baldwin steam engine, an antique truck, the original mine office, a 1910 blacksmith shop and even a real seam of coal. Cliff Cato, the museum manager, says you can do the self-guided tour (with map) in about 25 minutes.

Stringing chile ristras at Rancho de las Golondrinas.

Jack Parsons. Courtesy of Santa Fe
Chamber of Commerce.

**EL RANCHO DE LAS
GOLONDRINAS**
505-471-2261.
Exit 276 off I-25, 15 miles S.
of Santa Fe.
Season: Guided group
tours Apr.–Oct.; self-guided tours June–Aug.,
Wed.–Sun. 10–4.

El Rancho de las Golondrinas (the Ranch of the Swallows) has seen everything from settlers and traders to bishops and Indian raiders in its nearly 300-year history. Miguel Vega y Coca bought the ranch as a royal purchase in 1710, and it became the last stop before Santa Fe on the Camino Real from Mexico. Caravans of traders, soldiers

Fee (1996): Festivals $6 adults, $4.00 seniors & teens, $2.50 ages 5–12. General admission $4.00 adult, $3 seniors & teens, $1.50 ages 5–12. Gift shop.

and settlers regularly made the six-month round trip.

Visitors today can see an 18th-century *placita* house, a defensive tower, a molasses mill, a threshing ground, water mills, a blacksmith shop, a wheelwright shop, a winery, weaving rooms, outdoor ovens and more. The scene is complete with numerous farm animals.

Las Golondrinas celebrates Spring and Harvest festivals with costumed villagers portraying life in Spanish Colonial New Mexico. San Ysidro, the patron saint of farmers, is honored in the spring with a procession and Mass, and visitors may enjoy hot bread from the *hornos*. Music, dances and plays are part of the celebrations. These two festivals are usually held the first weekends in June and October.

The new Agnes Martin wing of the Harwood Museum is a temple to the art of light.

Karen Klitgaard

Taos

HARWOOD MUSEUM
505-758-9826.
238 Ledoux St., Taos, NM 87571.
Open: Daily 10–5 Tues.–Sat. 12–5 Sun. Closed Mon.
Fee (1998): $4 adults; children under 12 free.

The Harwood Foundation, New Mexico's second-oldest museum, is a treasury of Taos art. Founded in 1923, it contains paintings, drawings, prints, sculpture and photographs by the artists who made Taos famous. Included are works by Victor Higgins, Ernest Blumenschein, Andrew Dasburg, Patrocinio Barela, Earl Stroh, Joe Waldrum, Larry Bell and Fritz Scholder. There is also a collection of 19th-century *retablos*.

The museum is housed in a 19th-century adobe compound that was purchased by Burt and Elizabeth Harwood in 1916 and transformed into an outstanding example of Span-ish-Pueblo architecture. It is listed on the National Register of Historic Places. The brand-new splendid restoration features seven galleries altogether. This is a great place to view works of Taos Society of Artists and Taos modernists. Of special note is the stunning new Agnes Martin Gallery where you may view seven paintings by one of the nation's most acclaimed minimalists, a Taos resi-dent. The beauty of these luminous works, as with all the art within these walls, is highlighted by their setting in this magnificently-restored, light-filled adobe.

MILLICENT ROGERS MUSEUM
505-758-2462.
P.O. Box A, Taos, NM 87571.
4 miles N. of Taos off N.M. 522. Turn left on Museum Rd. *before* "the old blink-ing light" (which doesn't blink) & follow museum signs.
Open: Year-round, daily 9–5 except Easter, San Geronimo Day (Sept. 30), Thanksgiving, Christmas & New Year's. Closed Mon. Nov. 1–April 1.
Fee (1998): $6 adults, $1 ages 6–16, $12 families, $5 students with I.D.
Gift shop.

This outstanding private museum was founded in 1953 by relatives of Millicent Rogers, a stun-ning blonde model who moved to Taos in 1947. Her subsequent study of regional architecture and Indian and Spanish-Colonial art inspired an exten-sive collection of Native American jewelry, textiles, basketry, pottery and paintings. She died in 1953, but by that time her collection had become one of the most respected in the Southwest. Today it forms the core of a display that has been expanded to include religious and secular artwork of Hispanic New Mexico. The museum also holds one of the most important collections of pottery by famed San Ildefonso artist Maria Martinez. One of the museum's rarest and most striking pieces is a buf-falo kachina doll, circa 1875, from Zuni Pueblo. Exhibits here are rich in detail and cultural context. A must-see for an intensive in the art of the region.

Outside the Area

FLORENCE HAWLEY ELLIS MUSEUM OF ANTHROPOLOGY
505-685-4333.
Ghost Ranch Conference Center, Abiquiu, NM 87510.
On U.S. 84, 35 miles N.W. of Española.
Open: Jan.–Nov., Tues.–Sat. 9–11:45, 1–5; Sun. 1–5; closed Mon.
Suggested donation: adults $2; children and seniors $1.

The late Dr. Florence Hawley Ellis was a pioneer anthropologist who conducted excavations and research in Chaco Canyon and elsewhere. The museum specializes in excavated materials from the Ghost Ranch Gallina digs. The little-studied Gallina culture of northern New Mexico comprised the people who left Mesa Verde, Chaco Canyon and the Four Corners area during a long drought around A.D. 1200. Other exhibits feature the Spaniards of the area, Pueblo Indian clothing and prehistoric pottery making.

At the adjacent *Ruth Hall Museum of Paleontol-ogy,* be sure to see the copy of the *Coelophysis* dinosaur skeleton. The original was found near Ghost Ranch, one of the five best dinosaur quarries in the world. This sharp-toothed, birdlike carnivore, extinct for some 200 million years, is the official state fossil.

GHOST RANCH LIVING MUSEUM
505-685-4312.
HCR-77, Box 15, Abiquiu, NM 87510.
14 miles N. of Abiquiu on U.S. 84.
Open: Year-round, Tues.–Sat. 8–4:30; closed Mon.
Fee: $3 adults; $2 ages 12–17.

This small museum, renovated in 1991, is home to animals that have been injured and cannot return to the wild. Exhibits include native Southwest plants and animals such as bears, mountain lions, elk, bobcats, deer, eagles, snakes, foxes and raccoons. A new Gateway to the Past museum celebrates the tricultural area of Rio Chama, with oral history tapes, an interactive computer program, large-format photos, a small library and an auditorium.

MUSIC

Santa Fe

BIG RIVER CORPORATION
505-256-1777.
Big River Corp.
P.O. Box 8036, Albuquerque, NM 87198-8036.
Season: Summer only.
Tickets: Prices vary. Call TicketMaster, 505-884-0999.

The Paolo Soleri outdoor amphitheater at Santa Fe Indian School near downtown is the setting for this series of concerts by national and international performers. The amphitheater, designed by Italian-American architect Paolo Soleri, blends with the landscape. At night, it becomes a magical space where musicians and audience meld into one great show.

SANTA FE CHAMBER MUSIC FESTIVAL
505-983-2075.
P.O. Box 853, Santa Fe, NM 87504.
Season: July–Aug.
Tickets: Call for prices.

With dozens of internationally acclaimed musicians and a grand concert hall (the St. Francis Auditorium), the Santa Fe Chamber Music Festival is one of the biggest summer draws, and one of the primary reasons for Santa Fe's reputation as a music capital. Through its composer-in-residence program, the festival has brought in some of the foremost composers in the United States — among them Tobias Picker, William Schuman, Leon Kirchner and the late Aaron Copland. The festival's "Music of the Americas" series, launched in 1987, brings in jazz, folk and world music performers. Pre-concert lectures by composers, musicologists and instrumentalists give audiences a deeper appreciation of the music. Daytime rehearsals are free.

World renowned musicians perform each summer at the Santa Fe Chamber Music Festival.

Courtesy Santa Fe Chamber Music Festival

SANTA FE CONCERT ASSOCIATION
505-984-8759.
P.O. Box 4626, Santa Fe, NM 87502.
Season: Sept.–May.
Tickets: Prices vary with concert; season tickets available.

Since 1931, Santa Fe's oldest musical organization has been bringing outstanding musicians from all over the world to perform from a repertoire of classical and modern concert music. On the 1996–97 program were violinist Gil Shaham, the Prague Chamber Orchestra, mezzo-soprano Jennifer Larmore, among others. Association traditions include the Youth Concerts series and the all-Mozart Christmas Eve special. Most concerts are in St. Francis Auditorium at the Museum of Fine Arts.

SANTA FE DESERT CHORALE
505-988-7505, 800-244-4011.
P.O. Box 2813, Santa Fe, NM 87504.
Season: July–Aug.; also Christmas concerts.
Tickets: Call for prices.

One of the few professional choruses in the United States, the chorale has been described by the *Albuquerque Journal* as "a definitive choral performing ensemble." Founder and music director Lawrence Bandfield auditions between 24 and 30 singers each year. Twentieth-century works form the backbone of the chorale's repertory; however, major music from all periods is performed, particularly from the Renaissance and Baroque periods. World premieres have included Dominick Argento's *A Toccata of Galuppi's,* Brent Pierce's *El Pocito,* Steven Sametz's *O'Llama de Amor Viva* and Grace Williams' *The Call of the Sea.* Santa Fe concerts are performed at several downtown locations.

SANTA FE OPERA
505-986-5900, 505-986-5955 or 800-280-4654 (box office).

When the Santa Fe Opera opened in 1957, it filled a musical void and gave the city international stature. *Connoisseur* magazine has called it

Maria Spacagna sings the role of Cio-Cio-San in the Santa Fe Opera's 1996 production of Puccini's Madama Butterfly.

David Stein

P.O. Box 2408, Santa Fe, NM 87504.
Season: July 3–Aug. 29.
Tickets (1998): Seats $20–$200 except opening night; standing room $6–$8.

"the premiere summer opera festival in the United States . . . a daring, pioneering enterprise."

Founder and general director John Crosby mounts an ambitious repertoire each season and often takes chances on unknown or new operas, usually including popular standards along with a world premiere or some nearly forgotten masterpiece. Crosby is known for his careful choice of talent, attracting rising stars who often return to perform again after they've gained international reputations.

The opera's brand-new elegant amphitheater contributes to the mystique. Seven miles north of Santa Fe on U.S. 285, it sits on a hilltop with spectacular views of the Sangre de Cristo Mountains to the east and the Jemez sunsets to the west. The 2,126-seat facility, famous for its architectural design, excellent acoustics and views of the stage, now has a complete roof. (Curtain time is 9 p.m. Take along a warm coat and blankets; temperatures tend to plummet after dark. But you no longer need to sit through *Madama Butterfly* in a raincoat, holding an umbrella!)

SANTA FE PRO MUSICA
505-988-4640.
P.O. Box 2091, Santa Fe NM 87504.
Season: Sept.–May.
Tickets: Call for prices.

The Ensemble of Santa Fe and the Orchestra of Santa Fe merged in 1994 to form this new group, which presents orchestral and chamber ensemble concerts September through May. Full orchestral performances are at James A. Little Theater; the Chamber Ensemble Series is held at the Loretto Chapel and St. Francis Auditorium. Most special is the candlelight Christmas season concerts of Baroque music presented in the Loretto Chapel and played on period instruments.

SANTA FE SYMPHONY AND CHORUS
505-983-3530 or 800-480-1319.
P.O. Box 9692, Santa Fe, NM 87504.
Season: Sept.–May.
Tickets (1998): Singles $8–$35; season tickets available.

The Santa Fe Symphony and Chorus, a young and ambitious group founded in 1984, performs under the direction of guest conductors. The season consists of eight subscription concerts of classical and contemporary compositions. Most performances are held at the Santa Fe Convention Center, locally known as the Sweeney Center, 201 W. Marcy St. Imaginative programming is a hallmark of the symphony.

SUMMERSCENE
No phone.
P.O. Box 1808, Santa Fe, NM 87504.
Season: Mid-June–Aug., Tues. & Thurs. noon and 6 p.m.
Tickets: Free.

Every Tuesday and Thursday on the plaza, Summerscene sets the mood with casual entertainment. These popular concerts feature local, regional and national artists in more than 50 performances each season. Bankers, secretaries, construction workers and tourists alike bring lunch or buy a Frito pie at Woolworth's, grab a bench or a spot on the grass and enjoy the free show. There's something for everyone, from light opera to rhythm and blues, jazz, Cajun, salsa, Tex-Mex, bluegrass and Spanish folk. Schedules are widely available — in hotels, at the Sweeney Center and at downtown businesses.

OTHER MUSIC IN SANTA FE

Several smaller groups lend variety and flavor to the musical scene year-round: *Serenata of Santa Fe* (505-989-7988) is a chamber group of professionals who usually perform at the historic Santuario de Guadalupe, 100 S. Guadalupe St. The *Sangre de Cristo Chorale* (505-662-9717 evenings; P.O. Box 4462, Santa Fe, NM 87502) is an ensemble directed by Sheldon Kalberg that performs a repertory of classical, baroque, Renaissance and folk music. The *Santa Fe Women's Ensemble* (505-983-2137) comprises 12 semiprofessional singers who present a spring concert and four traditional Christmas concerts at the beautiful Loretto Chapel next to St. Francis Cathedral.

Taos

TAOS COMMUNITY AUDITORIUM
505-758-4677.
133 Paseo del Pueblo Norte, Taos, NM 87571.
Season: Year-round.
Tickets: Prices vary with performers, most $10.

Cutting edge, multicultural music, dance and theater performances with regional and national talent.

TAOS SCHOOL OF MUSIC SUMMER CHAMBER MUSIC FESTIVAL
505-776-2388.
P.O. Box 1879, Taos, NM 87571.
Season: Mid-June–early Aug.
Tickets (1998): $12–$15.

Established in the 1960s, this chamber music academy draws talented youngsters from all over the country to study piano and stringed instruments at Taos Ski Valley. Weekly performances at Taos Community Auditorium feature the young artists as well as groups such as the American String Quartet and the Brentano String Quartet.

Near Taos

Music at Angel Fire brings the melodious magic of Ani and Ida Kavafian to northern New Mexico each summer.

Courtesy Herbert Barrett Management

MUSIC FROM ANGEL FIRE
505-758-4667.
Total Arts Gallery, P.O. Box 1744, Taos, NM 87571.
Season: Late Aug.–early Sept.
Tickets (1998): $15, series tickets available.

This chamber music festival with a short but sweet season celebrated its 14th year in 1997. Internationally known musicians perform a series of concerts in Angel Fire, Taos, Raton and Santa Fe.

NIGHTLIFE

S anta Fe and Taos used to roll up their sidewalks at night, but lately they've been leaving them out a little longer. You won't find franchises here; tap-rooms tend to reflect local tastes, history and individuality. Here are some of the latest hot spots. (Remember, however, that night spots can change like the phases of the moon. For current happenings, check the Friday "Pasatiempo" section of the *New Mexican* in Santa Fe and the weekly *Taos News* in Taos.)

Santa Fe

If you enjoy flamenco, head to the **Eldorado Hotel Lobby Lounge** (505-988-4455; 309 W. San Francisco) to hear some of the best on weekends, specifically, Ruben Romero and Antonio Mendoza. There's a piano bar and a variety of per-formers most nights. Look to **Vanessie of Santa Fe** (505-982-9966; 434 W. San Francisco St.) for a cocktail-piano atmosphere, with live piano nightly.

Dance to live music nightly at the La Fonda.

Karen Klitgaard

La Fonda's **La Fiesta Lounge** (505-982-5511; 100 E. San Francisco St.) is another favorite place for locals and visitors to meet. Entertainment ranges from small jazz groups to flamenco guitar, to country and western with Bill and Bonnie Hearn. **El Farol** (505-983-9912; 808 Canyon Rd.) is a Santa Fe institution ensconced in an ancient adobe building. Cozy and dark with local landscape murals, it offers great Spanish appetizers, or *tapas,* bands both local and national, and dancing in a tight space. At **La Casa Sena Cantina** (505-988-9232; 125 E. Palace Ave.), the waitstaff comprises professional singers who belt out Broad-way musical tunes while toting margaritas. (See also Chapter Six, *Restaurants.*)

For more music and dance, there's the **Radisson Hotel Santa Fe** (505-982-5591; 750 N. St. Francis Dr.), which may offer jazz, oldies and soloists during any given week. ***Shooters Saloon and Grill*** (505-438-7777; 1196 Harrison Rd. off Cerrillos Rd. offers a large billiard parlor, Mexican and New Mexican dance bands, and draft beer.

If you want camaraderie and conversation, popular spots range from the Victorian elegance of ***La Posada de Santa Fe***'s bar (505-786-0000; 330 E. Palace Ave.), where you can hear the sultry voice of Chris Calloway (daughter of Cab) on weekends, to the funk of ***Evangelo's*** (505-982-9014; 200 W. San Francisco St.), where ersatz Polynesian decor achieves a remarkable grace, if not style. The ***Dragon Room***, the bar next door to the famous ***Pink Adobe Restaurant*** (505-983-7712; 406 Old Santa Fe Trail), features a collection of dragon figures and a glowing fireplace to soothe winter chills. In summer, it becomes the dragon patio with live music. The ***Mine Shaft Tavern*** in Madrid (505-473-0743; Main St., you can't miss it) is all that the name implies: a place where miners could and did feel very much at home. Occasional live music.

A dozen or so restaurants in Santa Fe and environs boast convivial bars and fairly regular live entertainment, such as Spanish classical guitar, flamenco, mariachi trios, jazz, Latin rhythms, country and western, and big bands. Here are a few: ***Mañana Restaurant and Bar***, (505-982-4333; Alameda and Don Gaspar); ***Maria's***, with mariachis nightly during the summer (505-983-7929 or 555 W. Cordova Rd.); ***Garduño's of Santa Fe*** (505-983-9797; 130 Lincoln Ave.) with a Cinco de Mayo ambience; the ***Ore House*** (505-983-8687; on the plaza); the ***Palace Restaurant*** (505-982-9891; 142 W. Palace Ave.), on the site of Dona Tules's notorious 1835 gambling saloon; and ***Tiny's*** (505-983-9817; St. Francis and Cerrillos Rd. in the Pen Road Shopping Center).The new and very popular ***Second Street Brewery*** offers a range of contemporary and folk, from "Celtic jazz" to the traditional Irish tin whistle of Gerry Carthy to a beloved local group called "The Silkies."

Check out the ***Santa Fe Music Hall*** (505-983-3311; 100 N. Guadalupe) for a variety of performances. ***Club Alegria*** is the spot where Father Frank Pretto and his salsa band now perform.

For C&W, the place in Santa Fe is ***Rodeo Nites*** (505-473-4138; 2911 Cerrillos Rd.).

Taos

A great spot to begin or end your evening is the Taos Inn's ***Adobe Bar*** (505-758-2233; 125 Paseo del Pueblo Norte). The inn itself is a lovingly restored historic landmark, and though the bar is compact, you can sit in the adjacent library, on the patio in summer or on one of the balconies overlooking the two-story lobby. There's live entertainment some nights, and you're likely to rub elbows with many Taoseños, from artists to laborers to business people. ***Fernando's Hideaway Lounge*** at the Holiday Inn (505-758-4444; 1005 Paseo del Pueblo Sur) is reputed to have the happiest happy hour in town, 5–7:30 p.m. weekdays, with free hors d'oeuvres.

There's live music nightly at the ***Sagebrush Inn*** (505-758-2254; 1508 Paseo de

Pueblo Sur), where some of the best local C&W performers play. Local bands also play weekends at the **Kachina Lodge** (505-758-2275; 413 Paseo del Pueblo Norte). **Tim's Chile Connection** (505-776-8787; Mile Marker 1, Ski Valley Rd.) is a favorite with locals on weekends. **Caffe Tazza** (505-758-8706; 122 Kit Carson Rd.) is the place to hear poetry readings and more off-beat performers. **Taos Coffee Co.** (505-758-3331;1807 Santa Fe Rd., Ranchos de Taos) has recently started offering music on weekends as well. And if you just want to relax with a beer, you can't beat **Eske's Brew Pub** (505-758-1517;106 Desgeorges Ln.).

PUEBLOS

The ancestors of Indians living today on New Mexico's 19 Indian Pueblos dwelled in the Southwest for many centuries; literally thousands of ruins dot the landscape. Their connection with the land gives Pueblo people a continuity hard to imagine for most Americans. Their prehistoric period was marked by frequent migration and resettlement, but the 16th century opened an era of new stresses. During that time, Spanish conquistadors and settlers arrived. Concurrently, nomadic tribes of Athapaskan Indians began making periodic raids on the pueblos for slaves, food and goods. Americans who came from the East in the 19th century brought more cultural, political and economic pressures.

Today's Pueblo Indians are justly proud not only of their cultural and artistic traditions but also of their growing economic self-sufficiency. The pueblo villages are self-governing, sovereign entities with their own schools, clinics and police forces. The Pueblo people operate numerous thriving businesses. Many speak English and Spanish in addition to their native tongues. Their artwork is in great demand by collectors all over the world, and they continue to nourish their spiritual roots in the ways that have been handed down from generation to generation.

One of the best times to visit is on a feast day, the major public celebration at each pueblo. Ostensibly, feast days are named after particular saints; however, the tradition predates the arrival of the Spanish priests, who applied the names of saints to what were already holy days for the Pueblo people. A feast day is a day of thanksgiving, when relatives return to visit and everyone gives thanks for the well-being of the people. Dancers spend many days preparing for the event. Families cook great quantities of food for visitors, and the intoxicating smells of *posole*, chile and bread baking in the wood-fired *hornos* (beehive-shaped ovens) waft through the air.

Feast days usually start with a Mass at the Catholic church. A priest may lead a procession of dancers to the church, and the dances begin sometime after Mass. In spring, summer and early autumn, dances like the Blue Corn Dance, Butterfly Dance and Harvest Dance may be performed in observance of the planting and harvest. In winter, the hunting cycle is celebrated with Deer, Elk and Buffalo dances. (See pueblo listings for dates of feast days.)

On Christmas Eve and Christmas Day, you may see the Matachines Dance at Taos, Picuris, San Juan, Santa Clara and San Ildefonso Pueblos. Dancers clothed in beaded headdresses with scarves over their mouths move to 16th-century Spanish folk tunes played on guitars and violins. The origins of the Matachines Dance are obscure, but it is probably rooted in Moorish customs brought from Spain. Similar dances are performed in neighboring Spanish villages and throughout the hemisphere.

A good time to see dances and buy artwork is the annual *Eight Northern Indian Pueblos Artist and Craftsman Show*, usually held in July at San Ilde-

---

Pueblo Etiquette

Here are some things to keep in mind when visiting a pueblo:

- Inquire ahead of time about visitor hours. Remember that some pueblos are closed to outsiders on certain days for religious activities.

- Drive slowly.

- Never bring drugs or alcoholic beverages to a pueblo.

- *Stop at the visitor center or tribal office when you arrive. This is a requirement at all the pueblos.* Some charge fees; others ask visitors to register.

- Do not walk into or on a *kiva* (circular ceremonial structures).

- Homes, *kivas* and cemeteries are not open to non-Pueblo visitors. However, if you are invited to come into someone's home to eat, it is considered impolite to refuse. (It's also considered polite to eat and leave promptly so that others can come in and eat.) Most pueblos have food concessions on feast days, when visitors can sample Pueblo cooking.

- Remember that dances are religious ceremonies, not performances. Conduct yourself as you were in a church. Revealing clothing, like shorts and halter tops, is not acceptable. Don't talk or obstruct the view of others during the dances, don't applaud afterward, and don't approach the dancers or ask about the meaning of dances. The Pueblo people prefer not to discuss their beliefs with outsiders.

- Do not cut across the plaza or area where the dances are being performed. Always walk along the perimeter.

- For your comfort, bring along folding chairs to watch the dances from.

- Observe each pueblo's regulations on use of cameras, tape recorders and drawing. Most pueblos forbid these activities during dances. (See pueblo listings for particulars.) If you want to photograph a pueblo resident, ask permission first and give a donation to the family.

fonso Pueblo, 25 miles northwest of Santa Fe. More than 600 Indian artists from Maine to California exhibit their work in this largest Native American-owned-and-operated arts-and-crafts show in the country. Pueblo pottery and jewelry dominate, but there's a wide variety of beadwork, kachina dolls, sculpture, painting, weaving and other crafts. Booths sell mutton stew, fry bread, Indian tacos, pies and outdoor-oven-baked breads. You may see both Plains and Pueblo Indian dances, and photography permits may be purchased. For location and dates, call or 505-852-4265 or 800-793-4955.

Key Numbers:
New Mexico Department of Indian Tourism
505-827-7382 or 800-545-2070.
Indian Pueblo Cultural Center
505-843-7270.
2401 Twelfth St. NW, Albuquerque, NM 871104.
Write or call for updated calendar of Pueblo events.

Near Santa Fe

COCHITI PUEBLO
505-465-2244.
Tribal Office, P.O. Box 70, Cochiti, NM 87072.
Cochiti Pueblo exit 264 from I-25 about 25 miles S. of Santa Fe.
Language: Keresan.
Feast Day: July 14, San Buenaventura.
Fee: None; cameras not allowed.

Cochiti Pueblo remains firmly rooted in its past while building a strong future. The church built in 1628 in honor of San Buenaventura still stands, remodeled and maintained. Not far away is *Cochiti Lake*, a recreational community built on land leased from the pueblo, which also operates Cochiti Lake services. Cochiti Lake has an 18-hole golf course, tennis courts, swimming pool, marina and shopping center. (See also "Swimming" and "Water Sports" in Chapter Seven, *Recreation*.)

Cochiti Pueblo is best known for its magnificent drums and evocative clay storyteller figurines. The popular storyteller figure was created in 1964 by Cochiti potter Helen Cordero, who says she was inspired by her grandfather telling stories to children. Now many Pueblo potters make these popular storytellers in human and animal forms, but Cochiti storytellers are still the most highly prized. Cochiti drums, which are essential to the pueblo's ceremonies, are also widely coveted by collectors. Individual pueblo artists sell crafts out of their home studios.

NAMBE PUEBLO
505-455-2036.
Rte. 1, Box 117-BB, Santa Fe, NM 87501.
Drive 15 miles N. of Santa Fe on U.S. 285, 3 miles E. on N.M. 503 to sign for Nambe Falls, then 2

A small pueblo set near the Sangre de Cristo Mountains in a piñon and juniper valley, Nambe (nam-BAY) retains a few original buildings, including the ruins of a mission. Many tribal members work at nearby Los Alamos National Laboratory, in Española or in Santa Fe. Beautiful Nambe

Murrae Haynes

Butterfly dancer from Nambe Pueblo.

miles to pueblo entrance.
Language: Tewa.
Feast Day: Oct. 4, St. Francis.
Fees (1996): Sketching $15, still cameras $5, movie/video cameras $10; fees subject to change.

POJOAQUE PUEBLO
505-455-3460
Rte. 11, Box 71, Santa Fe, NM 87501.
15 miles N. of Santa Fe on U.S. 285.
Language: Tewa.
Feast Day: Dec. 12, Our Lady of Guadalupe.
Fees: Contact Governor's Office (505-455-3901) before sketching or filming.

Falls, one of the state's few waterfalls, is the setting for the annual Fourth of July Ceremonials. From April through October, *Nambe Falls Recreational Site* offers fishing, picnicking, camping, boating and sightseeing. Fees are charged for each activity. For tours led by Native American guides, call *Nambe Pueblo Tours* (800-946-2623).

The 20 businesses that line the east side of U.S. 285 at Pojoaque speak of an enterprising spirit and prosperity; one would not guess that Pojoaque (po-WAH-kee) is a pueblo that has pulled itself back from near extinction. Only mounds of earth remain of the original pueblo, and in the late 1800s the people themselves were almost wiped out by a smallpox epidemic.

In the 1930s, a new Pojoaque was founded, and a milestone was reached in 1983 when tribal members danced for the first time in more than 100 years. Now they celebrate Our Lady of Guadalupe Day and All King's Day on January 6.

Next to the Pojoaque Pueblo Tourist Information Center on U.S. 285 is the Poeh Museum (pronounced POE), which hosts artist exhibits, weekend dance performances and occasional workshops. The museum also serves as a training complex for Tewa artists, with archives and Tewa art collections. Museum hours: Tues.–Sat. 8:00–4:30; closed Sun.–Mon.

SAN FELIPE PUEBLO
505-867-3381.
P.O. Box 4339, San Felipe
  Pueblo, NM 87001.
About 40 miles S. of Santa
  Fe off I-25.
Language: Keresan.
Feast Day: May 1, St.
  Phillip.
Fees : Admission fee
  may be charged. No
  photography, recording
  or sketching allowed;
  cameras may be
  confiscated.

This small pueblo on the banks of the Rio Grande
has a timeless feel, perhaps engendered by the
ceaseless flow of water past the softly contoured
adobe buildings. San Felipe is known for its beautiful Green Corn Dance on May 1, its feast day. Men,
women and children participate in day-long dances
under the spring sun. Dances are in the plaza,
which has been worn three feet below the ground
surface over the years by countless feet. A traditional and conservative pueblo, San Felipe is reviv-
ing its artisans' longtime skills in beadwork and
heishi (HEE-she), jewelry made of tiny, hand-carved
shell beads.

SAN ILDEFONSO
PUEBLO
505-455-3549.
Rte. 5, Box 315-A, Santa Fe,
  NM 87501.
Drive 15 miles N. of Santa
  Fe on U.S. 285, turn left at
  N.M. 502, then 6 miles to
  entrance on right.
Language: Tewa.
Feast Day: Jan. 23, San
  Ildefonso.
Fees: $3 per carload;
  sketching and filming
  $15, still cameras $5.
Fees subject to change.
No photography allowed
on feast days.

San Ildefonso is world famous for its black-on-
black pottery, a technique developed by Maria
Martinez and her husband, Julian, in the 1920s.
Maria was also among the first Pueblo potters to
sign her work. Her pots are prized by private collectors and museums nationwide, and her descendants
still make pottery, both innovative and traditional.
Other artisans sell wares out of their homes. Inquire
at the visitor and information center.

San Ildefonso also operates the *Maria Martinez
Museum* (505-455-3549, 8–5 summer, 8–4 winter)
with displays of local arts, embroidery, photography, pottery-making techniques and Pueblo history.
A stocked fishing lake is open March through October; permits can be obtained at the lake.

SAN JUAN PUEBLO
505-852-4400.
P.O. Box 1099, San Juan,
  NM 87566.
Drive 1 mile N. of
  Española on N.M. 68,
  turn left onto U.S. 74
  at San Juan Pueblo
  sign; entrance is 1 mile
  farther.
Language: Tewa.
Feast Day: June 24, San Juan.
Fees: Cameras, varies.
  Contact the tribal

In 1598, conquistador Don Juan de Oñate declared
this prosperous and friendly pueblo the first capital of New Mexico. When Spanish demands for
gold and slaves became too insistent, the San Juan
people asked Oñate to take his capital somewhere
else. (It ended up in Santa Fe.) A San Juan native
named Popé (Po-PAY) organized the Pueblo Revolt
in 1680. (See Chapter One, *History*.)

The largest and northernmost of the Tewa-speaking pueblos, San Juan has two central plazas with
its Catholic church and ceremonial *kivas* side by
side. It also runs the O'ke Oweenge Arts and Crafts

governor's office (505-852-4400) for photo permit and to see whether pueblo is open.

Cooperative, a multipurpose complex where visitors can view and buy the pueblo's distinctive red incised pottery, a ware whose luster and geometric designs are coveted by collectors worldwide. San Juan artisans also excel at jewelry making, carving, weaving and other arts.

Across the street from the crafts cooperative is the Tewa Indian Restaurant, where you can munch fry bread, dried fruit pies, red and green chile stews, *posole* and other traditional foods. It's open weekdays 10–2, closed holidays, weekends and June 24. Fishing at the tribal lakes is open winter and summer; contact the tribal office for regulations. The powerful Turtle Dance is performed each Dec. 26.

SANTA CLARA PUEBLO
505-753-7326.
P.O. Box 580, Española, NM 87532.
From Española drive 1.3 miles on N.M. 30, cross to W. side of Rio Grande and pueblo entrance on left.
Language: Tewa.
Feast Day: Aug. 12, Santa Clara.
Fees: Sketching and video cameras $15, still cameras $5. No cameras allowed at some events. Puye Cliff Dwellings self-guided tour $5 adults, $4 seniors & children. Adult fee includes still camera permit.

Set in the wide Rio Grande Valley, with vistas of mountains on either side, Santa Clara is home to 2,600 enterprising tribal members who farm, work at jobs outside the pueblo and create stunning red and black polished pottery, sculpture and paintings. They are the descendants of the ancient Puye cliff dwellers, and their name for their pueblo, *Kha P'o*, means "Singing Water."

Santa Clara potters are noted for their intricately carved pottery (*sgraffito*), particularly the etched miniatures. Look for "Pottery For Sale" signs on houses; you'll be invited to come in and meet the artist. Santa Clara also offers guided tours of the pueblo and its historical church. On the tours, you'll be allowed to photograph, see pottery demonstrations, buy native foods and perhaps see a dance. Tours are offered weekdays only, with five days' advance notice. Inquire at the tourism office, or phone the number above.

Santa Clara also operates the *Puye* (POO-yay) *Cliff Dwellings*, a National Landmark just west of the pueblo. The original dwellings were cave-like rooms hollowed out of cliffs made of volcanic tuff. Later, houses were built below the cliffs and atop the mesas. The site was abandoned around A.D. 1500 for the present pueblo site. You can follow three trails to see the ruins. Stairways in the rock connect the cliff dwellings with the 740-room pueblo ruins and *kiva* above. The mesa top affords spectacular mountain and valley views. Guided tours are available by prior arrangement. Before visiting Puye, inquire at the tourism office about road conditions.

Murrae Haynes

Puye Ruins

Santa Clara Canyon Recreational Area, a rugged natural spot, is open to visitors for camping, picnicking and fishing. It's open April through October; inquire about fees at the tourism office.

SANTO DOMINGO PUEBLO
505-465-2214.
P.O. Box 99, Santo Domingo Pueblo, NM 87052.
About 34 miles S. of Santa Fe on I-25.
Language: Keresan.
Feast Day: Aug. 4, Santo Domingo.
Fees: None; donations accepted. No cameras, sketching or recording allowed.

Santo Domingo is home to an amazing number of creative and enterprising artists. Many have transformed the traditional *heishi* and turquoise jewelry-making techniques into beautiful contemporary designs. Others have revived the ancient Santo Domingo pottery tradition and are producing superb blends of old and new. Santo Domingo jewelry is available from artists selling under the *portal* of the Palace of the Governors in Santa Fe and at shops at the pueblo.

The *August 4 Feast Day Corn Dance* is an unforgettable scene, with hundreds of dancers, singers and clowns participating in all-day ceremonies. Santo Domingo hosts an annual arts and crafts market each Labor Day weekend, with 300 booths of jewelry, pottery and other artwork along with Indian foods. For more information, call or write the *Santo Domingo Arts & Crafts Market* (505-465-2690; P.O. Box 369, Santo Domingo Pueblo, NM 87052).

TESUQUE PUEBLO
505-983-2667 or 800-483-1040.

Though close to Santa Fe and operating several successful businesses, Tesuque is one of the

Rte. 5, Box 360-T, Santa Fe, NM 87501.

9 miles N. of Santa Fe on U.S. 285. Main village is 1 mile W. of highway.

Language: Tewa.

Feast Day: Nov. 12, San Diego.

Fees (1996): No photography or video during dances; check with tribal office at other times.

most conservative of the pueblos. The site was occupied as far back as 1250; however, the original pueblo was at another location that was abandoned after the Pueblo Revolt of 1680. Tesuque Indians played a major part in the revolt. Two of its leaders, Catua and Omtua, secretly notified the other pueblos of the plan and were arrested when someone betrayed them to the Spaniards. Tesuque leaders then decided to stage the revolt three days earlier, and all the pueblos were successful in driving the Spaniards out of New Mexico for more than 12 years. (See Chapter One, *History*.)

The present pueblo was established in 1694. Listed on the National Register of Historic Places, Tesuque has a large central plaza with a Catholic church. The tribe operates a bingo parlor (505-984-8414) on U.S. 285, an RV park and store (505-455-2661), a campground in the Sangre de Cristo Mountains (505-983-2667) and Tesuque Natural Farm (505-983-2667), where certified organic blue corn, chile and other vegetables are grown. Several artists' studios are open to the public, selling mostly traditional Tesuque clay figurines, pottery, beadwork, drums, weavings and carvings. Inquire at the tribal office.

Near Taos

PICURIS PUEBLO
505-587-2957 or 505-587-2519.

P.O. Box 487, Peñasco, NM 87553.

Drive 17 miles N. from Española to junction with N.M. 75. Turn right and continue 13 miles to Picuris.

Language: Tewa.

Feast Day: Aug. 10, San Lorenzo.

Fees: Sketching $10, still cameras $5, movie/video cameras $10. Self-guided ruin tours $1.75. Fees also for fishing and camping; inquire at tribal office (505-587-2519). Call in advance about tours.

The last pueblo to be discovered by the Spaniards in 1519, Picuris (pee-ku-REES) is nearly hidden in the Sangre de Cristo Mountains. It was settled in the 1200s and about 200 years later had grown into a multistory adobe complex. Picuris was abandoned after the 1680 Pueblo Revolt and reestablished in the 1700s. It has never made a treaty with another government and retains its status as a sovereign nation and tribe.

The smallest of the pueblos, Picuris operates several facilities for visitors. The annual *Tri-Cultural Arts and Crafts Fair*, held the first week in July, uses proceeds to help with restoration of the pueblo's San Lorenzo Church. The *Hidden Valley Shop and Restaurant* includes a small convenience store and smoke shop, fishing equipment and arts and crafts. The restaurant, with Picuris and American foods, is open daily in the summer. Inquire at the tribal office about hours at other times. *Pu-Na* and *Tu-Tah Lakes* are stocked ponds with a picnic area. The *Picuris Pueblo Museum*, which displays authentic Indian arts and crafts, is open daily.

TAOS PUEBLO
505-758-1028 or
   505-758-9593.
P.O. Box 1846, Taos, NM
   87571.
2 miles N. of Taos off N.M.
   68.
Language: Tiwa.
Feast Days: Sept. 29–30,
   San Geronimo.
Fees: Admission $5 per car
   plus $2 for each person in
   car. Pueblo may be closed
   to non-Indians during
   Feb., March and Aug.;
   inquire at tribal office.
   No photography during
   feast days. Other times,
   sketching $15, painting
   $35, still cameras $5, and
   movie/video cameras
   $10.

Taos was well established long before Europe emerged from the Dark Ages. The present pueblo of multistoried adobe apartment buildings has been occupied since about A.D. 1450. Today, as then, the clear waters of the Rio Pueblo flow through the area from sacred Blue Lake in the Sangre de Cristo Mountains. Today, as then, residents draw their water from the stream. To honor their traditions, they live without indoor plumbing or electricity, just as their ancestors did. In less traditional parts of the pueblo, these conveniences are available.

Architecturally, Taos Pueblo is the most spectacular of the area's pueblos, capturing the imaginations of countless artists. Its beauty is the outward manifestation of its spiritual strength. Taos was the seat of the Pueblo Revolt of 1680, when the Spaniards were driven out of New Mexico. It also played an active role in the 1847 uprising of Hispanics and Indians against the U.S. government. (See Chapter One, *History*.)

With about 1,100 residents, Taos Pueblo is governed by a council of 50 men who are members of the secret *kiva* religion. The economy is based on government services, tourism, arts and crafts, ranching and farming. *San Geronimo Feast Day* is a highlight of the year, with a sunset dance on September 29, footraces, an arts and crafts fair, a ritual pole climbing, traditional dances and food. During the festivities, the "Black Eyes," a religious society, perform humorous acts that have spiritual significance for pueblo members.

Visitors are also welcome at the *Taos Pueblo Powwow*, held the second weekend of July each year. Native Americans from many tribes join in this colorful and popular social dance event. (The powwow is a Plains Indian tradition, but Taos has been influenced by contacts with Plains tribes for centuries.) Other dances open to the public (no cameras) are the *Turtle Dance*, January 1; *Buffalo or Deer Dance*, January 6; *Feast of Santa Cruz Corn Dance*, May 3; *San Antonio Corn Dance*, June 13; *San Juan Corn Dance*, June 24; and *Deer Dance or Matachines*, Christmas Day. Christmas Eve is a special time to visit, with bonfires and processions.

Taos Pueblo artists are noted for their mica-flecked (micaceous) pottery, tanned buckskin moccasins, silver jewelry and wonderful drums, made of hides stretched over hollowed cottonwood logs. A dozen or more shops on the pueblo plaza sell these goods, along with fragrant breads fresh-baked in outdoor adobe ovens called *hornos*.

SEASONAL EVENTS

U nless otherwise noted, admission is not charged for the following events.

Santa Fe

ALL SPECIES DAY

A pageant for all ages in which animals and plants have their outspoken but playful say about what we're doing to our environment. Usually held the Saturday before Earth Day in April, the big feature of this event is the *All Species Parade* in which kids dressed as antlered elk, stilt-legged storks, lumbering buffalo and papier mache birds parade and fly from the plaza to Fort Marcy Park. There the animals hold a "creature congress" in which they speak, squawk, howl and bay for the earth. There are also many festivities including dances, displays, floats, sideshows and storytelling. For dates and further information, call the *Santa Fe Visitors Bureau*, 800-777-2489.

CHRISTMAS

C hristmas in Santa Fe is a delight, a time when each culture celebrates its own traditions. The Palace of the Governors usually sponsors *Las Posadas*, a traditional Spanish reenactment of Joseph and Mary's search for shelter on the night Jesus was born. The plaza is the setting for the pageant, performed by an area church group, and a choir and audience members follow the Holy Couple around the plaza.

Many area musical ensembles conduct seasonal concerts in December; consult the Santa Fe Convention and Visitor Bureau or local newspapers for schedules. Also, many area pueblos hold special dances around Christmas (see introduction to "Pueblos," above). On Christmas Eve, Santa Fe is alight with thousands of *farolitos*, glowing candles placed in paper bags. The scent of piñon bonfires, or *luminarias*, fills the air as hundreds of people take to the streets in the Canyon Road neighborhood to see the *farolitos*, sing carols and socialize.

EIGHT NORTHERN INDIAN PUEBLOS ARTIST AND
CRAFTSMAN SHOW

T his is a large exhibition and sale of handcrafted Indian artwork and crafts, held at San Ildefonso Pueblo in mid-July. (See "Pueblos," above.)

FEAST DAY DANCES

Each pueblo has a special Feast Day celebration annually on its patron saint's day. (See "Pueblos," above.)

Artist Pablita Abeyta (r.) shows her wares to prospective buyers at the annual Indian Market.

Murrae Haynes

INDIAN MARKET
505-983-5220,
   fax 505-483-7647.
Southwestern Association
   for Indian Arts.
142 W. Palace, Santa Fe,
   NM 87501.
Time: Weekend following
   third Thursday in Aug.
Location: Plaza and
   vicinity.
Fee: None.

Indian Market is the biggest weekend of the year in Santa Fe, when more than 1,000 Native American artists exhibit and sell their work at outdoor booths on and around the plaza. Indian Market is the largest exhibition and sale of Indian art in the world. Begun more than 70 years ago as an effort to help Pueblo Indians revive their pottery and jewelry-making traditions, it has since been the springboard for countless successful artistic careers. All participants are carefully screened: they must be Native American, and their work must be totally handmade.

Activity starts before dawn on Saturday with artists unloading work at their booths and eager collectors lining up to get first chance at a coveted pot or necklace when the market officially opens at 8 a.m. Irresistible smells of fry bread, coffee, mutton stew and Navajo tacos fill the air, and the plaza slowly fills with people. Artists demonstrate skills like sand painting or basket weaving, and the drums sound for social dances in the courtyard of the Palace of the Governors. The array of artwork is mind-boggling, from pottery, jewelry, beadwork and weaving to basketry, paintings, drums and rattles. There's something for everyone, from a $3 corn necklace to a $5,000 Navajo rug.

Firedancer gyrates as Zozobra goes up in flames, beginning La Fiesta de Santa Fe.

Murrae Haynes

LA FIESTA DE SANTA FE
800-777-2489 (Santa Fe
  Convention and Visitors
  Bureau).
Time: Weekend after Labor
  Day.
Location: Plaza and
  vicinity.

The oldest continuously observed festival in the United States, La Fiesta is the quintessential celebration of New Mexico's Hispanic culture. The first Fiesta de Santa Fe was held in September 1712, with processions, sermons, candle lighting, pomp and circumstance in commemoration of Don Diego de Vargas's reentry into Santa Fe in 1692, following the 1680 Pueblo Revolt. (See Chapter One, *History*.)

Fiesta preparations begin long in advance, with the selection of a young woman as Fiesta Queen, along with her Court, and a young man as Don Diego de Vargas and his 17-member retinue. All play roles in a reenactment of Vargas's return. On the Friday after Labor Day, La Fiesta begins with the Pregón de la Fiesta and Mass at Rosario Chapel.

An extremely popular addition to La Fiesta is Zozobra, or "Old Man Gloom," a 40-foot-tall papier-mâché puppet that stands in Fort Marcy Park on Friday night of La Fiesta. Zozobra was born in 1926, the brainchild of Will Shuster, one of Los Cinco Pintores who started the Santa Fe art colony of that era. As fireworks flare and dancers gyrate wildly around him, Zozobra goes up in flames, symbolically burning away the year's troubles so that the celebrations can begin. The cheering crowd then heads for the plaza for food, music and dancing. Plaza festivities continue through the weekend.

RODEO DE SANTA FE
505-471-4300.
Rodeo Grounds, Rodeo Rd.
  near Richards Ave.
Time: Mid-July.
Fee: Admission charge; call
  for details.

(See "Rodeos" in Chapter Seven, *Recreation*.)

SANTA FE BANJO AND FIDDLE CONTEST

Time: Labor Day weekend.
Location: Rodeo Grounds, Rodeo Rd. near Richards Ave.
Fee: Admission charged; write or call the Santa Fe Convention and Visitors Bureau, 800-777-2489, for details.

You can see and hear just about every way to play a fiddle or pick a banjo at this festive weekend. Fiddle competitions include children's, bluegrass, Spanish and old-time. There are also mandolin, flatpick guitar and songwriting competitions, as well as workshops for a number of different instruments and playing styles. The weekend includes a jam session and performances by competition winners.

Spanish Market brings a feast of traditional Spanish Colonial art to Santa Fe the last weekend in July.

Corrie Photography

CONTEMPORARY HISPANIC MARKET

505-988-1878.
 Santa Fe Council for the Arts, P.O. Box 6863, Santa Fe, NM 87502.
Time: Last full weekend in July.
Location: Lincoln Ave., just off the plaza.

Contemporary work by Hispanic artists, including jewelry, fiber arts, painting, furniture and crafts, is exhibited and sold at this show, which operates alongside the traditional Spanish Market. This juried exhibition marked its 13th year in 1997.

SPANISH MARKET

505-983-4038.
Spanish Colonial Arts Society.
239-1/2 Johnson St. Santa Fe, NM 87501.
P.O. Box 1611, Santa Fe, NM 87504.
Time: Last full weekend in July.
Location: On the plaza.
Fee: None.

During the centuries when New Mexico was a Spanish colony, its isolation from Spain and distance from Mexico fostered the growth of unique folk arts. Many of these arts and crafts helped serve the religious needs of the settlers. Beginning in the 1920s, they have undergone a revival, and the work of New Mexican artisans is in great demand by collectors and museums.

At Spanish Market, which celebrated its 46th

year in 1997, you can see the finest Hispanic artwork produced in the region today: *santos, colcha* embroidery, woolen weavings, straw appliqué, carved and painted furniture, tinwork, forged iron, *reredos* and more. About 150 artists exhibit in booths around the plaza. The scene is complemented with native New Mexican folk music groups, food booths and artist demonstrations. There's also a winter market the first full weekend in December.

Taos

FIESTAS DE SANTIAGO Y SANTA ANA
505-758-3873 or
  800-732-8267.
P.O. Drawer I, Taos, NM
  87571.
Time: Late July.
Location: On the plaza.
Fee: None.

Taos's patron saints are honored in this traditional three-day festival that begins with a Friday night Mass and candlelight procession to the plaza. The weekend is filled with such goings-on as a satirical parade on local history, crowning of a Fiesta Queen, an arts and crafts fair and food booths.

MEET THE ARTIST SERIES
505-758-2233 or
  800-TAOS-INN.
Taos Inn, 125 Paseo del
  Pueblo Norte, Taos, NM
  87571.
Time: Sept., Oct.; call for
  dates and times.
Fee: None.

The historic Taos Inn created this semiannual event more than 15 years ago to give locals and visitors a chance to meet some of Taos's most accomplished artists. At informal get-togethers, artists discuss their work and present slide shows and demonstrations.

Eyeing a mountain man at the Old Taos Trade Fair.

Elaine Avery; courtesy Martinez Hacienda

OLD TAOS TRADE FAIR
505-758-0505.
P.O. Drawer CCC, Taos,
  NM 87571.

This two-day fair, which coincides with San Geronimo Day at Taos Pueblo (see "Pueblos," above, page 118) brings to life Spanish Colonial cul-

Time: Late Sept.
Fees (1998): $5 adults, $2.50 children under 16.

ture in the 1820s. Held at the Martinez Hacienda (see "Historic Sites," above), an authentically restored fortress-like home of that era, the fair features mountain men, traditional craft demonstrations, native foods, caravans, muzzle-loading rifle demonstrations and Hispanic and Indian music.

**TAOS FALL ARTS
  FESTIVAL**
505-758-3873 or
  800-732-8267.
P.O. Drawer I, Taos, NM
  87571.
Time: Late Sept.–early Oct.
Fee: None.

A roundup of arts festivities, this chamber-of-commerce-sponsored event celebrates the rich history, cultures and art of Taos County. Events include gallery openings, invitational and juried art exhibitions, an arts and crafts fair, and the *Wool Festival*, a great favorite with locals.

TAOS POETRY CIRCUS
505-758-0081.
SOMOS (Society for the
  Muse of the Southwest).
232 S. Santa Fe Rd.,
  Ranchos de Taos, NM
  87571.
P.O. Box 2615, Taos, NM
  87571.
Time: June.
Location: Call or write.
Tickets: Prices vary; call or
  write for details.

The Taos Poetry Circus is a marathon week of poetry workshops and readings by both established and emerging poets. The big night is the World Heavyweight Championship Poetry Bout, conducted like — you guessed it — a boxing match. You have to be there to believe it. You'll see performance poetry at its best in this thrilling event, especially when poets like Andrei Codresceu, Victor Hernandez Cruz, Anne Waldman, Ed Sanders and Deborah Salazar are pitted against each other. In a recent World Heavyweight Bout, the contenders were Quincy Troupe and Jimmy Santiago Baca.

TAOS PUEBLO POWWOW   (See "Taos Pueblo" in this chapter.)

**TAOS SPRING ARTS
  CELEBRATION**
505-758-3873 or
  800-732-8267.
P.O. Drawer I, Taos, NM
  87571.
Time: April-May.
Fee: None.

Taos shakes off winter with a blossoming of visual, literary and performing arts. Events include a major art show, arts and crafts, and many gallery and museum shows.

**TAOS TALKING
  PICTURE FESTIVAL**
505-751-0637
106 Padre Martinez Ln.,
  Taos, NM 87571
Time: Early mid-April
Fee: Varies.

This young, vital film festival presents an assortment of premieres, classics, independents and shorts along with panel discussions by filmmakers, actors and critics. An exhilarating and immensely stimulating experience. Get your tickets early. Many events sell out far in advance.

The Bear

By Linda Hogan

The bear is a dark continent
that walks upright
like a man.
It lives across the thawing river.
I have seen it
beyond the water,
beyond comfort. Last night
it left a mark at my door
that said winter
was a long and hungry night of sleep.
But I am not afraid; I have collected
other nights of fear
knowing what things walked
the edges of my sleep.

and I remember
the man who shot
a bear,
how it cried like he did
and in his own voice,
how he tracked that red song
into the forest's lean arms
to where the bear lay weeping
on fired earth, its black hands
covering its face from sky

where humans believe god lives
larger than death.

That man,
a madness remembered him.
It is a song in starved shadows
in nights of sleep.
It follows him.
Even the old rocks sing it.
It makes him want
to get down on his knees
and lay his own hands
across his face and turn away
from sky where god lives
larger than life.
Madness is its own country,
desperate and ruined.
It is a collector of lives.
It's a man
afraid of what he's done
and what he lives by. Safe,
we are safe
from the bear, and we have each other,
we have each other to fear.

Linda Hogan is a Chickasaw poet and associate professor at the University of Colorado who has participated in the Taos Poetry Circus.

YULETIDE IN TAOS
505-758-3873 or 800-732-8267.
P.O. Drawer I, Taos, NM 87571.
Time: Dec.
Fee: None.

Imagine Taos Plaza edged in snow, with colored lights and *farolitos* gleaming. This celebration incorporates Taos's Hispanic and Indian traditions in a series of community events: *farolito* tours, candlelight dinners, dance performances, ski area festivities, ethnic holiday foods, a crafts fair, and a Christmas parade and tree lighting on the plaza.

THEATER

Santa Fe

GREER GARSON THEATER
505-473-6511.
College of Santa Fe, St.
Michael's Dr., Santa Fe,
NM 87501.
Season: Oct.–May.
Tickets: Call box office,
open Aug.–May.

The Drama Department of the College of Santa Fe, a private liberal arts institution, stages four plays each season in a beautiful theater named for the department's benefactor, former Hollywood star Greer Garson, who owned a ranch near Santa Fe and spent much time here. Each season usually includes a drama, a comedy, a musical and a classic. These fine productions play to packed houses. The quality of professionalism is so high, you can't believe this is student work.

RAILYARD PERFORMANCE CENTER
505-982-8309.
430 W. Manhattan, Santa
Fe, NM 87501.
Next to Tomasita's
Restaurant on
Guadalupe St.
Season: Year-round.
Tickets: Prices vary with
productions.

This unique space is "a multi-use performance facility suitable for productions of theater, dance, and music." In operation since 1992, the center took over the space formerly occupied by the Santa Fe Actors' Theatre. It offers over 30 hours of classes a week in African, Haitian and Island dance and drama, as well as drumming and dance classes for kids. The theater seats about a hundred occupants.

SANTA FE PLAYHOUSE
505-988-4262.
142 E. De Vargas St.
Season: Year-round.
Tickets: Prices vary with
production.

Founded in the 1920s, the Santa Fe Playhouse started as the Santa Fe Community Theatre. It remains the longest-running theater group in New Mexico. Today it seems very much at home in its own intimate adobe theater building in one of Santa Fe's oldest neighborhoods. A favorite each fall is the Fiesta Melodrama, staged the week of La Fiesta. (See "Seasonal Events," above.) One of the best-kept secrets that week is who among the city's prominent citizens will be skewered in this irreverent satire. The season includes a program of classic and contemporary works.

SANTA FE STAGES
505-982-6683.
105 E. Marcy St., N.M. 107,
Santa Fe, NM 87501.

An international summer theater festival at the Greer Garson Theatre Center, the vital new Santa Fe Stages brings to town exciting, challenging, "best of the best" performances from England,

Elicia (Karen-Angela Bishop) plots the ways of love in "The Illusion" during the 1995 inaugural season of Santa Fe Stages.

Courtesy Santa Fe Stages

Box Office at Greer Garson Theatre Center, College of Santa Fe, 1600 St. Michael's Drive, Santa Fe, NM 87501.

Canada, U.S., France and Hungary, plus world premieres. For those with an appetite for artistic excellence and the total exhilaration only a superb evening of theater can deliver, this is a not-to-be-missed opportunity. Also brings outstanding contemporary theater and dance to Santa Fe during the winter. Order tickets early so as not to be disappointed. Many sorts of subscription series available.

SHAKESPEARE IN SANTA FE
505-982-2910.
310 N. Guadelupe St., #204, Santa Fe, NM 87501.
Performances held at St. John's College, about 1.5 miles E. of downtown.
Season: Summer.
Tickets: Admission free; first come, first served.

In 1998, Shakespeare in Santa Fe marked its tenth year of staging free professional productions of the bard's work in an idyllic outdoor setting. One play is produced each summer. The schedule varies from year to year. (Check the Pasatiempo section of the *New Mexican* for information.) Shakespeare in Santa Fe is supported by community contributions and grants. One popular summer pastime is arriving early and sharing a picnic supper on blankets before the performance.

Near Santa Fe

MINE SHAFT TAVERN MELODRAMA
505-473-0743.
Mine Shaft Tavern & Restaurant, N.M. 14 (Turquoise Trail), Madrid, NM 87010.

With audience-interactive theatrics at their most extravagant, the Engine House Theater adjacent to the Mine Shaft Tavern brings back the glorious days of villainy and heroism. Will the villain get the deed to the ranch? Will the dashing hero rescue the damsel in distress? Take the scenic 40-minute drive to Madrid, south of Santa Fe, and find

Season: Sat.–Sun., May–Oct. Call for schedule.
Tickets (1998): $9 adults, $7 seniors, $4 children; reservations suggested.

out. You can cheer the hero, throw marshmallows at the villain, and see a happy ending in a real Western ghost-town setting.

Taos

The Taos Art Association (505-758-4677), 45 years old, sponsors more than 50 performing arts events annually in the Taos Community Auditorium. People are still talking about the locally produced staging of *Godspell*. TAA also brings in exciting dance groups and performance art companies. Call for current happenings when you're in town.

SUMMER INSTITUTES

Santa Fe

SANTA FE PHOTOGRAPHIC WORKSHOPS
505-983-1400.
Mount Carmel Rd., Santa Fe, NM 87501.

Summer workshops in all aspects of photography, taught by photographers of national and international repute. Write for class schedule.

SANTA FE SCHOOL OF COOKING
505-983-4511.
116 W. San Francisco, Santa Fe, NM 87501.

Want to learn how to make a great salsa or serve an entire dinner of Southwestern cuisine? Contact the Santa Fe School of Cooking for a listing of classes.

Near Santa Fe

GHOST RANCH CONFERENCE CENTER
505-685-4333.
HC77 Box 11, Abiquiu, New Mexico 87510.

Classes and seminars in photography, writing, pottery, silversmithing, watercolor, weaving, history, spirituality, health and music are offered year-round at this retreat center in the heart of O'Keeffe's red rock country. Operated by the Presbyterian Church, rustic Ghost Ranch is a center of diversity. Many Elderhostel programs also available here. Write for schedule of classes.

Taos

TAOS INSTITUTE OF ARTS
505-758-2793.
Box 5280 NDCBU, Taos, NM 87571

For ten years, Taos Institute of Arts has offered accredited workshops with special emphasis on the cultures and arts of the Southwest. Students come from all over the world to take classes in painting, photography, writing and literature, textile, clay and ceramics, jewelry and Southwest culture from top-ranking instructors. Write or call for current brochure.

CHAPTER FIVE

*"God is everywhere, but His address is in Española"**
SACRED SITES, ANCIENT RUINS AND NATURAL WONDERS

New Mexico is home to a remarkable variety of spiritual paths. From Christian to Buddhist to Sikh, all have found the high mountains and desert expanses an inspiration to faith and practice. Contemporary spiritual seekers resonate with ancient Native American traditions, ongoing for thousands of years and still very much alive in New Mexico. The generations have imparted to the land itself a sense of the sacred, with the continuity of spiritual practice. Meditation, prayer and song are performed in time with the cycles of the year and the hours of the day. Here, people of all faiths are inspired to solitary contemplation as well as participation in community gatherings.

David Pascale

Kagyu Shenpen Kunchab (KSK) Stupa is a center of Tibetan Buddhism in Santa Fe.

New Mexico also has a tradition of pilgrimage. Each Holy Week, pilgrims may be seen walking the roads and highways to the Santuario de Chimayó,

---

*Sikh leader Yogi Bhajan .

long considered a site of miraculous healing. Catholic roots go five centuries deep into the land.

Worship often extends outside the church or *kiva*, into the plaza, the streets and the homes of the community. Prayer is more often than not accompanied with feasting, music and dance, considered vital elements of the ceremony. Gatherings, such as the Matachine dances performed in the Hispanic villages as well as on the Indian pueblos, are often open to the public. Any slightly-more-than-casual observer will be struck not only with the depth of religious observance, involving the entire community, but with the shared traditions; for example, the mixtures of Catholic and Indian ceremony that occur here as well as throughout Mexico and Latin America. Such sharing is a natural evolution for cultures that have lived side by side for centuries.

But sacred sites in New Mexico encompass more than shrines and altars built by human hands. Many believe the ancient ruins that stand on this land occupy power or holy spots. Some of these ruins contain places that in the past were used for prayer and ritual. Many consider certain natural wonders to be their own personal power spots, reminders of the power of the Creator, where they are able to feel a connection with the Divine.

Whatever your own spiritual path, you need not travel very far in northern New Mexico to receive inspiration and revitalization. Because of the variety of spiritual paths that have found a home here, northern New Mexico also offers a spiritual "educational opportunity" not generally available elsewhere. Whatever sacred sites you choose to visit, you will be joined in spirit to the many others who have stood there before you.

SACRED SITES

Santa Fe

KAGYU SHENPEN KUNCHAB TIBETAN DHARMA CENTER
505-471-1152.
751 Airport Rd.
Santa Fe, NM 87505.
KSK Noble Truth
    Bookstore.
505-471-5336.
Open noon–6 p.m. M–F,
    10–6 p.m. weekends.

Buddhist sitting meditations are held in this authentic Tibetan stupa, or temple. This center of Tibetan Buddhism was founded by the Venerable Kalu Rinposhe in 1975. Its spire is visible as you drive down Airport Rd. Visiting lamas and other teachers hold prayer and meditation services; they also give talks on Buddhist practices. The bookstore is an excellent place to find books by the Dalai Lama and other Buddhist thinkers. Resident Lama Karma Dorje leads sitting meditations on Wed. at 6 p.m., and Sun. at 8:30 a.m., 10:45 a.m. and 6 p.m., as well as at the new and full moon. If you would like to visit the stupa at other times, please pick up the key at the bookstore.

Prayer flags give their blessings to the wind at the Lama Foundation.

MOUNTAIN CLOUD ZEN CENTER

Old Pecos Trail, one mile south of the intersection with Zia Rd., across from the electric substation.
505-988-4396 or 505-988-5293 for Vipassana meditation information.
Formal sitting meditations are held: Mon. evening, 6:30–8:30 p.m.; Wed. evening 6–8 p.m.; Mon. and Wed. morning, 6:40–8 a.m. and Sun. morning, 8–10 a.m. Please call.

This Zen center was founded in 1981 by students of Philip Kapleau's Rochester Zen Center.

UPAYA

1404 Cerro Gordo Rd. Santa Fe, NM 87501. 505-986-8518.

A Buddhist retreat and learning center, Upaya offers weekday zazen meditation at 5:30–6:30 a.m. in the Cerro Gordo Temple; on Thurs. morning, from 7:30–8:30 a.m.; and various other practices on Sat. from 2–3:30 p.m. and Sun. at 1 p.m., 3–4 p.m. and 6–7 p.m. On Wednesdays, dharma talks by Joan Halifax, a lay priest in the Vietnamese tradition and leader of this center, are sometimes included. Please call if you would like a tour of the zendo at other times. Please write for a schedule of Upaya courses on subjects such as healing, dreams, and death and dying.

Española, Abiquiu and Chimayó

DAR AL-ISLAM
Off County Road 155 at
Sign #42A, above Ghost
Ranch.

Visitors are welcome to visit this world famous adobe mosque, built by Egyptian architect Hassan Fathy, called the world's foremost adobe architect. Check for information on the annual North American Muslim Pow-wow held in June. This Abiquiu site of a national organization educates Muslims and non-Muslims about Islam.

EL SANTUARIO DE CHIMAYÓ
505-351-4889.
PO Box 235.
Chimayó, NM 87522.
Masses and visiting hours:
Sunday Mass, noon;
Weekday Mass
Oct.–April, 7 a.m.;
May–Sept., 11 a.m. Open
daily in summer 9 a.m.–5
p.m.; winter 9 a.m.–4
p.m.
About 25 miles NE of Santa
Fe on U.S. 84/285 to
Española. Turn R. on
Hwy. 76. Follow signs to
Chimayó.

The site of this chapel is believed to be a former healing place of Pueblo Indians. The church was built between 1813–1816 by Bernardo Abeyta and other residents of El Potrero. They later finished the adobe chapel honoring Nuestro Señor de Esquipulas. Legend claims that Don Bernardo Abeyta, while deathly ill, received a vision that beckoned him to a spot on the ground beneath the cottonwoods, where he was immediately cured. He built the chapel on that spot. For generations, Hispanic villagers in these remote mountains have attested to the miraculous healing powers of the "holy dirt" from a certain spot in the chapel floor. Testimonials and crutches lining the walls of the anteroom to the chapel give weight to the Santuario's reputation as the "Lourdes of America." Pilgrims bring prayers for healing to the Santuario all year long, but on Good Friday, it is the destination of a pilgrimage when thousands walk to Chimayó from all over the state to receive blessings. The twin-towered Santuario, a classic example of Spanish-Pueblo church architecture, is also a favorite subject of artists.

MONASTERY OF CHRIST IN THE DESERT
No telephone. Send
inquiries to:

The primitive rock and adobe church of this remote Benedictine monastery along the Chama River was designed by a Japanese monk. Visits give guests the opportunity to share in the life of this

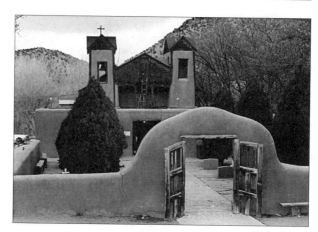

*Santuario de Chimayó is a
major pilgrimage site.*

Attention Guestmaster
Abiquiu, NM 87510
Sunday Mass, open to all, is
celebrated at 9:15 a.m.
The gift shop and book-
store are open daily.
75 miles north of Santa Fe
on U.S. 84/285. Go W. on
U.S. 84 past Ghost Ranch
Visitor's Center. Turn left
on Forest Service Rd. 151.
This 13 mile dirt winding
road ends at the
monastery grounds. If
wet, the road may be
impassable.

Benedictine order with the key elements of love,
prayer, reading, study and manual labor. To reserve
guest rooms for silent retreats, write the Guestmaster. Write for reservations well in advance, especially for Christmas and other Catholic holidays.
Correspondence takes several weeks.

SIKH DHARMA OF NEW MEXICO

505-753-6341 or
888-346-2420.
Rt. 2, Box 132-D.
Española, NM 87532.
Take U.S. 84/285 N. from
Santa Fe 26 miles. Before
Española, take a right on
N.M. 106 at stoplight.
Take right on first street,
Sombrillo. Go up and
over the hill. Look for the
gold dome of the gurd-
wara, or temple, on the
left. Parking lot on west
side of street.

Hacienda de Guru Ram Das, named for the
builder of the Sikh's Golden Temple in India,
is the location of this spiritual center, which is open
to visitors. The annual Peace Prayer Day, which
begins a week-long celebration, is held on the Saturday prior to summer solstice. Daily yoga classes,
sometimes taught by the ashram's spiritual leader,
Yogi Bhajan, welcome visitors. A full moon healing
celebration is held monthly.

Taos

LAMA FOUNDATION
505-586-1269 weekdays,
10 a.m.–noon MST.
Box 240.
San Cristobal, NM 87564.
Please write or call for
calendar of summer
events.

Nearly three decades old, the Lama Foundation has endured beyond the "be here now" revelations of the 1960s to become an ecumenical spiritual center where teachers of many paths— Buddhist, Catholic, Jewish, Sufi, Hindu—gather each summer to offer workshops to people from all walks of life. Since the Hondo Fire swept through the ponderosa pines on Lama Mountain early in the drought-stricken summer of 1996, Lama has strengthened its offerings of workshops on permaculture, creativity, relationships, sustainable agriculture and architecture, as well. The mountain, long reputed to be a link on the Kiowa Peace Path, where all could pass freely and safely, is recovering well from the fire, with meadows of wildflowers and stands of aspen shaping a new ecology.

NEEM KAROLI BABA ASHRAM
505- 758-3025.
Drawer W, Taos, NM 87571
or
416 Geronimo Lane, Taos,
NM 87571.
Hours: 7 a.m.–10 p.m. daily.
Chanting Tues., 7 p.m.

Inspired by the teachings of the Indian guru Neem Karoli Baba and his American disciple, Ram Dass (Richard Alpert), this ashram offers a quiet meditation room with an impressive statue of Hanuman, the monkey-faced Hindu god of service. The annual cycle of celebrations culminates with Maharaj-ji's Bhandara on the weekend in September closest to the full moon. Chanting begins Saturday at 4 a.m.; that afternoon, around 4 p.m., an enormous Indian feast is served to hundreds of participants.

Las Vegas

MONTEFIORE CEMETERY
About 65 miles N. of Santa Fe. Take I-25 to the second Las Vegas exit. Go left to the large cemetery. The Jewish section is in the back on the right.

In the old Jewish cemetery in Las Vegas, NM, it is possible to get a feeling for the life of Jewish pioneers of the west. Here one can walk among headstones dated 1848–Bavaria to 1926–Las Vegas. One can also begin to get a sense of the strength of the Jewish merchant-rancher community so instrumental in the development of the life of culture and commerce in northern New Mexico during the late 19th and early 20th century. Each September, the New Mexico Jewish Historical Society holds an annual cemetery cleaning celebration. People of all ages tend the graves and a picnic lunch is served.

For those who would like to learn more about Jewish pioneer life, contact the NMJHS at 505-989-6656 or PO Box 23056, Santa Fe, NM about their archive

ne State Record Center and Archives (at the intersection of Cerrillos
imino Carlos Rey in Santa Fe).

ANCIENT RUINS

Inspecting a cave dwelling at Bandelier National Monument.

Murrae Haynes

BANDELIER NATIONAL MONUMENT
505-672-3861 or 505-672-0343.
46 miles W. of Santa Fe. Take U.S. 285 N. to Pojoaque, W. on N.M. 502 and S. on N.M. 4.
Open: Year-round; daily except Christmas and New Year's. Summer 8–6; winter 9–5:30. Ruins trails open dawn to dusk.
Call for current conditions of backcountry trails.
Fee: $5 per car, campsites $8 per night.
No pets on trails.
Gift shop, snack bar.

This lush little Shangri-La tucked in a deep canyon on the Pajarito (pa-ha-REE-toe) Plateau was home to the ancestors of some Pueblo tribes between A.D. 1100 and 1550. The residents irrigated their corn, beans and squash with water from Frijoles (free-HOLE-ace) Creek and made their homes from the plentiful volcanic rock. Today you can climb among their cliff dwellings and view the village ruins and ceremonial *kivas*. The loop trail of the main Frijoles Canyon ruins takes about an hour. More agile visitors can climb ladders, as the residents once did, to enter Bandelier's restored dwellings—including a spectacular ceremonial cave with *kiva*. During summer, visitors can take ranger-led tours of the ruins after dark on special "night walks."

Bandelier's 50 square miles are federally designated wilderness, with 70 miles of maintained trails that go up onto mesas, down into volcanic canyons and through high-altitude pine forests. Those in good physical condition can take day hikes to more remote ruins. The visitor center and Frijoles Canyon ruins tend to be crowded, but solitude can be yours if you're willing to walk a bit. (See also "Hiking and Climbing" in Chapter Seven, *Recreation*.)

**PECOS NATIONAL
   HISTORICAL PARK**
505-757-6414.
28 miles S.E. of Santa Fe, off
   I-25.
Open: Daily 8–5 except
   Christmas; Memorial
   Day–Labor Day 8–6.
Fee (1997): $2 per adult or
   $4 per car; under 17 free.
Bookstore.

In 1540, before the Spaniards arrived, Pecos was a thriving Pueblo Indian village with apartment-like houses four or five stories high. In their green river valley, the Pecos people traded with other Pueblo villages and the Plains Indians to the east. Coronado's men visited in 1541, and by the early 1620s the Franciscans had arrived to build a mission and to convert the Indians to the Spanish way of life. The Franciscans also enlisted the Indians to help build a magnificent church, 150 feet from altar to entrance, with walls 22 feet thick in places. The foundations can still be seen, but the church and the Franciscans' efforts were destroyed in the Pueblo Revolt of 1680 (see Chapter One, *History*). A smaller church built atop the ruins in 1717 also lies in ruins.

What happened to the thriving village? Historians believe Pecos was decimated by European diseases and Comanche raids in the 17th century. The last residents left in 1838 to live with relatives at Jemez Pueblo, across the Rio Grande Valley. Today, a 1.25-mile trail on gentle terrain takes you around the mission and pueblo ruins, including a ceremonial *kiva* in which you can hear recorded Indian chants. In summer, weekend tours are offered at the Forked Lightning Ranch, the late actress Greer Garson's home.

PUYE CLIFF DWELLINGS
505-753-7326.
Please call for directions.
Closed during winter.
Fee: $5 per adult; children
   and seniors $4.

About 40 miles northwest of Santa Fe, near Española, the Puye Cliffs are the original habitation spot of the people of Santa Clara Pueblo. The tribe welcomes visitors, who can walk to the top of a mesa where a village once stood, and take in the magnificent views. Here you will find cliff dwellings dating from the 1200s. This ancient pueblo, built between 1450–1475, was once the center of numerous villages on the Pajarito Plateau. Many of the designs found on pottery here focus on a plumed serpent figure who guarded the springs which provided life-giving water. This site is a good example of the evolution of indigenous peoples architecture: first digging dwellings into the soft "tuff" (pressed volcanic ash) of the cliffs, then adding adobe fronts to cave dwellings and later building a pueblo on top of the mesa.

TSANKAWI
505- 672-3861.
About 30 miles W. of Santa
   Fe on Hwy. 84/285 to
   N.M. 502 then on N.M. 4
   on the way to Bandelier,
   immediately south of

An easy walk to unexcavated ruins, a visit to Tsankawi (pronounced tank-ah-WEE) offers a spectacular panoramic view across the Rio Grande valley to Santa Fe and the Sangre de Cristo Mountains. The site's name comes from the term that means "village between two canyons at the clump

White Rock. Look for the sign and gate on the W. side of N.M. 4, just S. of the Y-shaped stoplight intersection of E. Jemez Rd.
No entrance fee.

of sharp, round cactus." The enclave protects an important Rio Grande Anasazi (pre-historic Puebloan people) ruin. Take the 1.5 mile loop trail that begins at the parking area along N.M. 4. Descendants of the Chaco Canyon Anasazi lived here about 1300–1580 AD. Faint petroglyphs and hand and toe holds of the original Tewa-speaking dwellers are visible along the climb, aided in places by ladders. Please do not disturb the shards of black-on-cream pottery lying on the ground.

Outside the Area

CHACO CULTURE NATIONAL HISTORICAL PARK
505-786-7014.
60 miles S. of Bloomfield in N.W. New Mexico, via N.M. 44 and unpaved N.M. 57. All roads into the park are unpaved the last 20–26 miles.
Open: Daily except Christmas, dawn to dusk; visitor center open 8–6 Memorial Day to Labor Day, 8–5 off-season.
Fee: $30 for vehicles holding 1–6 passengers, $45 for vehicles holding 7–25 passengers, $100 for vehicles holding 26 or more passengers; campsites $8 per night; no hookups, no showers.

Known as the "Stonehenge of the West," Chaco is believed by many to be one of the great "power spots" on the globe. It is one of twelve World Heritage Sites in the United States on the United Nations list under the World Heritage Convention. Chaco Canyon is to North America what the Pyramids are to Egypt and what Machu Picchu is to South America. Humans have inhabited the area for 6,000 years or more. About A.D. 900, the Anasazi culture began to flower, and Chaco Canyon was its crowning achievement: six large pueblos and as many as 75 smaller towns, all built in a relatively short time. The largest, Pueblo Bonito, was a community of four-story masonry apartment buildings with solar orientation, hundreds of rooms and dozens of *kivas*. The Chacoan people farmed with an elaborate irrigation and terracing system and created stunning pottery and turquoise jewelry. They built an astonishing 400 miles of arrow-straight roads connecting the canyon with outlying settlements, and they traded with the people of Mezoamerica. Then, sometime around A.D. 1200, this thriving culture suddenly faded away. Archaeologists haven't yet come up with a totally satisfying theory as to why; prolonged drought seems the most likely answer.

The ruins were known to Spaniards and Indians in the region at least as far back as 1840, and the first archaeological excavations were started in 1896. Today, you can spend a couple of days or more exploring the ruins along the Chaco Wash. There are even more ruins atop the mesas. Rangers are available for guided walks, and the visitor center offers a good introduction with films and displays. The ruins are in surprisingly good condition, so it's easy to imagine Chaco Canyon alive again with the laughter of children and the sounds of men and women at work in the courtyards and fields.

Note: In 1996 the northern access route to Chaco was changed, so that County Road 7900 is the preferred route for accessing Chaco from N.M. 44. C.R. 7900 is approximately 3 miles east of the Nageezi trading post. The southern route into Chaco, from N.M. 57, has not changed. Consult a good map before setting out, and call the park to check on road conditions, since roads can become impassable during rain or snow. Also, there's no lodging, gasoline or food at the park; the nearest town is 60 miles away. Staples are available on weekdays at trading posts on N.M. 44. To make the most of your visit, plan to camp at Chaco. But get there early; campsites tend to fill quickly on weekends and most days during the summer.

NATURAL WONDERS

RIO GRANDE GORGE BRIDGE

At the intersection of N.M. 68 and N.M. 150 (Taos Ski Valley Road), go left for seven miles on U.S. 64. This bridge, completed in 1965, the nation's second highest arch, soars 2000 feet from rim to rim and rests 650 feet above the Rio Grande.

The gorge is known as America's first preserved "Wild and Scenic River. "The view from here of the river swirling through basalt boulders below, plus the panorama of the winding Rio Grande Gorge, the Taos Plateau and the Sangre de Cristo Mountains, is a New Mexico must-see. From this height, river rafters are only tiny specs on the winding river. The Gorge itself contains the Taos Box, a favorite whitewater run. Hang on to your hat! This is a mighty windy spot.

TENT ROCKS
About 40 miles SW of Santa Fe, just northwest of Cochiti Pueblo. Take I-25 S. to Cochiti exit.

This is the site of a fascinating miniature canyon. Soft, compressed volcanic rock has been eroded into tent-shaped formations, many with a harder material balanced on top. Smaller bases supporting a larger boulder are called hoodoos. A favorite hiking and camping spot among locals, believed by many to be a very spiritual place.

VALLE GRANDE
About 40 miles NW of Santa Fe. Continue on N.M. 4 past Bandelier about 15 miles.

Known as "the Caldera," this astonishing green basin, once considered the world's largest volcano, is now believed to be part of a large caldera, a basin formed during volcanic activity in the Pleistocene period. Located on a 137-year-old land grant named Baca Location No. 1, it is also called "Valle Grande" or "Baca Location," and is home to a herd of 45,000 elk. It is said that lava from this volcano has been found as far away as Kansas. This is a popular cross-country skiing area in winter.

CHAPTER SIX
Pleasing the Palate
RESTAURANTS & FOOD PURVEYORS

Interior of a New Mexico restaurant, ca. 1900.

The Santa Fe–Taos area offers more than 300 restaurants serving everything from New Mexican, American and Continental to French, Chinese, Thai and East Indian cuisine. In addition, scores of food purveyors offer unique drinks, pastries, baked goods, candies and delicacies. The combination is enough to satisfy the most far-ranging or ravenous appetite.

Our review team looked for a variety of places and price ranges — everything from gourmet dining spots to corner barbecue stands. We also looked for quality, and we avoided all but the most intriguing fast-food and chain restaurants. Fortunately, we were free to write honest reviews, since we were in no way beholden to these establishments. The results, we are confident, will steer you to some of the best dining the area has to offer. We have attempted to provide a range of dining opportunities, from the casual pizza or sandwich to the world-famous New Southwestern cuisine that has its home here. The combination of fresh local ingredients with some of the most creative and well-traveled chefs in the world make the dining scene in Taos and Santa Fe one of the most exciting on the planet.

One thing you'll find on your gastronomic travels in Santa Fe and Taos is a plethora of New Mexican restaurants. Remember: New Mexican cooking — particularly *northern* New Mexican cooking — is not Mexican or Tex-Mex; it's a peculiar mix of Spanish, Mexican, Pueblo Indian and local cuisine that includes many familiar foods like burritos, enchiladas and tacos, as well as less familiar foods like flautas, sopaipillas and chicharrones. It is derived from the native foods of corn, chile, beans and squash.

The most important single ingredient in northern New Mexican cuisine is *chile*, which should not be confused with *chili*, the familiar heavy tomato sauce. New Mexican chile sauces have little or no tomato. They're flavorful, spicy, sometimes hot sauces made with a mix of chile peppers and various spices, and they're served with almost every meal. In fact, some of the more traditional restaurants refuse to serve food without them. Chile can be red or green, hot or mild, and there's no telling from the color which is which. So when your waiter says, "Red or green?" don't be afraid to ask which is hotter. If you say "Christmas," you'll get a little of both.

Before you leap into this sea of restaurants, we suggest you first peruse one of two restaurant charts in the *Appendix*. One chart lists restaurants according to cuisine, the other according to price. Remember: all the restaurants listed in this book are given a price code based on the average cost of a single meal including appetizer, entree, dessert, tax and tip but *not* including alcoholic beverages.

Reviews are organized first by area, then alphabetically. Any restaurant that is outside the city limits of Santa Fe is listed under "Restaurants Near Santa Fe." Similarly, any establishment that is outside the town limits of Taos is listed under "Restaurants Near Taos."

Dining Price Codes

Inexpensive	Up to $12
Moderate	$12 to $25
Expensive	$25 to $50
Very Expensive	$50 or more

Credit Cards

AE — American Express
CB — Carte Blanche
D — Discover Card
DC — Diner's Club

MC — MasterCard
V — Visa

B = Breakfast, L = Lunch, D = Dinner, SB = Sunday Brunch, SSB = Saturday and Sunday Brunch.

RESTAURANTS IN SANTA FE

*Head to Bagelmania for your
lox and bagel fix.*

Murrae Haynes

BAGELMANIA
505-982-8900.
420 Catron St., Santa Fe,
    NM 87501 and
BAGELMANIA II
505-424-1200.
4056 Cerrillos Rd., Santa Fe,
    NM 87501.
Closed: Christmas.
Price: Inexpensive.
Cuisine: New York deli.
Serving: B, L, D.
Credit Cards: D, MC, V.
Handicap Access: Full.
Smoking: Patio only.
Reservations: None.

It was said that when Bagelmania opened six years ago, people no longer had to have their bagels flown in. True, Bagelmania outfits itself as the real New York item, and the owners are a long-time Queens bagel-making family. But service can often be spotty, and the food is inconsistent. Yet if you crave a smoked fish platter, a corned beef sandwich, or a bowl of matzoh ball soup, this is your best bet. You may prefer the omelettes, cheeses, garden salads and fresh-baked breads. Of course, there's a wide assortment of bagels with lox, cream cheese and the works.

CARLOS'S GOSP'L CAFE
505-983-1841.
125 Lincoln Ave., Santa Fe,
    NM 87501.
In First Interstate Plaza.
Closed: Sun., major
    holidays.

For a flavor of the Gospel South and hearty soups and sandwiches, drop in at noontime. Carlos brings the spirit of his native Tennessee, including soul music and service with a smile. His little enclave is a great place to refuel with spicy soups like the hangover stew or tortilla soup, delicious

Price: Inexpensive.
Cuisine: American.
Serving: L.
Credit Cards: None.
Handicap Access: Full.
Nonsmoking Section: No.
Special Features: Patio
dining; Gospel music.

salads or any one of a dozen huge sandwiches. Our favorite is the Miles Standish, fresh turkey breast with cranberries, cream cheese and mayonnaise. If you have room, don't miss Celeste's Green Chile Stew. And for dessert, Say Amen to the fresh, home-made pies, said by many local experts to be the best in town. Go for the lemon meringue!

CELEBRATIONS
505-989-8904.
613 Canyon Road, Santa Fe,
NM 87501
Closed: Hours vary, call.
Price: Inexpensive–
Moderate.
Cuisine: American,
Mexican.
Serving: B, L, D summer,
check winter hours.
Credit Cards: MC, V.
Handicap Access: Full.
Smoking: Front patio only.
Reservations: No.
Special features: Fireplaces;
Patios.

New Orleans in Santa Fe is the idea, and some-times it works in this funky old house on his-toric, arty Canyon Road. Service can be slow during the busy brunch. Summer breakfasts are best on the patio where the eggs Benedict with hollandaise are a bargain. Consider the Cobb salad or the New Orleans style oyster po'boy sandwich for lunch. Dinner can be extravagantly Creole with crawfish etouffee, earthily Southwestern with chicken fajitas or full of Nuevo Latino surprises with chiles rel-lenos and black beans. The menu changes periodi-cally, but the Louisiana homemade potato chips remain the speciality of this house. Celebrations has exceptional desserts. The white chocolate ice cream is worth the trouble of finding a parking place.

**CLOUD CLIFF BAKERY &
CAFE**
505-983-6254.
1805 2nd St., Santa Fe, NM
87505.
Closed: Christmas, New
Year's.
Price: Inexpensive.
Cuisine: New Mexican,
International.
Serving: B, L, SSB.
Credit Cards: D, MC, V.
Handicap Access: Full.
Nonsmoking Throughout.
Reservations: None.
Special Features: Patio din-
ing; Takeout; Art gallery.

A wonderful place to taste the local's Santa Fe, amidst the art in this light, bright warehouse. It's worth the trip for some of the best whole-grain, organic baked goods in town. Whether it's bread, pastries, scones or cookies, you simply can't go wrong. Breakfasts and brunches run the gamut, from eggs and pancakes to grilled nutloaf and Mex-ican potatoes. The spinach burrito served with black beans and rice is simply sublime. Best of all, breakfasts come with a basket of assorted breads, biscuits and muffins. Could be the best latte in town!

**COWGIRL HALL OF
FAME BAR-B-Q**
505-982-2565.

This restaurant is great for a full meal or a mid-afternoon snack. Beginnings include a variety of nachos, quesadillas, soups and chili. Their forte is the mesquite-smoked barbecue, but you'll find

319 S. Guadalupe St., Santa
Fe, NM 87501.
Closed: Thanksgiving,
Christmas.
Price: Moderate.
Cuisine: Barbecue, Western.
Credit Cards: AE, D, DC,
MC, V.
Handicap Access: Partial.
Non-Smoking Section: Yes.
Reservations: Recom-
mended for dinner.
Special Features: Patio;
Fireplaces; Takeout.

burgers and fish platters; smoked chicken-black
bean blue corn enchiladas; and good old T-bone
steaks. Sprinkled throughout are delicious vegetarian dishes, such as the vegetarian chili and butter-
nut casserole. An unusual item on any menu is
collard greens, and this dish is worth ordering at
the Cowgirl. If you're particular about spicy food,
ask. Finish up with chocolate espresso mud pie or
peach cobbler. The place is usually jumping, fre-
quented by a casual crowd, and on weekend nights
live music plays in the full bar. The spurs, saddles
and photographs of Prairie Rose, Faye Blessing and
other rodeo cowgirls on their rearing horses make a
fine memorabilia collection of Western lore.

The rooftop Coyote Cafe Cantina is a splendid place to enjoy an afternoon lunch.

Corrie Photography

COYOTE CAFE
505-983-1615.
132 W. Water St., Santa Fe,
NM 87501.
Open: Daily.
Price: Very Expensive.
Cuisine: Nouveau South-
western.
Serving: L (summer, week-
ends), D.
Credit Cards: AE, CB, D,
DC, MC, V.
Handicap Access: Full.

Santa Fe's Coyote Cafe is restaurateuring on a
grand scale. Mark Miller, its famous anthropologist turned owner-chef, publishes successful cookbooks, pops up on national talk shows and travels
constantly, spreading his popular nouvelle Southwestern cuisine. He is a great supporter of local
growers. Native ingredients are blended with
sophisticated flavors into dishes showing great creative imagination. Each dish is an inspired blend of
flavorful ingredients, usually with a spicy edge.
Start with an Abiquiu Tomato Salad or a Huitla-

Smoking in bar only.
Reservations: Strongly
recommended.
Special Features: Patio
dining.

coche Tamale; then feast on filet of salmon, grilled pork medallions or roasted quail. Finish up with one of a dazzling array of fruit-and-chocolate desserts. Dinners are prix-fixe three-course affairs in the $50 range.

The happy rooftop patio serves lower-priced fare during lunch and dinner, and service is also available at the Coyote's main bar. While you're there, be sure to try a Chimayó cocktail, a wonderful concoction made with apple juice, tequila and Cointreau.

DAVE'S NOT HERE
505-983-7060.
1115 Hickox St., Santa Fe,
NM 87501.
Closed: Sun.
Price: Inexpensive.
Cuisine: Burgers, New
Mexican.
Serving: L, D.
Credit Cards: None.
Handicap Access: Partial.
Nonsmoking Section:
None.
Reservations: None.
Special Features: Takeout.

This tiny, west-side favorite dining room was named for a former restaurateur named Dave who — you guessed it — is no longer here. Regardless of who or where Dave is, this funky hole in the wall serves great, filling meals at eminently affordable prices. The burger is the best, and ordered with the homemade fries will satisfy any burger craving. Vegetarians, do not despair! The Mexican food is also consistently flavorful, as substantial and delicious as the burgers. You can wash the meal down with a decent selection of beers — and save room for the homemade pies and cakes. The moist chocolate layer cake can heal a broken heart. You'll sit elbow-to-elbow with your neighbors, and there's no way to escape the cigarette smoke, but you may find these are mere trifles once the food arrives.

**EL FAROL RESTAURANT
AND LOUNGE**
505-983-9912.
808 Canyon Road, Santa Fe,
NM 87501.
Closed: Major holidays.
Price: Moderate.
Cuisine: Spanish tapas.
Serving: D.
Credit Cards: CB, D, DC,
MC, V.
Handicap Access: None.
Nonsmoking section: Yes.
Reservations: Recom-
mended.
Special Features: Patio
dining; Live music.

You're sitting at the bar when a stranger walks through the door, blinks at the dark low-ceiling room and plops down to tell you someone in Paris or London suggested he or she go to El Farol. It's that kind of place — the latest in Santa Fe's legendary succession of eccentric havens. Owner David Salazar says parts of the thick-walled adobe building date back to the 1830s; poets, prophets and punks have walked through its rustic doors. The Spanish-inspired tapas of zesty, contrasting flavors are for the adventurous, so leave the kids at home, and savor the differences between Boquerones Don Pedro, marinated fried whitefish with a mojo picon salsa; sautéed wild mushrooms with spaghetti squash, curried chicken salad with grapes and vinegary Moroccan eggplant. Four tapas make a good meal, with a carafe of Spanish wine, but consult your friendly if unconventional waitstaff as you go along. Dinner only, with live music every night turning the place into a full nightclub with Flamenco, Latin and blues, and a small dance floor. A bit smoky up front, but you can steal away to the nonsmoking back rooms or, in the summer, to the back patio. Parking can be a problem; look for the city lot across the street.

FRENCH PASTRY SHOP
505-983-6697.
100 E. San Francisco St. at
  La Fonda Hotel, Santa Fe,
  NM 87501.
Closed: Christmas.
Price: Moderate.
Cuisine: French.
Serving: B, L.
Credit Cards: None, cash
  only.
Handicap Access: Partial,
  enter from La Fonda
  Hotel.
Smoking: No.

Chocolate eclairs, croissants, palmiers, Napoleons, café au lait, espresso, fresh fruit tarts, chocolate mousse, dessert crepes, and fresh strawberries with Crème Chantilly. . . . Are you drooling yet? This little shop of gastronomic delights has provided the Santa Fe community with authentic French cuisine since 1974. A sign inside says "All pastries are made with pure butter and are made fresh daily." The menu, influenced by owner George Zadeyan's Marseille upbringing, includes ratatouille, torte Milanoise, and French onion soup as well as quiche Lorraine. If you want breakfast pastries, arrive early. They tend to sell out quickly. Bon appétit!

**GALISTEO CORNER
  CAFE**
505-984-1316.
201 Galisteo St., Santa Fe,
  NM 87501.
Open daily.
Price: Inexpensive.
Cuisine: Deli style.
Serving: B, L.
Credit Cards: AE, D, MC, V.
Handicap Access: Partial.
Nonsmoking throughout.
Special Features: Patio;
  Artwork.

Formerly known as the Galisteo News, a semi-funky newsstand and coffee bar, this deli is a local fixture. Though it changed ownership in 1997, it still draws the same business, tourist and local crowds who like to hang out talking, reading, people-watching and writing in any of several cozy nooks, or sipping cappuccinos on the street corner. The once-endless variety of magazines and newspapers has been greatly reduced but the expanded food selection somewhat offsets the loss. Order at the counter from an assortment of delicious coffee drinks, hot and iced teas, Italian sodas, soups, salads, sandwiches, foccacia pizzas and pastries. Popular breakfast choices include everything from French toast and breakfast burritos to strawberry blintzes and a bagel breakfast sandwich. For a different lunch taste, try the ratatouille crepe, a palate-pleasing mix of tomato, eggplant and zucchini smothered in a smooth béchamel sauce. The fruit smoothies are delicious.

**GARDUÑO'S OF SANTA
  FE**
505-983-9797.

Garduño's is a place you take anyone — your mother, your brother, your honey or a whole birthday party — and everyone should be happy.

130 Lincoln Ave., Santa Fe, NM 87501.
Open daily. Closed major holidays.
Price: Moderate.
Cuisine: Mexican.
Serving: L, D.
Credit Cards: AE, D, MC, V.
Handicap Access: Partial.
Reservations: Recommended for more than two.
Special features: Kids' menu; "Heart Healthy" meals (low fat tortillas and cheeses); Weekly specials; Catering; Speciality margarita menu.

With four restaurants in Albuquerque and one in Santa Fe, Garduño's popularity stems from its extensive, inventive menu and South of the Border feeling. Familiar offerings — fajitas, enchiladas, tacos and burritos — are served alongside more exotic fare such as "pescado rojo huachinango" (red snapper topped with crab, shrimp, and cheese) and "cilantro steak in rojas." All are served by a friendly, well-trained staff.

Though usually very busy, the spacious, colorfully-decorated restaurant is comfortable and relaxed. Thirteen margarita specialties tempt from the first page of the menu. Mariachi musicians (without the brass) pleasantly serenade as you dine. You might conclude with one of Garduño's original desserts — the fried ice cream or Taco Chocolate de Fresa are perfect examples of Garduño's ingenuity.

GERONIMO
505-982-1500.
724 Canyon Rd., Santa Fe, NM 87501.
Closed: Mon. lunch.
Price: Expensive.
Cuisine: Contemporary Southwest.
Serving: L, D, SB.
Credit Cards: AE, MC, V.
Handicap Access: Partial.
Smoking in bar only.
Reservations: Recommended.
Special Features: Fireplace; Courtyard.

Geronimo has been drawing raves since it opened in 1991. Housed in one of the city's finest old adobes, it's airy and elegant, and the food is delicious. The menu consists of American staples updated with Southwestern and other ethnic ingredients. Favorite appetizers include lobster-salad spring rolls with mango-ginger dipping sauce. Beautiful presentations arrive at the table in such creations as mesquite-grilled beef tenderloin with portobello mushroom orzo. Another favorite is house-made cannelloni of grilled free-range chicken.

To enjoy Geronimo without breaking your budget, try lunch or brunch; offerings are no less imaginative and about half the price. Desserts vary daily, and the entire menu changes at least once a season. For cool evenings, try the intimate bar with *kiva* fireplace and brass-topped tables. Quite pricy.

THE GREEN ONION
505-983-5198.
1851 St. Michael's Dr., Santa Fe, NM 87501.
Closed Christmas, Thanksgiving, Easter.
Price: Inexpensive.

Bostonians, Notre Dame fans and anybody else who worships Ireland in America have a place to go in Santa Fe, and they probably already have reservations for St. Patrick's Day and big football games. Other times, you might get a table at this friendly neighborhood sports tavern, bedecked

Serving L, D.
Credit Cards: AE, D, DC, MC, V.
Handicap Access: Full.
Smoking throughout.
Reservations: No.
Special features: TV sets throughout.

with shamrocks and pennants, and imbued with the good spirits of cops, volunteer firemen, baseball teams and journalists. No, it's not for intimate conversation. A dozen television sets, including one large screen, attest to that. Kids will love the special — a build-it-yourself hamburger with lots of add-ons. The carne guisada, an appetizer of cubed pork with fiery pico de gallo salsa makes a hearty meal by itself. Lighter fare includes the black bean and jalapeno soup with a flour tortilla and several substantial salads. The waitstaff puts on no airs about the wide selection of beers, including Guinness Stout on draft. Smoking is OK and there is a full bar with stools, video machines and even a pool table. Check out the music on weekend evenings.

GUADALUPE CAFE
505-982-9762.
422 Old Santa Fe Trail, Santa Fe, NM 87501.
Closed: Sun. eves, Mon.
Price: Moderate.
Cuisine: Northern New Mexican.
Serving: B, L, D, SB.
Credit Cards: D, MC, V.
Handicap Access: Partial.
Nonsmoking throughout.
Reservations: 6 or more.
Special Features: Takeout; Fireplace; Patio dining.

This friendly little cafe is a good place to start if you're new to northern New Mexican cuisine. Though relocated from the original Guadalupe St. digs, it's as reliable and enjoyable an experience as ever. It features authentic regional specialties plus a variety of American cafe standards like burgers, sandwiches and salads. Portions are generous — big enough to split, in many cases — and service is fast and exceptionally friendly. The main attraction is the northern New Mexican food. The chalupa plate — two corn tortilla baskets filled with chicken, beans, guacamole and sour cream — is a substantial treat. The Guadalupe's plain sopaipillas are also among the best in town: light, fragrant and tasty with a dab of honey. Try to save room for one of Laura's famous desserts. The Adobe Pie — coffee and vanilla ice cream packed into a rich chocolate cookie crust — is the runaway favorite. Sandwiches and gringo food available for those who prefer. An altogether wonderful experience.

HUNAN CHINESE RESTAURANT
505-471-6688.
2440 Cerrillos Rd., Santa Fe, NM 87501.
In College Plaza South shopping center.
Closed: Thanksgiving.
Price: Moderate.
Cuisine: Hunan and Peking Chinese.
Serving: L, D.

You needn't look any farther than Hunan for a tasty respite from chile, salsa and frijoles. This is the top pick among the various Chinese restaurants in town. Master Chef Alex Lee has more than 20 years' experience concocting authentic Hunan and Peking delights from recipes dating back to the Chin Dynasty. For starters, the Pu Pu Tray offers egg rolls, chicken, terrific spareribs, crisp and light fried wontons, tender barbecued beef and deep-fried shrimp. The menu can match any niche in

Credit Cards: D, MC, V.
Handicap Access: Partial.
Nonsmoking Section: Yes.
Reservations: Recom-
mended for large
parties.

taste, from Mongolian lamb to beef with a hot, orange-flavored sauce to sea-smoked duck. The mixed seafood delight is everyday ambrosia. Love the ginger chicken, and the lunch buffet is a real bargain. Plenty of vegetarian dishes to choose from as well. Go for the eggplant with garlic sauce.

Sandra Lee Tatum

Il Piatto brings a touch of Italy to the Southwest.

IL PIATTO
505-984-1091.
95 West Marcy St., Santa Fe,
NM 87501.
Open daily.
Price: Expensive.
Cuisine: Innovative Italian.
Serving: L, D.
Credit Cards: AE, MC, V.
Handicap Access: Full.
Nonsmoking throughout.
Reservations: Recom-
mended.
Special Features: Patio
dining; Takeout.

Named by *Esquire* magazine one of the top ten new restaurants, Il Piatto is a Santa Fe favorite. At lunch, try the green-lipped mussels baked in garlic aioli or the creamy wild mushroom risotto. The antipasto makes an excellent start to a meal. Lunch specials are a real bargain. Small, unpretentious, with superb food, Il Piatto features fresh soups and crisp salads, a variety of tasty antipasti and pastas, traditional Italian specials such as chicken cacciatore, and grilled selections. The chef shops for seasonal local produce at the farmers' market. Homemade desserts include such delectables as tiramisu (sponge cake soaked in coffee liqueur) and baked chocolate mousse with blackberries. There's also a moderately priced wine list and a selection of dessert wines and port. On warm days, you can dine on the little streetside patio, and in the evening Il Piatto creates a romantic mood with music and candlelight. A favorite of seasoned Santa Fe restaurant-goers.

IL PRIMO PIZZA & PASTA

505-988-2007.
234 N. Guadalupe St., Santa Fe, NM 87501.
Open: daily, closed major holidays.
Price: Inexpensive–Moderate.
Cuisine: Chicago-style pizza.
Serving: D.
Credit Cards: None.
Reservations: Large parties.
Handicap Access: None.
Nonsmoking Section: Yes.
Special Features: Delivery within limited area; Fireplace.

As you walk in the door, the smell of garlic, tomato sauce and baking bread fills the air. First impressions are everything. So follow your nose on this one. The interior of Il Primo is less than inviting but the excellent food, friendly staff and fireplace make up for the "early dorm" decor.

Il Primo's forte is the pizza. You have an extensive list of fresh toppings to put on five different types of pizza crusts, from extra thin to deep dish. Be warned: the thicker the crust, the longer the wait. It may take 40 minutes or longer to bake your pizza. You might prefer to order ahead. Order a salad to experience the creamy, homemade Italian garlic dressing. The wine is not great but the beers are cold.

INDIA PALACE

505-986-5859.
227 Don Gaspar, Santa Fe, NM 87501.
Open: Daily.
Price: Moderate.
Cuisine: East Indian.
Serving: L, D.
Credit Cards: AE, D, MC, V.
Handicap Access: Partial.
Smoking: Patio only.
Reservations: Recommended for dinner.
Special Features: Patio dining; Takeout; Lunch buffet; Indian art.

The India Palace offers the exquisite and complex tastes of the Indian subcontinent in an intimate and luxurious setting. A fountain plays and statues of gods smile serenely as diners sample delicacies from all regions of India.

Appetizers include the crisp fried patties called samosas and a many Indian breads, from leavened nan to paratha stuffed with spinach, all baked fresh daily. Tandoori specialties include several kinds of chicken and lamb. Curries abound, and can be prepared mild enough for any taste. There are also the vegetarian dishes for which India is famous, from creamed lentil dahl to bhindi masala, or spiced okra. The buffet lunch provides a cross-section of the menu — beautifully presented and a great bargain. At supper, the special dinners also select a variety of dishes, but be forewarned, the multiple portions are filling, and you'll want to leave room for saffron pudding or mango ice cream.

JULIAN'S RESTAURANT

505-988-2355.
221 Shelby Street, Santa Fe, NM 87501.
Closed: Thanksgiving.
Price: Very expensive.
Cuisine: Regional Italian.
Serving: D.
Credit Cards: AE, CB, D, MC, V.

Don't be fooled by the anonymous locale on a narrow, one-block, one-way street near the Santa Fe River. You could fall in love here. At the least, you'll get a memorable meal. Julian's is arguably the best eatery in town, blending classic Italian with modernity that you'll only find in America. Cozy rooms make for intimate settings, and the back room is adequate for a large party. For

Smoking: Patio only.
Reservations: Accepted.
Special Features: Fireplaces; Patio dining; Private dining.

romantic evenings, ask for the private patio or, in winter, a table by a beehive fireplace. Pay attention! This is serious dining and the waiters know their stuff, so consult and listen. You'll remember Julian's primi and piatti forte selections for years to come: spigola in guazzetto alla romana, a sea bass served in a virtual soup of tomatoes, garlic, mustard, raisins and pine nuts; homemade pasta dishes like delicate pumpkin-stuffed ravioli and fat cannelloni stuffed with veal, chicken, spinach and Parmesan cheese, and fresh tasty salads, all served with crusty bread. The wine list is massive. Share a dessert like crostata di mele, an apple tart, or fichi e zabaglione gratinate, fresh figs with custard and raspberry sauce.

Casa Sena has a great patio where you can sip a margarita.

Corrie Photography

LA CASA SENA
505-988-9232.
20 Sena Plaza/125 East Palace Ave. Santa Fe, NM 87501.
Open: Daily.
Price: Expensive–Very Expensive.
Cuisine: Fancy Southwestern.
Serving: L, D.
Credit Cards: AE, CB, DC, MC, V.
Handicap Access: Partial.
Nonsmoking Section: Yes.
Reservations: Recommended for both lunch and dinner.

For a romantic evening extraordinaire, you must have dinner on the patio at La Casa Sena. The surrounding courtyard is filled with huge cottonwood trees, a sensuous fountain, and heaters for chilly weather. Casa Sena's dishes are highly evolved Southwestern taste sensations, perfected by chef Kelly Rogers. Try the steamed Manilla clams with pico de gallo and lime for a first course. An intermezzo of watermelon-jalapeno granita will clear your palette for an entree of seared molasses duck breast with cranberry-hoisin sauce. Take advantage of the Chef's Tasting Menu, three courses each accompanied by a half-glass of carefully chosen wine and dessert with a porto not easily forgotten. The clay-pot trout is a favorite as well.

Special Features: Fireplace; Private dining; Cantina; Patio.

On the down side, the restaurant interior has a heavy, dark feel, and the food can be somewhat overpriced. If you'd rather be entertained for the evening, try the adjoining Cantina, where the waiters and waitresses sing from current Broadway hits. To get a good table, try to arrive a half-hour before showtime. At any rate, the patio at Casa Sena is an excellent spot for a margarita.

**LA PLAZUELA RESTAU-
RANT AT LA FONDA
HOTEL**
505-982-5511.
100 E. San Francisco, Santa
  Fe, NM 87501.
Open: Daily.
Price: Moderate.
Cuisine: Spanish, Mexican,
  New Mexican and Conti-
  nental.
Serving: B, L, D.
Credit Cards: AE, D, DC,
  MC, V.
Handicap Access: Full.
Nonsmoking throughout.
Reservations: Recom-
  mended for dinner.
Special Features: Covered
  patio; Hand painted
  windows; Hand carved
  wood furniture; Stone
  floor.

The enclosed central courtyard of the landmark La Fonda Hotel is a colorful dining space with brightly painted panes of glass from floor to ceiling, gaily covered with designs of birds and flowers by local artist Ernesto Martinez. Service is gracious and prompt.

The menu is known for its traditional Northern New Mexico specialties, including a combination plate that includes tamales, enchiladas and chile rellenos. Recent changes from chef Maurice Zeck have brought more Mexican and old-world Spanish dishes to the dinner menu. Some traditional dishes have a twist, such as the appetizers of tamales made with wild mushrooms and leeks or the even more unusual quesadilla with rattlesnake, which adds a meaty taste to the traditional ingredient of goat cheese. More conventional but still lavish is the Spanish paella, but allow some extra time for its preparation. Desserts are all made on the premises, and again feature traditional dishes with a twist — there are sweet enchiladas filed with raspberries and cream and flan de Naranja, with the caramel custard served in a halved orange.

**MARIA'S NEW MEXI-
CAN KITCHEN**
505-983-7929.
555 W. Cordova Rd., Santa
  Fe, NM 87501.
Closed: Thanksgiving and
  Christmas.
Price: Moderate.
Cuisine: New Mexican.
Serving: L, D.
Credit Cards: AE, CB, D,
  DC, MC, V.
Handicap Access: Partial.
Non-Smoking Section: Yes.

Nearly 50 years in the same location, Maria's continues to draw crowds. In an old adobe house with fireplaces tucked into corners and mariachi bands strolling between tables, this restaurant is known for its traditional Mexican dishes and atmosphere. Plates of enchiladas, tacos, and chile rellenos come steaming from the kitchen. Their tortillas are made right in the dining room and just may be the most tender in town. The food is all based on traditional recipes and cooking styles: fajitas served on metal platters in a forest of green pep-

Festive mariachis serenade diners at Maria's.

Murrae Haynes

Reservations: Recom-
    mended.
Special Features: Patio;
    Fireplaces; Mariachis.

pers and onions, tender and spicy carne adovada, huge servings of tacos and tamales, some of the freshest guacamole salad in town, and a mountainous egg flan that will send your taste buds home screaming for more. At Maria's it's hard to decide between red or green; both are tasty and neither sports too much spice. Owner Al Lucero's specialty has written a definitive book about margaritas and his bartenders can concoct over 70 different kinds. Dinners can be eaten in the bar, and patio dining in the warmer months makes Maria's just an enjoyable place to dine.

MU DU NOODLES
505-983-1411.
1494 Cerrillos Rd., Santa Fe,
    NM 87501.
Closed: Sun., major
    holidays.
Price: Inexpensive–
    Moderate.
Cuisine: Pacific Rim.
Serving: L, D.
Credit Cards: AE, D, MC, V.
Handicap Access: Yes.
Nonsmoking throughout.
Reservations: For parties of
    5 or more.
Special Features: Patio in
    season.

Don't pass by this restaurant now located in the site of the beloved, late Natural Cafe. It's far more than just noodles. Chef Mu is serving exquisite, healthful flavorful noodle combinations you can't resist. All in a bright, spare, low-key atmosphere where a single diner can be happy. Just the right combination for a Santa Fe success.

**OLD HOUSE RESTAU-
RANT & TAVERN**
505-988-4455 or
  505-995-4530.
309 W. San Francisco St.,
  Santa Fe, NM 87501 in
  the Eldorado Hotel.
Closed: Mon.
Price: Expensive.
Cuisine: New Southwestern.
Serving: D.
Credit Cards: AE, CB, D,
  DC, MC, V.
Handicap Access: Full.
Nonsmoking except in bar.
Reservations: Strongly rec-
  ommended.
Special Features: Private
  dining; Live entertain-
  ment in adjoining tavern.

During the many years we've been visiting the Old House, it has always been excellent. Now, if possible, it's even better. A gracious and knowledgeable waitstaff glides unobtrusively about the room while the elegant Southwestern decor and soft strains of jazz or classical music conspire to create a romantic, intimate atmosphere. As always, the fresh-baked breads are luscious, delivered with delectable maple coriander and prickly pear cactus butters. And the meals are still visual works of art— from the first tasty tortilla chips arranged like the petals of a flower to the meticulously crafted creme brulée and six-layer chocolate cake.

Rarely have we experienced a more delightful and original medley of flavors — partly the result, Chef Martín Rios says, of more emphasis on natural juices and light, creamless sauces that go with his new Asian, Mexican and Caribbean-influenced creations. Appetizers? Try barbecued roasted venison enchilada or Cajun cornmeal dusted oysters. Main dishes? Offerings change weekly, but there's always a variety of fresh fish, ultra-tender steaks and poultry, pasta and vegetarian plates. The extensive list of fine California and French wines is carefully selected to complement the food, and the dessert plate will take your breath away.

THE PALACE
505-982-9893.
142 W. Palace Ave., Santa
  Fe, NM 87501.
Closed: Christmas.
Price: Expensive.
Cuisine: Mediterranean
  with Italian accent.
Serving: L, D.
Credit Cards: AE, D, DC,
  MC.
Handicap. Access. Partial.
Nonsmoking Section: Yes.
Reservations: Recom-
  mended.
Special Features: Piano Bar;
  Patio in season.

There are occasions when no place but The Palace will do. When your aunt comes to visit, when impeccable, unobtrusive service is a requirement and when you want to show your old-fashioned side, head for the landmark with red-flocked wallpaper and red leather banquettes that was formerly the gambling saloon of Dona Tules. Order Caesar salad prepared with some pomp tableside and the profiteroles from the rolling dessert cart. Crab cakes, duckling in sun-dried tomato chutney, pasta and fresh fish can delight any appetite.

CAFE PASQUAL'S
505-983-9340.
121 Don Gaspar, Santa Fe,
  NM 87501.

Delightfully prepared food; friendly, attentive service; a bustling atmosphere spiced with colorful murals, chile ristras, and bright Mexican ban-

Pasqual's, a cheery haven of excellent food downtown.

Sandra Lee Tatum

Closed: Thanksgiving, Christmas.
Price: Moderate–Expensive.
Cuisine: New Mexican, New Southwestern.
Serving: B, L, D.
Credit Cards: AE, MC, V.
Handicap Access: Partial.
Nonsmoking throughout.
Reservations: Strongly recommended for dinner.
Special Features: Community table; T-shirts; Cookbooks.

ners—these are a few of the reasons folks are so willing to brave long lines in front of this longtime Santa Fe eatery near the plaza. To avoid the crowd, arrive early or sit at the congenial community table.

For breakfast, you'll ooh and aah over the Genovese omelette with sun-dried tomatoes and pine nuts. For lunch, savor the tangy taste of a zesty shrimp cocktail, a heavenly grilled salmon burrito, or a healthful Yucatan free-range chicken breast salad. You can slice hefty dinner costs with half orders and still come away satisfied. And you'll drool over the rich assortment of desserts and pastries. (Hint: Try the toasted piñon ice cream with caramel sauce.) Your visit to Santa Fe is incomplete without a stop at Pasqual's. And FYI, Kathy Kagel is almost as well-known for her organizing to feed the hungry in New Mexico as she is as a chef!

PAUL'S RESTAURANT OF SANTA FE
505-982-8738.
72 West Marcy Street, Santa Fe.
Open: Lunch Monday–Saturday; Dinner daily.
Price: Moderate.
Cuisine: American and International.
Serving: L, D.
Credit Cards: AE, D, MC, V.

Paul's Restaurant is a cozy bistro, tucked away off a busy street just north of Santa Fe's plaza. Inside, all is cheerful serenity, as diners eat beneath a collection of wooden fish dangling from the ceiling, while from a high shelf a friendly lion watches a painted rabbit munch on a slice of watermelon.

The cooking style derives from California cuisine, with an emphasis on fresh ingredients and a mix of international dishes. Local produce is used as much as possible. Appetizers such as crawfish ravioli in a tomato, saffron, and jalapeno sauce or

Handicap Access: Full.
Smoking: Non-Smoking throughout.
Reservations: Recommended for dinner.
Special Features: Folk art collection.

red chile duck wonton in a soy ginger sauce add some surprising elements to traditional dumplings. Sauces play an important part in the main dishes as well. The filet mignon is enhanced with a delicate ginger sesame sauce, while chef Paul Hunsicker's award-winning pecan-crusted salmon with sorrel sauce remains the most popular.

A special feature of the menu is the selection of Twilight Specials, for diners arriving between 5:30–7 p.m. This is an excellent value, with an appetizer, main dish, and dessert for the fixed price of twenty dollars. This is the perfect place to go before a performance or concert.

PEPPER'S RESTAURANT & CANTINA
505-984-2272.
2239 Old Pecos Trail, Santa Fe, NM 87505.
Closed: Christmas, Thanksgiving.
Price: Moderate.
Cuisine: Northern New Mexican, American.
Serving: B, L, D.
Credit Cards: AE, D, DC, MC, V.
Handicap Access: Full.
Smoking in bar only.
Reservations: None.
Special Features: Banquet room; Full Service Cantina; Takeout; Patio.

Peppers Restaurant & Cantina lies at the crossroads of two historic Old West trails: the Santa Fe Trail and the Old Pecos Trail, an ancient Indian footpath. It's a great place for kids and fun for all ages. From the Mexican paper *banderas* to the festively painted wooden chairs, this is probably the most colorful restaurant in Santa Fe — the mood is relaxed and festive with bright colors, carved parrots, south-of-the-border tunes and a friendly, efficient staff.

The menu includes excellent Silver Coin margaritas and an assortment of New Mexican and American dishes. Nachos grandes (an appetizer) is almost a meal in itself. Stick with specialties like fresh chile rellenos, flame-broiled half-pound burgers with green chile, or choose from a wide assortment of vegetarian dishes. Kids get lots of attention with a creative coloring menu and tic tac toe page, with dino chicken nuggets, power tostadas and root beer floats with whipped cream. Also recommended are the sizzling fajitas and the Lemon Herb Chicken. If you have room, order a dessert of Bourbon Street pecan pie (made with a hint of Jim Beam) or an incredibly rich chocolate cake that can satisfy two voracious chocoholics!

PINK ADOBE
505-983-7712.
406 Old Santa Fe Trail, Santa Fe, NM 87501.
Closed: Major holidays.
Price: Expensive.
Cuisine: Continental, New Mexican with Cajun twist.

The Pink Adobe is well over 50 years old; now it's the grande dame of Santa Fe restaurants. Though its rough-hewn wooden chairs and tables are a bit closely spaced, its dark, cozy nooks create a romantic atmosphere for all occasions, and service is quick and friendly. In wintertime, fires crackle in the *kiva* fireplaces, and the place is magic. However,

The Pink Adobe features classic Santa Fe dining.

Karen Klitgaard

Serving: L (Mon.–Fri.), D.
Credit Cards: AE, CB, D, DC, MC, V.
Handicap Access: Partial.
Smoking in bar only.
Reservations: Recommended.
Special Features: Fireplaces; Patio dining.

many think the Pink Adobe is riding on its reputation these days. Nonetheless, regardless of the quality of the food, it remains one of the choice "see and be seen" spots in town.

The menu at the Pink has changed little over the decades. There are four appetizers and about 15 entrees including steak, chicken, shrimp, lamb, pork and various New Mexican dishes. The emphasis is on hearty fare rather than delicacy and the steaks are superior. This is one place where it's best to stick with standards, rather than go for the daily specials. For lunch, try the perfectly seasoned green chile stew, the succulent roast tenderloin of beef or the pecan-crusted fresh salmon. Be sure to leave room for hot apple pie with New Orleans-tinged hard sauce.

PRANZO ITALIAN GRILL
505-984-2645.
540 Montezuma, Santa Fe, NM 87501.
Open: Daily.
Price: Moderate to Expensive.
Cuisine: Northern Italian.
Serving: L, D.
Credit Cards: AE, CB, DC, MC, V.
Handicap Access: Partial.
Nonsmoking Section: Yes.
Reservations: Recommended for both Lunch and Dinner.

Pranzo Italian Grill in the historic Sanbusco railroad district is a local's restaurant with a balanced menu and carefully made food at very accessible prices. The bar is a wonderful place to meet a friend over a pizza or frito misto and an aperitif. In Italian, "pranzo" means the main meal of the day, and the grill draws a hundred percent of its inspiration from Italy. The key here is consistency; Pranzo's can boast that their sage cream ravioli will satisfy a patron from one year to the next.

Begin by pouring a saucer of olive oil provided at your table, salt and pepper the surface, then dip in hunks of light sourdough bread. Choose from one of the most extensive wine lists in town. Don't for-

Special Features: Terrace;
  Full service bar.

get to include some grilled item in your evening's enjoyment, like an appetizer of portobello mushroom as big as a hat with diced pancetta and goat cheese, or an entree like osso buco served with saffron risotto. Highly recommended for a casual yet special night out.

SAKURA
505-983-5353.
321 W. San Francisco St.,
  Santa Fe, NM 87501.
Closed: Mon., Christmas,
  New Year's.
Price: Moderate.
Cuisine: Japanese.
Serving: L, D.
Credit Cards: AE, MC, V.
Handicap Access: Partial.
Nonsmoking Section: Yes.
Reservations: Recom-
  mended.
Special Features: Tatami
  rooms; Patio dining.

The menu in this modest but fine Japanese restaurant is largely limited to Japanese staples, but they are served up very well and usually satisfy. At lunch, Sakura is a favorite spot for local business people, who feast on a series of "jumbo platters" including salmon, beef or chicken teriyaki or shrimp and vegetable tempura at good prices. The salmon is excellent. There's an ample assortment of sushi both at lunch and dinner (when the prices rise sharply). Conventional table service as well as private tatami rooms and a comfortable sushi bar are available. In warm weather, tree-shaded patio tables overlook a green lawn. It does what it does very well.

**SAN FRANCISCO
  STREET BAR & GRILL**
505-982-2044.
114 W. San Francisco St.,
  lower level of Plaza Mer-
  cado.
Closed: Christmas, New
  Year's, Thanksgiving.
Price: Inexpensive–
  Moderate.
Cuisine: American.
Serving: L, D.
Credit Cards: MC, V.
Handicap Access: Partial.
Nonsmoking Section: Yes.
Reservations: None.
Special Features: Indoor
  patio; Takeout.

This is a casual restaurant perfectly suitable for the whole family. The wine list is short, the service professional, the atmosphere casual. A huge, juicy hamburger with fries or coleslaw tops the menu. The meat is rich and tasty, but if you like it rare, make sure you insist. The sausage dishes are also juicy and tender, and the fish dishes well worth ordering. At dinnertime (when the crowds generally thin out), seafood and pasta dishes complement the lunch-hour staples. For dessert, we suggest a piece of Dutch apple pie. The place is also open till 11 p.m. seven nights a week, making it one of the best late-night noshes in the downtown area. A reliable favorite of locals and visitors alike.

SANTACAFE
505-984-1788.
231 Washington Ave., Santa
  Fe, NM 87501.
Closed: Christmas, New
  Year's.

SantaCafe serves complex fare in quietly elegant surroundings, and the stunning arrangements are almost too beautiful to eat. Of course, this glorious show comes at a price, but you can have the SantaCafe experience at lunch for considerably less.

The elegant SantaCafe: dining at its best.

Frederick G.S. Clow

Price: Very Expensive.
Cuisine: New American
   with Southwest and
   Asian flair.
Serving: L (Mon.–Sat.), D.
Credit Cards: AE, D, MC, V.
Handicap Access: Full.
Nonsmoking throughout.
Reservations: Strongly
   recommended.
Special Features: Patio
   dining; Fireplace.

A knockout lunch might start with coriander crusted ahi tuna with cilantro vinaigrette, or a generous Caesar salad kissed with a mild garlic dressing. Depending on the season, other delectable items might include filet mignon or flash-fried calamari. Dinners must be among the world's most imaginative and beautiful: fresh, warm breads; East-West duck breast with black currant-*hoisin* sauce; grilled quail with sage sauce; and lobster-filled red chile ravioli with fennel. As might be expected, the wine list is extensive, and the desserts are exquisite. Save your allowance for this one — but go!

**SANTA FE BAKING CO.
   & CAFE**
505-988-4292.
504 W. Cordova Rd., Santa
   Fe, NM 87501.
Closed: Christmas.
Price: Inexpensive.
Cuisine: American,
   Southwest.
Serving: B, L.
Credit Cards: MC, V.
Handicap Access: Full.
Nonsmoking throughout.
Reservations: None.

This popular breakfast spot is light, bright, friendly, delicious and cheap. Located in the Coronado Shopping Center, it's off the beaten tourist path and offers plenty of parking. Here you'll find standard American breakfasts and a variety of tasty coffees and juices, along with a case of freshly baked croissants, scones and pastries. Lunches include an assortment of delicious sandwiches both hot and cold, as well as a variety of salads and soups.

THE SHED
505-982-9030.
113 1/2 E. Palace, Santa Fe,
  NM 87501.
Closed: Sun., Thanksgiv-
  ing, Christmas and New
  Years.
Price: Moderate.
Cuisine: Mexican,
  American.
Serving: L; D Wed.–Sat.
Credit Cards: AE, MC, V.
Handicap Access: Partial.
Non-Smoking Section: Yes.
Reservations: Recom-
  mended.
Special Features: Patio,
  enclosed during winter;
  Fireplaces.

Located in an adobe dating back to 1692, this long-established restaurant is a definite landmark. The winding rooms and narrow hallways add to the historic atmosphere. Wear casual, go stylish. This restaurant, off the street and tucked back into an enclosed patio, appeals to serious Mexican food lovers of all stature. Aside from the many blue corn entrees, what sets this restaurant apart is the chile. Straight from the farm, the chiles are ground on the premises and for more subtle palates, the freshness is indeed noticeable. Selections of fish and beef dishes help widen the choice for those a little timid about Mexican food. Wine is served by the glass or the bottle; beer is on draft. In summer the patio makes perfect dining, and a table by one of the corner fireplaces can take the winter chill off and add to the romance of a good meal. What a lovely place to dine! You'll know you can't be anywhere on earth but Santa Fe.

SHOHKO-CAFE
505-983-7288.
321 Johnson St., Santa Fe,
  NM 87501.
Closed: Sun. (winter),
  major holidays.
Price: Moderate–Expensive.
Cuisine: Japanese.
Serving: L (Mon.–Fri.), D
  (Mon.–Sat.).
Credit Cards: AE, D, MC, V.
Handicap Access: Partial.
Nonsmoking Section: Yes.
Reservations: Recom-
  mended eves.
Special Features: Sushi bar.

Dining at Shohko is a delight for many reasons, including the seamless blend of Japanese and Southwestern decor; the warm, damp towel you're given when you're seated; the clear taste of warm sake; the steaming miso soup; and the efficient service. The menu offers an array of sushi selections, Japanese entrees and a few Chinese specials. Salads are wonderfully light and tasty. Excellent entrees include the ginger beef, shrimp-and-scallop tempura or one of the festive sushi combinations, rounded out by chocolate mousse or vanilla pound cake for dessert. Shohko also offers a specially prepared macrobiotic dinner, Japanese curry, weekend Dim Sum luncheons and a wide assortment of appetizers, desserts, wine and beer. If you like Japanese food, you'll love this place. Can be crowded at lunch, so best plan to arrive either early or late.

STEAKSMITH AT EL GANCHO
505-988-3333.
Old Las Vegas Highway (1
  mile east of intersection
  with Old Pecos Trail).

Eating at Steaksmith, the restaurant at El Gancho Country Club, is like dining in an old fashioned mountain lodge beneath huge *vigas* and beside an open fireplace — and it's a reliable place for a festive meal.   As the name implies, the restaurant

Open: Daily. Closed major holidays.
Price: Expensive.
Cuisine: American and regional steakhouse.
Serving: D. Cocktails from 4 p.m.
Credit Cards: AE, D, DC, MC, V.
Handicap Access: Full.
Smoking: Smoking section in bar, lounge, and smoking section in restaurant.
Reservations: Strongly recommended.
Special Features: Fireplaces; Wood *vigas*.

TIA SOPHIA'S
505-983-9880.
210 W. San Francisco, Santa Fe, NM 87501.
Closed: Sun., major holidays.
Price: Inexpensive to Moderate.
Cuisine: New Mexican.
Serving: B, L.
Credit Cards: MC, V.
Handicap Access: Yes.
Nonsmoking Section: Yes.

TINY'S RESTAURANT & LOUNGE
505-983-9817.
1015 Pen Rd. (Southeast corner of St. Francis and Cerrillos Rd.)
Closed: Sunday.
Price: Inexpensive.
Cuisine: New Mexican.
Serving: L, D.
Credit Cards: AE, D, DC, MC, V.
Handicap Access: Full.
Nonsmoking Section: Yes.

serves an excellent selection of beef — aged on the premises. But it is equally well known for its seafood, considered by many diners to be the best in the area. Steaksmith also boasts a tapas menu so extensive that several of these make a meal in themselves, and will make vegetarians happy. The approach here is international, with shrimp wrapped in prosciutto, chile cheese balls, and tuna yakitori as well as the more prosaic Buffalo wings on the list. Don't neglect dessert either — the homemade ice creams and frozen ice cream pie are particularly luscious. Steaksmith also offers a varied children's menu, which includes a tortilla pizza designed to please even a finicky young eater. Service is efficient and attentive, and the meal is a leisurely one, from start to pie.

Located just across the street from the famous Andrew Smith Gallery, Tia Sophia's is an unassuming little restaurant that serves good New Mexican meals in a family atmosphere. Daily breakfast and lunch specials are popular and affordable. The breakfast burritos and huevos rancheros are worth ordering for those with a hearty a.m. appetite. For lunch, order one of the homemade stuffed sopaipillas. If you have restless little ones, there is a book case at the front of the restaurant filled with wonderful regional and classic children's stories. Please note that Tia Sophia's closes promptly at 2 p.m. Eat, then go shopping.

Tiny's bar and its attendant restaurant has been a hang-out for local politicians and business people for fifty years; it is an old-fashioned neighborhood restaurant, designed for socializing as well as eating. Although the family-owned restaurant has expanded, and added a more spacious dining area, Tiny's retains its feeling of being an authentic Santa Fe institution, decorated with original paintings. The food at Tiny's is basic New Mexican cooking at its best — from guacamole and chips appetizer to flautas, enchiladas, carne adovado, and fajitas, topped as always with a choice of chile. Also, there

Reservations: Recom-
mended for dinner.
Special features: Patio
dining; Live music on
weekends.

are light menu items that still have a traditional feeling, such as fajita or taco salad, served with a low calorie dressing.

This is a relaxed place for family dining; service is prompt and there is a limited but appealing menu for children under twelve. Tiny's also has dancing on the weekends, where the Jose Gonzales Trio has been performing for over twenty years.

TOMASITA'S
505-938-5721.
500 S. Guadalupe St., Santa
Fe, NM 87501.
Closed: Sun., major
holidays.
Price: Moderate.
Cuisine: Northern New
Mexican.
Serving: L, D.
Credit Cards: MC, V.
Handicap Access: Partial.
Nonsmoking Section: Yes.
Reservations: None.
Special Features: Takeout;
Patio.

Located near the Sanbusco Market in Santa Fe, Tomasita's specializes in traditional New Mexican cuisine. Tomasita's also comes with a warning. Santa Feans frequent this establishment to get their chile — Hot. If you do not have a tolerance for spicy food, ask for the chile on the side. Although Tomasita's receives awards each year for its food, some feel it is overrated. Tomasita's has ample parking and reasonable service once you are seated. However, you should expect a significant wait during peak eating hours, especially during the summer, when service and quality may both be off. Daily specials are worth trying and vegetarian entrees are available. If you are a railroad enthusiast, note that Tomasita's is in the old Guadalupe Station area.

TORTILLA FLATS
505-471-8685.
3139 Cerrillos Road at Calle
de Ceilo, Santa Fe, NM
87501.
Open: Daily. Closed: Major
Holidays.
Price: Moderate.
Cuisine: New Mexican.
Serving: B, L, D.
Credit Cards: D, MC, V.
Handicap Access: Yes.
Nonsmoking Section: Yes.
Reservations: Unnecessary.
Special Features: Children's
menu; Full bar.

Santa Fe locals head to unpretentious Tortilla Flats for traditional hearty New Mexican meals served in a friendly, family atmosphere. This establishment will satisfy any appetite without emptying your wallet. House specialties such as carne adovada, huevos rancheros, blue corn flautas, and chorizo burritos will knock your socks off. Each entree is served your choice of pinto or black beans, posole or queso calavacitas con maiz (squash, melted cheese, and corn) and a flour tortilla or sopaipilla. If you have a wait (you will have a wait on the weekends), saddle up in the cantina and order a round of margaritas and a guacamole appetizer (seasonal). Also, remember to save room for the sopaipilla helada (with ice cream) as your postres or dessert. You will not be disappointed.

UPPER CRUST PIZZA
505-982-0000.
329 Old Santa Fe Trail,
   Santa Fe, NM 87501.
Closed: Thanksgiving.
Price: Inexpensive.
Cuisine: Pizza; Sandwiches.
Serving: L, D.
Credit Cards: MC, V.
Handicap Access: Partial.
Nonsmoking Section: Yes.
Special Features: Free
   Delivery; Patio and front
   porch dining; Live Music;
   Parking in rear.

Delicious! This clean, casual eatery is nestled in an old adobe structure with *vigas*, skylights, and Saltillo tile floors. Weekday lunches, you'll encounter a line out the door and down the street. Locals know that between 11 and 1 p.m., they can get a huge piece of pizza, salad, and a drink for a few bucks, made to order with fresh ingredients, and the service is prompt. Even high maintenance people are accommodated with a smile. Pizzas such as the Grecian gourmet specialty pizza are made with either traditional Italian or whole wheat crusts. Sandwiches and house specials come with a side salad and chips. Try the house special whole wheat calzone filled with a blend of three cheeses, spinach, pesto and tomatoes. Be sure to order a side of mouth-watering garlic bread made with fresh diced garlic and herbs sautéed with butter. If you like live music, the Upper Crust features folk and country sets at least three nights a week.

Cozy and sophisticated, Whistling Moon Cafe serves excellent Mediterranean food.

Murrae Haynes

WHISTLING MOON CAFE
505-983-3093.
402 N. Guadalupe, Santa Fe,
   NM 87501.
Closed: Major holidays.
Price: Moderate.
Cuisine: Mediterranean.
Serving: L, D.
Credit Cards: MC, V.
Handicap Access. Yes.
Nonsmoking throughout.
Reservations: For parties of 6
   or more.
Special Features: Patio in
   season.

If you enjoy a platter of crispy calamari lightly seasoned with cumin, fresh pasta primavera or roast lamb gyros, served in a cozy and cosmopolitan atmosphere while you recline in a deeply-cushioned booth, come here, where the food is light and imaginative. Great for a lunch date or appetizers with a glass of wine. One of our reviewer's favorite Santa Fe spots.

ZIA DINER
505-988-7008.
326 South Guadalupe St.,
    Santa Fe, NM 87501.
Open: Daily, Closed major
    holidays.
Price: Moderate.
Cuisine: Modern American
    Cuisine.
Serving: L, D.
Credit Cards: MC, V
Handicap Access: Yes.
Nonsmoking Section: Yes.
Special Features: Patio;
    Counter seating; Full bar;
    Kid's menu; Takeout;
Limited vegetarian selec-
    tion; Parking in rear.

If you've had your fill of New Mexican food and simply want a good, filling meal that won't break the bank, head to Zia Diner for lunch or dinner. Located just east of Sanbusco Market Center, this clean, spacious eatery has something for everyone: fresh salads, great sandwiches, blue plate specials, made-to-order pizza, pot pies, and don't forget dessert. Try the chicken satay or artichoke hearts Parmesan appetizer while deciding your entree. Traditional yet lighter versions of diner favorites like chicken fried steak, green chile-piñon meatloaf and shepherd's pie pepper the menu; fresh steamed vegetables accompany these items. Ask your server about daily specials. Finally, save room for Zia's Aroma coffee and a piece of deep dish strawberry-rhubarb pie, à la mode! Some people who think they know pie believe the Zia's is the best! However, food here can be inconsistent; certain nights portions may be small.

RESTAURANTS NEAR SANTA FE

ANGELINA'S
505-753-8543.
1226 North Railroad Ave.,
    Española, NM 87532.
Closed: Christmas.
Price: Inexpensive.
Cuisine: Northern New
    Mexican.
Serving: B, L, D.
Credit Cards: MC, V.
Handicap Access: Partial.
Nonsmoking Section: Yes.
Reservations: Large groups
    only.
Special Features: Takeout.

The laid-back service in this family restaurant is often spotty, and the food can also vary in quality. But if you're here on a good day, you'll be glad you came. Chips with Angelina's dipping sauce are usually a delight. Good entree bets are chile rellenos, soft-shell tacos, lamb fajitas and carne adovada. An assortment of beers and a few wines are also available. Bring the Tums!

**ANTHONY'S AT THE
    DELTA**
505-753-4511.
228 Paseo de Oñate N.W.,
    Española, NM 87532.
Open: Daily. Closed: Major
    holidays.
Price: Expensive.

Anthony's is an elegant cluster of Garcia family enterprises that started as a humble neighborhood bar in 1949. Today Anthony's is a delta in the middle of the desert. This Spanish Colonial haven includes a spacious, high-ceilinged restaurant, a flower market and a candy shop — all with plushly decorated rooms, handcrafted furniture, brilliant

Cuisine: Steak and Seafood.
Serving: D.
Credit Cards: AE, D, DC,
MC, V.
Handicap Access: Partial.
Nonsmoking Section: Yes.
Reservations: Recom-
mended.
Special Features: Patio; Full
Bar; Fireplace; Private
dining.

flower gardens and landscaped terraces. In the restaurant, this sensual feast continues with leafy fig trees, soft classical music, and an impressive list of domestic and imported wines. The food is good but not great. Most entrees fall short of expectations generated by the price. The salad bar is above average, and Chef Jerry Cross' specials are usually good. For those interested in lighter entrees, vegetarian selections are available. If nothing else, stop in to enjoy an aperitif at the bar and take a moment to experience a lovely interlude on your travels between Santa Fe and Taos.

*Many say the Bobcat Bite
serves the best burger in the
west.*

Karen Klitgaard

**BOBCAT BITE
RESTAURANT**
505-983-5319.
Old Las Vegas Highway
(4.1 miles east of the Old
Pecos trail intersection).
Open Wednesday–Satur-
day.
Price: Inexpensive.
Cuisine: Hamburgers and
more.
Serving: L, D.
Credit Cards: None.
Handicap Access: Full.
Smoking Throughout.
Reservations: No.

The Bobcat Bite is a small adobe that once served as a trading store and gun shop. Forty years ago the original owner ran a working ranch and named the restaurant for the enterprising bobcats who came to investigate, and perched in full sight on the roof.

Today they serve a premier hamburger, and not much else. But there are many who swear this is the best burger available. The menu emphasizes beef, in a cheeseburger, 13 oz. hamburger steak, a 13 oz. rib eye, or the special of an 8 oz. New York strip steak with salad and garlic bread. Portions are generous, and the mostly local crowd is congenial despite the small table and counter space. The chef credits the delicious burgers to his well-seasoned and much used grill. There is also strict attention paid to grilling each individual order, with the menu listing definitions of rare ("dark red — warm center") to well done ("fully cooked — no pink"). Whatever the reason, the Bobcat's beef puts mere fast food to shame, and still attracts the occasional bobcat.

THE BLUE WINDOW
505-662-6305.
800 Trinity Dr., Suite H,
  Meri-Mac Mall, Los
  Alamos, NM 87544.
Closed: Sun.
Price: Moderate.
Cuisine: International.
Serving: L, D.
Credit Cards: D, MC, V.
Handicap Access: Partial.
Nonsmoking Section: Yes.
Reservations: Recom-
  mended.
Special Features: Private
  dining; Takeout.

You don't expect to find a restaurant expertly serving fine food at reasonable prices in a little mall in Los Alamos, but this is it. Gentle Spanish guitar music plays in the background, and soft lighting illuminates the plant-filled room.

Chef-owner Bill Oschwald's menu changes seasonally. Most popular are the homemade pastas. You can also count on daily fish specials such as grilled marlin and grilled sea scallops, both served with delicious sauces. The roast duckling with sparkling fruit compote is likewise superb. The Blue Window shines with Continental fare such as crepes and London broil served with béarnaise and bordelaise sauces. Even the most ambitious Santa Fe diner would not be making a mistake to drive up the hill for a visit.

JOANN'S RANCH-O-
CASADOS
505-753-3837.
411 N. Riverside Dr.,
  Española, NM.
Closed: Sun., major holidays.
Price: Inexpensive.
Cuisine: Northern New
  Mexico.
Serving: B, L, D.
Credit Cards: AE, D, DC.
  MC, V.
Handicap Access. No.
Nonsmoking Section.
Reservations: No.

If you'd like to feel as though you're eating in the kitchen of a wonderful, smiling New Mexico cook, go to JoAnn's. She is the high priestess of chile, and her restaurant, serving the produce of the family ranch, is a favorite among locals for its warmth as well as its good food.

THE LEGAL TENDER
505-466-1223.
Across from train station in
  Lamy.
Special features: Live
  music; Dancing.

For a trip back into western history, dine in the Victorian Legal Tender, across from the old Lamy train station. Even though it's largely a tourist restaurant catering to those who travel on the Santa Fe Southern, the menu offers a reasonably-priced, tasty selection of sandwiches, appetizers, salads and main dishes from pasta to prime rib to suit any appetite.

PO SUWAE GEH RESTAURANT

505-455-7493.
Pojoaque Pueblo Plaza,
about 15 miles N. of
Santa Fe on U.S. 285.
Open: Daily.
Price: Inexpensive.
Cuisine: Pueblo, American,
New Mexican.
Serving: B, L, D.
Credit Cards: MC, V.
Handicap Access: Full.
Nonsmoking Section: Yes.
Reservations: Not necessary.

Conveniently located near the Pojoaque Pueblo Museum and Tourist Information Center, the Po Suwae Geh (meaning "Drink Water Place") serves up generous portions of Pueblo Indian and New Mexican fare in several pastel-shaded eating spaces. Choose a padded booth or dining table, and enjoy some traditional Indian atole, blue corn pancakes or Indian tacos. A great place to get your chile fix. There's also an assortment of sandwiches and a selection of pies, shakes and sundaes. A favorite stopping place on the drive north.

Dining on the enclosed patio at Rancho de Chimayó.

Murrae Haynes

RANCHO DE CHIMAYÓ

505-351-4444.
P.O. Box 11, Chimayó, NM
87522. On Hwy. 520.
Closed: Mon. from
Nov.–May.
Price: Moderate.
Cuisine: Northern New
Mexican.
Serving: L, D.
Credit Cards: AE, DC, MC,
V.
Handicap Access: Full.
Nonsmoking Section: Yes.
Reservations: Recommended.

This beautifully remodeled ranch house has been in the Jaramillo family since the 1880s. A restaurant since 1965, it still has the feel of old northern New Mexico, including wood floors, whitewashed adobe walls, hand-stripped *vigas* and a lushly terraced patio. Moreover, the food is prepared from recipes that have been in the Jaramillo family for generations.

After many visits over the years, we've found the food fairly good, the portions enormous and the service friendly and efficient. It's lovely in wintertime to sip a margarita beside the blazing piñon fire. The menu includes about a dozen traditional northern New Mexican plates plus steak and trout

Special Features: Fireplaces; amandine. The nachos are particularly crisp. A
  Patio dining; Musicians huge, flaky sopaipilla relleno is stuffed to bursting
  in summer. with beef, beans and Spanish rice. And the Chi-
mayó chicken is usually moist and flavorful. For
dessert, we recommend the flan, a rich, creamy
caramel custard with a pleasing tapioca consistency. There's also a small selection of house wines, brandies, liqueurs and coffee drinks. A visit to the Santuario de Chimayó followed by a lunch at the Rancho de Chimayó will give the
visitor a better feeling for New Mexico tradition than just about anything else.

RENATE'S
505-757-2626.
Hwy. 50 , 1/2 m. from
  Glorieta exit 299 off I-25.
Closed: Tues.
Price: Moderate.
Cuisine: German.
Serving: L, D.
Handicap Access. Partial.
Nonsmoking throughout.
Reservations: Recom-
  mended.
Special Features: Live piano
  music.

Dine in this cozy, lace-curtained cottage near
Pecos and you'll swear you're in the Alps, tasting crispy potato pancakes, sauerbraten, homemade hearty mushroom soup and Renate's famous
rum cake and poppy seed cake. The wait for the
eight tables can be long, so try to arrive in the off-
hours.

ROADRUNNER CAFE
505-455-3012.
Pojoaque, N.M., 16 miles N.
  of Santa Fe on N.M. 285.
Closed: Thanksgiving,
  Christmas.
Price: Inexpensive.
Cuisine: New Mexican,
  American.
Serving: B (all day), L, D.
Credit Cards: MC, V.
Handicap Access: Partial.
Nonsmoking Section: No.
Reservations: Large parties.

A truck stop nestled in the scenic Pojoaque Valley, the Roadrunner is just what you'd expect:
inexpensive, friendly, loud and down-home. But it
also offers some remarkably fresh and tasty dishes.
The menu offers hearty, served-anytime breakfasts,
an assortment of burgers, sandwiches, seafoods
and steaks, and a variety of New Mexican specialties served with rice and beans. Don't miss Lorraine's delicious whole-wheat sopaipillas. And for
dessert, try one of her fresh fruit pies.

**TESUQUE VILLAGE
  MARKET**
505-988-8848.
P.O. Box 231, Tesuque, NM
  87574.
Junction of N.M. 591 and
  Bishop's Lodge Rd.
Open: Daily.
Price: Inexpensive.
Cuisine: New Mexican,
  American.

When you walk into the Tesuque Market, you
find an upscale grocery store with shelves
and coolers stocked with beer, cookies, ice cream,
candies, canned goods, and elaborate selections of
mustards and salsas. There's an entire room full of
California and local wines. The deli bar offers an
inviting assortment of gourmet cheeses, meats,
cakes and breads for takeout. Farther on, in the nar-

Hang out, take out or dine in at the homey Tesuque Village Market.

Murrae Haynes

Serving: B, L, D.
Credit Cards: MC, V.
Handicap Access: Partial.
Nonsmoking Section: Yes.
Reservations: None.
Special Features: Patio
dining; Takeout.

row dining hall and "gallery," prompt waitresses scurry over creaking floors, and regional artwork adorns the walls.

The menu includes a varied selection of New Mexican and American offerings, from huevos rancheros and bean burritos to sandwiches and seafoods. Popular lunches include a huge green chile burger with spicy fries and a tasty green chile stew with tender meat chunks. Desserts, made fresh daily, include glurpy cakes, pies, cobblers, eclairs, cheesecakes and more. Indoors or outside on the front porch, you'll find a great place to hang out with a coffee and read. Another famous see-and-be-seen place, but absolutely comfortable.

**WOLF CANYON
BREWING COMPANY**
505-438-7000.
9885 Cerrillos Rd., Santa Fe,
NM 87505.
Open: Daily.
Price: Moderate.
Cuisine: New Mexican,
American.
Serving: L, D.
Credit Cards: AE, DC, MC,
V.
Handicap Access: Full.
Nonsmoking Section: Yes.
Reservations: Recom-
mended for dinner.
Special Features: Brewery;
Patio Dining; Catering.

Three miles south of Villa Linda Mall, between State Road 14 and Interstate 25, this young eatery and microbrewery has found a happy niche on the hilly outskirts of Santa Fe. And no wonder. The food is good, the brew is great, and the atmosphere is inspiring. On a sunny day, you can sit on the spacious patio under the wide blue sky, sipping your favorite ale or sampling the various house brews. Alternatively, you can retire to the bright, friendly bar or any of several other spacious rooms within the soaring, two-story structure.

Notice the ten gleaming, stainless-steel brew vats visible through plate-glass windows, then order a half dozen four-ounce samples of Brewmaster Brad Kraus's best — amongst them, Copper Mesa

Amber, Piñon Nut Brown and the deliciously malty Lobo Negro Porter. Choose from the daily specials or a wide assortment of American and classic New Mexican dishes. Best bets are the less expensive family standbys like fish and chips, hefty burgers and chicken fried steak. The sausage and bratwurst platters are excellent, and the calamari not bad at all. Desserts, ranging from chocolate eclair pie to turtle cheesecake, are unique and delectable.

RESTAURANTS IN TAOS

Patio dining at the elegant Apple Tree.

Murrae Haynes

APPLE TREE
505-758-1900.
1 block north of plaza at
    123 Bent St., Taos, NM
    87571.
Open: Daily.
Price: Expensive.
Cuisine: New Mexican,
    Continental.
Serving: L, D, SB.
Credit Cards: AE, D, DC,
    MC, V.
Handicap Access: Partial.
Nonsmoking throughout.
Reservations: Recom-
    mended.
Special Features: Fireplaces;
    Patio dining.

Located in a charming Victorian house., dinner at the Apple Tree is a convivial, candlelit affair, with impeccable service, superb food and an atmosphere reminiscent of a country inn. The menu offers a creative combination of Mexican, Continental, East Indian and New Mexican-influenced dishes — for example, Thai red curry, Catalonian almond chicken and tangy Yucatan chicken with roasted tomatillo sauce. Appetizers such as savory wild mushroom pate are both hearty and delicate. Don't miss the richly spiced curry vegetable soup or the fresh salad with exquisite honey-mustard dressing. A favorite entree at the Apple Tree is the grilled tiger shrimp quesadilla, guaranteed to become a mouthwatering memory. The wine list offers excellent value and variety. Try to save room for dessert — the nut torte, mixed berry cobbler and chocolate pecan pie are all superb. A favorite restaurant in all New Mexico!

BRAVO
505-758-8100.
1353 Paseo Del Pueblo Sur,
   Taos, NM 87571.
Closed: Sun., Christmas,
   Easter, New Year's Day.
Price: Moderate.
Cuisine: California,
   Mediterranean, Home-
   style European.
Serving: L, D.
Credit Cards: AE, MC, V.
Handicap Access: Full.
Smoking: Patio only.
Reservations: For parties of
   10 or more.
Special features: Deli take-
   out with wine and beer;
   Fresh salad bar; Patio.

You'd never guess from the strip-mall exterior about the splendid culinary experience inside that has made Bravo a favorite among Taos locals. The by-the-pound salad bar is far more than beets and carrots, it includes exquisite and extraordinary combinations and marinations. The sourdough bread is said to be the best. Also, the soups and home-cooked dishes, whether you eat them for lunch, supper or take out, will suit any appetite. Fabulous desserts and imported goodies as well.

CASA DE VALDEZ
505-758-8777.
1401 Paseo del Pueblo Sur,
   Taos, NM 87571.
Closed: Wed.
Price: Moderate.
Cuisine: New Mexican,
   Barbecue.
Serving: L, D.
Credit Cards: AE, D, DC,
   MC, V.
Handicap Access: Partial.
Nonsmoking Section: Yes.
Reservations: Recom-
   mended.
Special Features: Patio
   dining; Private dining.

A popular après-ski spot, Casa de Valdez is a chalet-style building with views of the Sangre de Cristo Mountains. It offers traditional New Mexican cuisine, a mouthwatering selection of char-broiled steak and shrimp dishes, and hearty beef, chicken and spareribs barbecued in a backyard pit. Many local families are regulars here — the food is satisfying and wholesome.

Owner Peter Valdez, who wants to pass on his hard-earned lessons about heart disease, serves only organically raised poultry and the leanest cuts of aged beef. Salad dressings are homemade, and dinner rolls often arrive piping hot from the oven. Service is prompt and friendly, and there's a narrow but fine selection of Napa Valley wines and fine French champagnes.

DOC MARTIN'S
505-758-1977.
125 Paseo del Pueblo Norte,
   Taos, NM 87571, in the
   Taos Inn.
Open: Daily.
Price: Expensive.
Cuisine: Contemporary
   Southwestern.
Serving: B, L, D.
Credit Cards: AE, CB, DC,
   MC, V.

Next to the Taos Inn, ensconced in an adobe building that was home to physician T. P. Martin from the 1890s to the early 1940s, this is one of the town's top people-watching spots. If he were alive, Doc Martin himself would probably enjoy sidling up to the bar or grabbing a table by a front window.

The decorous-feeling restaurant has a well-deserved reputation for fine food and drink, and the service is attentive and friendly. The menu

Handicap Access: Full.
Smoking: Patio only.
Reservations: Recom-
  mended for dinner.
Special Features: Patio; Live
  music; Fireplace; Private
  dining.

offers imaginative variations of New Mexico standards plus a well-rounded selection of contemporary American dishes. Dinner entrees range from
Southwest lacquered duck to red chile, sesame
crusted, tierra mignon on noodle cake with spicy
eggplant sauce. Prix fixe dinner specials can be a
great bargain.

Doc Martin's wine list has many times earned the
Wine Spectator's award of excellence. Some can be sampled by the glass. For
dessert, try the mouthwatering Aztec mousse flavored with Kahlùa.

FRED'S PLACE
505-758-0514.
332 Paseo Del Pueblo Sur,
  Taos, NM 87571.
Closed: Sun., Major Holi-
  days.
Price: Inexpensive.
Cuisine: Mexican, New
  Mexican.
Serving: D.
Credit Cards: AE, D, DC
  MC, V.
Handicap Access: Partial.
Smoking throughout.
Reservations: None.

When you eat at Fred's Place, you'll be seated
in a room wildly and totally painted in a version of the Apocalypse. The waitresses may be
dressed accordingly, or as though prepared for
inter-galactic travel. The menu is limited to classic
Mexican entrees, the food is fresh and tasty, with
the distinctive taste of fresh spices and good cheese,
and the place is always packed. If you're a smoker,
you can eat and smoke in peace.

JOSEPH'S TABLE
505-751-4512.
4167 Paseo Del Pueblo Sur,
  Ranchos de Taos, NM
  87571.
Closed: Mon., Major holi-
  days.
Price: Expensive.
Cuisine: Continental.
Serving: L, D.
Credit Cards: MC, V.
Handicap. Access: Partial.
Nonsmoking throughout.
Reservations: Recom-
  mended.

Out of a funky hole-in-the-wall in a crumbling
adobe emerges the select few tables of this fine
restaurant, highly regarded as among the best in
Taos. A lovely place for a winter dinner of roasted
lamb shank, crisped sweet potatoes, creme brulée.
Both the wine and the service are excellent. Reminiscent of an off-the-beaten-path European restaurant.

MAINSTREET BAKERY
505-758-9610.
Guadalupe Plaza, Taos, NM
  87571.
Closed: Christmas, New
  Year's.

This bakery with politically conscious cafe space
advertises itself as "all organic, all natural —
almost." Although it offers inexpensive lunches
(mostly fresh soups, salads and sandwiches) and
moderately priced dinners (New Mexican dishes,

Price: Inexpensive.
Cuisine: Natural,
 Vegetarian.
Serving: B, L, D.
Credit Cards: None.
Handicap Access: Partial.
Nonsmoking throughout.
Reservations: None.
Special Features: Patio
 dining.

**MARCIANO'S
 RISTORANTI**
505-751-0805.
112 C Placita, Taos, NM
 87571.
Closed: Tues.
Cuisine: Italian, Healthy
 Nouvelle.
Serving: D.
Credit Cards: AE, D, MC, V.
Nonsmoking throughout.
Reservations: Recom-
 mended.

pastas and seafoods), its most popular draw is breakfast: fresh breads, egg and tofu dishes, French toast, granola and heavy-duty buckwheat pancakes. Our favorite is the Mainstreet Special, a piquant scramble of hormone-free eggs, mushroom, spinach, green onion and cream cheese. The Guadalupe Special, with eggs, cheddar and green chile, is a close second. Coffee at Main Street is fresh-ground. Alternatives to this wicked brew are provided in the form of Cafix, herbal teas and fresh-squeezed orange juice.

It may be tricky to find, but Marciano's, near the Harwood Museum, is worth it, especially if you're a health-conscious person or on a special diet. The fresh, organic food, from the salad to roast chicken, is of the highest quality. Pasta is homemade. Try the specials, like the Puttenesca. The dinner salad is a constructed artwork. Simple adobe interior, nothing fancy, candlelit, a bit romantic in the Taos manner. Emphasis is on local produce.

Michael's Kitchen: a rustic cafe serving a little of everything.

Murrae Haynes

MICHAEL'S KITCHEN
505-758-4178.
304C Paseo del Pueblo, .3
 miles N. of Taos Plaza.

Michael's Kitchen has maintained the Taos communities' loyalty for over 23 years. Owned by the Ninneman family, Michael's Kitchen

Open: Daily 7 a.m. to 8:30
p.m., closed the month of
November, major
holidays.
Price: Moderate.
Cuisine: American, New
Mexican.
Serving: B, L, D any time of
day.
Credit Cards: AE, D, MC, V.
Handicap Access: Partial.
Nonsmoking Section: Yes.
Special Features: Fresh
baked pastries and
desserts; Counter seating;
Children's menu;
Takeout.

OGELVIE'S BAR & GRILL

505-758-8866.
East side of Taos Plaza,
Taos, NM 87571.
Open: Daily, closed major
holidays.
Price: Moderate–Expensive.
Cuisine: American.
Serving: L, D.
Credit Cards: AE, MC, V.
Handicap Access: Yes.
Nonsmoking Section: Yes.
Reservations: Not required.
Special Features: Patio; Full
Bar.

ORLANDO'S NEW MEXICAN CAFE

505-751-1450.
1.8 miles north of Taos
Plaza on the left.
Closed: Sun., Christmas.
Price: Inexpensive.
Cuisine: Northern New
Mexican.
Serving: L, D.
Credit cards: None.
Handicap Access. No.
Smoking: Patio only.
Reservations: None.
Special Features: Patio.

serves delicious hearty dishes — fried chicken to enchiladas, chosen from their tabloid sized menu. As you walk in the door, you will notice the large display cases full of breakfast pastries, breads, pies and other mouth-watering desserts baked fresh daily at the restaurant. Once you finish gawking at the salad-plate sized cinnamon rolls with cream cheese icing and confetti sprinkles on top (Orville Rolls), have a seat at the counter or at a table in one of the main dining rooms and settle in for awhile. If you have any Taos questions, this is the place to inquire; just ask your server or one of the Taoseños probably sitting at the next table. If you come for breakfast, you may have a wait, but it's worth it.

After visiting the many art galleries and boutiques on Taos Plaza, stop by Ogelvie's for lunch or dinner. They offer fresh salads, pastas, traditional New Mexican dishes and unique entrees such as Australian lamb sirloin and prawn brochette. The main dining room is spacious and cheerfully illuminated. It is a great setting for family or large party dining. If the weather is warm, ask for a table on Ogelvie's second story patio overlooking the plaza. A good place for a margarita. Make sure you order the garlic mashed potatoes if they do not accompany your meal. The food can be a bit disappointing, and you can find more authentic Mexican dishes elsewhere.

If you're in the market for authentic Northern New Mexico cooking without the lard, you can't do better than Orlando's. The decor of colorful Mexican folk art, the bright colors, the scrumptious desserts and the gracious hosts, Orlando and Yvette, all contribute to a delightful experience. Try the chile bowl, "with everything." Summer dining on the patio is a joy.

PIZZA EMERGENCY
505-751-0911.
316 Paseo del Pueblo Sur,
Taos, NM 87571.
Closed: Major holidays.
Price: Inexpensive.
Cuisine: New York-style
pizza.
Serving: L, D.
Credit Cards: None.
Handicap Access: Partial.
Nonsmoking Section: Yes.
Reservations: None.
Special Features: Free
delivery.

Though this modern little pizza bar changed hands a while back, it still offers New York-style pizzas that are almost as good as those originally made by its founder. The crusts are light and delicious; the cheese smooth and savory; and there's an assortment of wonderful toppings, from pepperoni, Canadian bacon and ground beef to pineapple, plum tomatoes and artichoke hearts. Pizza Emergency also serves hot sandwiches — the eggplant parmesan isn't bad — pastas, calzones and a few delicious cookies and pastries. Video games and the foods of choice make this a haven for youngsters.

RESTAURANTS NEAR TAOS

**THE BAVARIAN SKI
RESTAURANT &
LODGE**
505-751-6661.
Taos Ski Valley, Taos, NM
87525.
Open: 7 days during winter;
call for summer hours.
Price: Expensive–Very
Expensive.
Cuisine: German.
Serving: L, D, après-ski.
Credit Cards: AE, D, DC,
MC, V.
Handicap Access: Yes.
Reservations: Recom-
mended.

You can ski to this mid-mountain European log lodge or call for a van to pick you up at Taos Ski Valley. Featuring German specialties like sauerbraten, spaetzel and beer imported from the oldest brewery in Munich. A beautiful sun deck surrounds this re-creation of an Alpine ski lodge. Be sure to try this one.

COYOTE CREEK CAFE
505-377-3550.
Mini Mart Plaza, Angel
Fire, NM 87110.
Closed: Mon., usually.
Price: Inexpensive.
Cuisine: American,
Continental.
Serving: L, D, SB.
Credit Cards: D, MC, V.
Handicap Access: Partial.
Nonsmoking Section: Yes.
Reservations: Recom-
mended ski season.

This little place offers a folksy flair along with inexpensive food, including a serviceable sandwich. The menu includes four or five homemade daily lunch and dinner specials that vary from double-decker pizzas, to cream vegetables Alfredo, to blue corn enchiladas with green chile. One of the Coyote's hottest sellers is shrimp brochette, eight spiced shrimp wrapped in bacon and skewered, broiled and served on a bed of dark rye toast. Desserts include homemade pies and cheesecakes, plus other delectables that will knock your socks off. Warning: daytime service can be sullen.

Murrae Haynes

Embudo Station: a welcome oasis beside the Rio Grande.

EMBUDO STATION
505-852-4707.
N.M. 68 between Taos and
  Santa Fe.
Closed: Nov.–April.
Price: Moderate.
Cuisine: Barbecue smoke-
  house with brewery.
Serving: L, D.
Credit Cards: AE, MC, V.
Handicap Access: Full.
Smoking: Patio only.
Reservations: Recom-
  mended.
Special Features: Riverside
  patio; Live music on
  weekends; Brewery
  tours; Bakery-deli.

During the 1880s, this little cluster of buildings beside the river was home to the narrow-gauge Chile Line railroad. It's also the place where John Wesley Powell measured the flow of the Rio Grande. Now it's home to a variety of delights, including patio dining under giant cottonwoods, home-brewed beer, local wines and mouthwatering meats cooked long and lovingly in a stone smoke-house. This is a must-stop for travelers en route from Taos to Santa Fe, if only for one of the fine microbrews and an appetizer.

When you first walk in, you can smell the barbe-cued and slow-smoked bacon, turkeys, hams and trout that have made Embudo Station famous. You can order your brew by the glass or pitcher and slurp it within a few strides of the Rio Grande's rushing waters, accompanied by a plate of juicy meats and crusty baguettes. Embudo Station serves heaping dishes of fries, a black bean soup that's one of the best anywhere, a Greek salad fit for an Aegean king and some outstanding desserts. Try the smoked trout as well.

There's always six home-brewed beers on tap. You can visit the beautiful stone brewery, the country smokehouse or the nearby deli-bakery. In season you can take the Sunset Dinner Float, a two-hour raft trip that starts five miles north at Lover's Lane and ends up with dinner at Embudo.

NORTHTOWN
  RESTAURANT
505-758-2374.

Just an unpretentious, popular little breakfast and lunch spot serving tasty, healthful fare. Stop by for breakfast sometime on your way to the Taos Ski

908 Paseo del Pueblo Norte,
Taos, NM 87571.
Closed: Thanksgiving,
Christmas, New Year's.
Price: Inexpensive.
Cuisine: New Mexican,
American.
Serving: B, L.
Credit Cards: None.
Handicap Access: Partial.
Nonsmoking Section: No.
Reservations: None.

THE OUTBACK
505-758-3112.
712 Paseo del Pueblo Norte,
Taos, NM 87571.
Closed: Thanksgiving,
Christmas.
Price: Inexpensive.
Cuisine: Taos Pizza.
Serving: L, D.
Credit Cards: MC, V.
Handicap Access: Partial.
Nonsmoking Section: Yes.
Reservations: None.
Special Features: Takeout.

**RANCHOS PLAZA
GRILL**
505-758-0719.
8 Rancho Plaza, Ranchos de
Taos, NM.
Closed: Mon.
Price: Inexpensive.
Cuisine: Traditional Ameri-
can with Southwest flavor.
Serving: B, L.
Credit Cards: None.
Handicap Access. Partial.
Nonsmoking Section: Yes.
Reservations: Yes.
Special features: View of
the most painted and
photographed church in
America; Ancient adobe
building.

Valley and down a stack of blueberry or pecan hot-cakes. Or try the huevos rancheros. Here you'll find zucchini and banana bread, blueberry and pump-kin muffins, rich coffee cakes and a variety of hearty northern New Mexican lunches. Veggie-burgers available. You can browse the lending library shelves while you wait for your lunch. All this and more, you can eat to pleasant conversation and the busy sounds of clanking dishes and silver-ware.

This funky little pizza joint slightly outside the Taos town limits is well named. You may have to hunt around a bit to find it on your first visit, but it's well worth the trek. Outback is the undisputed local favorite pizzaria. This is one of the hippest pizza parlors you've ever seen, complete with an old-fashioned gas pump in the corner and cus-tomers' crayoned works of art hanging on the walls. The Outback specializes in "Taos-style gourmet pizza," lovingly made to order from organic Colorado wheat. As the place is often packed, you may want to order in advance or do takeout. Try the Florentine, with chicken, garlic and herbs sautéed in white wine, or the new portobello mushroom pie. Servings are more than generous, and they don't scrimp on the toppings.

The charming Ranchos Plaza Grill, originally a spin-off of the popular Trading Post Cafe, pro-vides delicious, hearty breakfasts and interesting lunch specials in addition to all that charm. Our reviewer pronounced the pancakes the best she'd ever tasted, and their interpretation of huevos rancheros is a pleasing change. Look for chicken fried steak and other homestyle dishes, as well as vegetarian selections for lunch.

The Stakeout overlooks the Santa Fe Trail and miles of mountains.

Sandra Lee Tatum

THE STAKEOUT
505-758-2042.
P.O. Box 453, Ranchos de
    Taos, NM 87557.
On Stakeout Dr. off N.M.
    68, about 8 miles S. of
    Taos.
Open: Daily.
Price: Expensive.
Cuisine: Steak and Seafood.
Serving: D.
Credit Cards: AE, CB, DC,
    MC, V.
Handicap Access: Partial.
Nonsmoking Section: Yes.
Reservations: Recom-
    mended.
Special Features: Live
    music; Fireplace; Patio
    dining.

Located in a rambling white adobe overlooking miles of mountainous terrain, the Stakeout is a semiformal oasis in a remote corner of dry scrubland located on Outlaw Hill, part of the original Santa Fe Trail and a lookout where desperadoes once stopped to rest. The restaurant offers spectacular views, huge picture windows, crackling woodstoves and fireplaces, a warm, wood-paneled bar and a selection of relatively inexpensive domestic, imported and dessert wines.

This casual-elegant place offers outstanding steaks and seafood, plus daily specials and seasonal game and lobster dishes. For appetizers, start with the house-cured smoked salmon—the best! Some succulent specialties include scaloppini of veal sautéed with fresh asparagus, fresh crabmeat stuffed with crayfish and topped with Mornay sauce; and duck roasted with apples and prunes, served with an orange currant sauce. There's also a kids' menu and a selection of homemade desserts. You won't go wrong with a steak. Service is absolutely lovely.

**TIM'S STRAY DOG
    CANTINA**
505-776-2894
Taos Ski Valley, NM 87525.

A lively hangout for all ages where they're not afraid to serve the chile good and hot. A great place for that après-ski brew. A perennially popular spot, for good reason. The food is plentiful and

Closed: Easter; Memorial Day.
Price: Inexpensive
Cuisine: New Mexican.
Serving: B, L, D during ski season. L, D in summer.
Credit cards: AE, MC, V.
Handicap Access: Yes.
Smoking section.
Reservations: For parties of six or more.

TIWA KITCHEN
505-751-1020.
Taos Pueblo Rd., Taos, NM 87571. 1.7 m. from Allsup. Call ahead.
Price: Inexpensive.
Cuisine: Native foods, New Mexican.
Serving: B, L.
Credit Cards: MC, V.
Handicap Access. Partial.
Nonsmoking Section: Yes.
Reservations: None.

inexpensive, the service friendly, and the atmosphere warm.

Dine on the Taos Pueblo on such delicacies as stuffed frybread, blue corn pancakes with wild plum jelly, fantastic red and green chile dishes, buffalo and oven bread fresh from the *horno*—with a view of majestic Taos Mountain.

Dine in relaxed elegance in Taos' Trading Post Cafe.

Karen Klitgaard

TRADING POST CAFE
505-758-5089.
4179 Hwy. 68 at Hwy. 518; P.O. Box 698, Ranchos de Taos, NM 87557.
Closed: Sun., Christmas, New Year's.

Located right along the Taos Highway, this bustling, superbly-run eatery opened in November 1994 on the old Ranchos Trading Post. Up until 1981, the trading post had been the largest general store in the Taos area, and was also the area's most popular meeting place, a true commu-

Price: Moderate.
Cuisine: European.
Serving: L, D.
Credit Cards: MC, V.
Handicap Access: Partial.
Nonsmoking Section: Yes.
Reservations: Recom-
    mended for parties of
    five or more.
Special Features: Fireplace;
    Patio dining.

nity center. Today, the owners of the Trading Post Cafe are doing their best to revive that same community spirit, inviting residents and travelers alike to come in and warm their feet by the *kiva* fireplace, nestle into a comfy corner table, or sit counterside on tall, wrought-iron swivel stools.

The menu includes a wide array of good to delicious lunch and dinner offerings — generous portions to suit everyone's palate, at a wide variety of prices. There are salads, fish, pastas, soups, Creole pepper shrimp, escargot, and meats from roast duck to Sonoma lamb chops to Florentine beefsteak. How about a paella with a glass of Vouvray? The pasta specials are superb. The waitstaff's list of daily specials is nothing short of astounding. Service is especially generous and professional, and there's an excellent and moderately priced list of red and white wines, as well as an array of wonderful, homemade desserts. The patio is glorious in warm weather. The Trading Post is the last word in the casual sophistication that marks the best of Taos. The author has eaten here many, many times and never been disappointed.

FOOD PURVEYORS

A butcher shop on Water Street, Santa Fe, ca. 1900.

Courtesy Museum of New Mexico

As agricultural communities, Santa Fe and Taos have been bastions of local produce and home cooking for the better part of 400 years. After the 1940s, the emphasis shifted to mass production, with chain grocery stores and fewer independent food purveyors. However, vendors still sell seasonal fare, from sweet corn and chile to apples and *bizcochitos* (the anise-flavored "state cookie") at roadside stands. During the past decade, specialty establishments, including ice cream and candy shops, delis, bakeries and gourmet markets, have become more abundant. Following are some of the special places and products, both old and new, that make the modern Santa Fe–Taos area such a gastronomic delight. And if you are fortunate to drive past one of the still-existing old-time general stores, such as Bode's in Abiquiu, do venture in. It's possible to find gourmet delights, a hand-made tamale in the crockpot or a great bowl of chile, amidst the pots and pans, hardware and sacks of beans.

BAKERIES

Santa Fe

ATALAYA RESTAURANT & BAKERY
Owner: John O'Brien.
505-982-2709.
320 S. Guadalupe, Santa Fe, NM 87501.
Closed: Major holidays.

A most civilized place to breakfast on a beautiful pastry and latte, or take home a lovely loaf of fresh-baked bread. Order the fragrant buttery apple pancake for breakfast and be prepared to split it. Lunch on the patio is always pleasant.

CLOUD CLIFF BAKERY
Owner: Willem Malten.
505-983-6254.
1805 2nd St., Santa Fe, NM 87505.
Closed: Major holidays.

Cloud Cliff supplies many local grocers and restaurants with bread, rolls, muffins, scones and the like, but nowhere are these goodies fresher than at the restaurant and bakery itself. The cinnamon rolls are particularly mouthwatering. Cloud Cliff offers a wide variety of breads, including Aztec Amaranth, Crunchy Millet, Cinnamon Raisin and traditional breads such as Levain and Cibatta.

COYOTE CAFE GENERAL STORE
Owner: Mark Miller.
505-982-2454.
132 W. Water, Santa Fe, NM 87501.
Closed: Sunday.

Downstairs from the famous Coyote Cafe, you can find a shop stocked with all manner of salsas and chile-lovers accoutrements, selling fabulous loaves of blue corn-chile roasted garlic bread and other delights.

FRENCH PASTRY SHOP
Owner: George Zadeyan.
505-983-6697.
100 E. San Francisco St., Santa Fe, NM 87501.
Closed: Christmas.
No credit cards.

George Zadeyan and his brother started their first French Pastry Shop in Santa Fe in 1972. Two years later, they moved to La Fonda Hotel on the plaza. The location, along with a delicious array of pastries and crepes, has made this little cafe a tourist mecca in the summertime and a year-round destination for many locals. The reasons are obvious enough once you've been there: croissants, raisin rolls, apple turnovers, Napoleons, strawberry tarts, eclairs, quiches, sandwiches, crepes, coffees, cappuccinos — you get the idea.

HAAGEN DAZS/PLAZA BAKERY
Owner: Fred Libby.
505-988-3858.
56 E. San Francisco St., Santa Fe, NM 87501.
Closed: Thanksgiving, Christmas.

You know about the ice cream, but do you know about the baked goodies? With seven full-time bakers, the Haagen Dazs/Plaza Bakery is Santa Fe's largest bakery, wholesaling to numerous local coffee shops, hotels and restaurants. Stuffed chocolate croissants, cream cheese brownies, fruit pies, bearclaws, strudel, scones and herb baguettes are just a few of the delectables offered — along with 33 flavors of ice cream. Sandwiches, coffee, tea and a variety of espresso drinks are also served. Located on the plaza, this is a great people-watching spot and usually very crowded.

SAGE BAKEHOUSE
Owners: Andree Falls and Amy Cox.
505-820-7243.
535-C Cerrillos Rd., Santa Fe, NM 87501.
Closed: Major holidays.

When the Sage Bakehouse opened its doors four years back, it changed Santa Feans' concepts of the staff of life. From their special ovens come loaves of kalamata olive and pecan breads, all made of the purest, most basic ingredients. Try a sandwich of black forest ham and gruyere cheese for lunch, and by all means, taste their hearth breads.

Taos

DAYLIGHT DONUTS
Owners: John and Jaxene Collier.
505-758-1156.
312 Paseo del Pueblo Sur, Taos, NM 87571.
Closed: Sun., Christmas.

Hungry for a real sticky bun and a plain old-fashioned doughnut just out of the oven? The Daylight, which opens promptly at 4 a.m., prides itself on doughnuts deep fried in soybean oil. It also has biscuits with sausage gravy and an astounding array of Daylight Donuts accessories, including coffee mugs, T-shirts, pop-sippers and caps.

MAINSTREET BAKERY
Owner: Mike Griego.
505-758-9610.
112 Dona Luz, Guadalupe Plaza, Taos, NM 87571.
Closed: Major holidays.

This famous local bakery is really one large kitchen/warehouse space with cafe. Watch the bakers labor over the goods that make the place famous: 15 wholesome breads, including chile-anadama and carrot poppy seed, plus huge cinnamon rolls, bearclaws and more. Most Mainstreet baked goods are sweetened with honey and use organic ingredients and healthy substitutes like carob instead of chocolate chips.

Near Taos

CASA FRESEN BAKERY, GOURMET MARKET & CATERING
Owner: Debra Cole.
505-776-2969.
482 Hwy. 150, Arroyo Seco, NM 87514.
Closed: Tues.

Many national food writers have literally beaten a path to this funky stop en route to Taos Ski Valley. There they find not only exquisite scones, breads, pies and cookies, but what some consider "as good a sandwich as I've ever eaten," made on fresh-baked crisp sourdough with locally grown tomatoes, greens and imported cheeses. A veritable must-stop for anyone who loves food.

BREWERIES AND BREWPUBS

Santa Fe

SANTA FE BREWING COMPANY
Manager: Carlos Muller.
505-424-3333.
#18 E. Frontage Rd., Santa Fe, NM 87505.
Closed: Sun.

In 1988, a wine-bottle distributor named Mike Levis opened New Mexico's first commercial brewery on his 65-acre ranch outside Galisteo. Today, the brewery's best-known product is Santa Fe Pale Ale, available in bars, restaurants, liquor and grocery stores. The company makes seven other beers that are available only at the brewery itself: Fiesta Ale, Porter, Wheat Beer, Barley Wine, Nut Brown Ale, Raspberry Ale and Russian Imperial Stout. Tour the brewery (no reservations required), and pick up a T-shirt, cap or poster emblazoned with the company label.

SECOND STREET BREWERY
Owner: Peter Allen.
505-982-3030.
1814 2nd St., Santa Fe, NM 87501.
Closed: Christmas, Easter, Thanksgiving.

As a relatively new entry on the micro-brewery scene, this one is already winning major awards for its custom suds. The brewery has been an instant success with locals, who enjoy the relaxed pub and its fish and chips, soups and salads after work or on the weekends, with their families, when they can hear live music in the evening. Particularly welcoming of women, who need not fear entering alone.

Taos

ESKE'S BREW PUB
Owner: Steve and Wanda Eskeback.
505-758-1517.
106 Desgeorges Ln., Taos, NM 87571.
Closed: Christmas.

Ever try a green chile beer or an apricot ale? This is the place, where the fresh home-brewed beers are served with a menu of green chile stew, bratwurst and delicious grilled sandwiches. A relaxed hangout.

BUTCHERS

There are a number of small groceries and health-food markets in Santa Fe and Taos that offer specialty and custom-cut meats. The following are some of the better ones (see also "Health Food Stores," below).

Santa Fe

Close to the center of town, you'll find **Kaune Food Town** (505-982-2629; 511 Old Santa Fe Trail), one of the oldest groceries around. It offers a wide variety of meats, including natural beef and poultry, Colorado lamb, and game meats from venison and buffalo to rabbit and pheasant. You can also find a variety of natural meats, fish and poultry at Santa Fe's three health-food stores, *The Marketplace* (505-984-2852, 627 W. Alameda), **Wild Oats Market** (505-983-5333; 1090 S. St. Francis Dr.) and *Alfalfa's,* (505-986-8667, 333 W. Cordova).

Cid's Food Market (505-758-1148; 822 Paseo del Pueblo Norte) has a little butcher department worth a special mention. Here you'll find Coleman natural beef and lamb from Colorado, as well as Shelton's grain-fed, hormone-free chicken. At **Graham's Superette** (505-758-2924; 910 Paseo del Pueblo Norte) owners Robert and Dilia Graham oversee the only old-fashioned, full-service meat rack in town. They offer a mind-boggling array of range-fed lamb, pork, beef and buffalo; free-ranging fryers and turkeys; and cuts from T-bones and top round to beef tongue and *burrinate* (lamb intestine). If you ask, they'll even give you recipes and cooking tips.

CANDY AND ICE CREAM SHOPS

In addition to *Baskin-Robbins* (505-982-9031, 1841 Cerrillos Rd., Santa Fe, NM 87501; 505-758-0031, Calvary and Pueblo Rd., Taos, NM 87571) and *Haagen Dazs Ice Cream Shoppe* (505-988-3858; 56 E. San Francisco St., Santa Fe, NM 87501, discussed under "Bakeries," above), Santa Fe and Taos have other sweet-tooth centers worth mentioning.

SEÑOR MURPHY CANDYMAKER
Owner: Michael Monahan.
505-983-9243 at 223 Canyon Rd.
505-983-0461 at La Fonda Hotel, Santa Fe, NM 87501.
505-471-8899 at Villa Linda Mall.
Closed: Sun.

Neil Murphy, whose ancestors sold candy in Dublin, Ireland, started in 1972 with one tiny candy store. Today, the Santa Fe outlets are going strong. Their specialty is anything with piñon nuts — for example, piñon toffee and piñon fudge — as well as two new spicy chile concoctions with peanut brittle and chocolate cream. They also make chile jellies and outstanding condiments for meats and hors d'ouvres. Great gifts for yourself, those back home or abroad.

TAOS COW ICE CREAM
Owner: Jamie Leeson.
505-776-5640.
591 Arroyo Hondo, Arroyo
  Seco, NM 87514.
Closed: Christmas, New
  Year's, Thanksgiving.

There is such a thing as insisting on going to the source, and if you're an ice cream lover, you'll want to make the pilgrimage up the Taos Ski Valley Rd. to the still-funky, somewhat tucked away ice creamery known as Taos Cow for the creamiest, most exquisite ice cream you've ever tasted, in seasonal flavors.

CATERERS

Santa Fe

ADOBO CATERING
Owner: Peter Dent.
505-989-7674.
1807 2nd St., Unit 7, Santa
  Fe, NM 87505.
Closed: Sun., caters 7 days.

Adobo is a full-service caterer with lots of experience. The staff offers buffet tables with menus for almost any occasion or cuisine, from Russian, Latin American and Mediterranean to American and New Mexican. If needed, they'll even provide flowers, photography and music.

**CELEBRATIONS
  RESTAURANT &
  CATERERS**
Owner: Sylvia Johnson.
505-989-8904.
613 Canyon Rd., Santa Fe,
  NM 87501.
Caters daily.

In a quaint old adobe bistro on Canyon Rd., Celebrations serves hearty breakfasts, lunches and dinners to the public by day and rents space for dinner parties at night. Though northern New Mexican and Creole are their specialties, they'll do any cuisine that suits your fancy.

**WALTER BURKE
  CATERING**
Owner: Walter Burke.
505-473-9600.
1209 Calle de Commercio,
  Santa Fe, NM 87505.
Open: Daily.

If you want absolutely impeccable catering for any occasion, call Walter Burke. In Santa Fe, the name speaks for itself. About the only thing they don't provide is a location, but they can help you find one. In business since 1981, they're one of the largest catering firms in town, and they've prepared just about every kind of cuisine imaginable.

Taos

**APPLE TREE
  RESTAURANT**
Owners: Ginny and Arthur
  Greeno.
505-758-1900.
123 Bent St., Taos, NM
  87571.
Open: Daily. All year.

The Apple Tree caters a little bit of everything, with traditional New Mexican cuisine among its most popular offerings. Birthdays, weddings, special dinners — whatever the need, the Apple Tree prides itself on adaptability, fresh foods, local produce and outstanding desserts.

COFFEE SHOPS

There are so many good places to sip coffee in Santa Fe and Taos that it's difficult to list them all, much less do them justice. Here we simply call your attention to a number of choice spots where you can find good, fresh coffees, teas, espressos and cappuccinos. The rest is up to you.

Browsing after coffee and pastries at Downtown Subscription.

Murrae Haynes

In **_Santa Fe_**, good coffee spots include the **Aztec Street Cafe** (505-983-9464; 317 Aztec St.) a rather smoky spot with a hip-beat-punk ambiance; **The Backroom Coffeebar** (505-988-5323; 616 Canyon Rd.), a sunny, peaceful spot with a contemporary crafts gallery; **Cloud Cliff Bakery & Cafe** (505-983-6254; 1805 2nd St.); **Downtown Subscription** (505-983-3085; 376 Garcia St.), a spacious, cheerful bar and patio with rack upon rack of newspapers and magazines, plus great coffees and pastries; **Galisteo Corner Cafe** (505-984-1316; 201 Galisteo St.), also serving delicious soups, sandwiches, pastries and such with newspapers and magazines; **Haagen-Dazs** (505-988-3858; 56 E. San Francisco St. on the plaza) with rich, deep coffee and unbelievable pastries; **Ohori's** (505-988-7026; 507 Old Santa Fe Trail), with fresh-roasted beans and a different coffee each time the urn empties; and **Portare Via** (505-988-3886; 540 Montezuma in the Sanbusco Center), a delightful little mall bar with killer espresso and yummy salads, sandwiches and pastries.

In **_Taos,_** you'll find some good brews at the **Taos Mountain Tea and Coffee Purveyors,** (505-751-7184; 124-F Bent St.). This aromatic hole in the wall in the Dunn House complex becomes a pleasant wake-up spot as locals gather for a shot of coffee and some conversation before going to work. There's no place to sit, but you can get your coffee by the cup or the pound in flavors ranging from chocolate hazelnut to Sumatra. Other good sipping spots include the **Bent Street Deli & Cafe** (505-758-5787; 120 Bent St. in the Dunn House complex);

Caffe Tazza (505-758-8706; 122 Kit Carson Rd.), the very popular *The Bean* (505-758-7711; 900 Paseo del Pueblo Norte) and the fine *Taos Coffee Co.* (505-758-3331; 1807 Santa Fe Rd., in Ranchos de Taos).

COOKING SCHOOL

SANTA FE SCHOOL OF COOKING
Owner: Susan Curtis.
505-983-4511.
116 W. San Francisco St.,
   Santa Fe, NM 87501.
Closed: Easter, Christmas,
   New Year's.
Classes several times
   weekly; call for reservations.

If you're interested in learning to cook traditional New Mexican and contemporary Southwestern food, take a lesson from the Santa Fe School of Cooking. The school and its food market, under the deft direction of Susan Curtis, are located on the upper level of the Plaza Mercado, a block from the plaza. Curtis offers regional cooking classes almost daily, ranging from $25 to $47, including a meal. The class packs in 2-1/2 hours' worth of technique, information, hints and farmer's wisdom. When the class is over, students eat all that delicious food for lunch.

You'll find fresh local produce at the Santa Fe Area Farmers' Market.

Corrie Photography

FARMERS' MARKETS

The most common farmers' markets in the Santa Fe–Taos area are those you find along the highway — little shacks or temporary stands strung with red chile *ristras* and offering a variety of homegrown fruits, vegetables and piñon nuts. In season, the most abundant cluster of such spots can be found on N.M. 68 between Velarde and Dixon. From time to time, families even gather to cook and sell their freshly harvested green chile in shopping centers. Keep in mind that not all the produce is locally grown. When in doubt, ask the vendor.

Between June and October, there are a number of excellent farmers' markets in the Santa Fe–Taos area. The largest is the *Santa Fe Area Farmers' Market*

(505-983-4098; 530 S. Guadalupe), held Tuesdays and Saturdays from 7 to 11:30 a.m. at the Sanbusco Market Center, a collection of specialty retail shops and restaurants. Here you can get ultra-fresh, locally grown produce (much of it organic), as well as prepared foods such as salsas, jams and jellies — even apple cider and honey. Saturday mornings are an event here, with live music, tastings and cooking demonstrations.

Three other regional markets offer similarly fresh local produce and specialty items between July and October. They include the *Taos Farmers' Market* (505-758-3982), which meets Saturday mornings around 7 a.m. near the county courthouse on Paseo del Pueblo Sur; the *Española Farmers' Market* (505-753-5340), which meets Monday afternoons from 3 p.m. to dark at the Big Rock Shopping Center on Riverside Drive; and the *Los Alamos Farmers' Market* (505-662-6594), held Thursday mornings from 7 till noon on Central Ave., just north of the county municipal building. Santa Fe and Los Alamos sometimes host monthly indoor markets in the winter. Call for specific information.

FAST FOODS

As in most places, fast-food spots are abundant in the Santa Fe–Taos area. Some are so ubiquitous and predictable as to need no mention, and they are equally easy to find. Others, particularly those unique to the area, are worth looking for.

In **Santa Fe**, one of the best and most popular is the **Burrito Company** (505-982-4453; 111 Washington Ave.), less than a block from the plaza. Breakfast and lunch menus feature such favorites as fast burritos, Mexican plates, hot dogs, hamburgers and New Mexico-style chile dogs. Here you can get a good blue corn chicken enchilada for a song. They also sell their own salsa and chile by the quart. It's a convenient local hangout, highly recommended for families and folks in a hurry.

While on the plaza, you can get a delicious lunch for about $3.00, plus the cost of a lemonade, at *Roque's Carnitas.* Just follow the delicious aroma to Roque's cart on the corner of Washington and Palace Ave.

Possibly the most popular Mexican food takeout stand in town is *Baja Tacos* (505-471-8762; 2621 Cerrillos Rd.) with its healthy ingredients, tasty ample portions and "happy hour" discounts. Specializes in tofu and vegetarian Mexican food. Also excellent for a quick Mexican food fix is *Felipe's Tacos,* (505-473-9397; 1711 Llano), for healthy authentic quesadillas, burritos and tacos, with a choice of fresh salsas to accompany.

If you're after a quick burger, try *Blake's Lotaburger,* a New Mexico chain that's popular for quick and easy family outings. Blake's raises their own beef, and if you want a New Mexico chile cheeseburger, this is a good place to find one. In or near Santa Fe there are Lotaburgers on Airport Rd., Cerrillos Rd., St. Michael's Dr., N. Guadalupe and in Pojoaque. Near Taos you'll find Lotaburgers on Paseo del Pueblo Sur and in El Prado, just north of town.

Baja Tacos remains the choice of locals for Mexican fast food.

Karen Klitgaard

Another spot worth mentioning is **Bert's Burger Bowl** (505-982-0215; 235 N. Guadalupe) in Santa Fe, where the menu is written half in English and half in Spanish. The grease in these tasty burgers may shut down your arteries, but the green chile will open them right up again. A bit more upscale in ingredients, though hardly in price, is the **Ramblin' Cafe** (505-989-1272; 1420 2nd St.) with fresh, delicious made-to-order soups, sandwiches and daily specials. They also deliver and cater.

In <u>Taos</u>, look for **Mante's Chow Cart** (505-758-3632; 402 Paseo del Pueblo Sur) where the specialty of the casa is the chile relleno and the breakfast burrito is all you could ever want. If you've got a burrito craving, head for **Rita's Mexican Food** (505-758-8556; 4133 State Rd. 68, Ranchos de Taos), exactly the kind of hole-in-the-wall gem, with a few outdoor picnic tables, travelers pride themselves on discovering. Whether you get the chicken, chorizo or fajita burrito, you'll walk away full and happy. In Arroyo Seco, **Abe's Cocina**, (505-776-8516; 489 State Rd. 150) is the place to pick up a breakfast burrito.

When traveling to and from Santa Fe and Taos, do as the locals do and stop at **El Parasol** (505-753-8852; 602 Santa Cruz Rd.) for the takeout version of the next-door restaurant, El Paragua. There's no better place to take in the local color or the red chile. Low-riders and movie stars alike flock here.

GOURMET SHOPS

Santa Fe

KAUNE FOOD TOWN
Owner: Jim Downey.
505-982-2629.
511 Old Santa Fe Trail,
  Santa Fe, NM 87501.
Closed: Sun., major holidays.

If this little community grocery store looks a bit outdated, that shouldn't be surprising; it's about 50 years old. What *is* surprising is that it offers a dazzling array of gourmet foods, from imported prosciutto, truffle mousse and vegetarian terrines;

to exotic spices and high-end canned goods like hearts of palm and white asparagus; to an entire wall of mustards. In addition, it has gourmet ice creams and fresh breads, jellies and teas. It also has a variety of fresh meats (see "Butchers," above).

Kokoman Circus is stocked with an overwhelming array of gourmet goodies.

Karen Klitgaard

KOKOMAN CIRCUS
Owner: Keith Obermeyer.
505-983-7770.
301 Garfield, Santa Fe, NM
   87501.
Closed: Sun., Christmas,
   Thanksgiving, New
   Year's.

Cater yourself a gourmet picnic of a lifetime from the incredible assortment of imported and domestic cheeses, meats, olives, wines and desserts. This is the Zabar's of Santa Fe. This is where you can have the most fun in Santa Fe for under $25. Also has sit-down tables, daily specials, wine and coffee bar.

Taos

**BENT STREET DELI &
   CAFE**
Owners: Tom Kennedy and
   Charlene DuLong.
505-758-5787.
120 Bent St., Taos, NM
   87571.
Closed: Sun.

When this little deli opened in 1990, it was so deluged with customers that the owners had to close their doors on the first day. The appreciative throngs still descend morning, noon and night for a cup of coffee, a bagel with lox, a pound of smoked Gouda cheese, warm Brie with apples and almonds, a jar of chile or chutney, a slice of homemade apple pie — even a Bent St. Sub or a dinner of shrimp with green chile pesto. Bent Street is a cozy place with comfy tables, pleasant music, picture windows, a *placita* and lots of greenery — all in all, a delightful spot.

HEALTH FOOD STORES

Santa Fe

Murrae Haynes

Order a fresh carrot juice or a latte in Alfalfa's Juice Bar.

ALFALFA'S
505-986-8667.
333 W. Cordova Rd.

A wonderful market with an orientation similar to *Wild Oats*, Alfalfa's opened under the same ownership just up the street. This is an especially congenial place with a charming, sunny patio and an outstanding food and juice bar and deli. The juice bar patio is the place to hang out these days. Should you be in the mood for a meal, for a dollar or two more than Furr's Cafeteria, you can have your choice of delicious healthy daily entrees and specials cafeteria-style. You can fix yourself a fresh salad to go from the impressive salad bar and pay by the pound.

THE MARKETPLACE
Owner: Jill Markstein,
Judith Sedlow.
505-984-2852.
627 W. Alameda St., Santa
Fe, NM 87501.
Closed: Major holidays.

Santa Fe's locally owned and operated Marketplace specializes in wholesome natural foods that are largely free of chemical preservatives, including local organic produce and non-sugar products. They also feature a range of gourmet and deli items (specialty cheeses, etc.); chemical-free meats and fish; lots of bulk grains, herbs and coffees; plus a wide variety of vitamins and health and beauty aids. Still retains its air of a neighborhood market.

**WILD OATS
COMMUNITY
MARKETS**
Managers: Ramone Lovato,
Dimid Hayes.

This airy, innovative market specializes in quality grains, meats and produce devoid of harmful chemicals. The bulk department offers some 70 different foods, from grains and granolas to flours

505-983-5333 at 1090 St. Francis Dr.
505-473-4943 at St. Michael's Village West, Santa Fe, NM 87501.
Closed: Christmas.

and seaweeds; more than a hundred herbs and spices; and even bulk oils, soaps and lotions. Full-spectrum lighting and fresh flowers add a special touch to this market, as do the gracious and helpful personnel.

Besides all this, Wild Oats offers a plethora of fresh breads and baked goods from numerous local bakeries, a full-service juice bar with cappuccino, espresso and irresistible ice creams, a colorful salad bar, and a deli with such exotic offerings as Egyptian hummus, Moroccan carrots and French Niçoise olives. There's also a festive community air about the place, including such innovations as back rubs for tired shoppers and monthly food and education festivals.

Taos

AMIGOS FOOD CO-OP
Manager: Daniel Carmona.
505-758-8493.
326 Paseo del Pueblo Sur, Taos NM 87571.
Closed: Major holidays.

Amigos offers good prices on natural food staples, from grains and granolas to beans and teas. Walls and aisles are lined with well-ordered shelves and bins stocked with healthful cereals, juices, vitamins and baked goods. Eighty percent of Amigos's produce is organic, and a popular vegetarian restaurant serves fruit and vegetable juices, smoothies, sandwiches, salads, baked goods and deli items. Nearby is a well-stocked magazine rack replete with periodicals on healthy living and a better environment. Also offers a modest wholesome soup lunch.

CID'S FOOD MARKET
Owners: Cid and Betty Backer.
505-758-1148.
822 Paseo del Pueblo Norte, Taos, NM 87571.
Closed: Sun., major holidays.

Since Cid's opened in 1986, owners Cid and Betty Backer have made it a point to purchase the freshest, purest food available. In addition to a colorful array of organic fruits and vegetables and shelves of gourmet items, Cid's offers a variety of natural soaps, herbs, vitamins, non-animal-tested cosmetics and biodegradable cleansers. At the same time, it caters to the less fanatic with such items as Lindt chocolates and a selection of non-organic fruits and vegetables. Cid's has a first-rate meat department (see "Butchers," above). In season, it buys and sells locally grown produce and eggs. Here you can find organic purple potatoes from Colorado. It even offers a variety of rare seeds for far-West gardens, including such exotics as Tarahumara Scarlet Runner Beans, Violet Queen Broccoli, and Cocozelle, an Italian straight summer squash. It's also the place to run into everyone you know in town and catch up on the latest.

WINE AND LIQUOR STORES

Following are some convenient places to lift your spirits in Santa Fe and Taos. Most of them sell a wide selection of beers, wines and hard liquor — and many have employees who can make recommendations and help you find what you're looking for. Be sure to shop early, though; sale of alcoholic beverages is illegal on Sunday.

Santa Fe

Cliff's Packaged Liquor Store 505-988-1790; 903 Old Pecos Trail, Santa Fe, NM 87501.

Kaune's Grocery Co. 505-983-7378; 208 Washington Ave., Santa Fe, NM 87501.

Lamplighter Liquor Store 505-438-9132; 2411 Cerrillos Rd., Santa Fe, NM 87505.

Owl Liquors 505-982-1751; 913 Hickox, Santa Fe, NM 87501.

Rodeo Plaza Liquors 505-473-2867; 2801 Rodeo Rd., Santa Fe, NM 87505.

Near Santa Fe

Kokoman Wines & Liquors 505-455-2219; Pojoaque, on U.S. 285, 15 miles N. of Santa Fe. One of the largest selections of fine wines, beers and liquors.

Tesuque Village Market 505-988-8848; Tesuque, NM, about 5 miles north of Santa Fe off U.S. 285.

Taos

Del Norte Lounge 505-758-8904; S. Santa Fe Rd., Taos, NM 87571.

Wine Cellar at the Taos Inn 505-758-8209; 125 Paseo del Pueblo Norte, Taos, NM 87571.

Near Taos

Andy's La Fiesta Discount Liquors 505-758-9733; St. Francis Plaza, Ranchos de Taos, NM.

El Prado Liquor Store 505-758-8254; El Prado, NM, 1 mile N. of Taos on N.M. 3.

WINERIES

The first grapevines in the Rio Grande Valley were planted by missionaries in the late 1500s, from cuttings originally brought from Spain. Thanks to the valley's long, warm days and cool nights, wine making flourished here for hundreds of years — all the way up to Prohibition in the 1920s. Finally in the early '70s, after a hiatus of 50 years, commercial wine production began making a comeback — partly with the help of French, German and Swiss investments. Today there are about a dozen wineries scattered throughout the state, a few of

Santa Fe Vineyards produces fine local wines.

them located in the mountainous Santa Fe–Taos area. Most have tasting rooms and welcome visitors.

BALAGNA WINERY
Owner: John Balagna.
505-672-3678.
223 Rio Bravo Dr., Los
   Alamos, NM 87544.
In White Rock.
Open: Daily.

John Balagna first began making wine with his grandfather in Colorado. When he retired in 1986, he went into winemaking full time, and today he makes a number of unique wines on his Pajarito Acres property. Among them are Celeste Blanco, a blend of Seyval and Muscat Canelli white grapes, a humorous blend called Dago Red ("I'm Italian," he laughs) to go with pastas and tacos, and a selection of more conventional whites and reds from Chardonnay and Riesling to red Zinfandel and rosé. In 1993, he marked the 50th anniversary of the atomic bomb with his "La Bomba Grande." A most congenial host, Balagna loves nothing more than to give tours and to talk to folks.

BLACK MESA WINERY
Owners: Gary and Connie
   Anderson.
800-852-MESA.
1502 Highway 68, Velarde,
   NM 87582.
Closed: Sun.

A retired orthopedic surgeon, Gary Anderson began making wine at home for fun in the 1970s. Now he and Connie live on the road to Taos, in fruit country where grapes have been grown for centuries. This is the place to taste big reds fermented in oak barrels, and the proprietors love to share their love of their occupation.

SANTA FE VINEYARDS
Owner: Len Rosingana.
505-753-8100.

Len Rosingana learned about wines from his Italian grandparents in California and later restored the old Ruby Hill winery in the Livermore

Rte. 1, Box 216, Española,
NM 87532.
20 miles N. of Santa Fe on
U.S. 285.
Closed: Major holidays.

Valley. He started Santa Fe Vineyards in 1982 hoping to embody the spirit of northern New Mexico. That first year, Rosingana produced some 200 cases of wine; today he's making upwards of 8,000 cases a year, and his wines have repeatedly won top awards in state competitions. Stop by for a tour. Just the smell of the place is enchanting, not to mention the array of Peña T-shirts and prints, green chile, tortilla chips, pastas, pine nuts and wonderful, inexpensive wines. If your tastes are anything like ours, you'll particularly enjoy the 1993 Chardonnay, a delightfully fruity and spicy selection.

LA CHIRIPADA WINERY
Owners: Mike and Patrick
Johnson.
505-579-4437.
P.O. Box 191, Dixon, MM
87525.
About 3 miles E. of N.M. 68
on N.M. 580.
Open: Daily.

Sometime when you're shuttling between Santa Fe and Taos on N.M. 68, take a detour at the Dixon turnoff for a taste of heaven. Mike and Patrick Johnson started this little family vineyard in 1977 and began making wine in 1981. At 6,100 feet, La Chiripada is the highest commercial vineyard in the United States, where they successfully cultivated the heartiest of grapes (two Pinot Noir hybrids, for example) that ripen into intense flavors. Each year they crush some 50 tons of fruit — a third from their own little vineyards and two-thirds from those at lower elevations. The combined results, several of which have won bronze medal awards in the *Dallas Morning News* National Wine Competition, speak for themselves. These wines are surprisingly good. We recommend the Primavera, a blend of Riesling and French hybrids, served at the Santa Fe School of Cooking.

CHAPTER SEVEN
For the Fun of It
RECREATION

Two campers in New Mexico, 1893.

With high mountain terrain, clear blue skies and several million acres of forest lands, the Santa Fe–Taos area offers a bountiful backdrop for year-round outdoor fun. Fishing, hunting, camping, golfing, boating, biking, horseback riding, running — every sport has its place and season. In the spring, rafters buck the frothing rapids of the Rio Grande and balloonists float high over scenic hills. Summer hikers roam backcountry trails between 7,000 and 13,000 feet, while windsurfers sweep across the choppy waters of wide-open lakes. In the fall, hunters and fishermen take to rivers and hills with visions of lunker trout, kokanee salmon, and trophy deer and elk. The winter mountains become a snowy wonderland, offering world-class ski areas, myriad cross-country trails and challenging snowmobile highways.

BALLOONING

The Taos Mountain Balloon Rally attracts over 70 hot air balloons each year.

For a blessedly quiet bird's-eye view of the Santa Fe–Taos area, there's nothing better than to hop in a basket and cast your fate to the wind. In **Santa Fe**, the place to call is **Santa Fe Detours** (505-983-6565 or 800-338-6877), located on the plaza above Haagen-Dazs at 54-1/2 E. San Francisco St. They can arrange a ballooning experience for $135 a person.

In **Taos**, **Paradise Hot Air Balloon Adventures** (505-751-6098; Box 6466, Taos, NM 87571) offers valley and Rio Grande Gorge flights year-round for $215 a person, which includes an hour flight and breakfast or brunch; as well as a $155 45-minute flight. Paradise will arrange for special flights, too; they've flown weddings, anniversaries and even one divorce! Ask about the special full-moon flight. **Pueblo Balloon Company in Taos** (505-751-9877; NDCBU 7213, Taos, NM 87571) is also available to take you aloft.

BICYCLING

From smooth country highways to rugged mountain trails, you can't beat the Santa Fe–Taos area for road biking and knobby-tired mountain bike adventure. If your heart is set on road biking, be sure to bring your own bike; it's almost impossible to get touring rentals in Santa Fe or Taos. And if you're mountain biking, remember: (1) mountain bikes are not allowed in wilderness areas; (2) be considerate of hikers and those on horseback; (3) trails are usually steeper and more difficult than forest roads; and (4) trail conditions change markedly with the weather. For a listing of bike races throughout the state, call **City Different Cyclery**, 505-983-4473.

Santa Fe Area

One of the best ways to start pedaling in Santa Fe is to get hold of a *Santa Fe Bicycle Map* in the Public Works office at City Hall (505-984-6620; 200 Lincoln Ave., Santa Fe, NM 87501) or at one of the bicycle dealerships listed below. This map, compiled by the members of the **Sangre de Cristo Cycling Club,** shows both recreational and utilitarian routes in and around the city. Other good publications are the *New Mexico Bicyclist's Guide,* compiled by the state Highway Department, and *Santa Fe on Foot: Walking, Running and Bicycling Routes in the City Different,* by Elaine Pinkerton. Both of these are available at most local bookstores and sports shops. The best mountain bike guides to the area are *The New Mexico Mountain Bike Guide* and *The Mountain Bike Guide to the Jemez Mountains,* by Chris Shaw and Brant Hayenga.

There are some great mountain biking trails minutes from downtown Santa

Murrae Haynes

Racers hang together in the early going of the Santa Fe Classic's opening hill climb.

Fe and a couple of places to rent the sturdy-framed, low-geared contraptions. (Rental prices in 1997 ranged from $15–$18 for a half day, $18–$30 for a full day and $75–$110 for a week.) Camino La Tierra accesses a number of easy trails on city-owned land close to town. For more aggressive riding, try the arroyo behind St. John's College, the Chamiso Trail, Pacheco Canyon Road or any of the myriad trails off the Aspen Vista parking lot near the top of the Ski Basin Road. For other good routes, call the *Santa Fe National Forest* at 505-438-7840.

Places offering bike tours in the Santa Fe area include: *Bike N Sport* (505-820-0809); *Dayrider Mountain Bike Tours* (505-474-7660) and *New Mexico Mountain Bike Adventures* (505-474-0074).

Taos Area

Mountain biking trails in the Carson National Forest off U.S. 64 will take you all the way to Angel Fire. A favorite route for families is Rio Chiquito, a long Forest Service road off N.M. 518 that connects with Garcia Park, including beaver ponds and good picnicking. Picuris Peak, also with access off N.M. 518, is a good intermediate-to-expert route with a steep grade but a great view. For more detailed recommendations, call or stop in at the *Carson National Forest* office (505-758-6200; 208 Cruz Alta Rd., Taos, NM 87571).

BICYCLE DEALERS

Santa Fe

Ace Mountain Bikes (505-982-8079; 825 Early St.). Mountain bike repairs and information.

City Different Cyclery (505-983-4473; 1161 St. Michael's Dr.). Sales and service, mountain bike rentals and a wealth of road-bike information.

Known World Adventures (505-983-7756 or 800-983-7756); 825 Early St. Hourly, half day and full day rentals, with guides available.

Palace Bike Rentals (505-984-2151; 409 E. Palace). Mountain bike rentals, including helmet, lock, water bottle, map and advice.

rob and charlie's (505-471-9119; 1632 St. Michael's Dr.). Specialists in retail, parts and repair, with over 4,000 parts in stock; good biking info and BMX stud bikes for kids.

Santa Fe Mountain Sports (505-988-3337); 518 Old Santa Fe Trail. Offers new suspension bikes; open every day.

Sun Mountain Bike Rental (505-983-5155); 121 Sandoval, in Alpine Sports, just off the Plaza. Hotel delivery available.

Tees & Skis (505-983-5637); 107 Washington Ave, on the Plaza.

Taos Area

Cottam's Ski & Outdoor (505-758-2822) offers a selection of specialized bikes, right by the Plaza.

Gearing Up (505-751-0365; 129 Paseo del Pueblo Sur). Centrally-located sales and service, mountain bike rentals, books, maps and info. Geared toward general bike users.

Hot Tracks Cyclery (505-751-0949; 729 Paseo del Pueblo Sur, Suite D). Sales and service, mountain bike rentals, maps, books and info. Geared toward enthusiasts, friendly and knowledgeable.

Native Sons Adventures (505-758-9342 or 800-753-7559; 1033 Paseo Del Pueblo Sur). Mountain bike sales, rental, service, tours and info.

Taos Mountain Outfitters (505-758-9292; 114 S. Plaza). Mountain bike rentals.

BOATING

(See "Water Sports")

CAMPING

(See also "Hiking and Climbing")

Many first-time visitors are surprised and delighted to find a land of lush mountain wilderness, including scores of idyllic campsites. Public, vehicle-accessible sites in national forest and state park areas are usually open from May through October and available on a first-come, first-served basis. There are also myriad backcountry campsites for those on the trail (usually requiring overnight permits) plus a number of private camping areas that offer trailer hookups and tent sites with all the amenities. For maps and specifics on public areas, contact the government agencies listed under "Hiking and Climbing." For information and reservations at private RV campgrounds, contact the following:

PRIVATE CAMPGROUNDS

Near Santa Fe

Camel Rock RV Campground (505-455-2661; Rte. 5, P.O. Box 360-H, Santa Fe, NM 87501). About 10 miles north of Santa Fe on U.S. 285 near Camel Rock. Owned by Tesuque Pueblo, it includes 68 full hookups and pull-through sites, tent sites, security gate, fishing pond, laundry, phones, restrooms, and handicapped-accessible showers. Open year-round.

Los Campos Recreation Vehicle Park (505-473-1949; 3574 Cerrillos Rd., Santa Fe, NM 87501). One of two full-service RV parks within the city limits, with 94 full hookups, four tent sites, restrooms, shower, laundry, swimming pool and car rentals.

Pecos River Campground (505-421-2211; Off I-25 toward Las Vegas on exit 319, 40 miles north of Santa Fe). A popular resting spot near Pecos National Monument with convenience store, full hookups and pull-through sites, movie and VCR rentals, laundry, fishing, showers and "Santa Fe Trail wagon ruts."

Rancheros de Santa Fe Camping Park (505-466-3482; 736 Old Las Vegas Highway, Santa Fe, NM 87505). Exit 290 off I-25 and drive one mile east on Old Las Vegas Highway. Wooded and open sites for tents, trailers and motor homes with pool, showers, restrooms, groceries, hiking trail, laundry and propane.

Santa Fe KOA (505-982-1419; Rte. 3, Box 95-A, Santa Fe, NM 87501). Exit 290 off I-25 and drive three miles east on Old Las Vegas Highway. Full hookups, pull-through sites, tent sites, groceries, laundry, bathrooms and rec room.

Near Taos

El Bordo Trailer Park (505-377-6617; 3063 N.M. 434, Angel Fire, NM 87710). Ten RV spaces in the pines, electric, septic and water. Open May 15–Oct. 15.

Golden Eagle RV Park (505-377-2286 or 800-388-6188, P.O. Box 458, Eagle Nest, NM 87718). Off N.M. 64, a 531-space RV park, including 30 pull-throughs, restrooms, showers, pay phone, RV supplies, gas and game room.

Questa Lodge (505-586-0300; P.O. Box 155, Questa, NM 87556.). A quarter mile off N.M. 522 in Questa, on the Red River. Motel and RV park with 26 full-service hookups, five cabins, tent sites, laundromat, restrooms and children's playground, open May 1 through October.

Roadrunner Campground Group (505-754-2286; P.O. Box 588, Red River, NM 87558). On Main Street. Camping for 150 vehicles with 89 full hookups, laundry, showers, tennis court, restrooms, cable TV, playground, barbecue area, picnic tables, fire ring, tipis and gazebo.

Valley RV Park (505-758-4469; Box 7204, NDCBU, Taos, NM 87571). At 120 Estes Road. Complete commercial campground including 35 full hookups, 75 water and electric hookups, 18 tent sites, playground, rec room, showers, phones, convenience store and laundromat. Open March 15 through Oct. 31; Nov. 1–March 15 with limited services available.

CASINOS

You can't drive very far in northern New Mexico without running into one of the new Indian-run gambling casinos. While the pros and cons of gambling are hotly debated, on the streets and in the courts, the casinos remain up and running, with packed parking lots. If you yearn to try your luck without going all the way to Las Vegas, Nevada, just join the crowd. Many also serve lavish, low-cost buffets.

Camel Rock Casino (800-GO-CAMEL). Ten minutes north of downtown Santa Fe on U.S. 84/285. Run by Tesuque Pueblo, Camel Rock offers slots, blackjack, bingo, roulette and a $1.99 breakfast buffet.

Cities of Gold Casino (800-455-3313). Fifteen miles north of Santa Fe on U.S. 84/285. Cities of Gold is run by Pojoaque Pueblo and has over 700 slot machines, in addition to other games, as well as an "extravagant" 24-hour buffet spread.

Ohkay Casino (505-747-1748). Just north of Española on U.S. 84/285. Operated by San Juan Pueblo, this popular casino is well-known for its breakfast buffet.

Taos Mountain Casino (505-737-0777). Taos Pueblo. The only non-smoking casino in the state, Taos Mountain offers slots but no bingo.

FITNESS CENTERS

Whether it's weight training, aerobics, racquetball, stretching, swimming or yoga, rest assured there are plenty of gyms to suit your needs. Most of them also employ fitness experts who are ready and eager to help you with a program tailored to meet your needs. Many offer racquetball facilities. In 1997, membership rates varied between $45–$75 a month or $330–$720 a year, and rates for nonmembers were between $5 and $10 a day.

Santa Fe

Bulldog Gym (505-988-5117; 1512 Paseo de Peralta). Specializes in one-on-one personal fitness training.

Carl and Sandra's Conditioning Center (505-982-6760; 153-A Paseo de Peralta, in the DeVargas Center). Run by Olympic trainer Carl Miller and his wife, this gym specializes in individualized personal weight training, aerobics, nutrition, stress management and exercises for pregnant women.

Club International (505-473-9807; 1931 Warner Ave.). Separate rooms specialize in Nautilus, free weights, aerobics (including bench step) and cardiovascular exercise. Also offers lap pool with water exercises, six racquetball courts, treadmills, Stairmasters, Lifecycles, Biocycles, Combi-Cycles, whirlpool, individualized fitness programs, sauna, steam room and child care.

Fitness Plus (505-473-7315; 1119 Calle del Cielo off Cerrillos Rd.). A club for women only, with varied fitness classes, Nautilus, free weights, toning tables, massage, facials, acupuncture, body wraps and child care.

Fort Marcy Complex (505-984-6725; Fort Marcy Park off Washington St.). The city's major sports complex, with gym, weight room, jogging course, racquetball courts, aerobic and workout room. Rates in 1997 were $4 per visit with a $25/year membership card. Nonmember and student rates also available, at $35 a month.

Mandrill Gym (505-988-2986; 708 W. San Mateo). A serious weight training center with free weights, Flex machines, aerobics, women's body shaping classes and sports massage.

Momentum (505-992-8000;1807 2nd St.). Offering fitness programs including "the method" taught by Joseph Pilates and other mind-body connecting fitness programs.
Santa Fe Spa (505-984-8727; 786 N. St. Francis Dr., just north of Picacho Plaza Hotel). Includes indoor lap pool, racquetball courts, free weights, Nautilus and Cybex equipment, treadmills, Lifecycles, Stairmasters, classes in aerobics (including Step Reebok), belly dance and yoga, individual training, sauna and steam rooms, whirlpool, massage and physical therapy.

Taos Area

Northside Health and Fitness (505-758-2855; Box 4701, Taos, NM 87571). A new, very friendly, handicap-accessible, community-oriented fitness center with indoor and outdoor pools, four tennis courts, Cybex weight equipment, aerobics classes, cardiovascular room with Cybex rowers and Nordic Track skiers, physical therapy, kids' activities and great drumming classes! Day passes available for $9.
Taos Spa & Court Club (505-758-1980; 111 Dona Ana Dr., across from the Sagebrush Inn). Includes racquetball, tennis, indoor and outdoor pools, aerobics, weight room with free weights and machines, personalized instruction, hot tubs, sauna, steam rooms, child care and summer kid camps. Day passes available for $10.

GOLF

Most people don't think of New Mexico as a golf haven, but the sport is becoming increasingly popular in these parts. Local courses, varying between 6,000 and 8,600 feet in elevation, offer some of the highest fairways in the world, with terrain ranging from brushy plains to rolling hills thick with conifers. Most clubs hold seasonal tourneys, with schedules available at the pro shops.

GOLF CLUBS

Santa Fe

Santa Fe Country Club (505-471-0601; Airport Rd., P.O. Box 28125, Santa Fe, NM 87502). Designed by one of the first PGA members more than 50 years ago, this 18-hole, par-72 course features tree-shaded golfing close to town. Usually open March through November, it has four sets of tees with distances between 6,703 and 7,091 yards and a ladies' course measuring 5,955 yards. It also includes a driving and chipping range and a practice putting green. In 1997, resident greens fees were $25 weekdays, $35.00 weekends; nonresident $45 weekdays and weekends. Pro on duty is Joe Tiano.

Golfers tee off at 7,000 feet in Northern New Mexico.

Corrie Photography

Near Santa Fe

The Cochiti Lake Golf Course (505-465-2239; 5200 Cochiti Hwy., Cochiti, NM 87083) is rated number five in the state and among the top 25 public courses in the country. Set against a stunning backdrop of red-rock mesas and steep canyons, it features an 18-hole, par 72 course of 6,400 yards along with a driving range, putting green, pro shop and restaurant complete with green chile cheeseburgers. Pro on duty is Bill Winfield. In 1997, greens fees were $20 weekdays, $25 weekends or $30 and $35 respectively to ride. Open all year, weather permitting.

Los Alamos Golf Course (505-662-8139; 4250 Diamond Drive, Los Alamos, NM 87544). This course is 18 holes, par 71, 6,500 yards. It includes driving range, putting green, bar and snack bar. Pros on duty are Dennis McCloskey, Donny Torrez and Mike Clancy. In 1997, greens fees were $17.50 weekdays, $22 weekends.

Pendaries Village Golf & Country Club (505-425-6076; P.O. Box 820, Rociada, NM 87742). About an hour-and-a-half out of Santa Fe, on the north side of Las Vegas. With a well-deserved reputation as one of the state's most beautiful golf courses, Pendaries is an 18-hole, par 72 mountain course at 7200 feet. 1997 greens fees are $36 weekdays; $40 weekends, with a $22 golf cart rental charge. Has a pro shop, snack bar and restaurant with bar. Pro on duty is Tom Neilsen. Open April 15–Oct. 15.

Near Taos

Angel Fire Golf Course (505-377-3055; Angel Fire Resort). At 8,600 feet, this is one of the highest and most lushly wooded regulation courses in the world. Usually open from mid-May to mid-October, it's an 18-hole, par-72 course with driving range and putting greens, club and cart rentals, and a restaurant and bar. Pro instruction is offered by Chris Stewart. In 1997 the greens fee was $45 weekdays; $50 weekends.

Red Eagle Golf Course (505-754-6569; P.O. Box 10, Red River, NM 87558). At 8,800 feet, this 18-hole, par-72 course is even higher than that of Angel Fire, with a pro shop. It's located halfway between Red River and Eagle Nest. 1997 fees were $20 weekdays and weekends. Pro on duty is Charlie Houts.

HIKING AND CLIMBING

Cradled by mountains containing two national forests and numerous wilderness areas and state parks, north central New Mexico offers more than three million acres of public forest land with hundreds of miles of lakeshores and cold mountain streams. Most of this land is truly wild and forested. It is also laced with more than a thousand miles of well-maintained trails that vary from a half-hour's guided nature walk to a two-week pack trip.

The primary recreation areas are the *Santa Fe* and *Carson National Forests*. A few of the gems within these two massive preserves include the 223,333-acre *Pecos Wilderness*, east of Santa Fe with magnificent aspen and evergreen forests; the 5,200-acre *Dome Wilderness* in the volcanic Jemez Mountains to the west; the 41,132-acre *San Pedro Parks Wilderness* with rolling, spruce-studded mountaintops and open meadows; and the rugged *Wheeler Peak* and lake-strewn *Latir Peak Wilderness* areas northeast of Taos.

Hikers of all levels enjoy the beauty of trails through the Sangre de Cristos.

Corrie Photography

NATIONAL FOREST OFFICES

Santa Fe Area

Santa Fe National Forest, Supervisor's Office (505-438-7840; 1220 St. Francis Dr., P.O. Box 1689, Santa Fe, NM 87504). Contact this office for general information, maps of the Santa Fe National Forest and detailed topo maps of Pecos and San Pedro Parks Wilderness areas.

Coyote Ranger District (505-638-5526, in Santa Fe; Coyote, NM 87012). Handles San Pedro Parks Wilderness area.

Española Ranger District (505-753-7331; P.O. Box R, Española, NM 87532; Corner of Santa Clara St. and Los Alamos Hwy., Española).

Jemez Ranger District (505-829-3535; Jemez Springs, NM 87025, between Los Alamos and Jemez Springs on N.M. 4).

Pecos Ranger District (505-757-6121; P.O. Box 429, Pecos, NM 87552; Exit 299 Glorieta, Pecos, N.M. 50).

Taos Area

Carson National Forest, Supervisor's Office (505-758-6200; 208 Cruz Alta Rd., Taos, NM 87571).

El Rito Ranger District (505-581-4554; P.O. Box 56, El Rito, NM 87530; at junction of N.M. 110 and N.M. 96).

Peñasco Ranger District (505-587-2255; P.O. Box 68, Peñasco, NM 87553).

Questa Ranger District (505-586-0520; P.O. Box 110, Questa, NM 87556; two miles east of Questa on N.M. 38). Handles 20,000-acre Latir Peaks Wilderness Area north of Red River.

Tres Piedras Ranger District (505-758-8678; P.O. Box 38, Tres Piedras, NM 87577; one mile west of junction of U.S. 64 and U.S. 285).

NATIONAL MONUMENTS (NEAR SANTA FE)

Bandelier National Monument (505-672-3861; National Park Service, Los Alamos, NM 87544) includes nearly 50 square miles of mesa and canyon country with myriad walking, hiking and overnight camping opportunities in the land of the Anasazi. Short trails in Frijoles Canyon lead through ancient ruins and cliff dwellings; longer trails lead south through canyons and west to the Dome Wilderness. Tsankawi (SANK-a-wee), located off N.M. 4, a smaller monument area near White Rock, offers several miles of trails through unexcavated ruins.

Pecos National Monument (505-757-6414; National Park Service, Drawer 11, Pecos, NM 87552) is two miles south of Pecos off N.M. 63. It includes a handicapped-accessible, self-guided trail through ruins of the old Pecos Pueblo and church. (For more information on Pecos or Bandelier, see Chapter Five, *Sacred Sites*.)

STATE PARKS

New Mexico State Parks and Recreation (505-821-7173 or 888-667-2757; P.O. Box 1147, Santa Fe, NM 87504).

Near Santa Fe

Hyde Memorial (505-983-7175; 12 miles northeast of Santa Fe via Ski Basin Rd.) Offers 350 acres of mountains and streams with trails and camping and picnic areas.

Santa Fe River (505-827-7173). Includes five narrow acres of greenery with a few picnic tables along Alameda Street, a few blocks from the center of town.

Taos Area

Cimarron Canyon (505-377-6271; three miles east of Eagle Nest via U.S. 64). A 33,000-acre mountainous preserve with numerous wonderful trails and camping and picnic areas.

Kit Carson Memorial Park (505-758-4160; in Taos). Offers short walks and a playground on 22 acres.

Rio Grande Gorge Park (505-758-4160; 16 miles southwest of Taos on N.M. 570). Includes shelter, barbecues, drinking water and campgrounds along the road by the river. Now under jurisdiction of the Town of Taos.

ORGANIZATIONS, BOOKS & MAPS

Santa Fe Area

For an excellent introduction to some of the fine trails in the Santa Fe–Taos area, we suggest you contact the *Santa Fe Sierra Club* (505-983-2703; 440 Cerrillos Rd., Santa Fe, NM 87501). During the spring and summer months, they run two or three trips of varying difficulty every weekend. They've also published a book entitled *Day Hikes in the Santa Fe Area,* detailing numerous short hikes, many of which can be made into overnight journeys. Another good hiking contact is the *Randall Davey Audubon Center* (505-983-4609).

For equipment, detailed maps and excellent advice on Santa Fe area hiking and climbing, we also suggest you contact *Base Camp* (505-982-9707; 322 Montezuma) or *Wilderness Exchange* (505-986-1152; 513 W. Cordova Rd.) The bookshelves of these two shops include some popular guides you might also want to peruse.

You can also get topo maps of the northern New Mexico area at *New Mexico Office Solutions* (505-988-8991; 515 Cerrillos Rd., Santa Fe, NM 87501).The *Bureau of Land Management* (505-438-7400; P.O. Box 27115, Santa Fe, NM 87502-0115) has an invaluable series of 1:100,000 scale maps based on the USGS series showing roads, trails and land ownership by color. For a variety of hiking and backpacking treks, call Bill Neuwirth at *Tracks* (505-982-2586). He'll arrange for anything from birding to wild edible hikes to animal tracking.

Taos Area

In Taos, one of the best wilderness contacts is **Taos Mountain Outfitters** (505-758-9292; 114 S. Plaza, Taos, NM 87571). In addition to routes and rentals, most of their salespeople are avid hikers and climbers. They also have a little publication called *Taos Rock*, which will steer you toward the best rock climbing in the area. Another bet is **Native Sons Adventures** (505-758-9342; 715 Paseo del Pueblo Sur, Taos, NM 87571), which rents backcountry gear and offers a variety of wilderness treks. **Sipapu Lodge and Ski Area** (505-587-2240; Rte. Box 29, Vadito, NM 87579) also offers hiking opportunities.

HORSEBACK RIDING

Packing through the Pecos Wilderness is a high alpine delight.

Murrae Haynes

(See also "Hunting and Fishing")

Horse travel may not be as common today as it was in the days of yore, but it's definitely alive and well. You can still get a whiff of the Old West as you saddle up and head on out, whether for a few turns around the corral, a picnic ride or a week-long pack trip. Following are some local outfitters. In 1997, prices ranged from $20–$35 per hour, with special rates for longer trips.

Santa Fe Area

B Bar C Stables (505-471-3331; W. Alameda, Santa Fe). Riding year-round, by appointment, easy access from town, sunset rides, beginners can learn.

Bear Creek Adventures (505-757-6229; Rte. 1, Box 21-D, Pecos, NM 87552). Operating out of the Glorieta Conference Center, Eric Roybal and his family offer a variety of horseback and horsedrawn experiences, from trail rides to sleigh rides and hay rides.

Bishop's Lodge (505-983-6377; P.O. Box 2367, Santa Fe, NM 87504, Bishop's Lodge Rd.). Approximately two-hour guided trail rides within the lodge's 1,000-acre grounds, starting at 9:30 a.m. and 2 p.m. most days except Sundays. Also 7:30 breakfast rides. Call for reservations.

Broken Saddle Riding Co. (505-470-0074; 26 miles from Santa Fe plaza in Cerrillos). 360 degree views along the Turquoise Trail.

Galisteo Inn (505-466-4000; Box 4, Galisteo, NM 87540; about 1/4 mile east of N.M. 41 in Galisteo). Trail rides in Galisteo Basin. Limited to riders over 12.

Rancho Encantado (505-982-3537; Rte. 4, Box 57-C, Santa Fe, NM, 87501). About eight miles north of Santa Fe off N.M. 592. Trail rides for guests only.

Rancho las Palomas (505-466-3874; 15 miles N. of Santa Fe in Canoncito). Children welcome.

Terrero General Stores and Riding Stables (505-757-6193; P.O. Box 12, Terrero, NM 87573). Owners Huie and Sherry Ley run sightseeing and photography trips, as well as seasonal hunting, fishing and pack trips into the Santa Fe National Forest and the Pecos Wilderness.

Taos Area

Adventures in the Great Outdoors (505-758-7332; Taos). Wildlife viewing, fishing trips.

Bitter Creek Guest Ranch (505-754-2587; P.O. Box 310, Red River, NM 87558, 2-1/2 miles north of Red River on Bitter Creek Rd.). High country trail rides, elk photo and video trips.

Bobcat Pass Wilderness Adventures (505-754-2769; Red River). Elk and other wildlife viewing, gold mine tours, city slicker ranch rides.

Rio Grande Stables (505-776-5913 or 888-508-7667; Taos Ski Valley). Mountain riding in the Taos Ski Valley.

Roadrunner Horseback Tours (505-377-6416 or 800-377-6416; N.M. 434, Angel Fire). Cattle drives, fishing trips.

Shadow Mountain Guest Ranch (505-758-7732; Taos Canyon, U.S. 64, six miles from Taos). Trail rides through alpine country.

Taos Indian Horse Ranch (800-659-3210; P.O. Box 3019, Taos, NM 87571; on Miller Rd, Taos Pueblo). For well over two decades, Stormstar and Sandy have offered horseback and sleigh rides with big draft horses, Southwest studies and cookouts, Indian storytellers and Taos Mountain music. Reservations required.

HUNTING AND FISHING

The Santa Fe–Taos area is a hunting and fishing paradise. Gun or bow hunters can bag not only deer, elk, squirrels, game birds and waterfowl but also wild turkey, antelope, elk, bighorn sheep, javelina — even exotic species such as ibex and oryx. Lake fish include bass, perch, catfish and walleye. Koka-nee salmon (introduced from the Pacific Coast) and five species of trout abound in stocked lakes and streams.

Before you go, be sure to get licenses and current rules and regulations from the *New Mexico Department of Game and Fish* (505-827-7911; 408 Galisteo St., Santa Fe, NM 87501) or from a local sporting goods store. You may also call or write them for their list of registered guides and outfitters. For information on hunting and fishing on Indian lands, see "Pueblos" in Chapter Four, *Culture*. You don't need a license to hunt or fish there, but you must have written per-mission and an official tribal document showing legal possession of any game or fish taken.

Rainbows and browns abound in the streams of northern New Mexico.

Corrie Photography

For information on conditions and places to go, talk to any local guide or out-fitter. They can take you to prime fishing and hunting territory, both public and private. If you decide to use a guide, check with the National Forest Service or the Bureau of Land Management to make sure the outfit has proper permits and insurance. Prices for guides and outfitters vary widely, depending on the kind of hunt and the accommodations. In 1997, they ranged from $220 for a day of fishing to around $4,000 for a five-day elk hunt, with the most luxurious trips going as high as $10,000, depending on a variety of factors such as quarry, des-tination and time.

GUIDES AND OUTFITTERS

Santa Fe

Base Camp (505-982-9707; 322 Montezuma St.). Specializes in hike-in flyfishing.
High Desert Angler (505-988-7688; 435 S. Guadalupe St., Santa Fe, NM 87501). This is *the* fly-fishing center of Santa Fe, including instruction and guide ser-

vice, rentals, equipment sales and expert, friendly advice from owner Jan Crawford. She can also tell you about She Fishes!, a popular local women's flyfishing club with many scheduled trips.

Known World Guide Service (800-983-7756; Santa Fe). Takes you to the Wild and Scenic Rio Grande, Red River, the Pecos River and Santa Fe National Forest.

Oshman's Sporting Goods (505-988-4466, De Vargas Center Mall). Here you'll find anything from spinning and fly rods to rifles and shotguns with all the eggs, lures, flies and accessories you'll ever need.

The Outdoorsman of Santa Fe (505-983-3432; 506 W. Cordova Rd. in the Coronado Center). An archery and bowhunting headquarters with an indoor archery range.

Ron Peterson Guns (505-471-4411; 509 Airport Rd., Santa Fe). Guns, ammo, rods, reels, bows, black powder, scopes — the works. Also the home for Imperial Taxidermy, which does game heads, fish, reptiles and life-size animals.

Santa Fe Flyfishing School Guide Service (505-986-3913; Santa Fe). Trips throughout northern New Mexico.

Near Santa Fe

Bear Creek Adventures (505-757-6229; Rte. 1, Box 21-D, Pecos, NM 87552). Operating out of the Glorieta Conference Center, native New Mexican Eric Roybal leads all kinds of hunting and fishing trips into the Sangre de Cristos.

Terrero General Stores and Riding Stables, Inc. (505-757-6193; P.O. Box 12, Terrero, NM 87573). Owner Huie Ley leads minimum four-day hunting and fishing trips into the wildest areas of the Sangre de Cristo Mountains. A native of Terrero, he's one of the best outfitter-guides anywhere.

Taos

Los Rios Anglers (505-758-2798; 226-C North Pueblo Rd., Taos, NM 87571). Owners Van Beacham and Jack Woolley are two of the best fly-fishing guides in the state. They've got a complete fly-fishing shop offering gear, information and year-round pack and float trips — including trips into the Rio Grande Gorge and isolated fishing on private lands.

Near Taos

Bitter Creek Guest Ranch (505-754-2587; P.O. Box 310, Red River, NM 87558). Fully licensed outfitter and guide, featuring deer and elk hunts into the mountain area of Valle Vidal.

Deep Creek Wilderness (505-776-8423; P.O. Box 721, El Prado, NM 87529). This family outfit is operated by Jesse Gonzales, whose ancestors have hunted and fished in the Taos area for generations. He offers hunting, fishing, horseback, camping and sightseeing trips in the Carson National Forest, Latir

Lakes Wilderness and Valle Vidal area, reputed to have one of the biggest elk herds in the country.

Eagle Nest Marina (505-377-6941; P.O. Box 66, Eagle Nest, NM 87718). Owner Mo Finley offers fishing equipment and trips for cutthroat, rainbow, coho and kokanee all seasons at Eagle Nest Lake, including ice fishing in the winter.

High Mountain Outfitters (505-377-2240; P.O. Box 244, Eagle Nest, NM 87718). Run by Pancho Trujillo, one of the best licensed hunting guides in northern New Mexico. He specializes in big-game trophy hunts with gun and bow for elk, deer, antelope, sheep, bear, mountain lion and turkey, plus summer fishing and backpacking trips. All hunts include food, lodging, guides and transportation.

Rio Costilla Park (505-586-0542; P.O. Box 111, Costilla, NM 87524). Fishing and hunting trips on a 79,000-acre private reserve in the Latir Lakes area about 40 miles north of Taos. Trespass fee required for private hunting; call to arrange for guided trips.

PARKS IN TOWN

Following is a list of parks in Santa Fe and Taos that offer open space, quiet and recreational opportunities for everyone. For maps and further information, contact the *Santa Fe Parks and Recreation Division* (505-473-7228 or 505-473-7236; 1142 Siler Rd., Santa Fe, NM 87501 or the *Taos Parks and Recreation Department* (505-758-4160).

Santa Fe

Amelia White (Old Santa Fe Trail and Corrales Rd.). A small, natural park with pleasant sitting spots, walking paths and access for the handicapped.

Asbaugh (Cerrillos Rd. and San Jose Ave.). A long, narrow finger of green next to the Santa Fe Indian Hospital. Includes picnic tables, tennis court, baseball and soccer fields, walking paths, basketball court and access for handicapped.

Cathedral (Palace Ave. and Cathedral Pl.). A quiet, fence-enclosed lunch spot with picnic tables a block east of the plaza.

Fort Marcy-Magers Field (Washington Ave. and Murales Rd., north of Paseo de Peralta). A major facility complete with picnic tables, restrooms, grills, tennis court, baseball field, indoor swimming pool, fitness room, gymnasium, playground, walking paths, par course and handicapped access.

Frank S. Ortiz (Camino de las Crucitas). A large neighborhood park with shelter, tennis courts, soccer field, walking paths, playground and handicapped access.

Gen. Franklin E. Miles (Siringo Rd. and Camino Carlos Rey). Many square blocks' worth of sports fields and fun, including rest rooms, picnic tables, shelter, softball field, indoor swimming pool, paths, playground and handicapped access.

Larragoite (Agua Fria Rd. and Potencia St., near Larragoite Elementary School). A neighborhood park offering picnic tables, tennis courts and softball field.

The Plaza. The city's oldest and most-used facility with benches and trees in the very heart of town.

Ragle (W. Zia Rd. and Yucca St.). Many acres of athletic fields near Santa Fe High School, offering picnic tables, grills, shelter, restrooms, baseball fields, pathways, playground and handicapped access.

Randall Davey Audubon Center (see under "Historic Buildings and Sites," in Chapter Four, *Culture*).

Salvador Perez (Alta Vista and Letrado Sts.). A square block of open, green playground with picnic tables, restrooms, tennis courts, softball field, indoor swimming pool, horseshoe pit, racquetball, volleyball, fitness room, trails and handicapped access.

Santa Fe River (Along Alameda St.). A refreshing sliver of green with picnic tables bordering the Santa Fe River.

Villa Linda (Rodeo Rd. at Villa Linda Mall). Picnic tables, soccer field, playground and handicapped access.

Washington (Washington Ave. and S. Federal St.). A quiet, landscaped park with benches and big shade trees right next to the post office and courthouse. A great picnic spot.

Taos

Filemon Sanchez Park (Slightly outside the south side of town). Includes baseball diamonds and other recreation facilities.

Fred Baca Memorial Park (505-758-8234; Camino del Media, just outside the town limits). A four-acre municipal park with picnic tables, restrooms, two tennis courts, basketball court, soccer field, volleyball court and playground.

Kit Carson Park (505-758-8234;N. Pueblo Rd., a block from the plaza). A 20-acre park with bike and walking path, picnic tables, grills, playground, tennis court, basketball court, amphitheater and ice skating. Includes the graves of Kit Carson, Mabel Dodge Luhan, Padre Martinez and other famous Taoseños.

RAFTING, CANOEING, KAYAKING

Northern New Mexico's wild and scenic waters provide some of the best whitewater thrills in the country. The best time for such trips is usually late May through late July, but stretches along the Rio Grande from the Colorado border all the way to Cochiti Dam are negotiable all year. You can also float several stretches of the Pecos River between Cowles and Las Vegas. For recorded information on river flows, call 505-758-8148. For maps and information on permits, seasons and conditions, contact the *Bureau of Land Management* (505-758-8851; 224 Cruz Alta Rd., Taos, NM 87571).

Most commercial float companies provide half-day, full-day and overnight rafting trips on the Rio Grande and the Chama. A relatively serene float, ideal for families, is the **Lower Rio Grande Gorge**. Two of the most popular white-water stretches are the **Racecourse** and the **Taos Box** on the upper Rio Grande, with foaming Class IV waters that are bound to awaken your wild side. The Chama's Wild and Scenic waters offer beautiful overnight trips. Prices in 1997 were $38–$45 for half-day trips, $84–$97 for a full day with lunch, and around $225 for overnights with all equipment and meals provided. Three-day trips and special discounts are also available. With increasing restrictions on river use, early booking is advised.

COMMERCIAL FLOAT TRIPS AND RENTALS

Rafting one of the gentler rapids of the Rio Grande's frothing Taos Box.

Murrae Haynes

Santa Fe

New Wave Rafting Company (505-984-1444; 107 Washington Ave. or Rte. 5, Box 302-A, Santa Fe, NM 87501). One of the largest and most reputable rafting outfitters in the area.

Rio Grande River Tours (505-758-0762 or 800-525-4966; Box 1-D, Pilar Route, Embudo, NM 87531).

Santa Fe Detours (505-986-0043; 52-$^1/_2$ E. San Francisco St., Santa Fe, NM 87501). Books tours with numerous rafting companies.

Santa Fe Rafting (505-988-4914 or 800-467-RAFT; 1000 Cerrillos Rd., or P.O. Box 23525, Santa Fe, NM 87502).

Southwest Wilderness Adventures (505-983-7262 or 800-869-7238; 142 Lincoln Ave., Suite 103, or P.O. Box 9380, Santa Fe, NM 87504).

Whitewater Information and Reservations (800-338-6877). Clearinghouse that books approved local rafting companies.

Taos Area

Far Flung Adventures (505-758-2628 or 800-359-2627; P.O. Box 707, El Prado, NM 87529).

Los Rios River Runners (505-776-8854 or 800-544-1181; 23 Ski Valley Rd., or P.O. Box 2734, Taos, NM 87571).

Native Sons Adventures (505-758-9342 or 800-753-7559; 1033 Paseo del Pueblo Sur, Taos, NM 87571).

Rio Grande River Tours (505-758-0762; Box 1-D, Pilar, Rte. Embudo, NM 87531).

RODEOS

The Santa Fe–Taos area has its roots in the Old West. No event emphasizes this more clearly than the rodeo, which hearkens back to the 19th century when much of New Mexico was dominated by the cattle industry and its rough-and-tumble cowboys.

In July, you can attend the *Rodeo de Santa Fe*, with some of best riding and roping anywhere. A downtown parade of riders from all over the country kicks off the festivities. (Before July 4, call Carl Fisher at 505-988-5043; after July 4, call 505-471-4300.)

Toward the end of July, you can drift on down to the *Rodeo de Galisteo*, a somewhat smaller though no less exciting Wild West event. Up north toward the end of June, you can take in the *Rodeo de Taos* (800-732-8267) at the Taos County Fairgrounds.

RUNNING

Runners here enjoy an exceptional variety of terrain and unusually clean, clear skies. From mountain highways and trails to secluded city byways, there's no better place to develop your legs and lungs while enjoying the unspoiled open spaces. For a comprehensive listing of races throughout the state, call the *New Mexico Track and Field* (505-865-8612; 118 Amherst N.E., Albuquerque, NM 87106).

Santa Fe

The *Santa Fe Striders* running club (505-983-2144; P.O. Box 1818, Santa Fe, NM 87504) starts fun runs from the plaza every Wednesday evening at 6 p.m. in the summer months. Contact them for information on seasonal running events. A few good running spots in Santa Fe include the east side, the banks of the Santa Fe River along Alameda Street, the Old Santa Fe Trail and the St. Cather-ine's cross-country course. For more information on these and other good routes, consult John Pollak of the Striders (505-983-2144) or *Santa Fe on Foot*, by Elaine Pinkerton. For longer jaunts, try the Ski Basin Road and some of the routes listed under "Biking."

Taos

Each year, Taos hosts at least one 10-kilometer race, plus a triathlon in the fall and a marathon in June. Since there's no organized running club, your best bet is to check for dates and times with the **Taos County Chamber of Commerce** (800-732-TAOS; P.O. Drawer I, Taos, NM 87571). Another popular event in the area is the annual **Wheeler Peak Mountain Run** (800-348-6444), a half marathon usually held the last weekend in June. For training runs, the outskirts of Taos quickly lead to fairly flat, wide-open spaces, particularly toward the north, east and west.

SKIING

DOWNHILL SKIING

Santa Fe–Taos is a skier's paradise, boasting a half dozen areas with some of the most popular world-class slopes in the country. Many of the ski areas start at 9,000–10,000 feet and rise to 12,000 or more, making for vertical drops in excess of 2,500 feet with annual snowfalls up to 300 inches.

A few hardy souls began skiing at the Santa Fe Ski Basin shortly after World War II, and Lloyd and Olive Bolander set up the first rope tow at Sipapu in 1952. The sport really began to take off in 1955, when pioneer Ernie Blake began carving out a mountain niche for families at the Taos Ski Valley. Other spots such as Red River and Angel Fire followed during the 1960s. Since then, lifts, lodges, lounges, snowmaking and myriad cross-country trails have created a major resort area that now draws skiers from all over the world.

In general, you can count on some of the beginner and intermediate runs to be open by late November, the remaining runs by the middle of December. Snowmaking usually creates a number of good trails by Thanksgiving at Angel Fire, Red River, Santa Fe and Taos Ski Valley. All areas are open daily from 9 a.m. to 4 p.m. with the exception of Pajarito Mountain near Los Alamos, which is open only on Wednesdays, weekends and federal holidays.

NEW MEXICO SKI INFORMATION

New Mexico Snophone (505-984-0606). Recordings 24 hours a day, updated daily at 1 p.m.

Ski New Mexico, Inc. (505-984-0606 or 800-755-7669; P.O. Box 1104, Santa Fe, NM 87504). Call to order your free copy of *New Mexico Skiers and Snowboarders Guide*.

Near Santa Fe

A skier goes airborne at the Santa Fe Ski Basin.

Don Strel

SANTA FE SKI BASIN
505-982-4429 (information), 505-983-9155 (snow report) or 800-982-SNOW (reservations).
1210 Luisa St., Suite 5, Santa Fe, NM 87501; (505-983-9155) in-town office number.
15 miles N.E. of Santa Fe via N.M. 475 (Ski Basin Rd.).
Peak Elevation: 12,000 ft.
Vertical Drop: 1,650 ft.
Annual Snowfall: 225 in.
Snowmaking: 30% of area.
Trails: 38 Downhill (20% beginner; 40% intermediate; 40% advanced. No X-C.
Lifts: 4 Chairlifts (1 quad, 1 triple, 2 double); 1 poma, 2 Mitey Mites.
Tickets (1997/98): Adults $39; half-day $25; seniors & children $24.
Ski School Pro: Bill Gould.

The Santa Fe Ski Basin got its start in the 1930s with sheep and Indian trails as the basis for runs. The first ski area was developed a few miles down from its present site, at Hyde Park. By 1947, two dogleg rope tows with Cadillac engines lugged a few hardy skiers to the top of a nearby hill. In the early '50s, the first chairlift was built at the present site — using Army Air Corps surplus seats from a B-24 bomber and a 50-year-old cable from a nearby mine.

Currently, five modern lifts ferry skiers to 12,000 feet, the second highest slope in the country. At the top of the triple chair, you can take in 80,000 square miles of awe-inspiring views. You'll also find relatively short lift lines and some of the best family skiing in the state. Beginner and intermediate skiers can always find comfortable slopes, while advanced stretches like Parachute and Wizard — not to mention Tequila Sunrise and Big Rocks with their deep powder and ungroomed moguls — provide challenges and thrills for the very best.

The ski school at the basin, which includes Telemark and snowboard classes, will take kids as young as three. You can get day care for the younger kids if you arrange for it in advance. There's also the on-slope Totemoff Bar and Grill, La Casa Mall at the base of the mountain, a cafeteria, a boutique and over 1,500 pairs of rental skis.

PAJARITO MOUNTAIN
505-662-5725 (information); 505-662-SNOW (snow report).
Los Alamos Ski Club, Inc. P.O. Box 155, Los Alamos, NM 87544.
7 miles W. of Los Alamos via N.M. 502 and F.R. 1.
Peak Elevation: 10,441 ft.
Vertical Drop: 1,241 ft.
Annual Snowfall: 153 in.
Snowmaking: None.
Trails: 37 Downhill (20% beginner, 50% intermediate, 30% advanced). No X-C.
Lifts: 5 Chairlifts (1 triple, 3 double, 1 quad); 1 rope tow.
Tickets (1997/98): Adults $32; half-day $23, seniors & children $21.
Ski School Pro: Jerry Byrd.

Pajarito was started in 1957 by a group of Los Alamos National Laboratory employees who wanted a convenient place to ski. The area is owned and operated by the Los Alamos Ski Club, whose members are mainly Los Alamos employees or residents; however, it's also open to the public.

Pajarito is geared toward the serious day skier. Its runs are steeper, shorter and rougher than most areas, which can be frustrating for beginners. On the other hand, some experts consider its runs the most challenging in the state. "If you can ski bumps, you're in heaven," says one of our friends. "If you're a novice who gets stuck on a bumpy run or goes into the trees, it's just hell." In recent years, there's been an effort to increase grooming to accommodate all levels of skiers.

There's no resort atmosphere at Pajarito — you won't find bars, lounges or day care for the kids — but you will find a three-story lodge with ski rentals and a nice cafeteria. You'll also find one of the rarest pluses of any ski area: no lift lines. Also, with only three skiing days a week, the snow at Pajarito lasts a relatively long time. Because of this and its small-town family atmosphere, many consider it an undiscovered gem.

Near Taos

TAOS SKI VALLEY
505-776-2291 (information); 505-776-2916 (snow report) or 800-776-1111 (reservations).
P.O. Box 90, Taos Ski Valley, NM 87525.
18 miles N.E. of Taos via U.S. 64 & N.M. 150.
Peak Elevation: 11,819 ft.
Vertical Drop: 2,612 ft.
Annual Snowfall: 320 in.
Snowmaking: 35% of area.
Trails: 72 Downhill (24%

Dreaming of his own resort, Taos Ski Valley (TSV's) indefatigable founder Ernie Blake spent countless hours flying his small plane over the Sangre de Cristo Mountains, scouting for the perfect site. The valley he finally located got an inauspicious start as a ski resort, with unreliable investors and near inaccessibility. But Blake persevered. When TSV opened as a fledgling family ski area in 1955, a 300-foot, diesel-driven T-bar was its first lift. TSV has never looked back.

The tradition at TSV is service, and that begins with excellent engineering and design. From lift

Steep runs make for big thrills at Taos Ski Valley.

Ken Gallard; courtesy Taos Ski Valley

beginner, 25% intermediate, 51% advanced); No X-C.
Lifts: 10 Chairlifts (4 quad, 1 triple, 5 double); 1 surface lift.
Tickets (1997/98): Adults $40, half-day $27, children $25, teen $30, seniors 65–69 $24, 70 & over free.
Ski School Pro: Max Killinger.

line management to trail marking to cafeteria food to ski school programming, the pattern is consistently high quality. Even with a record-breaking abundance of snow and people, the whole system usually works flawlessly. Exceptions are the parking lots, which because of the lay of valley tend to be long and narrow.

Lowlanders will definitely feel the elevation here. Drink plenty of water (no alcohol) and take frequent rests. The views across the valley and over to neighboring Kachina Peak (12,481 feet) are worth a pause. The skiing is challenging, even for experts, but there are plenty of intermediate and novice slopes as well, including a few from the very top. The combination of trails called Honeysuckle, Winklereid and Rubezahl can bring even a first-day skier down safely from the peak. If you're into pushing the envelope, you'll do no better than to bump and pump your way down such mogul-studded trails as the infamous Al's Run (under the #1 and #5 lifts) or to try the steep trails off the West Basin Ridge.

Amenities are provided at mid-station snack bars (Phoenix and Whistlestop) and in numerous lodges and restaurants at the base. Families are efficiently accommodated, with day care for tots ages six weeks and up, ski school for the kids, convenient lockers and storage baskets, and a most welcome addition: ski patrollers who actually patrol the slopes and slow traffic down in tight quarters. In or near the base lodge, you'll find about 2,000 pairs of rental skis, lodging for more than a thousand skiers, all manner of books and souvenirs, and numerous festive events.

ANGEL FIRE RESORT
800-633-7463 (information,
  snow report and reservations).
P.O. Drawer B, Angel Fire,
  NM 87710.
22 miles E. of Taos via U.S.
  64 & N.M. 434.
Peak Elevation: 10,650 ft.
Vertical Drop: 2,180 ft.
Avg. Snowfall: 210 in.
Snowmaking: 60% of area.
Trails: 62 Downhill (33%
  beginner, 51% intermediate, 16% advanced); new
  groomed 35K X-C track.
Lifts: 5 Chairlifts (4 double,
  1 high-speed quad); 1
  surface tow.
Tickets (1997/98): Adults
  $36, children $20, over 65
  free. X-C $5 a day.
Ski School Pro: Robin May.

Texan Roy H. Lebus started Angel Fire Resort in 1967, with little more than a dream and a handful of dedicated workers. Today it is known as a family resort and a "cruiser's mountain," featuring a variety of long, well-groomed trails (the longest is 3.5 miles).

Angel Fire is predominantly tailored to beginning and intermediate skiers; however, it also offers a number of outstanding expert runs, as evidenced by the fact that the 1982 World Cup Freestyle championships were held here. Widespread snowmaking guarantees 2,000 vertical feet of skiing even in the driest of years, and only in the very busiest of times does the lift line require more than a five- or 10-minute wait. Another plus is the large picnic pavilion on the mountain that can accommodate several hundred skiers at a time.

With 3,000 beds, Angel Fire has one of the largest, most affordable lodging bases in the state. During reduced-rate periods, it's possible for Dad and Mom and two kids under 12 to stay for little more than $100 a night. The resort also boasts more major (and offbeat) events than almost any other area — for example, the world shovel race championships, featuring the wild antics of riders careening down the mountain at over 60 miles an hour on scoop shovels.

RED RIVER SKI AREA
505-754-2220 (information,
  snow report) or 800-331-
  SNOW (reservations).
P.O. Box 900, Red River,
  NM 87558.
37 miles N. of Taos via
  N.M. 522 & N.M. 38.
Peak Elevation: 10,350 ft.
Vertical Drop: 1,600 ft.
Avg. Snowfall: 190 in.
Snowmaking: 78% of area.
Trails: 57 Downhill (32%
  beginner, 38% intermedi-
  ate, 30% advanced); X-C
  available nearby at
  Enchanted Forest.
Lifts: 6 Chairlifts (4 double,
  2 triple); 1 surface lift.
Tickets (1997/98): Adults
  $37, half-day $27, teen

Red River was started in 1961 by a well-loved oilman and character named John Bolton, and its first lift consisted of used derricks and cables Bolton imported from an oil field in Texas. Located in the northern arc of the Enchanted Circle, Red River is another family-friendly ski area, with extensive snowmaking and numerous wide, beginner and intermediate trails. Runs like Kit Carson and Broadway allow plenty of room for everybody to fall down, while expert speedways like Cat Skinner and Landing Strip are enough to get anyone's adrenaline pumping. The area rents about 1,000 pairs of skis, with another 2,000 pairs available in Red River. It also hosts on-slope bars and restaurants.

Red River features a 4,500-bed lodging base less than a block from the ski area; an annual winter carnival with dogsled races and horsedrawn sleighs;

$30,children & seniors $23.
Ski School Pros: Dick Pelton, Ron Pockrandt

the annual New Mexico Cup in February; and February's "Mardi Gras in the Mountains," when the whole town turns to cooking Cajun food and dressing in festive Southern garb. There's also a Kinderski school for ages 4–10 and Buckaroo Child Care for ages six months to four years.

SIPAPU LODGE & SKI AREA

505-587-2240 (information, snow report).
Rte. Box 29, Vadito, NM 87579.
25 miles S.E. of Taos via N.M. 68 & N.M. 518.
Peak Elevation: 9,065 ft.
Vertical Drop: 865 ft.
Avg. Snowfall: 110 in.
Snowmaking: 30% of area.
Trails: 20 Downhill (20% novice, 50% intermediate, 30% advanced); X-C available in nearby Carson National Forest.
Lifts: 3 Lifts (1 triple chair, 2 pomas).
Tickets (1997/98): Adults $28, half-day $20, children $21.

Sipapu was started by Lloyd and Olive Bolander, who first brought a small portable rope tow to the area in 1952. The next year, they offered 30 pairs of rental skis with "bear-trap" bindings. Now, more than 40 years later, Sipapu is many times its original size, but it's still owned and operated by the same family. (Lloyd and Olive teach skiing, and their son Bruce gets up early to tend to the snow.) The Bolanders like to think of their guests as family, too, and the area's laid-back atmosphere helps everyone feel at home.

This refreshingly small, quiet, ski area focuses mainly on beginner and intermediate fun. (The longest run, Beep-Beep, is about 1.5 miles from top to bottom.) It is also known as a telemark mountain. Lots of times after a pleasant run, you can jump right back on the lift with no wait at all. The area includes a restaurant and a snack bar, about 750 pairs of rental skis, on-slope lodging for nearly 200 and another 375 beds nearby. Though it lacks high-tech equipment and plush lodging, Sipapu is just about custom made for families on a budget.

WHERE TO BUY AND RENT SKI EQUIPMENT

All the ski areas listed offer a good supply of on-slope rental equipment. You can also find ski rentals, sales and service at numerous shops in Santa Fe, Taos and other towns near the ski areas.

Santa Fe

Ace Mountain Wear (505-982-8079; 825 Early St., Suite B). Custom clothing for skiers and snowboarders.
Alpine Sports (505-983-5155; 121 Sandoval). Downhill and cross-country sales and rentals.
Base Camp (505-982-9707; 322 Montezuma). Cross-country sales and rentals.
rob and charlie's (505-471-9119; 1632 St. Michael's Dr.). Snowboard sales and rentals.

Ski Tech Ski Rentals (505-983-5512; 905 S. St. Francis Dr.). Cross-country rentals, fast computerized service.

Skier's Edge (505-983-1025; 1836 Cerrillos Rd.). Downhill, cross-country and snowboard rentals.

Wild Mountain Outfitters (505-986-1152; 513 W. Cordova Rd.). Cross-country and Telemark sales.

Near Santa Fe

Cottam's Ski Rentals (505-982-0495; Hyde Park, Ski Basin Rd.). Downhill and cross-country rental and accessories, snowboards, inner tubes and sleds.

Sports Bag (505-662-2454; Los Alamos Community Center, Los Alamos). Downhill and cross-country sales, cross-country rentals.

Taos

Adventure Ski Shops (505-758-9744 or 800-433-1321; 303 Paseo del Pueblo Norte; 505-758-1167; S. Santa Fe Rd.). Downhill and cross-country sales, service and repairs.

Cottam's Ski Shops (505-758-8242 or 800-322-8267; 707 S. Santa Fe Rd., across from Furrs; 505-758-1697, Kachina Lodge in north Taos). Downhill and cross-country rentals and service, and snowboards.

Taos Mountain Outfitters (505-758-9292; 114 S. Plaza). Cross-country rentals only.

Terry Sports (505-776-8292; 314 Paseo del Pueblo Norte, next to Thunderbird Lodge). Downhill and cross-country sales, rentals and repair.

Near Taos

Alpine Ski Rentals and Lodging (505-377-2509 or 800-530-8754; N.M. 434, Angel Fire). Downhill sales, rentals and repairs; snowboard rentals.

Cottam's Ski Shops (505-776-8719 or 800-322-8267; Taos Ski Valley). Downhill and cross-country rentals and tuning.

8000 Plus (505-377-3516; Mini Mart Plaza, Angel Fire). Downhill ski rentals and tuning.

High Country Ski Rentals (505-377-6424 or 800-344-6424; Red River). Downhill rentals and service.

Mickey's Ski Rental (505-377-2501; 212 Main St., Eagle Nest). Downhill ski rentals and repair.

Millers Crossing Ski and Sportswear (505-754-2374; Millers Crossing, W. Main Red River). Cross-country sales, service, rentals and lessons.

Mountain Sports (505-377-3490; N. Angel Fire Rd., Angel Fire). Downhill ski sales and rentals, boots, clothing, snowboards.

Roadrunner Tours Ltd. (505-377-6416; 3404 NM 434, Angel Fire). Downhill ski and clothing rentals.

Sitzmark Sports (505-754-2456 or 800-843-7547; Main & Malletta, Red River). Downhill ski and snowboard sales, rentals, repair and clothing.

Ski Tech (505-377-3213; Village Center, N. Angel Fire Rd., Angel Fire). Downhill ski sales, rentals, repair, accessories.

Terry Sports (505-776-8292; Taos Ski Valley). Downhill and cross-country sales, rental and repair.

Valley Ski Rental (505-377-2286; U.S. 64, Eagle Nest). Downhill sales, rentals and repair.

Whitewater Ski Rentals (505-776-1842 or 800-544-1181; 23 Ski Valley Rd., near the blinking light north of Taos). Downhill, cross-country and Telemark sales, rentals and repair.

Wild Bill's Ski Shop (505-754-2735 or 800-659-8879; Main St., Red River). Downhill ski rentals and repair.

CROSS-COUNTRY SKIING

If you're looking for solitude and the quiet sound of skis sliding over back-country trails, take a break from the lift lines and go touring or Nordic. Almost anytime from December through March, you can find myriad snow-covered trails lacing national forests and wilderness areas, plus countless public trails and a few privately groomed trails within the area. For current snow conditions and maps, contact the national forest offices listed below. Some of the more popular books on the subject include: *Ski Touring in Northern New Mexico,* by Sam Beard; *Skiing the Sun,* by Jim Burns and Cheryl Lemanski; and *Cross-Country Skiing in Northern New Mexico* by Kay Matthews.

PUBLIC SKI TOURING

Santa Fe Area

Some of the best ski touring in the Santa Fe area is in the *Santa Fe National Forest* (Santa Fe office 505-438-7840; 1220 St. Francis Dr., Santa Fe, NM 87501). A few of the more popular trails include those starting from Black Canyon Campground, about nine miles from town via the Ski Basin Rd.; Borrega and Aspen Vista Trails about 13 miles up the Ski Basin Rd; and Winsor Trail just off the Ski Basin parking lot. These and other trails in the area are administered by the *Española Ranger District* (505-753-7331). Ask for recreation staff.

In the Jemez Mountains, Peralta Canyon Rd., the East Fork of the Jemez and Corral Canyon are all good touring areas, as are Fenton Hill and Jemez Falls in the *Jemez Ranger District* (505-829-3535).

Cross-country skiing near Taos.

Murrae Haynes

Taos Area

The *Carson National Forest* offers numerous public ski-touring trails, some of them located right next to the Taos, Red River and Sipapu ski areas. One of the more popular areas in the *Camino Real Ranger District* (505-587-2255) is Amole Canyon off N.M. 518 between Taos and Sipapu. Here the national forest, in cooperation with the Taos Norski Club, maintains set tracks and signs along a three-mile loop that's closed to snowmobiles and ideal for skating. There are also six- and seven-mile unmaintained loop trails at the same location. Another popular snowmobile-free route off N.M. 518 is Picuris Lookout, with exceptional mountain views. Capulin/La Sombra, about five miles east of Taos off U.S. 64, is a flat, 1.5-mile trail that's great for skating.

Popular routes in the *Tres Piedras Ranger District* (505-758-8678) include Maquinita Canyon, Biscara Trail, Burned Mountain, and Forest Road 795. In the *Questa Ranger District* (505-586-0520 or 505-758-6200), try East Fork, Ditch Cabin, Long Canyon or Goose Creek.

Detailed guides for many of the trails listed are available at Carson National Forest offices. Remember that some trails are designated for skiers or snowmobiles only, and some are shared. Restrictions are posted, but be sure to check with the Forest Service for detailed information. Also get hold of the Forest Service's *Winter Recreation Safety Guide,* which lists winter hazards and how to prepare for them.

TOURS AND PRIVATE TOURING CENTERS

Santa Fe Area

For instruction, tours and overnight ski-touring packages in the Santa Fe area, call Bill Neuwirth at *Tracks* (505-982-2586; P.O. Box 173, Santa Fe, NM

87504). *Santa Fe Detours* (505-983-6565 or 800-338-6877) will arrange half or full-day trips. *Southwest Wilderness Adventures* (505-983-7262 or 800-869-7238; P.O. Box 9380 Santa Fe, NM 87504) also offers Nordic ski programs with rentals, clinics and tours.

Taos Area

For cross-country ski instruction and tours in the Taos area, your best bet is to call *Millers Crossing* (505-754-2374) in Red River, or *Whitewater Ski Tours* (505-776-8854 or 800-544-1181). *The* place to go touring near Taos is the *Enchanted Forest Cross Country Ski Area* (505-754-2374; P.O. Box 521, Red River, NM 87558). Just east of Red River atop Bobcat Pass, it offers 30 kilometers of groomed and ungroomed trails amid 600 forested acres. Here you'll find not only prime ski terrain for classical, freestyle and Telemark, but also instructors, patrols, warming huts and rentals. Tickets in the 1997–98 season were $10 a day or $18 for two days; rentals were $10.50 a day or $18 for two days.

SNOWMOBILING

There's an exhilarating network of trails for snowmobilers through both the Santa Fe and Carson National Forests. Many of these regularly groomed mini-highways twist and turn through thick forests to high alpine meadows where speedsters can zoom across wide-open spaces to their hearts' content. Be sure to check with district Forest Service offices (listed under "Public Ski Touring" above) before you choose a trail. Remember to slow down and stay clear of skiers and snowshoers. For maximum safety and fun, choose a trail that's designated for snowmobiles only. Three of the best are Fourth of July Canyon, Old Red River Pass and Greenie Peak in the *Questa Ranger District* (505-586-0520) near Red River. A number of businesses in Red River also provide safe, guided snowmobile tours, complete with mountaintop hot-dog cookouts. And in January the *Angel Fire Ski Area* (800-446-8117) hosts the *Angel Fire Snowmobile Festival*, with races, free rides, buffet dinner and prizes.

SPAS AND HOT SPRINGS

Still bubbling and steaming in the aftermath of its relatively recent volcanic activity, northern New Mexico is dotted with natural hot springs. Private bath houses have been built over two such spots, at Ojo Caliente and Jemez Springs (outside the area), and numerous other gurgling hotspots can be found in the open air. Just outside Santa Fe there's even a Japanese bathhouse offering everything you could want in a natural spring, and more.

Near Santa Fe

*Go up to Ten Thousand
Waves for a luxurious soak
in a hot tub overlooking
Santa Fe.*

Mary Neiberg

TEN THOUSAND WAVES
Japanese Health Spa.
505-982-9304.
Ski Basin Rd., Santa Fe, NM
    87501.
Open daily.
Reservations: Strongly
    recommended.

Only 10 minutes' drive from the Santa Fe Plaza, Ten Thousand Waves can confidently claim to be the most beautiful and peaceful spa in the Santa Fe–Taos area. Disengagement from everyday cares begins when you park in the lot and walk up a winding, stepped path illuminated at night by ground-level Japanese lanterns. Up top, gurgling water and giant goldfish slip by as you cross a bridge and ascend to the lobby. Here you may sign in for any of a host of pleasures, including hot tubs public or private, with special men's and women's tub hours scheduled.

Some of the mountainside tubs, though discreetly screened, have lovely views through the pines. The public tubs (including coed and women's tubs) are convivial places where idle conversation and subdued jollity prevail, while private tubs have the allure of romance or the challenge of solitary meditation. Locker rooms are stunningly handsome, with thoughtful extras ranging from kimonos and thongs to soap, shampoo and cedar lotion. Massage therapy runs the gamut, from Swedish to Shiatsu.

A special feature is an especially relaxing massage in water called Watsu, plus a new "Master's Massage" given by a practitioner with over 20 years' experience. There are salt rubs, herbal wraps and more. A well-stocked health-food snack bar in the lobby and a cozy fireplace make lingering an added pleasure. Services are not cheap (in 1997, private tubs ran $18–$25 per person per hour, massages $65 an hour and facials $65), but the pleasures are priceless.

Near Taos

**OJO CALIENTE
  MINERAL SPRINGS**
505-583-2233.
P.O. Box 68, Ojo Caliente,
  NM 87549.
S.W. of Taos on U.S. 285.
Closed: Christmas.
Reservations: Required for
  private tubs.

This is the most popular mineral springs spa in northern New Mexico, featuring natural hot waters with therapeutic iron, arsenic and lithium. Attendants in separate men's and women's locker areas pamper and guide you either to individual cubicles with fresh water for 15-minute arsenic soaks (great for arthritis and rheumatism) or to a large, enclosed outdoor grotto area with hot iron water. There's also a coed bathhouse with individual rooms for couples. After your soak, an attendant will put you on a table and cover you head to toe with steaming hot cotton blankets for further relaxation or in preparation for a full-body massage.

Before returning to the "real" world, you're invited to take a shower (soaps and shampoos provided), a swim in the heated outdoor pool, a peaceful walk beside giant cottonwoods, or to fill cannisters with any of the three healthful mineral waters. You can even go riding if you want. Prices have been going up quite a bit in recent years, but as of 1997 they were: $16 for an all-day pass including soak and sweat wrap Mon.–Fri.; $22 for the same on weekends and holidays; and $59 an hour for massage. The *Inn at Ojo* (see "Lodging Near Taos," in Chapter Three, *Lodging*) also offers overnight packages for couples, including breakfast and two mineral baths apiece.

SWIMMING

Opportunities for swimming abound in the Santa Fe–Taos area, from lakes and rivers to numerous fine municipal and private pools. Popular swimming lakes within the area include *Cochiti* (505-465-0307), *Abiquiu* (505-685-4371), *Heron* (505-827-7173), *El Vado* (505-827-7173), *Storrie* (505-827-7173) and *Eagle Nest* (505-377-2420). Swimming in the Rio Grande is discouraged, due to the rocky bottom and strong undertow, but you can spend time near the river at the Wild Rivers Recreation Area north of Taos and the Orilla Verde Recreation Area on the south end of Taos (505-758-8851).

Santa Fe

In Santa Fe you'll find four indoor public pools and one outdoor pool, available for a small fee for adults and free for children seven and under. For details on times, classes and activities, call the city swimming pools division (505-984-6758). For numbers and addresses of private pools, see "Fitness Centers" and individual entries in Chapter Three, *Lodging*. Municipal pools include:

Bicentennial Pool (505-984-6773; on Alto St.). Open only in summer.
Fort Marcy Pool (505-984-6730; 490 Washington Ave.).
Salvador Perez Pool (505-984-6755; 601 Alta Vista).
Tino Griego Pool (505-473-7270; on 1730 Llano St.).

Taos

For swimming opportunities in Taos, there's one municipal pool (505-758-9171; 120 Civic Plaza), which charges a small fee for a swim and shower. There are also pools at the *Quail Ridge Inn* (505-776-2211; Taos Ski Valley Rd.) and the *Taos Spa & Court Club* (505-758-1980; 111 Dona Ana Dr.) available to nonmembers for about $10 a day. Other pools are available in various hotels and motels (see individual entries in Chapter Three, *Lodging*).

TENNIS

With clean air and clear skies most of the year, courts in the Santa Fe–Taos area are usually popping with tennis balls — except when they're snow covered during winter. Even then, both towns have numerous private indoor courts that can be rented any time of the year.

Santa Fe

The City of Santa Fe offers some 27 public tennis courts and four major private tennis facilities, including indoor, outdoor and lighted courts. Some public parks with tennis courts include Fort Marcy, Ortiz, Larragoite, Herb Martinez and Salvador Perez. For specifics and other locations, call the *City Recreation Department* (505-984-6864). The city also offers two four-week instruction sessions in June and July, including an hour-long class daily with a tournament at the end. Costs in 1997 for the entire month plus the tourney was $40 for adults, $30 for kids, tots seven and under $20.

Santa Fe-area clubs with tennis courts include the following:

Bishop's Lodge (505-983-6377; Bishop's Lodge Rd.).
El Gancho (505-988-5000; Old Las Vegas Hwy.).
Sangre de Cristo Racquet Club (505-983-7978; 1755 Camino Corrales).
Santa Fe Country Club (505-471-3378; off Airport Rd.).

Taos

In Taos, the town *Parks and Recreation Department* (505-758-4160, 505-758-8234) maintains two tennis courts at Kit Carson Park and two at Fred Baca Park. There are another five outdoor courts and two indoor courts at the *Taos Spa and Court Club* (505-758-1980; 111 Dona Ana Dr. — $10 an hour per person in 1997), and two indoor courts at the *Quail Ridge Inn* ($35 an hour for non-guests in 1997). Memorial Day through Labor Day this 110-room inn hosts tennis programs, clinics and tournaments. Each summer Quail Ridge offers tennis pros and three USPTA-sanctioned tournaments each year.

WATER SPORTS

(See also "Hunting and Fishing.")

Surprisingly, New Mexico boasts more small boats per capita than almost any other state in the union. Some say it's because of the yearning for water in a state so high and dry. Others say it's because of the spirit of a land once covered by inland seas. But those who really know say it's simply because New Mexico has a lot of good boating. Canoeing, water skiing and fishing as well as boating activity can be found at the following lakes.

Near Santa Fe

Cochiti Lake (505-465-0307; Army Corps of Engineers, P.O. Box 1238, Pena Blanca, NM 87041). About half an hour southwest of Santa Fe off I-25, Cochiti is a "no-wake" lake with free public boat ramps and rentals of canoes, rowboats and fishing boats. There's also a recreation center about a half mile from the lake, with pool and ping pong tables, a swimming pool and a basketball court.

Nambe Reservoir, about 20 miles north of Santa Fe via U.S. 285 and N.M. 503 (take turnoff to Nambe Falls). For boating information, contact, Nambe Pueblo (505-455-2036; Rte. 1, Box 117-BB, Santa Fe, NM 87501).

Santa Cruz Reservoir, a small lake and recreation area near Española (505-438-7400; Bureau of Land Management, 1474 Rodeo Rd. Santa Fe, NM 87505. A "no-wake" lake with a small-boat ramp and a 5-mph speed limit. Swimming allowed only in the northeast picnic area.

Near Taos

Eagle Nest Lake, east of Taos on the edge of the Enchanted Circle. Two shops there can give you information on boat rentals and activities: *Eagle Nest Marina* (505-377-6941; P.O. Box 66, Eagle Nest, NM 87718) and *Lakeshore Marina* (505-377-6966; Eagle Nest Lake, Eagle Nest, NM 87718).

Outside the Area

Abiquiu Lake (505-685-4371; Army Corps of Engineers). About 65 miles Northwest of Santa Fe on U.S. 84. The large, scenic reservoir behind Abiquiu Dam offers a little of everything, from canoeing and windsurfing to fishing and water skiing. No boat rentals are available.

Heron and El Vado Lakes, near the town of Chama. Both are administered by the *New Mexico State Parks and Recreation Division* (505-827-7173), and both have boat ramps and camping facilities. Heron is a "no-wake" lake, especially popular for small sailboats and hobies. Water skiing is allowed at El Vado. For further information, contact the *Stone House Lodge* (505-588-7274; HC 75 Box 1022, Rutheron, NM 87551). From April through Nov., Stone House rentals include 24-foot pontoon boats with awnings and outboard engines, 20-foot Bass Buggies and 14-foot fishing trollers, plus 15- and 17-foot canoes.

Storrie Lake (505-827-7465) six miles north of Las Vegas via N.M. 518, one of the most popular windsurfing spots in the state. It includes a boat ramp and courtesy dock but no boat rentals.

For more information on ramps, rentals and activities, contact the *New Mexico State Park and Recreation Division* (505-827-7173 or 888-NM-PARKS). For new and used boats, motors, parts and accessories and a full-service shop, contact *High Country Marine* (505-471-4077; Race Track Frontage Rd., Rte. 14, Box 315-MC, Santa Fe, NM 87505).

WINDSURFING

A boardsailor bucks wind and waves at Cochiti Lake.

Murrae Haynes

Clear weather and strong breezes wafting across easily accessible lakes combine to make windsurfing one of New Mexico's fastest growing sports. Much of the good surfing, both recreational and competitive, is less than an hour's drive away. The most popular nearby lakes are *Cochiti* (505-465-0307) near Santa Fe, *Eagle Nest* (505-377-6941) near Taos, and *Storrie* (505-827-7465) and *Abiquiu* (505-685-4371) outside the area. Storrie in particular, with its warm water and great winds, becomes a boardsailing mecca in the summer, hosting numerous regattas and family-style beach parties. At most lakes the strongest winds tend to come up in the afternoon, whipping up whitecaps and whisking surfers across the water at dizzying speeds. Watch out for thunderstorms, though; they sometimes blow in with the afternoon winds.

For more information on these and other windsurfing lakes, see "Water Sports." For details on windsurfing events, sales and rentals, contact the *Santa Fe Sailboard Fleet* (P.O. Box 15931, Santa Fe, NM 87506) or *Santa Fe Windsurfing* (505-473-7900; 1086 Siler Rd., Santa Fe, NM 87501).

YOGA

(See also "Fitness Centers" in this chapter).

Santa Fe

Bikram's Yoga College of India (505-988-2887; 110 Valencia Rd., Santa Fe, NM 87501). Practice the Yoga developed by Bikram, the "Yogi to the Stars."

High Energy Yoga Center (505-471-8450; 2754 Agua Fria , N.M. 1, Santa Fe, NM 87501). Pain relief and relaxation offered in beautiful studio with heated floor.

Santa Fe Community Yoga Center (505-820-9363; 1807 2nd St., Santa Fe, NM 87501). A complete Yoga network with 10 instructors of various lineages, prenatal, men's and children's classes, as well as instruction in nutrition and meditation.

White Iris Yoga Studio (505-986-8212; 2214 W. Alameda #D, Santa Fe, NM 87501). Instructor Gail Ackerman and her associates teach classes in Iyengar yoga mornings and evenings. Call for a complete schedule.

Yoga Moves (505-989-1072; 825 Early St., Santa Fe, NM 87501). Excellent instruction and philosophical understanding.

CHAPTER EIGHT
Antique, Boutique and Unique
SHOPPING

T. Harmon Parkhurst; courtesy Museum of New Mexico.

Candelario's original curio store on San Francisco St., Santa Fe, ca. 1915.

Santa Fe and Taos are both cities where cultures converge, and as such they have always been centers of trade. Santa Fe of course sits at the end of the Santa Fe Trail; Taos is perched on the Rio Grande, at the northernmost point of the eight Pueblos. The towns are places where people have always met and exchanged ideas and goods — both decorative and utilitarian.

The contemporary scene is no different — Taos and Santa Fe are shopping centers for Native American art and jewelry, for the painting of both local and international artists, and for the crafts of the entire world. The area presents unique shopping, whether in galleries and boutiques or in the more informal settings of vendors on the plaza.

Trader Jack's Flea Market in Santa Fe is a wonderful example of goods arrayed from as far away as Africa and as nearby as the studios of local artisans. A huge outdoor shopping arena, it is situated next to the Santa Fe Opera (10

The flea market north of Santa Fe is a bargain hunters' paradise; an international bazaar.

Murrae Haynes

minutes north of Santa Fe on U.S. 84/285. Open seasonally Friday–Sunday, 8 a.m.–5 p.m.) where the shopper can browse for fine jewelry and leather, furniture, masks and the occasional odd lot. Beneath a turquoise sky and within sight of the Sangre de Cristo Mountains this is a relaxed place to shop, and prices are generally good.

There's more to discover in the shopping meccas of Taos and Santa Fe than any one guide can easily cover, so we focused on the best of Southwestern arts and our favorite choices from the world bazaar. We kept an eye out for quality and value so whatever your budget, you can find the right keepsake.

Remember that the closer you are to the main plazas, the higher the prices. Whenever you are buying, ask what materials were used to make the craft item you're considering. Don't assume everything for sale here is made locally. Find out where the item came from. You may want to drive out to the pueblos (see "Pueblos" in Chapter Four, *Culture*) to buy handmade Indian pottery, jewelry and other crafts directly from the artists.

A word about bargaining: Haggling over prices is not a widely accepted practice in New Mexico. Much time and work go into the creation of a pot, a carving or a piece of jewelry, and artists know the value of their work. However, if you have talked to the artist and feel he or she is receptive, a diplomatic discussion of price may be appropriate. Also remember that shop hours may vary with the amount of traffic. It's always wise to call ahead if you're making a special trip.

ANTIQUES

Santa Fe

Antique Warehouse (505-984-1159; 530 South Guadalupe St. #B, at the Railyards). Spanish Colonial antiques, including hard-to-find architectural elements, doors, unusual tables and gracious benches.

Just some of the captivating memorabilia at Arrowsmith's Relics of the Old West.

Murrae Haynes

Arrowsmith's Relics of the Old West (505-989-7663; 402 Old Santa Fe Trail, across from the San Miguel Chapel). A repository of western myth, replete with everything from saddles, spurs, chaps and guns to Indian pottery, rugs, pawn jewelry and bead work to Spanish Colonial religious art.

Claiborne Gallery (505-982-8019; 608 Canyon Rd.). Owner Omer Claiborne, a respected expert on Spanish Colonial antiques, travels the world in search of items for his shop. Antiques from Mexico, Spain, Guatemala, the Philippines and South America are featured.

Susan Tarman Antiques and Fine Art (505-983-2336; 923 Paseo de Peralta). This collection is built around 17th through 19th century antiques from Europe, Asia and America. The porcelain, pewter and silver are highlights of the store, as is the elegant antique furniture.

Things Finer (505-983-5552; inside La Fonda Hotel). Nestled in the classic Pueblo Deco lobby of the La Fonda Hotel, Things Finer is a treasure trove of jewelry, antiques, silver, miniatures and rare icons from Russia. The staff will also do appraisals on items you bring in.

<u>*Taos*</u>

El Rincon (505-758-9188; 114 Kit Carson Rd.). This is part museum and part retail store. In the dim, dusty interior of this centuries-old trading post — said to be the oldest in Taos — you'll see Kit Carson paraphernalia as well as other southwestern relics. The store sells Spanish Colonial antiques, as well as artifacts from Pueblo and Plains Indians. Good contemporary souvenirs, too. Some of the finest contemporary silversmiths market their wares here.

Hacienda de San Francisco Galeria (505-758-0477; 4 St. Francis Church Plaza, Ranchos de Taos). The 18th century Romero Hacienda has seven rooms full of Spanish Colonial antiques from the 17th through the 19th century, hailing from New Mexico, Mexico, Spain and Argentina. Includes furniture, silver, paintings and *santos*.

Old Taos (505-758-7353; 108 Teresina Lane). This antique shop fills the potential buyer with a sense of adventure, as hunting down the right object seems likely in this collection of Pueblo pots, fine pawn jewelry, religious artifacts, Spanish colonial furniture, folk art and fishing memorabilia.

BOOKS

S anta Fe and Taos are both towns full of writers — and readers. Most stores have sections emphasizing publications on the arts, history and culture of the region. Second-hand bookstores are the perfect place to discover a treasure, and all shelves invite some browsing before buying. Keep in mind that most museums and historic sites listed in Chapter Four, *Culture* have bookshops as well.

<u>*Santa Fe*</u>

Alla' Spanish Language Books (505-988-5416; 102 W. San Francisco St.). In keeping with the history of the region, Alla' is devoted to books in Spanish — with about 20,000 general titles and over 2,000 books for kids. Also has Spanish language records and tapes.

Ark Books (505-988-3709; 133 Romero St. off Agua Fria, west of downtown). This New Age bookstore is a complete environment, with an aviary twittering with finches, a tiny garden, statues and crystals galore. Six rooms of book specialize in healing, word religions, relationships, mythology and magic. You can also buy tapes of soothing music, an extensive collection of Tarot cards, jewelry, incense and magical accouterments. A splendid place for a relaxing browse.

Blue Moon Books & Video (505-982-3035; 329 Garfield at Guadalupe St.). Blue Moon Books is a quintessential second hand book store, complete with an array of cats and a knowledgeable owner, Carmen Blue. The store's shelves are strong in the areas of literature, poetry, women's issues, psychology, religion and spirituality. Vintage videos for rent include those of opera and some hard-to-find children's favorites.

Books & More Books (505-983-5438; 1341 Cerrillos Rd.). A collection of antique blue bottles greets the visitor to this spacious used bookstore. Owners poet Leo Romero and painter Elizabeth Cook-Romero keep the large inventory dynamic by buying books all over the country. The art section is excellent, as are those devoted to Southwestern books, fiction, poetry, religion and the natural sciences. There are often unusually good prices on children's classics such as the illustrated Scribner's.

Collected Works (505-988-4226; 208-B W. San Francisco St.). This is the place to go if you are in the mood to read something — but don't yet know what. A fine selection of current fiction and memoir greets you at the entrance. Also has extensive Southwestern books — from local guidebooks to the history and literature of the region.

Dumont Maps and Books of the West (505-988-1076; 301 E. Palace Ave., Suite 1). Formerly Parker Books, Dumont continues to offer a fine selection of antiquarian maps as well as rare and out-of-print Western and Americana books.

Garcia Street Books (505-986-0151; 376 Garcia St. at Acequia Madre). An open, airy space with a wide array of new titles by regional authors, as well as general interest titles and an excellent collection of affordable paperback classics. Specializes in fast special orders. Buy a book, then go next door to the Downtown Subscription, grab an espresso, and enjoy a quiet moment at a little outdoor table.

Browsers delight in the range of titles at Palace Avenue Books, Santa Fe.

Karen Klitgaard

Palace Avenue Books (505-986-0536; 209 E. Palace Ave.). Specializes in Southwestern books, both general interest and scholarly. This is a good source for rare books on Western history, Native Americans and museum art books. Also has a full general stock, including philosophy and religion.

Nicholas Potter, Bookseller (505-983-5434; 211 E. Palace Ave.). A well-loved Santa Fe bookstore of the old school, Nicholas Potter specializes in matching the customer with the right book. The store has rare and used hardbacks, as well as photographs and a collection of classical and jazz records.

Railyard Books (505-995-0533; 340 Read at Guadalupe St.). The newest bookstore in town, the Railyard has well stocked shelves and tables of contemporary literature and non-fiction. There is also a small newsstand, and a cafe for coffee and snacks.

Taos

The Brodsky Bookshop (505-758-9468; 218 Paseo del Pueblo Norte). An intimate shop with a wide range of Western and Southwestern fiction and non-fiction, maps and cards — plus general interest titles. Long a reader's landmark in Taos, the bookstore under new owners Morris Witten and Rick Smith still encourages readers to sit with a book in one of many quiet nooks.

Fernandez de Taos Book Store (505-758-4391; 109 N. Plaza). A nexus of information, the bookshop has both a complete newsstand and a large selection of new books, whether history of the Southwest or the newest Tony Hillerman murder mystery.

G. Robinson Old Prints & Maps (505-758-2278; 124-D Bent St.). Need an 1885 hand-colored map of Alaska or an 1830 steel-engraved map of Tierra del Fuego? This is the place. Some maps are expensive, but many are available for under $100.

Moby Dickens Bookshop (505-758-3050; 124-A Bent St.). A browser's heaven, with several rooms of carefully selected current fiction and non-fiction, as well as at least one requisite friendly cat. The shop also has an upstairs section devoted to rare and out-of-print books.

Taos Book Shop (505-758-3733; 122-D Kit Carson Rd.). At a half-century, this is the oldest book shop in New Mexico. Within the five rooms in a rambling old adobe resides an excellent selection of Southwestern books, both in and out of print, as well as local authors. Cafe Tazza's gracious patio neighbors on the store. You'll find parking in the rear.

CHILDREN'S

Kids do love to shop, whether spending their hard earned pennies, allowance, or their parents' money! However, shopping with children doesn't have to be a stressful experience or even an advanced case of the gimmes. The stores listed here are small, and stocked with toys that can educate as well as entertain.

Santa Fe

Captain Kid Toys (505-988-CAPT; 333 Montezuma St.). SORRY — WE'RE OPEN reads the sign on this toy store which is crammed full of educational toys, building block classics and treasure chests of teeny-tiny treats. But certainly kids will only be sorry to leave.

Doodlet's (505-983-3771; 120 Don Gaspar Ave.). A truly unique store, Doodlet's stocks treasures from chocolate sardines to tin mermaids. Grown ups as well as children won't be able to stop browsing through postcards, stickers, teacups, Victoriana, charms and miniatures.

Horizons—The Discovery Store (505-983-1554; 328 Guadalupe St.). Science and natural history play a part in the fascinating displays here of everything in the world around us, from magnets to dinosaurs. A visit to the store is a trip to a mini-museum — books, globes and guides all help stimulate learning in both children and adults.

Taos

Moretti's for Kids (505-751-7141; 122 D. Paseo del Pueblo Sur). All the children's clothing in the store — from tie dye to brightly colored appliqué — is made locally by a consortium of designers and seamstresses. A great place to find an original new baby gift.

Tiovivo (505-758-9400;103 Paseo del Pueblo Norte). Everything a toy store should be to enchant young patrons. Kites hang from the ceiling, an erector set Ferris wheel turns, and there are enough stuffed animals to stock the most exotic menagerie. Also has books, games, kits and toys for all ages.

CLOTHING

Santa Fe style — or a Southwestern style of dressing — combines traditional elements with individual taste. It emphasizes longer skirts, luscious fabrics and lots of accessories. For men, it combines Western shirts and boots with the decorative bolo tie. Historically, the look comes from western dress, fiesta costumes and Native American styles. It is also contemporary and fashionable, mixing elements together. It may take years to create your own look. Start by shopping in Santa Fe and Taos for items that are uniquely you — and don't be afraid to try unusual combinations as you go. As one turquoise-and-velvet-clad doyenne of Santa Fe declared: "I don't worry about styles. These clothes have been good for 400 years; they'll be good for another year."

CONTEMPORARY

Santa Fe

Blue Fish Clothing, Inc. (505-986-0827; 220 Shelby St.). Blue Fish's signature look is hand printed fabric, resplendent with bright colors and cheerful primitive designs. You can't help but feel relaxed and playful in these comfortable clothes of natural fiber. Also has hats, sweaters, soaps and scents.

Chico's (505-984-1132, 328 S. Guadalupe; 505-989-7702, 101 W. Marcy St.; 505-984-3134, 135 W. Palace Ave.). Chico's clothes for women are sporty yet comfortable, featuring relaxed styles in natural fabrics. Bold prints mix well with basics here, and the costume jewelry collection provides the perfect finishing touches. Excellent for the traveler's wardrobe.

Crazy Fox Boutique (505-984-2224; 227 Don Gaspar Ave. at Santa Fe Village Mall). This outlet for San Francisco designer Karen Alexander shows her trademark style of dresses in flowery prints, as well as other sophisticated styles for women. Good buys here — don't overlook the designer fabrics.

Judy's Unique Apparel (505-988-5746; 714 Canyon Rd.). Judy's has a plethora of simple dresses in showy fabrics — from velveteen to flowered rayon. The collection of scarves is an enticing rainbow of chiffon and chenille, and don't hesitate to try on one of the charming hats. A local favorite.

Lucille's (505-983-6331; 223 Galisteo St.). This store is hung from floor to ceiling with racks of soft loose dresses and separates, many designed in ethnic fabrics. This is the place to find the perfect moderately priced outfit for a special event. Sizes run to the roomy. Another favorite of the well-dressed Santa Fe woman.

Spirit Clothing (505-982-2677; 109 W. San Francisco St.). This top of the line boutique carries clothes from European, Japanese and American designers. A small gallery of contemporary painting graces its walls, and the clothes too are individual works of art.

Zephyr Clothing (505-988-5635; 125 E. Palace Ave.). Unique pieces of women's clothing in velvet, silk, wool and rayon. The coats are specially designed for sale in the store. The place to find that one-of-a-kind.

Taos

Spotted Bear (505-758-3040; 127 Paseo del Pueblo Sur). One of the most extraordinary clothing stores anywhere, Spotted Bear is worth a pilgrimage. Women's clothing here is exotic and exquisite, from velvet animal print scarves to amusing flowered hats. There are dresses of hand painted silk and vintage design outfits, as well as unique raincoats in rich materials. Period look — choose your era — to right-now metallic and faux leopard.

ETHNIC

Santa Fe

Origins (505-988-2323; 135 W. San Francisco St.). One of the best wearable-art shops in the country, Origins is an Aladdin's cave of treasures. Fabrics from around the world mingle with designer clothing and one-of-a-kind art creations. Explore the store to discover tribal arts, antique jewelry, fantasy hats, embroidered shawls and the new gold-and-antiques room. Find the perfect outfit for the opera or your class reunion. The owner's motto is: "We feature forever dressing."

Near Santa Fe

Maya Jones Imports Warehouse (505-473-3641; in the town of Madrid, on N.M. 14 south of Santa Fe). Maya Jones's casual, colorful clothing is based on handwoven Guatemalan cotton textiles. The store also offers jewelry, accessories and folk art from around the world. Prices and the scenery make it well worth the half-hour drive.

Taos

From the Andes (505-758-0485; 103 E. Plaza). Owner Maria Isabel Peterson travels to South America to bring back beautiful handmade woolen sweaters, skirts, dresses, vests, ponchos, hats, bags, wall hangings, dolls and more.

LEATHER

Santa Fe

Char Designs Inc. (505-455-2264; Cuyamungue, 10 miles north of Santa Fe on 285; 505-988-5969; 104 Old Santa Fe Trail). The two stores share a designer—Santa Fe's Char, but the Old Santa Fe Trail store is a high end boutique, which also features Canadian designer Linda Lundstrom's parkas and other dressy cold weather gear. The Cuyamungue store takes a more casual approach, with suedes, Mexican pottery and gift items.
Desert Son (505-982-9499; 725 Canyon Rd.). Custom leather work for men and women, including boots, moccasins and a particularly good selection of belts. The store also features bags and hats—in Western and other styles.

Taos

Overland Sheepskin Co. (505-758-8820; three miles north of Taos on N.M. 522. Also in Santa Fe at 505-983-4727; 217 Galisteo St.). Shearling coats to see you through the coldest winters, plus hats, slippers, mittens and more. Overland has its own production facility near Taos, where you can watch the wool pro-

Overland Sheepskin; rack upon rack of warm, wonderful clothing.

ducers grazing in the fields. The Santa Fe store (505-983-4727; 217 Galisteo St.) has a somewhat larger stock of goods to chose from.

Taos Moccasin Company Factory Outlet (505-751-0032 or 800-747-7025; 216-B Paseo del Pueblo Sur, Box 5279, Taos, NM 87571). This is the place to buy Taos "Indian Maid Mox" manufactured locally since 1953. The outlet stocks mocs for all ages and sizes in factory firsts, plus other leather and suede garments. Check the bargain table for discontinued and factory seconds.

SHOES

Santa Fe

Goler Fine Imported Shoes (505-982-0924; 125 E. Palace). If shoes have personalities, then these range from the saucy to the chic to the downright elegant, in materials from leather to brocade. Upscale shoes from everywhere on the fashion map.

Hopalong Boot Company (505-471-5570; 3908 Rodeo Rd. west of the Rodeo Grounds). If you haven't been left a great pair of boots in a cowboy's will, this is the place to shop. Specializing in "broken in cowboy boots," Hopalong also has a wide array of clothing. There are Navajo-style velvet skirts, as well as denim and fiesta skirts. For men, there are western shirts, vests and more. Before you go dancing, stop in here.

On Your Feet (505-983-3900; 530 Montezuma St., Sanbusco Market Center). For comfortable shoes that look good and cute shoes that feel good, this is the place for both men and women. Also has fabulous socks.

Santa Fe Boot Company (505-983-8415; 950 W. Cordova Rd.). The right boots are certainly necessary to a cowboy, and they are also the basis for a Santa Fe style outfit. Luckily, Santa Fe Boot company offers both working boots and just boots that work well with your wardrobe. A large selection includes trusted brand names, prices are reasonable and there are hats as well, to outfit you literally from head to toe.

Street Feet (505-984-2828, 100 E. San Francisco St.; 505-984-8181, 435 S. Guadalupe St.; 505-984-3131, 221 Galisteo St.). Street Feet has shoes galore from Italy and South America, as well as Canadian boots. About half the stock is clothing, with an emphasis on soft fabrics, including leggings, bags, scarves and belts. For the least formal atmosphere, shop with the locals at the Guadalupe location.

Taos

Steppin' Out (505-758-4487; 120 Bent St.). Two floors of fine leather goods, from shoes to belts to hand bags. Some high end waterproof boots make bad weather not only endurable but a chance for chic. Also a selection of gracious soft clothing.

SOUTHWESTERN

Santa Fe

Monte Cristi Custom Hat Works (505-983-9598; 322 McKenzie). For a hat as individual as you are, hats are made to order at Monte Cristi. They feature western hats, Dick Tracey style fedoras and a few ladies' styles. Prices run $300 and up, but hats will last a lifetime.

Pinkoyote (505-983-3030 or 800-257-PINK; 330 Old Santa Fe Trail). The look here is colorful and casual, featuring unique clothing with Southwestern motifs for any occasion.

Santa Fe Western Mercantile (505-471-3655; 6820 Cerrillos Rd.). This is where cowboys and ranchers shop for real working clothes. Denims, shirts, boots, hats and chaps are available along with saddles and racing tack.

Taos

Martha of Taos (505-758-3102; 121 Paseo del Pueblo Norte, just south of the Taos Inn). Martha was the original designer of classic Taos women's clothing. New owner Sheryl Shockley-Wallace continues to offer traditional and contemporary Southwestern women's clothing as well as art and jewelry.

Yukio's (505-758-2269; 226 Paseo del Pueblo Norte). The store is a collaboration between wife and husband. JoAnn Obara creates the multi-print tiered skirts and broomstick skirts while the silver jewelry is designed by Berny Obara. The little girls' reversible skirt and vest outfits are charming. All items designed and made in the workshop on the premises.

VINTAGE

Santa Fe

Double Take (505-989-8886; 320 Aztec). Santa Fe's premier resale shop, the store has an extensive well-chosen stock, from wardrobe basics to more exotic items. Also has an excellent selection of children's clothing, much of it in mint condition.

Open Hands Thrift Store (505-989-7209, 905 W. Alameda; 505-438-9240, 3965 Cerrillos Rd.; 505-989-1077, 851 W. San Mateo Rd.). There is good hunting here at the thrift stores which benefit Open Hands charities, from clothes to furniture, with particularly good buys in coats and jackets. The West Alameda location is favored by locals for its stock, but may also be picked over, so try and visit more than once.

Serendipity (505-983-6666; 333 Montezuma St.). This consignment store offers the buyer elegant choices in contemporary and Southwestern style clothing and jewelry at considerable savings. A seamstress on the premises can help customize the fit.

Wild Things (505-983-4908;316 Garfield). The sixties aren't dead — nor are the forties and fifties — in this store's warren of rooms filled with tie-dye, vintage dresses and crinolines. The clothes here are fun, costumey and one of a kind.

FURNISHINGS AND RUGS

Santa Fe

Artesanos (505-983-1743, 222 Galisteo St.; 505-471-8020, 1414 Maclovia). The largest distributor of Mexican tile in the U.S., Artesanos features cheerful tiles of birds and flowers that also enliven many local kitchens and bathrooms. Consider individual ones as wall hangings or trivets.

Arius Tile (505-988-1196, 114 Don Gaspar; 505-988-1125, La Fonda Hotel/100 E San Francisco). Since 1972, Arius Tile has been providing Santa Fe with original hand-glazed tiles, both individual designs and as parts of larger mosaics. Has a beautiful collection of Judaica, as well as Virgin of Guadalupe designs.

Design Warehouse (505-988-1555, 101 W. Marcy St.; 505-473-4555, Villa Linda Mall). This is where the locals shop for smooth contemporary design in everything from candles to couches, lunch boxes to beds. Has an excellent selection of modern glass and dinnerware.

El Paso Import Company (505-982-5698; 418 Cerrillos). For the home decorator looking to add a touch of the warmth of Old Mexico, this is the place to shop.

El Paso Import has chairs, tables, sideboards and a wide variety of painted wooden furniture. The store also features pots, pot stands, ceramic candle holders, trunks, ironwork lamps, hardware for doors and old spurs. A second store (505-986-0037; 1519 Paseo de Peralta) carries architectural items such a doors and large benches, in addition to household items.

Heriz Oriental Rugs (505-983-9650; 651 Cerrillos Rd.) is owned by Shahin Medghalchi, who lovingly restores rugs as well as selling old and new kilims. The store features Navajo, Persian and Afghani rugs, as well as custom furniture. Prices are comparatively low and a visit is an educational experience in the world of rugs.

Morrelli (505-992-8867; 540 S. Guadalupe St.). Jeremy Morrelli is the designer who creates heirloom-quality doors and architectural elements that grace the homes of the rich and famous. The showroom is full of the hand-carved and hand-made, from furniture to doorways.

Seret & Sons Rugs and Furniture (505-983-5008, 224 Galisteo St.; 505-988-9151, 149 E. Alameda). Ira Seret has been importing from Afghanistan for over 30 years. In the main showroom on Galisteo, see carved wood and custom-covered couches, chairs and chaises fit for a scene from the Arabian Nights. The Alameda shop has a bazaar layered with lush dhurrries, kilims and carpets.

Southwest Spanish Craftsmen (505-982-1767; 328 S. Guadalupe St.). This is the showroom for the oldest furniture company in the Southwest, founded in 1927. Although the company specializes in Southwestern styles, they work with the customer and have designed everything from English desks to Italian beds. Wood, finish and texture can all be chosen; and books of design help the customer select something individual and beautiful. Work is done painstakingly by local artisans.

Taos Furniture (505-988-1229; 1807 Second St.). This showroom / workshop features furnishings for home and office in a variety of Southwestern based styles. A wide selection of handcrafted, durable, Ponderosa pine furniture.

Taos

Country Furnishings of Taos (505-758-4633; 534 Paseo del Pueblo Norte). Unique and appealing folk-art furniture painted by local artists. In the same design vein are home accessories, jewelry and a panoply of gifts by some of the state's top craftspeople.

Lo Fino Handcrafted Furniture (505-758-0298; 201 Paseo del Pueblo Sur). More than 30 designers of furniture and lighting showcase their work here. Many of the styles and colors draw their inspiration from northern New Mexico. Furniture can be found in both Spanish Colonial and Southwestern contemporary styles. Ask about custom design.

GALLERIES

S anta Fe has about 200 galleries and Taos about 85, certainly enough to keep the most avid art enthusiasts on their toes. Here, we've included the "don't-miss" galleries as well as others that stand out because of their unusual themes, excellent reputation or both. Friday evenings are the traditional time for gallery openings. Check the *Santa Fe New Mexican*'s Friday "Pasatiempo" section for times and places. Gallery categories below include Contemporary Art, Hispanic Folk Art, Indian Art, Photography and Traditional Art. (See also "Posters" in this chapter.)

CONTEMPORARY ART

Santa Fe

These fine-art galleries feature recent paintings, sculpture and prints in both representational and abstract styles. Some focus on Southwestern-inspired work; others are nonregional.

Edith Lambert Galleries, Limited (505-984-2783; 300 Galisteo, Suite 201). Brilliantly-colored work from the Caribbean and some of the most innovative shows in town, including the annual "Art of the Book."

Hand Graphics Gallery (505-988-1241; 418 Montezuma St.). Exciting lithographs, monotypes and photogravures by prominent Southwestern artists like Page Allen, Eric Lindgren and Emmi Whitehorse. Tours of the adjacent printmaking studio are available.

LewAllen Contemporary, Inc. (505-988-8997; 129 W. Palace Ave.). Respected gallery owner Arlene LewAllen features fine contemporary paintings, drawings, sculpture and photography displayed in spacious rooms. Other media are also represented: "I like to have the best examples in clay, glass and steel — one artist in each," Ms. LewAllen says.

Laurel Seth Gallery (505-988-7349;1121 Paseo de Peralta). Represents a younger generation of northern New Mexico artists painting in traditional styles. A great place to begin collecting Southwest art.

Linda Durham Contemporary Art (505-466-6600; 12 La Vega, Galisteo; P.O. Box 601, Galisteo, NM 87540). Long a Canyon Road landmark, Linda Durham Contemporary Art is now a short drive away in quiet Galisteo, where the canvases of Durham's contemporary artists hang on ancient adobe walls. Featuring abstract and contemporary paintings, sculptures and drawings by mostly N.M.-based artists, this gallery is highly respected by serious collectors.

See Canyon Road's finest at The Munson Gallery.

The Munson Gallery (505-983-1657; 225 Canyon Rd.). Beautiful watercolors, oils and drawings by master artists. Represents some of the most highly-regarded and interesting New Mexico artists, such as Melissa Zink and Eddie Dominguez.

Shidoni Foundry and Galleries (505-988-8001; Bishop's Lodge Rd., five miles north of Santa Fe). A must visit. This eight-acre sculpture garden in the lush Tesuque River valley is internationally known. Bronze pourings are on Saturday afternoons; call for times. Open year-round.

Waxlander Gallery (505-984-2202 or 800-342-2202; 622 Canyon Rd.). A strong sense of color characterizes the work of the ten or so New Mexico contemporary artists featured in a 150-year-old adobe. Owner Phyllis Kapp represents an all-too-rare combination of successful painter and gallery operator.

Taos

Bareiss Gallery (505-776-2284; 15 Rt. 150 at the base of the road to Taos Ski Valley). Startling contemporary work, well worth a visit.

The Fenix Gallery (505-758-9120; 228-B Paseo del Pueblo Norte). A small, excellent gallery with paintings, prints and sculpture mostly by Taos artists of national and international repute. Director Judith Kendall has an eye for work that's nonrepresentational but "with a lot of content." Also featured are the expressionistic landscapes of Alyce Frank.

Lumina Fine Art & Photography (505-758-7282; 239 Morada Ln.). A visual feast of art and architecture. The house was built in the 1930s by Tony Luhan, husband of the legendary Mabel Dodge Luhan, and later became the home of Taos Founder artist Victor Higgins. It may be New Mexico's most beautiful gallery, elegantly furnished and filled with the works of Taos artists, northern New Mexico folk artists and contemporary and vintage photographers. The newly opened sculpture garden is a spectacular must-see.

Art lovers can't miss the Ridwan Sculpture Garden at Lumina in Taos.

Karen Klitgaard

New Directions Gallery (505-758-2771; 107-B North Plaza). Some of the deepest and most challenging contemporary art is on display here, including the work of Taos artists Larry Bell, Anita Rodriguez and the sculpture of Ted Egri.

Parks Gallery (505-751-0343; 140 Kit Carson Rd.). High-quality contemporary painting, photography, sculpture, prints and jewelry. Eye-opening, thoughtful work.

HISPANIC FOLK ART

Santa Fe

Courtesy Davis Mather Folk Art Gallery

Cat by Felipe Archuleta, Davis Mather Folk Art Gallery.

Davis Mather Folk Art Gallery (505-983-1660 or 505-988-1218; 141 Lincoln Ave. a block north of the plaza). One of the best collections of New Mexico animal woodcarvings and Mexican folk art. Owner Davis Mather delights in recounting how he discovered the work of Felipe Archuleta, the New Mexico artisan who popularized the whimsical animal carvings in the 1960s.

Montez Gallery (505-982-1828; 125 E. Palace Ave., #33, Sena Plaza courtyard). Excellent New Mexico folk art by a large group of *santeros*, many of whom have worked in the Smithsonian Institution. *Santos, retablos, bultos*, tinwork, furniture, paintings, pottery, weavings and jewelry from $3 to $3,000.

Near Santa Fe

Chimayó Trading and Mercantile (505-351-4566 or 800-248-7859; N.M. 76 at Chimayó). Chimayó weavings, New Mexico folk art, Indian art, pottery and jewelry, antiques and furniture. Open daily.

Galeria Ortega and Ortega's Weaving Shop (505-351-2288 or 505-351-4215; N.M. 520 at N.M. 76, on the High Road to Taos). Watch Andrew Ortega, a seventh-generation weaver, at work in his studio. Authentic woolen blankets, rugs, coats, vests and purses made in the Chimayó weaving style. Also Santa Clara Pueblo pottery and Southwestern books. Snacks available at the adjoining Cafe Ortega.

Theresa's Art Gallery (505-753-4698; N.M. 76 between Española and Chimayó; write Rte. 1, Box 12, Santa Cruz, NM 87567). A small gallery operated out of the home of Theresa and Richard Montoya, artists who paint Spanish Colonial folk art. They also carry wood carvings, *retablos* and *bultos* made by area artists and Santa Clara Pueblo pottery and more. Reasonably priced.

Taos

Act 1 Gallery (505-758-7831; 226 N. Paseo del Pueblo Norte). Features the work of local folk artist Lydia Garcia, as well as marvelous jewelry, ceramics and the pastels of Dinah K. Worman.

Martinez Hacienda (see "Historic Buildings and Sites" in Chapter Four, *Culture*). Quality New Mexico folk art, from carvings and paintings to tinwork.

Millicent Rogers Museum (see "Museums" in Chapter Four, *Culture*). *Santos, retablos*, tinwork and Rio Grande and Chimayó weavings.

Studio de Colores Gallery (505-751-3502; 119 Quesnel St.). Showcases the colorful, distinctively New Mexican work of Ed Sandoval and the haunting, moody landscapes and interiors of Ann Huston.

NATIVE AMERICAN ART

Santa Fe is an international center for the sale of Native American art and antiquities. Most Native American artisans from the Southwest make pottery and jewelry, but there are also traditions of weaving, basket making, carving and painting. Some of these artists have international reputations.

Most potters tend to work within the context of their own pueblo's traditions, though they usually find room for innovation. Each pueblo's pottery has distinctive designs, shapes and colors, but traditional pottery is all made by the same labor-intensive process. The clay is gathered and cleaned by hand, and pots are shaped by the coil method, in which the artist winds a long, thin roll of clay into the desired shape. Paints and slips (thin clay soup painted on the outer surface of the pot to smooth it) are made by hand from plant and mineral materials, and the pot is fired in an outdoor kiln. Many hours and great skill are required to create even a small pot. The pueblos best known for their fine pottery are San Ildefonso, Santa Clara, San Juan and Acoma, as well as the Hopi villages of northeastern Arizona.

If you want to buy an authentic traditional pot, be sure to ask whether it's handmade or slip-cast (commercially molded). Some artists buy slip-cast pots and paint them. These are fine decorator items, but they will never appreciate in value; a well-made hand-coiled pot will.

Jewelry-making is also an ancient art among the Pueblo Indians. They have been crafting fine turquoise and shell beads for many centuries. As with pottery, jewelry-making by traditional methods is a painstaking, time-consuming process, and an artisan may apprentice for several years.

The Navajo (who are not a Pueblo tribe) are the acknowledged masters of silverwork, crafting the turquoise and silver jewelry and *concha* belts that epitomize the Southwest. The Hopi produce a unique kind of silverwork called overlay, characterized by angular geometric repeat patterns on rings, bracelets, necklaces, bolos, etc. The Zuni of west-central New Mexico make the finest lapidary work, such as needlepoint and petitpoint, in which tiny bits of turquoise are individually shaped and inlaid precisely into silver settings. The Santo Domingo Pueblo natives are the most skilled creators of *heishi,* or finely carved beads made of shell.

Shopping under the portal of the Palace of the Governors is a definite must-do for visitors.

Corrie Photography

If you're buying from artists who sell under the *portal* at the Palace of the Governors on Santa Fe's plaza, it is good to know that this area is reserved only for New Mexican Indians and that all items must be made by hand, either by the seller or by members of his or her family. In shops, clerks should be able to provide information on who made an item and something of its tradition. Following are some shops and galleries that specialize in Indian art. If you have time, though, we suggest you visit the pueblos (see "Pueblos" in Chapter Four, *Culture*). Also included below are some reputable shops that deal in Indian antiquities; most of these offer contemporary artwork as well.

Santa Fe

Dewey Galleries Ltd. (505-982-8632; 53 Old Santa Fe Trail). This venerable gallery features Southwest Indian and Hispanic art and old Navajo textiles.

Glenn Green Galleries (505-988-4168; 50 E. San Francisco St., on the plaza). Gaze in awe at the monumental works of Apache artist Allan Houser, the grandfather of contemporary Native American sculpture and 1992 recipient of the National Medal of Arts.

Keshi — the Zuni Connection (505-989-8728; 227 Don Gaspar Ave., inside Santa Fe Village). Keshi carries a fine selection of Zuni fetishes — small stone carvings in the shapes of totem animals.

Morning Star Gallery (505-982-8187; 513 Canyon Rd.). One of Santa Fe's most reputable dealers in antique Indian art: pottery, weavings, clothing, basketry, blankets, kachina dolls and more.

Niman Fine Arts (505-988-5091; 125 Lincoln Ave., N.M. 116). The exclusive representative for Dan Namingha, a Tewa-Hopi artist with a growing international reputation. Namingha's paintings, mixed media pieces and sculptures evoke a powerful spiritual response in many people, and he's also become a spokesman for native cultures worldwide.

Dog by Hispanic artist Miguel Rodriguez; chicken by Navajo artists Lula Herbert and Guy Johns, at the Rainbow Man.

Murrae Haynes

Palace of the Governors Museum Shop (505-982-3016; entrance at Palace Ave. and Washington St.). All authentic, Indian-made artwork in all mediums and a wide variety of books on the Southwest. No state sales tax charged here.

The Rainbow Man (505-982-8706; 107 E. Palace Ave.). Indian trade blankets are the passion of owners Bob and Marianne Kapoun. Their eight-room shop is a little museum of Western art and memorabilia. Blankets, pawn jewelry, Edward S. Curtis photographs, railroad items, Indian art and fine crafts and contemporary Hispanic folk art.

Ray Tracey Galleries (505-989-3430, 135 W. Palace Ave.). Award-winning Native American jewelers Ray Tracey, Ben Nighthorse and Carlton Jamon design stunning work in silver and gold with hand-inlaid coral, sugulite, turquoise, lapis, opal and diamonds.

Robert Nichols (505-982-2145; 419 Canyon Rd.). Longtime Santa Fe art dealer Robert Nichols specializes in quality contemporary Southwestern Indian pottery and traditional Southwestern Indian paintings. With these, he blends antique Americana, folk art, decorative arts and country furnishings.

Taos

Taos artist R.C. Gorman at work.

Don Laine; courtesy Taos Chamber
of Commerce.

Don Fernando Indian Art Gallery (505-758-3791; 104 W. Plaza). The oldest Indian arts shop on the plaza, Don Fernando's has storyteller figures by Cochiti Pueblo potters, black-on-black pottery, folk art carvings, jewelry and books on the Southwest.

La Unica Cosa (505-758-3065; 117 Paseo del Pueblo Norte). The Zapotec Indians, who live in the mountains of southern Mexico, use nonautomated looms to create their intricate weavings. Wool is processed by hand and dyes are made from indigenous plants. Be sure to see these unusual and beautiful rugs, pillows and art hangings.

Navajo Gallery (505-758-3250; 210 Ledoux St.). A flamboyant Navajo artist whose stylized depictions of Indian women have made him practically a household word, R.C. Gorman owns this gallery as a showcase for his work. Paintings, drawings, prints, sculptures, cast paper, etched glass and more.

R.B. Ravens (505-758-7322; Ranchos de Taos, south of Taos in the St. Francis Church plaza). Even if your budget can't handle an antique Navajo weaving, you'll enjoy viewing the museum-quality Pueblo, Navajo and Rio Grande textiles here. The beautiful adobe building also houses antique Indian jewelry, paintings by Taos Founders, pottery, kachina dolls and pre-Columbian art. An excellent selection of books on Navajo textiles.

Southwest Moccasin & Drum (505-758-9332 or 800-447-3630; 803 Paseo del Pueblo Norte). Art and craftwork, much of it from Taos Pueblo, displayed in a 150-year-old adobe chapel. Hand-painted drums, moccasins, musical instruments, weavings, fetishes, sculptures and jewelry.

Taos Drums (505-758-DRUM or 800-424-DRUM; five miles south of the plaza; look for teepees). Internationally known, Taos Indian drums are made by hand from hollowed-out logs and tanned hides. This retail-wholesale shop features craft demonstrations daily. A large selection of drums, plus native artifacts, crafts, rattles, fans, lamps and more.

PHOTOGRAPHY

Santa Fe

Andrew Smith Fine American Photography (505-984-1234; 203 E. San Francisco St., on the plaza). A large inventory of the masters of 19th- and 20th-century photography, both European and American. Ansel Adams, Edward Curtis, Laura Gilpin and contemporary photographers of the Western landscape. Definitely the place to look at photographs.

Taos

See Lumina under "Contemporary Art."

TRADITIONAL ART

Santa Fe and Taos attracted a number of artists from the East Coast and Europe in the early decades of this century. The painting movements they started became known as the "Santa Fe School" and the "Taos School." Today, their works are in great demand, and many artists who live here continue to work in the style popularized by these earlier artists. Most of the galleries below also carry traditional paintings and sculptures of artists of the greater West.

Santa Fe

Gerald Peters Gallery (505-988-8961; 439 Camino del Monte Sol). This international gallery features classic Western and Taos Society artists as well as contemporary paintings, sculpture and photography. Peters is known for his O'Keeffes. The gallery is moving during the summer of 1998 — check for their new location.

The Jamison Galleries (505-982-3666; 560 Montezuma St. in Sanbusco Market Center). Feast your eyes on the work of some of the Southwest's legendary artists in the Jamison's large, new space at Sanbusco. Paintings by the Santa Fe and Taos Founders and Alfred Morang. Also early works by new lights like Earl Biss, R.C. Gorman, Fritz Scholder, Kevin Red Star and Edward Borein.

Nedra Matteucci's Fenn Galleries (505-982-4631; 1075 Paseo de Peralta). Perhaps Santa Fe's best-known gallery, Fenn occupies a huge adobe house full of the finest classic Western and American art of the 19th and 20th centuries. Their specialty is historical American art, but you'll also find some top contemporary Southwestern painters and sculptors.

Owings-Dewey Fine Art (505-982-6244; 76 E. San Francisco St., on the plaza). A part of Dewey Galleries, Owings-Dewey shows 19th- and 20th-century American art, including Western, traditional and contemporary painting, watercolors and original graphics.

Taos

Hirsch Fine Art (505 758-2478; 146B Kit Carson Rd.). Deals in museum-quality works on paper by early Southwest artists, including the Taos Founders. Some surprisingly affordable pieces.

The Shriver Gallery (505-758-4994; 401 Paseo del Pueblo Norte). Traditional fine art with a Western emphasis, including a selection of paintings, drawings, bronze sculptures and etchings.

Total Arts Gallery (505-758-4667; 122-A Kit Carson Rd.). For more than 24 years, this six-room gallery has presented a cross section of fine art that embraces traditional and contemporary artists of national and international repute.

WORLD ART AND GIFTS

Santa Fe

Beauty and the Beads (505-982-5234; 407 S. Guadalupe St.). To make a necklace of charms or antique glass beads, step into Beauty and the Beads. Beads are arranged to catch the eye and set the imagination going. There is help available for simple or more elaborate projects.

Fourth World Cottage Industries (505-982-4388; 102 W. San Francisco St., upstairs). Imports from Central and South America in a range of prices. Casual cotton and wool clothing for men and women adds a bit of ethnic chic to any wardrobe. The store also has art hangings, pottery, masks and Guatemalan handwoven fabric.

Glorianna's Fine Crafts (505-982-0353; 55 W. Marcy St.). Exotic beads tell tales of trade and travel, and there are strands and strands of everything from amber to crystal to glass at Glorianna's. Also has bead books and other craft information.

Guadalupe's #1, A-OK Rubber Stamps and Crosses (505-982-9862; 102 W. San Francisco St., upstairs). Stamp your own creative mark on the world by choosing from hundreds of imaginative and outrageous rubber stamps. Also pads, inks and handmade icons.

Jackalope (505-471-8539 or 800-753-7757; 2820 Cerrillos Rd., about three miles south of downtown). Jackalope's motto is "Folk art by the Truckload" and its wealth includes handmade furniture from Mexico, folk art imports, famous chile lights and more than two acres of irresistible pottery from around the world. With a patio restaurant, greenhouse, prairie dog village, tiny carousel and occasional entertainment — from mariachis to puppet shows — Jacka-lope is an enchanted world unto itself. A must-do.

Maya (505-989-7590; 108 Galisteo). An international boutique, Maya features clothing and jewelry from around the world, as well as Oaxacan animal carv-ings, Huichol bead and yarn art and carvings from Tibet. The Day of the Dead items are charming, if a bit scary, and there is one of the best earring selections in town. Clothing in sensuous fabrics is well-selected.

Pachamama (505-983-4020; 223 Canyon Rd.). An entrancing collection of antiques and traditional folk art from Latin America in a wide range of prices. Specializes in magical and religious objects such as *santos, retablos* and *milagros*, as well as furniture, masks, jewelry, toys, baskets and musical instruments.

Spiritwerks (505-989-7550; 533 Old Santa Fe Trail). "Unique Trashique" is the self-advertised slogan of this charming store which features wild handmade pins, altars, magnets, angels, key chains and more. Each piece is unique, dec-orative and irreverent — a great place to search for your own guardian angel.

Susan's Christmas Shop (505-983-2127; 115 E. Palace Ave.). Santa himself couldn't do better than this dazzling array of hand-made Christmas orna-ments from New Mexico, Mexico and beyond. Look for seasonal changes too — hearts on Valentine's day and collector quality decorated eggs for Easter.

Taos

Follow Your Heart (505-758-4881; 124 Bent St.). Delights from around the world include Chinese porcelain, glassware, unique boxes, baskets, ethnic clothing, candles and toiletries.

FX/18 (505-758-8590; 1018 Paseo del Pueblo Norte in El Prado). Whimsical sculptures guard the entrance to the store and inside there is a voluminous display of silver jewelry, much also with a playful touch. The store shows the work of younger cutting edge local jewelers, as well as locally made soaps, notecards and gifts.

The Market (505-758-3195; 125 Kit Carson Rd.). For more than thirty years, The Market has been showing the work of Southwestern potters, in particular those from Colorado and New Mexico. A large selection of bright contemporary designs to grace any kitchen and table.

Taos Blue (505-758-3561; 101 Bent St.). Saints and angles brush halos and wings in this gift shop specializing in objects with divine inspiration — from pottery to paintings on wood to luscious hand-knit sweaters. The place to find a unique gift by a local craftsperson.

JEWELRY

Santa Fe

James Reid, Ltd. (505-988-1147 or 800-545-2056; 114 E. Palace Ave.). offers breathtaking concha belts and belt buckles in silver and gold, in both traditional and contemporary designs.

Luna Felix, Goldsmith (505-989-7679; 116 W. San Francisco St.). Designer Luna Felix pioneered the Etruscan revival look in fine jewelry, lavish stones in neoclassical, almost architectural, settings. A renowned goldsmith, her name is synonymous with the romantic in jewelry. Rings and earrings are particularly compelling in this collection.

Ornament (505-983-9399; 209 W. San Francisco St.). This jewelry store features both innovative and traditional work, in gold, silver and gemstones. It shows the work of a hundred designers of wearable art — jewelry and as well as suede clothing. An impeccable choice for a purchase.

Ortega's On the Plaza (505-988-1866; 101 W San Francisco St.). This venerable trader has a first class selection of Indian jewelry, emphasizing traditional designs in turquoise and silver. Also has pottery, kachinas and some elegant velvet clothing.

Palace of the Governors' Portal (Palace Avenue — entire north block of the Plaza). One of the best places in town to shop for traditional Indian jewelry is beneath the portal of the historic Governor's Palace. Artists and artisans assemble from the surrounding pueblos and as far away as the Navajo Reservation to sell traditional silver and turquoise jewelry, as well as small pots and other items. Prices are reasonable, and there is a special pleasure in buying from the jeweler or a family representative. Earrings, necklaces, bolo ties and rings are in particular abundance, and a tiny bracelet makes a special baby present. Vendors are assigned slots daily by lottery, so if you find something you love, buy it — it may be difficult to trace later.

Sissel's Discount Indian Jewelry (505-471-3499, 2900 Cerrillos Rd.; 505-438-9155, 8380 Cerrillos Rd.). Turquoise and silver jewelry, from fetish necklaces to bolo ties, at a discount price. This is the place to adorn yourself with squash blossom necklaces, earrings and belts without bankrupting your wallet.

Tin-Nee-Ann Trading Co. (505-988-1630; 923 Cerrillos Rd.). The trading company is a quintessential old fashioned curio shop, with great deals on Indian jewelry, from earrings to squash blossom necklaces. Also features kachinas, pottery and sand paintings.

Tresa Vorenberg Goldsmiths (505-988-7215; 656 Canyon Rd.). Tresa Vorenberg represents her own work as well as that of forty other designers specializing in precious metals and gems. The wedding rings here are finely handcrafted; and special services include insurance appraisal and a resident gemologist.

Taos

Artwares Contemporary Jewelry (505-758-8850 or 800-527-8850 mail order; on the plaza). Known for its stylized Zuni bear, executed in precious metals and used to adorn earrings, necklaces and pins. There is fine lapidary work, and a mix of Native American and contemporary style jewelry in a reasonable price range.

Emily Benoist Ruffin, Goldsmith (505-758-1061; 119 Bent St.). Custom and limited-edition sterling and gold jewelry with gemstones in contemporary designs by Ms. Ruffin. Fine jewelry by upwards of thirty other international artists.

KITCHENWARE

Santa Fe

Cookworks (505-988-7676; 322 S. Guadalupe St.). Copper pans glisten, waiting for a cook to start sautéing. Elegant gear from gourmet cookery mingles with linens, glassware, scented candles and imported tableware.

Nambe Mills Inc. (505-988-5528, 924 Paseo de Peralta; 505-988-3574, 112 W. San Francisco St.). Nambe (nam-BAY) ware is a secret metal alloy that does not include silver, lead, or pewter. It shines like sterling silver yet can be used for cooking and retains heat or cold for hours. Nambe dishes, platters, trays, plates and bowls are cast at a foundry in Santa Fe. The pieces make classic wedding or housewarming gifts.

Off The Wall (505-983-8337; 616 Canyon Rd.). These witty teapots, cups, cookie jars, clocks and lamps look as if they could walk and talk. Every piece has its own personality. And don't miss the coffee bar in back, with espresso, bagels and sweet treats.

Santa Fe Pottery (505-989-3363; 323 S. Guadalupe St.). Features handmade pottery by Southwestern artisans, from clocks to dinner plates. Colorful, vivid designs give both functional and decorative pieces a bold, eye-catching appeal.

Taos

Monet's Kitchen (505-758-8003; 124 Bent St.). A nicely apportioned kitchen shop with espresso makers, woks, pottery, aprons and table linens. Some gourmet foods and coffees as well, for a complete gift basket.

Taos Cookery (505-689-2354; 113 Bent St.). Besides featuring general kitchenware, Taos Cookery also represents many local potters. Among the most eye-catching designs are the multicolored productions of Ojo Sarco Pottery, whose husband and wife team creates dishwasher and microwave safe pottery emblazoned with patterns taken from the New Mexico landscape.

MALLS

Santa Fe

De Vargas Center Mall (505-982-2655; 159 Paseo de Peralta). The oldest mall in Santa Fe is a shopping center for residents on the northern half of town. It has about fifty stores, with Ross Dress for Less, Hastings Books Music and Video and Albertsons Food Center as the largest. The mall also has jewelry stores, movie theaters, pizza, ice cream and a cafeteria.

Sanbusco (505-989-9390; 500 Montezuma St.). In the renovated historic Railyard area, Sanbusco has a pleasant indoor arcade atmosphere. It features high end clothing boutiques such as Bodhi Bazaar as well as beauty products and home accessories. From late spring through mid-autumn, its parking lot is the site of the nationally-known Santa Fe Area Farmers Market.

Santa Fe Factory Stores (505-474-4000; located 8 miles south of the Santa Fe Plaza at 8380 Cerrillos Road). Over forty outlet stores pleasantly situated just south of Santa Fe, the Santa Fe Factory Stores offer the shopper good prices on many name brands. You'll find shoes from Joan and David, leather goods by Coach and Mark Cross, housewares from Dansk and Royal Doulton, as well as books, children's clothing and more.

Villa Linda (505-473-4253; 4250 Cerrillos Rd.). The Villa Linda mall is the largest mall in Santa Fe, with 110 stores, including Dillard, J.C. Penney, Mervyn's and Sears Roebuck. It has movie theaters, a video arcade, post office, public library branch and a food court.

POSTERS

Santa Fe

The Santa Fe Opera, Chamber Music Festival, Santa Fe Indian Market and Santa Fe Spanish Market all publish quality art posters each year that become collector's items. In particular, the Chamber Music Festival's Georgia O'Keeffe poster series remains popular. Some Southwestern artists and photographers also publish their work as posters. The following shops are in the plaza area:

Fox Gallery/ New Millenium Fine Art (505-983-2002; 217 W. Water St.).
Posters of Santa Fe (505-982-6645 or 800-827-6745; 111 E. Palace Ave.).
Posters of the West — White Hyacinth Frame Shop (505-983-2831 or 800-828-9557; 208 W. San Francisco St.).

Taos

Eloise Contemporary (505-758-3230; 122-C East Kit Carson Rd.).
Festival Posters (505-758-4667; 122-A Kit Carson Rd.).
Final Touch Frame Shop (505-758-4360; 102-B Padre Martinez Lane).

TEXTILES AND FIBERS

Santa Fe

Down & Outdoors in Santa Fe (505-988-4355; 32 Burro Alley). An outlet for warm specialty items made of down, the store guarantees all its comforters, pillows and feather beds. Also has sheets, baby clothes, pillows and of course cozy jackets.
Handwoven Originals (505-982-4118; 211 Old Santa Fe Tr.). Handwoven clothing and painted silk are the hallmarks of the store. Much of the work is done by local artists and designers. Features shawls, skirts, vests, jackets, hats and scarves
Quilts Ltd. (505-988-5888; 652 Canyon Rd.). Antique traditional, Southwestern and Plains Indian quilts, plus clothing made from quilted fabrics.
Santa Fe Weaving Gallery (505-982-1737; 124-$^1/_2$ Galisteo St.). The gallery shows clothing designed by 25 nationally recognized fiber artists. Fabrics include handwoven chenille, cotton knots, silk appliqué and painted wool and silk. Take home some art you can wear.

Taos

Clay & Fiber Gallery (505-758-8093; 126 W. Plaza Dr.). An excellent, unusual selection of textiles, ceramics, jewelry, glass and sculpture by contemporary artisans.

La Lana (505-758-9631; 136 Paseo del Pueblo Norte). La Lana is stocked with warm and colorful handwoven and hand knit items: shawls, coats, sweaters and jackets. They also sell yarn to inspire your own creations.

Rio Grande Weaver's Supply (505-758-0433; 216-B Paseo del Pueblo Norte, Taos, NM 87571. Send $3 for mail-order catalog and price list.) Here is everything a weaver needs, from hand-dyed yarns for apparel, rugs and tapestries to weaving and spinning equipment, including the Rio Grande Loom. Next door is their retail outlet, Weaving Southwest, which exhibits bold abstract designs by local weavers.

Twining Weavers and Contemporary Crafts (505-758-9000; 135 Paseo de Pueblo Norte). The stock here includes handwoven wool rugs, pillows made from hand-dyed yarns, Guatemalan cotton runners, place mats, napkins and baskets from around the world. Owner Sally Bachman will work directly with the customer to customize colors and designs.

CHAPTER NINE
Practical Matters
INFORMATION

Courtesy Museum of New Mexico

Office interior of the Santa Fe New Mexican, *early 1900s.*

H ere is a modest encyclopedia of useful information about the Santa Fe and Taos area. Our aim is to ease everyday life for locals and help ensure that vacation time goes smoothly for visitors. This chapter covers the following topics:

AMBULANCE, FIRE & POLICE

The general emergency number (fire, police, ambulance) for Santa Fe and Taos is 911. Other emergency numbers are as follows.

Santa Fe

Crisis Intervention	505-473-5200
Poison Control	800-432-6866
Rape Crisis Center	505-986-9111

Taos

Ambulance	505-758-9591
Fire	505-758-3386
Poison Control	800-432-6866
Police	505-758-4656
Sheriff	505-758-4709

State Police

Española	505-753-2277
Santa Fe	505-827-9300
Taos	505-758-8878

AREA CODE, ZIP CODES, CITY HALLS & LOCAL GOVERNMENT

AREA CODE

The *Area Code* for all of New Mexico is **505**.

CITY HALLS & LOCAL GOVERNMENT

Santa Fe, New Mexico's capital, is governed by an eight-member city council (the mayor breaks tie votes). It is the county seat of Santa Fe County, which is headed by a five-member county commission. Taos is governed by a four-member town council (again, the mayor breaks tie votes). It is the county seat of Taos County, which is headed by a three-member county commission. The two other major cities in the region with sizable local governments are Española and Los Alamos. In addition, there are 11 Indian pueblos in the area located on reservations. Politically and legally, each pueblo is a sovereign nation led by a tribal governor and a tribal ruling council. Each also has its own police force. For general information, call the following numbers or write to the city or county clerk, care of the city or county in question; or to the tourist information centers at the pueblos.

Town or Pueblo	Telephone	Zip Code
Cochiti Pueblo	505-465-2244	87072
Española	505-753-2377	87532
Los Alamos County	505-662-8105	87544
Nambe Pueblo	505-455-2036	87501
Picuris Pueblo	505-587-2519	87553
Pojoaque Pueblo	505-455-3460	87501
Rio Arriba County	505-753-2992	87532
San Felipe Pueblo	505-867-3381	87001
San Ildefonso Pueblo	505-455-3549	87501
San Juan Pueblo	505-852-4400	87566
Santa Clara Pueblo	505-753-7326	87532
Santa Fe	505-984-6500	87501
Santa Fe County	505-986-6200	87504
Santo Domingo Pueblo	505-465-2214	87052
Taos	505-751-2000	87571
Taos County	505-758-8834	87571
Taos Pueblo	505-758-9593	87571
Tesuque Pueblo	505-983-2667	87574

BANKS

Most banks in Santa Fe and Taos are linked electronically to nationwide automatic teller systems. Here is a list of telephone numbers and addresses of some of these banks' main offices.

Santa Fe

The Bank of Santa Fe (505-984-0500; main office at 241 Washington Ave.). Linked to MasterCard, Money, Lynx, Cirrus and Plus systems.

First National Bank of Santa Fe (505-992-2000; main office on the plaza). Linked to Lynx, Plus, Pulse and Bank Mate systems.

First State Bank (505-982-6050; main office at 201 Washington Ave.). Linked to Bank Mate, Plus, Pulse, Lynx, Cirrus and Discover Novus systems.

NationsBank (505-471-1234; main office at 1234 St. Michael's Dr.). Linked to Plus, MasterCard Maestro, Lynx, Pulse, Visa and Bank Mate systems.

Norwest Banks (505-984-8500; main office at 1048 Paseo de Peralta). Linked to Cirrus, Plus, Lynx, Pulse MasterCard, Visa, Discover Novus and American Express Cash systems.

Taos

First State Bank of Taos (505-758-6652; main office at 120 W. Plaza). Linked to Plus, Pulse Bank Mate, Cirrus, Discover Novus, MasterCard and Lynx systems.

Peoples Bank (505-758-4500; main office at 1356 Paseo del Pueblo Sur). Linked to Cirrus, Lynx, Pulse and Money systems.

Sentinel Bank of Taos (505-758-6700; main office at 512 Paseo del Pueblo Sur). Linked to Cirrus, Lynx and Pulse systems.

BIBLIOGRAPHY

For the traveler who enjoys reading about a region as well as visiting it, we've put together a list of some of the many books that have been written on the Santa Fe–Taos area. *Books You Can Buy* lists books available at most Santa Fe and Taos bookshops, bookstores elsewhere or from the publishers. (For information on Santa Fe–Taos booksellers, see "Bookstores" in Chapter Eight, *Shopping*.) *Books You Can Borrow* lists books that are out of print or no longer for sale. The best sources for book borrowing are described under "Libraries" in Chapter Four, *Culture*.

Books You Can Buy

AUTOBIOGRAPHIES, BIOGRAPHIES & REMINISCENCES

Brandt, Karen Nilsson and Sharon Niederman. *Living Treasures: Celebration of the Human Spirit.* Santa Fe: Western Edge Press, 1997. 191 pp., $32.50.

Cabeza de Baca, Fabiola. *We Fed Them Cactus.* Albuquerque: University of New Mexico Press, 1954 and 1994. 186 pp., $9.95.

Chavez, Fray Angelico. *But Time and Chance: The Story of Padre Martinez of Taos 1793–1867.* Santa Fe: Sunstone Press, 1981. 171 pp., $11.95.

Church, Peggy Pond. *The House at Otowi Bridge: The Story of Edith Warner and Los Alamos.* Albuquerque: University of New Mexico Press, 1959. 149 pp., $9.95.

Horgan, Paul. *Lamy of Santa Fe.* New York: The Noonday Press, 1975. 523 pp., $17.95.

Luhan, Mabel Dodge. *Winter in Taos.* Taos: Las Palomas de Taos, 1935. 237 pp., $14.95.

Magoffin, Susan Shelby. *Down the Santa Fe Trail and into Mexico: The Diary of Susan Shelby Magoffin, 1846–1847.* Lincoln: University of Nebraska Press, 1982. 284 pp., $6.95.

Miller, Michael, ed. *A New Mexico Scrapbook: Memoirs de Nuevo Mexico. Twenty-Three New Mexicans Remember Growing Up.* Huntsville, Ala.: Honeysuckle Imprint, 1991. 161 pp., $18.

Niederman, Sharon. *A Quilt of Words: Women's Diaries, Letters & Original Accounts of Life in the Southwest, 1860–1960.* Boulder: Johnson Books, 1988. 220 pp., $11.95.

Ortega, Pedro Ribera. *Christmas in Old Santa Fe.* Santa Fe: Sunstone Press, 1973. 102 pp., index, $6.95.

Russell, Marian. *Memoirs of Marian Russell Along the Old Santa Fe Trail.* Albuquerque: University of New Mexico Press, 1954. 163 pp., illus., index, $10.95.

CULTURAL STUDIES

Bullock, Alice. *Living Legends of the Santa Fe Country.* Santa Fe: The Lightning Tree — Jene Lyons Publishers, 1978. 96 pp., illus., $7.95.

Chavez, Fray Angelico. *Origins of New Mexico Families: A Genealogy of the Spanish Colonial Period,* revised edition. Santa Fe: Museum of New Mexico Press, 1992. 441 pp., $33.00.

Edelman, Sandra A. *Summer People, Winter People: A Guide to the Pueblos in the Santa Fe Area.* Santa Fe: Sunstone Press, 1986. 32 pp., index, $4.95.

Gibson, Arrell Morgan. *The Santa Fe and Taos Colonies: Age of the Muses, 1900–1942.* Norman, Okla.: University of Oklahoma Press, 1983. 345 pp., illus., index, $13.95.

Julyan, Robert. *The Place Names of New Mexico.* Albuquerque: University of New Mexico Press, 1996. 385 pp., $21.00.

Kutz, Jack. *Mysteries and Miracles of New Mexico: Guidebook to the Genuinely Bizarre in the Land of Enchantment.* Corrales, N.M.: Rhombus Publishing Co., 1988. 216 pp., $7.95.

Simmons, Marc. *Witchcraft in the Southwest: Spanish and Indian Supernaturalism on the Rio Grande.* Lincoln, Neb.: University of Nebraska Press. 183 pp., $6.95.

Steele, Thomas J. *Santos and Saints: The Religious Folk Art of Hispanic New Mexico.* Santa Fe: Ancient City Press, 1974. 220 pp., index, $12.95.

Weigle, Marta. *Brothers of Light, Brothers of Blood: The Penitentes of the Southwest.* Santa Fe: Ancient City Press, 1976. 300 pp., $12.95.

Weigle, Marta and Kyle Fiore. *Santa Fe and Taos: The Writer's Era 1916–41*. Santa Fe: Ancient City Press, 1982. 229 pp., illus., index, $16.95.

Weigle, Marta and Peter White. *The Lore of New Mexico*. Albuquerque: University of New Mexico Press/American Folklore Society. 1988. 523 pp., $37.00.

LITERARY WORKS

Anaya, Rudolfo A. *Bless Me Ultima*. Berkeley, Calif.: Tonatiuh-Quinto Sol International, 1972. 247 pp., $11.95.

Bradford, Richard. *Red Sky at Morning*. New York: Harper & Row, 1968. 256 pp., $8.95.

Cather, Willa. *Death Comes for the Archbishop*. New York: Vintage, 1927. 297 pp., $8.95.

Crawford, Stanley. *Mayordomo: Chronicle of an Acequia in Northern New Mexico*. New York: Anchor Books Doubleday, 1988. 231 pp., $8.95.

Hillerman, Tony ed. *The Spell of New Mexico*. Albuquerque: University of New Mexico Press, 1976. 105 pp., $9.95.

Horgan, Paul. *The Centuries of Santa Fe*. Santa Fe: William Gannon Publishers, 1956. 363 pp., index, $9.95.

La Farge, Oliver. *Laughing Boy*. Boston: Houghton Mifflin Co., 1929. 192 pp., $4.95.

Nichols, John. *The Milagro Beanfield War*. New York: Ballantine Books, 1974. 629 pp., $5.95.

Niederman, Sharon and Miriam Sagan, eds. *New Mexico Poetry Renaissance*. Santa Fe: Red Crane Books, 1994. 224 pp., $13.00.

Querry, Ron. *Death of Bernadette Left-Hand*. Santa Fe. Red Crane Press, 1993. $11.95.

A rack of paperbacks at La Fonda newsstand.

Murrae Haynes

Waters, Frank. *The Man Who Killed the Deer*. New York: Farrar Rinehart, 1942. 217 pp., $3.95.

LOCAL HISTORIES

Chauvenet, Beatrice. *Hewett and Friends: A Biography of Santa Fe's Vibrant Era*. Santa Fe: Museum of New Mexico Press, 1983. 248 pp., illus., index, $16.95.

DeBuys, William. *Enchantment and Exploitation: The Life and Hard Times of a New Mexican Mountain Range*. Albuquerque: University of New Mexico Press, 1985. 394 pp., index, illus., $15.95.

Gregg, Josiah. *The Commerce of the Prairies*. Lincoln, Neb.: University of Nebraska Press, 1967. 343 pp., index, $9.95.

Hemp, Bill. *Taos Landmarks & Legends*. Los Alamos: Exceptional Books Ltd., 1996. 134 pp., $19.95.

Horgan, Paul. *Great River: The Rio Grande in North American History*. Austin, Tex.: Texas Monthly Press, 1984. 1020 pp., index, $14.95.

Jenkins, Myra Ellen and Albert H. Schroeder. *A Brief History of New Mexico*. Albuquerque: University of New Mexico Press, 1974. 87 pp., illus., index, $8.95.

La Farge, Oliver. *Santa Fe: The Autobiography of a Southwest Town*. Norman, Okla.: University of Oklahoma Press, 1959. 436 pp., illus., index, $15.95.

Roberts, Susan A., and Calvin A. Roberts. *New Mexico*. Albuquerque: University of New Mexico Press, 1988. 215 pp., index, $14.95.

Rudnick, Lois Palkin. *Utopian Vistas: The Mabel Dodge Luhan House and the American Counterculture*. Albuquerque: University of New Mexico Press,

Simmons, Marc. *New Mexico: An Interpretive History*. Albuquerque: University of New Mexico Press, 1988. 207 pp., $10.95.

Tobias, Henry. *A History of the Jews in New Mexico*. Albuquerque: University of New Mexico Press, 1990. 294 pp., $19.00.

PHOTOGRAPHIC STUDIES

Brewer, Robert and Steve McDowell. *The Persistence of Memory: New Mexico's Churches*. Santa Fe: Museum of New Mexico Press, 1991. 152 pp., $39.95.

Cash, Maria Romero. *Built of Earth and Song: A Guide to New Mexico Churches*. Santa Fe: Red Crane Press, 1993. $11.95.

Clark, William, Edward Klanner, Jack Parsons, and Bernard Plossu. *Santa Fe: The City in Photographs*. Santa Fe: Fotowest Publishing, 1984. 72 pp., $14.95.

Gregg, Andrew K. *New Mexico in the 19th Century: A Pictorial History*. Albuquerque: University of New Mexico Press. 196 pp., index, $15.95.

Nichols, John and William Davis. *If Mountains Die: A New Mexico Memoir*. New York: Alfred A. Knopf, 1987. 144 pp., $19.95.

Robin, Arthur H., William M. Ferguson, and Lisa Ferguson. *Rock Art of Bandelier National Monument*. Albuquerque: University of New Mexico Press, 1989. 156 pp., index, $29.95.

Sherman, John. *Taos: A Pictorial History*. Santa Fe: William Gannon Publishers, 1990. 164 pp., $19.95.

Warren, Nancy Hunter. *Villages of Hispanic New Mexico*. Santa Fe: School of American Research, 1987. 109 pp., $18.00.

RECREATION

Anderson, Fletcher and Ann Hopkinson. *Rivers of the Southwest: A Boater's Guide to the Rivers of Colorado, New Mexico, Utah and Arizona*. Boulder, Colo.: Pruett Publishing Co., 1982. 129 pp., illus., index, $8.95.

Kaysing, Bill. *Great Hot Springs of the West*. Santa Barbara: Capra Press, 1984. 213 pp., illus., index, $10.95.

Matthews, Kay. *Cross-Country Skiing in Northern New Mexico: An Introduction and Trail Guide*. Placitas, N.M.: Acequia Madre Press, 1986. 96 pp., maps, $7.95.

Pinkerton, Elaine. *Santa Fe on Foot: Walking, Running and Bicycle Routes in the City Different*. Santa Fe: Ocean Tree, 1986. 125 pp., illus., maps, $7.95.

Santa Fe Group of the Sierra Club. *Day Hikes in the Santa Fe Area*. 1990. 192 pp., index, $8.95.

Ungnade, Herbert E. *Guide to the New Mexico Mountains*. Albuquerque: University of New Mexico Press, 1988. 235 pp., index, $10.95.

TRAVEL

Chronic, Halka. *Roadside Geology of New Mexico*. Missoula, Mont.: Mountain Press Publishing Co., 1987. 255 pp., index, $11.95.

Fugate, Frances L. and Roberta B. *Roadside History of New Mexico*. Missoula, Mont.: Mountain Press Publishing Co., 1989. 483 pp., index, $15.95.

Smith, Toby. *Odyssey*. Albuquerque: University of New Mexico Press, 1987. 182 pp., $11.95.

Books You Can Borrow

Blacker, Irwin. *Taos*. Cleveland, Ohio: World Publishers, 1959. A fictional account of the 1680 Pueblo Indian Revolt that drove the Spaniards out of New Mexico for 12 years.

Boyd, E. *Popular Arts of Spanish New Mexico*. Santa Fe: Museum of New Mexico Press, 1974. A color photographic study of the entire spectrum of Hispanic art in the Land of Enchantment.

Hackett, Charles Wilson. *Revolt of the Pueblo Indians of New Mexico and Otermín's Attempted Reconquest, 1680–1682*. Albuquerque: University of New Mexico Press, 1942.

Henderson, Alice Corbin. *Brothers of Light: The Penitentes of the Southwest*. New York: Harcourt, Brace & Co., 1937. One of the best treatments of the Penitente phenomenon.

Kendall, George. *Narrative of the Texan–Santa Fe Expedition*. Albuquerque: University of New Mexico Press, 1844. Illus., maps. Outlines the beginning of the conflict between Texas and New Mexico that is still evident today, mostly in attitudes.

Knee, Ernest. *Santa Fe, New Mexico*. New York: Chanticleer Press, 1942. An unpretentious, classic photographic study of authentic, old Santa Fe charm accompanied by text.

Robertson, Edna. *Artists of the Caminos and Canyons: The Early Years*. Peregrine, 1976. A study of the turn-of-the-century artists in Santa Fe and Taos.

Ross, Calvin. *Sky Determines*. Albuquerque: University of New Mexico Press, 1948. A unique book. Covers New Mexico history, weather, art, landscape, etc.

Spivey R. *Maria*. Flagstaff, Ariz.: Northland Press, 1979. About the famous San Ildefonso Pueblo potter.

CHAMBERS OF COMMERCE

Local chambers of commerce and visitors' bureaus are usually a quick and convenient way of getting information about the specific area you want to visit. In Santa Fe, your best bet is the **Santa Fe Convention and Visitors Bureau** (505-984-6760 or 800-777-2489, 201 W. Marcy St., in the Sweeney Center); and the **Santa Fe County Chamber of Commerce** (505-988-3279 or 800-777-2489, 510 N. Guadalupe St., in the DeVargas Mall near Montgomery Ward). In the Taos area, call or stop in at the **Taos County Chamber of Commerce** (505-758-3873 or 800-732-8267, 1139 Paseo del Pueblo Sur), or call the **Taos Bed & Breakfast Association** (505-758-4747 or 800-876-7857, PO Box 2772, Taos, NM 87571). Other chambers of commerce in the Taos area include the **Angel Fire/Eagle Nest Chamber of Commerce** (505-377-6661 or 800-446-8117; PO Box 547, Angel Fire, NM 87710) and the **Red River Chamber of Commerce** (505-754-2366 or 800-348-6444, PO Box 870 Red River, NM 87558).

CLIMATE AND WEATHER REPORTS

CLIMATE

Santa Fe and Taos are blessed with a healthful, dynamic, high-desert climate. The air is dry all year, and at 7,000 feet (the approximate elevation of both cities) nights are always cool. There are 300 days of sunshine a year.

Sound wonderful? It is. But you'll enjoy it more if you take a few precautions. Bring and use sunscreen (with a protection level of at least 30), chapstick and skin

Kitty Leaken

Santa Fe's night sky lit up by an electrical storm.

lotion. Be sure to take it easy when you first get here to give your body a chance to adjust the altitude. To keep your energy up, eat foods that are high in carbohydrates. Go easy on alcohol, tranquilizers and sleeping pills. And drink lots of water.

For current weather information in the Santa Fe area, call 505-473-2211 at NationsBank or 505-988-5151, Journal North Weather Forecast Service. There is no similar number for Taos, but you can get information on road conditions by calling the State Police at 505-758-8878 or New Mexico Road Conditions at 800-432-4269. You can reach the National Weather Service in Albuquerque at 505-243-0702.

GUIDED TOURS

There are a number of fun and informative sightseeing tours in the Santa Fe–Taos area. Local cab drivers can usually be persuaded to drive you around, adding colorful histories that only a cabbie might know. For more organized, detailed tours, consider the following:

Santa Fe

Grayline Tours (505-983-9491), a bus and trolley service, provides numerous sightseeing tours of Santa Fe and vicinity. A three-hour historical tour of the city is offered year-round (open coach in summer, closed van in winter). The 1997

A Roadrunner tour bus on
the streets of Santa Fe.

rate was $17 per person. A briefer tour of the city (1.25 hours) can be had by boarding **Grayline's Roadrunner** bus, an open coach that departs from La Fonda Hotel every hour during the summer. The 1997 fare was $8 for adults, $4 for children under 12. Grayline also visits Bandelier National Monument (a half-day tour cost $50 per person in 1997).

Frank Montaño, a Santa Fe City Councilor, will take you on **Fiesta Tours on the Plaza** (505-983-1570). The focus here is on downtown historic sites. Tours depart from the corner of Palace and Lincoln on the NW corner of the Plaza at 10 a.m., noon, 2 p.m., 4 p.m. and 6 p.m. The tour of the historic district lasts 1-1/4 hours. Purchase your tickets ($7 adults; $4 children under 12) from the bus driver.

If you want a leisurely walking tour of the downtown area, there are a number of options to choose from. One of the best is **Afoot in Santa Fe Walking Tours** (505-983-3701), led by longtime resident Charles Porter. In the winter, there's one tour a day, seven days a week, beginning at 9:30 a.m. In summer he offers two tours a day Monday through Saturday and one on Sunday. Departure times are 9:30 a.m. and 1:30 p.m. (the Sunday tour is in the morning). Meet him at the southeast side of the parking lot at the Inn at Loretto, located at 211 Old Santa Fe Trail, a block southeast of the plaza. The tour lasts approximately 2.5 hours and is well worth the fee ($12 in 1997).

Another first-rate walking tour of the downtown area is offered by **Santa Fe Detours** (505-983-6565 or 800-338-6877), which will provide you with guides who are longtime residents and who have knowledge of local history and anthropology. Departure times, rates and length of tours are identical to Afoot in Santa Fe. Meet under the T-shirt tree next to the Burrito Co. at 107 Washington Ave. Reservations aren't necessary; the 1997 rate was $10 per person. Stop by the Santa Fe Detours office (54-1/2 E. San Francisco St. above Haagen Dazs on the Plaza) for a discount. They also offer a hotline for unique area B&B's and lodging.

RojoTours and Services (505-474-8333) provide customized expeditions not only of Santa Fe but also of nearby Indian pueblos and other sites, as well as an all-day excursion to Chaco Canyon. *Pathways Customized Tours* (505-982-5382) provides a similar variety of excursions, including trips to the magnificent red-rock country of Abiquiu, an hour north of Santa Fe, where Georgia O'Keeffe lived and painted.

Recursos de Santa Fe (505-982-9301 or 800-732-6881) is a non-profit organization specializing in educational tours that include excursions to archaeological sites, lectures in Georgia O'Keeffe country, and visits to the homes and studios of local artists.

Nambe Pueblo Tours (505-820-1340 or 800-946-2623) offers tours led by local Indians of some of the pueblos north of Santa Fe (including Taos Pueblo) and Bandelier National Monument. They'll even take you to a traditional pueblo feast, complete with traditional dances and storytelling.

Aboot About (505-988-2774) will take you to places in and near the Santa Fe Plaza that are reputed to be haunted. Reservations are required. (The 1997 rate was $10 for adults.) In winter, dinner or dessert parties with ghost stories told by the fire are available. For a taste of the Santa Fe region circa 1890, *Santa Fe Southern* (505-989-8600 or 888-989-8600) offers a ride aboard a passenger train to Lamy, 25 miles to the southeast. You can have lunch there at the historic Legal Tender restaurant or walk off into the peaceful landscape with your own picnic. The train departs from Santa Fe every Tuesday, Thursday and Saturday at 10:30 a.m. at the Santa Fe Railyards, six blocks southwest of the plaza. The 1997 fare for adults was $21; $16 for children 7–13 and seniors 60 and over; $5 for children 3–6 and children under 3 are free.

Taos

Grayline Tours (505-983-9491) in Santa Fe makes round-trip tours to Taos daily in the summer ($55 per person). Highlights include a ride on the High Road to Taos and a stop at Taos Pueblo. *Faust's Transportation* (505-758-3410) provides afternoon tours of Taos with stops at museums, shops, Taos Pueblo and the Rio Grande Gorge Bridge (the 1997 ticket price was $20 for adults). *Pride of Taos* (505-758-8340) offers a 2.5-hour trolley tour of Taos once a day for $20 per person (1997 rate).

For foot tours of Taos, try *Arsenio Cordova's Taos Walking Tours* (505-758-4020). Cordova is a sixth-generation Taoseño with a wealth of information on the history of the Taos region. From May through September, he offers one tour daily. During the rest of the year, appointments must be made in advance. The price in 1997 was $10 per person. For art lovers, there's *Artours* (505-758-4246 or 800-582-9700), headed by Marcia Winter. Winter's great-grandfather was O.E. Berninghaus, one of the founding members of the Taos art colony. She specializes in small, customized tours of art museums, artists' studios and private collections.

HANDICAPPED SERVICES

To obtain a copy of a booklet that identifies handicap facilities, call 505-827-6329 or 505-827-6465 or write the *Governor's Committee on the Concerns of the Handicapped*, 491 Old Santa Fe Trail, Lamy Building, Room 117, Santa Fe, NM 87501. For further information about handicapped issues in Santa Fe, call the non profit group *New Vistas* (800-737-0330) or write *City of Santa Fe, Community Services Division*, P.O. Box 909, Santa Fe, NM, 87504. Out-of-state handicapped visitors can obtain a temporary placard for handicapped parking by calling the *New Mexico Motor Vehicle Division* at 505-827-4636. *Capital City Cab Co.* (505-438-0000) offers disabled people a 75-percent discount on fares with a coupon available from City Hall. You must have proof of American Disabilities Act qualification to receive a 21-day visitors pass. Please call 505-438-1463 for more information on pass discounts. Your best bet for information on handicapped-accessible facilities and parking in Taos is the *Taos County Chamber of Commerce* (800-732-TAOS).

HOSPITALS

<u>Española</u>

Española Hospital 505-753-7111; 1010 Spruce St.

<u>Los Alamos</u>

Los Alamos Medical Center 505-662-4201; 3917 West Rd.

<u>Santa Fe</u>

St. Vincent Hospital 505-983-3361; 455 St. Michael's Dr.

<u>Taos</u>

Holy Cross Hospital 505-758-8883; 630 Paseo del Pueblo Sur.

LATE NIGHT FOOD AND FUEL

If the munchies hit or your fuel gauge drops perilously low in the wee hours, there are places you can go. Santa Fe in particular has an abundance of convenience stores, restaurants and gas stations that stay open 24 hours a day.

CONVENIENCE STORES

Allsup's, 3000 Cerrillos Rd., Santa Fe.
Allsup's, 1899 St. Michaels Dr., Santa Fe.
Allsup's, S. Santa Fe Rd., Taos.

GAS STATIONS

Allsup's, S. Santa Fe Rd., Taos.
Giant Service Station, St. Francis Drive at Sawmill Rd., Santa Fe.
Santa Fe Chevron Food Mart, 3354 Cerrillos Rd., Santa Fe.

RESTAURANTS

Carrows, 505-471-7856, 1718 St. Michael's Dr., Santa Fe.
Denny's, 505-471-2152, 3004 Cerrillos Rd., Santa Fe.
Dunkin' Donuts, 505-988-2090, 1085 S. St. Francis Dr., Santa Fe.
The Kettle, 505-473-5840, 4250 Cerrillos Rd. at Villa Linda Mall, Santa Fe.

MEDIA

MAGAZINES AND NEWSPAPERS

Albuquerque Journal North (505-988-8881 or 800-641-3451; 328 Galisteo St., Santa Fe, NM 87501). A statewide, daily morning newspaper that includes a "Journal North" section published Tuesday through Saturday and distributed in northern New Mexico.

The New Mexican (505-983-3303; 202 E. Marcy St., Santa Fe, NM 87501). A general-interest daily distributed in northern New Mexico.

New Mexico Magazine (505-827-7447; Joseph M. Montoya Building, 1100 St. Francis Dr., Santa Fe, NM 87501). A general-interest monthly published by state government, covering New Mexico culture, history and travel.

Sangre de Cristo Chronicle (505-377-2358; Drawer I, Angel Fire, NM 87710). A news weekly covering Taos, Angel Fire, Red River and Eagle Nest.

The Santa Fe Reporter (505-988-5541; 132 E. Marcy St., Santa Fe, NM 87501). A general-interest weekly published each Wednesday and distributed free of charge throughout Santa Fe and vicinity.

Santa Fe Sun (505-989-8381; 1807 2nd St., Santa Fe, NM 87501). A community-oriented monthly that focuses on grassroots activism, local news and feature stories, and New Age issues.

Santa Fean Magazine (505-983-8914; 1440-A St. Francis Dr., Santa Fe, NM 87501). A monthly arts-oriented publication.

The Santa Fe Reporter *on*
E. Marcy St.

Murrae Haynes

Taos Magazine (505-758-5404; P.O. Box 1380, Taos, NM 87571). An arts magazine published eight times a year, in January, March, May, July, August, September, October and November.

Taos News (505-758-2241; 120 Camino De La Placita, Taos, NM 87571). A
weekly newspaper covering local news and human interest. Comes out
every Thursday.

THE Magazine (505-982-5785; 520 Franklin Ave., Santa Fe, NM 87501). A
monthly magazine of the arts with regional, national and international per-
spectives.

RADIO STATIONS

KBOM-FM 106.7 (505-471-1067) Santa Fe; oldies.
KDCE-AM 950 (505-753-8131) Española; Spanish.
KKIT-AM 1340 (505-758-2231) Taos; news, sports, weather, music.
KNYN-FM 95.5 (505-982-5696) Santa Fe; country and western.
KTAO-FM 101.5 (505-758-8882) Taos; adult rock.
KVSF-AM 1260 (505-982-2666) Santa Fe; all news, talk.

TELEVISION STATIONS

KASA FOX TV Channel 2 (505-982-2422) Santa Fe; old movies and sitcoms.
KCHF TV Channel 11 (505-473-1111) Santa Fe; religious.

The major television stations are located in Albuquerque.

KNME TV Channel 5 (505-242-5555) Albuquerque; Public.
KOAT TV Channel 7 (505-884-7777) Albuquerque; ABC affiliate.
KOB TV Channel 4 (505-243-4411) Albuquerque; NBC affiliate.
KRQE TV Channel 13 (505-243-2285) Albuquerque; CBS affiliate.

REAL ESTATE

If owning a home in the Land of Enchantment sounds like a dream come true, then you might be interested in a little housing information.

If you're shopping for real estate in the Santa Fe or Taos areas, you can get information in a variety of ways. For a list of Realtors, consult the Yellow Pages or contact the chambers of commerce. The *Santa Fe County Chamber of Commerce* (505-983-7317) is located at 510 N. Guadalupe, Santa Fe, NM 87501. The mailing address for the *Taos County Chamber of Commerce* (505-758-3873 or 800-732-8267) is P.O. Drawer I, Taos, NM 87571. Both organizations will send lists of their Realtor members.

If you're thinking about buying property here, it's a good idea to study local zoning laws, building permits, restrictive covenants and so forth. A good source of information is a small book titled *Understanding Santa Fe Real Estate* by Karen Walker, available at most Santa Fe bookstores or from *Ancient City Press* (505-982-8195; 517 Alarid, Santa Fe, NM 87501). For phone numbers to city halls and county offices, see "Area Codes" in this chapter.

Another way of getting real estate information is to follow the market in the newspapers (see "Media" in this chapter. Or pick up a copy of the *Santa Fe Real Estate Weekly.* It includes useful information on real estate prices and trends and is free at news stands throughout the city. You could also try any of the various periodicals published by realty agencies. *Homes and Land of Santa Fe and Northern New Mexico,* a free monthly publication that provides up-to-date information on the housing market, is distributed monthly at various shops around town. You can order a copy by calling 505-982-2210 or 800-277-7800, or by writing 1600 Capitol Circle SW, Tallahassee, FL 32310. Please specify which area of New Mexico interests you. Another homebuyers' guide is *The Santa Fe Real Estate Source* from Santa Fe Properties (505-982-4466 or 800-374-2931; 1000 Paseo de Peralta, Santa Fe, NM 87501). Similar publications in Taos can be obtained by calling the following realty agencies: *Coldwell Banker* (505-758-8673 or 800-829-8673), *Prudential-Schantz Realty of Taos* (505-758-1924) or *Century 21* (505-758-0080; 800-336-4826). For further information on the Taos real estate market, call the *Taos County Board of Realtors* (505-758-7511).

ROAD SERVICES

Here is a listing of some 24-hour emergency road services in the Santa Fe–Taos region.

Santa Fe

A-1 Towing   505-983-1616

A-Jack Towing   505-438-6042
Flores Wrecker Service   5050-471-5271 or 800-406-5271 (outside Santa Fe)

Taos
AA-1 Wrecker Service   505-758-8984
Vigil's Towing   505-758-3793

Española
Holmes Wrecker Service   505-753-3460
Lujan's Towing   505-753-0483

Los Alamos
Knecht Automotive   505-662-9743
RPM Automotive Towing   505-662-7721

IF TIME IS SHORT

The more time you spend in New Mexico, the more you will want to see. If your time is limited, however, you won't want to miss these attractions. The suggestions here are but a few personal favorites, each with its own distinctive flavor. If you must make your visit brief, try to come back soon and create your own list of favorites.

LODGING

Santa Fe

El Rey Inn (505-982-1931; 1862 Cerrillos Rd., Santa Fe). An oasis on the roadside, very comfortable and very reasonable.

Inn of the Animal Tracks (505-988-1546; 707 Paseo de Peralta, Santa Fe). Cozy and whimsical, the friendly owners create a warm, welcoming atmosphere.

Water Street Inn (505-984-1193; 427 W. Water St., Santa Fe). Ultimate luxury at an intimate getaway.

Taos

Casa Europa (505-758-9798; 840 Upper Ranchitos Rd., Taos). The best in contemporary comfort in a centuries-old adobe.

Dobson House (505-776-5738; Arroyo Hondo). Unforgettable views in a solar "castle" on a hill overlooking the Rio Grande Gorge.

Old Taos Guesthouse (505-758-5448; 1028 Witt Rd., Taos). Casual and relaxing, with owners who are superlative hosts.

Salsa del Salto (505-776-2422; north of Arroyo Seco on the Ski Valley Rd.). Spectacular fireplace, light and luxury in a true getaway.

CULTURAL ATTRACTIONS

Santa Fe

Georgia O'Keeffe Museum (505-995-0785; 313 Read St., Santa Fe). View the evolution of the artist's vision in an elegant setting even she would have approved.

Museum of International Folk Art (505-827-6350; 706 Camino Lejo, Santa Fe). You simply cannot visit Santa Fe and skip this rich, colorful treasure trove.

Santuario de Chimayó (505-351-4889; in Chimayó 26 miles NE of Santa Fe on NM 76). Nowhere can you get a better understanding of the spirit of northern New Mexico than at this holy shrine.

Taos

Harwood Museum (505-758-9826; 238 Ledoux St., Taos). Excellent overview of Taos School Modernist painters plus the spectacular new Agnes Martin wing.

Martinez Hacienda (505-758-0505; 2 miles S. of plaza on NM 240). The best place to get a feel for Spanish Colonial life is at this well-preserved hacienda.

Millicent Rogers Museum (505-758-2462; 4 m. n. of Taos on NM 522). The very best all-around collection of Native American jewelry, pottery, painting and textiles, including the Martinez' family collection of Maria's pottery.

RESTAURANTS

Santa Fe

Guadalupe Cafe (505-9882-9762; 422 Old Santa Fe Trail, Santa Fe). Excellent homestyle New Mexico cooking where the chile is good and hot and the portions are huge.

Il Piatto (505-984-1091; 95 W. Marcy St., Santa Fe). Sophisticated northern Italian that is beyond the best.

Rancho de Chimayó (505-351-4444; around the bend from the Santuario de Chimayó). A beautiful renovated 1880s ranch house that lives and breathes the traditions of northern New Mexico. A must for first-time visitors.

SantaCafe (505-984-1788; 231 Washington Ave., Santa Fe). The perfect place for a splurge, where cooking is the highest form of art.

Taos.

The Apple Tree (505-758-1900; 123 Bent St., Taos). All-time, favorite classic New Mexico dining in a country inn atmosphere, lovely patio, dishes from wild mushroom pate to tiger shrimp quesadillas to duck fajitas.

The Bavarian (505-770-0450; Taos Ski Valley). Re-creation of Alpine ski lodge serving authentic German food and the finest imported beer. Very romantic and you can ski in.

Cafe Fresen Bakery & Gourmet Market (505-776-2969; 482 Hwy. 150, Arroyo Seco). Superlative sandwiches and baked goods on the way to the Ski Valley, rustic atmosphere.

Orlando's New Mexican Cafe (505-751-1450; 1.8 m. north of the plaza). The place for authentic, wholesome, fresh native New Mexican lunch and dinner, served in a delightful Mexican folk art setting.

Trading Post Cafe (505-758-5089; Ranchos de Taos). If there were such a thing as a perfect restaurant, this could be the one. Wide choice of pasta, fresh fish, roasts and wines

RECREATION

To relax:

Ojo Caliente Hot Springs (505-583-2233; Ojo Caliente). With four kinds of mineral waters and a variety of heated pools, this is the place to soak and unwind.

Ten Thousand Waves (505-982-9304; Ski Basin Rd., Santa Fe). Pamper yourself in this spectacular Japanese spa with private tubs overlooking the city.

For adventure:

Bandelier National Monument (505-672-3861; 46 m. w. of Santa Fe). Hike and climb amidst cliff dwellings and view village ruins and ceremonial *kivas* through Frijoles Canyon.

Rafting the Rio Grande Gorge, specifically, the Taos Box, (see Chapter Eight, *Recreation*) can be an unforgettable white water adventure.

Glossary

For the most part, Spanish pronunciation is phonetic. That is, it sounds the way it looks with a few exceptions: *ll* sounds like "yuh"; *j* sounds like "h"; *qu* sounds like "k," and *ñ* sounds like "ny." There are also a few tricky rules — for example, double *r*'s are trilled and *d* is often pronounced "th" — but we'll leave these details for Spanish classes. Following, then, are reasonable pronunciations and short definitions for Spanish words (and a few other terms) that are commonly used in the Santa Fe–Taos area.

acequia (Ah-SEH-kee-ya) — irrigation ditch.

Anasazi (An-a-SAH-zee) — Navajo word meaning "ancient strangers," used to refer to the peoples who inhabited such places as Chaco Canyon, Mesa Verde and Bandelier National Monument from 900–1300 A.D.

arroyo (a-ROY-oh) — dry gully or streambed.

arroz (a-ROSS) — rice.

banco (BONK-oh) — adobe bench, usually an extension of an adobe wall.

bulto (BOOL-toh) — traditional Hispanic, three-dimensional carving of a saint.

burrito (Boo-REE-toh) — flour tortilla usually wrapped around a filling of beans, meat, cheese and sauce.

canales (ka-NAL-ess) — gutters, rainspouts.

cantina (kan-TEE-na) — saloon or barroom.

capirotada (ka-pi-ro-TA-da) — bread pudding.

carne (KAR-ne) — meat.

carne adovada (KAR-ne ah-do-VA-da) — meat chunks (usually pork) marinated in red chile sauce.

carne asada (KAR-ne ah-SA-da) — roast beef.

carreta (ka-RET-ah) — wagon.

casita (ka-SEE-ta) — cottage, one-room guest house.

chile, or *chili* (CHEE-leh) — sauce made from either red or green chile peppers that is used for seasoning most foods in northern New Mexico.

chile relleno (CHEE-leh re-YEH-no) — crisp, batter-fried green chile pepper stuffed with chicken and/or cheese.

chorizo (cho-REE-so) — spicy Mexican sausage.

con queso (cone KEH-so) — with cheese.

concha (KON-cha) — belt of inscribed silver plates originally made by the Navajo Indians.

corbel (Kor-BELL) — wooden beam support, usually ornately carved.

chimenea (Chee-me-NEH-ya) — chimney.

curandera (Coor-an-DEH-ra) — female Hispanic healer who uses a combination of herbal and other folk remedies.

empanada (em-pa-NAH-da) — fried pie stuffed with seasoned, chopped meat and vegetables or fruit, then sealed and deep fried. In northern New Mexico often filled with pinon nuts, currants, spices and wine.

enchilada (en-chi-LA-da) — flour tortilla filled with cheese, chicken or meat and covered with red or green chile.

fajitas (fa-HEE-tas) — small strips of highly seasoned, charbroiled meat eaten in a rolled tortilla with guacamole and sour cream.

farolito (far-oh-LEE-toh) — paper bag containing a glowing candle, often displayed in rows around Christmastime to symbolize the arrival of the Christ Child.

flan (flan) — caramel custard covered with burnt-sugar syrup, a traditional northern New Mexican dessert.

fry bread (not "fried bread") — *sopaipillas* made by the Pueblo Indians.

guacamole (gwok-a-MOLE-eh) — a thick sauce or paste made with a mix of mashed avocados and salsa.

hacienda (AH-see-EN-da) — a large estate, dwelling or plantation.

horno (OR-no) — beehive-shaped outdoor oven for the making of bread, originally brought from Spain.

huevos (WEH-vose) — eggs.

huevos rancheros (WEH-vose ran-CHEH-ros) — fried eggs with red chile sauce, cheese and lettuce.

jalapeño (HALL-a-PEN-yoh) — small hot pepper.

kachina doll (ka-CHEE-na) — a small wooden doll representing a Hopi spirit, usually carved from cottonwood.

kiva (KEE-va) — circular underground chamber used by the Pueblo Indians for ceremonial and other purposes.

kiva fireplace — traditional adobe fireplace, usually small, beehive-shaped and placed in a corner.

latillas (la-TEE-ahs) — network of thin wooden strips placed over beams or vigas just beneath the roof.

luminaria (loo-mi-NA-ree-ah) — hot, smoky bonfire made of pitchy pirlon pine to celebrate the Christmas season.

nachos (NA-chos) — tortilla chips covered with a mix of beans, cheese and chile, baked and served as hors d'oeuvres.

natillas (na-TEE-ahs) — vanilla custard, a traditional northern New Mexican dessert.

nicho (NEE-cho) — recessed niche in an adobe wall for holding a statue or other ornament.

panocha (pan-OH-cha) — wheat flour pudding.

placita (pla-SEE-ta) — patio.

pollo (PO-yo) — chicken.

portal (por-TALL) — covered patio or sidewalk with supports and fixed roof.

posada (po-SA-da) — resting place or inn.

posole (po-SOLE-eh) — a hominy-like corn stew.

pueblo (PWEB-loh) — a Native American communal village of the Southwest consisting of multi-tiered adobe structures with flat roofs around a central plaza.

quesadillas (KEH-sa-DEE-yas) — lightly grilled tortillas stuffed with chicken, beef or beans.

reredo (reh-REH-doh) — carved altar screen for church.

retablo (reh-TAB-loh) — traditional Hispanic painting of a saint on a wooden plaque.

ristra (REES-tra) — string of dried red chiles, often hung on front porches.

salsa (SAL-sa) — traditional northern New Mexican hot sauce composed of tomatoes, onions, peppers and spices.

santero (San-TEH-roh) — artist who depicts saints.

santo (SAN-toh) — a painted or carved representation of a saint.

sopaipilla (so-pie-PEE-ya) — Spanish popover. These "little pillows" puff up when fried, providing convenient hollows to fill with honey or butter.

taco (TA-koh) — folded corn tortilla usually filled with beans, meat, cheese, tomato and lettuce.

tamale (ta-MAL-eh) — corn meal stuffed with chicken or pork and red chile, wrapped in corn husks and steamed.

tapas (TAP-ahs) — appetizers.

tortilla (tor-TEE-ya) — thin pancake made of corn meal or wheat flour.

tostados (tos-TA-dos) — corn tortillas quartered and fried until crisp, usually eaten as hors d'oeuvres.

trastero (tras-TER-oh) — wooden, free-standing closet or chest of drawers dating from the 17th century; usually ornately carved.

vigas (VEE-gas) — heavy ceiling beams usually made of rough-hewn treetrunks, traditional in Southwest architecture.

zaguan (zag-WAN) — long, covered porch.

Index

LODGING BY PRICE

Lodging Price Codes
Inexpensive: Up to $65
Moderate: $65 to $100
Expensive: $100 to $150
Very Expensive: Over $150

RESTAURANTS BY PRICE

RESTAURANTS BY CUISINE

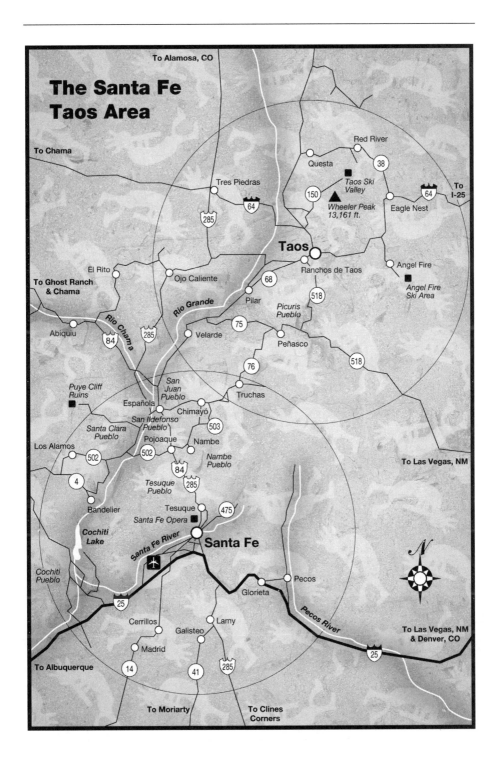

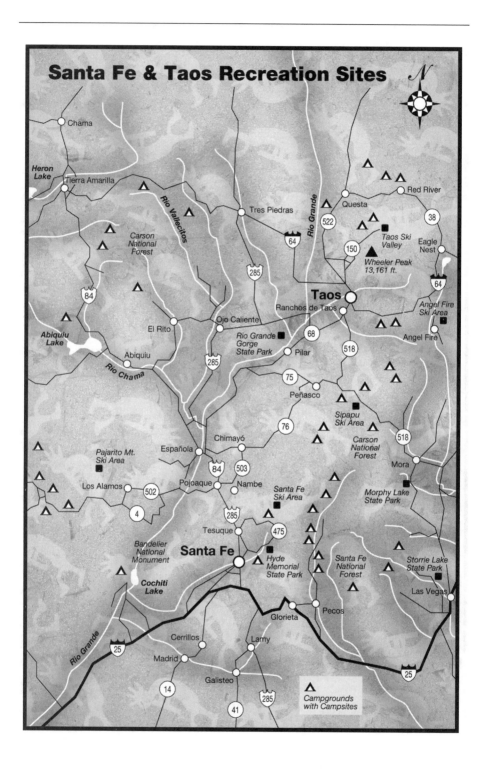

Santa Fe & Taos Recreation Sites

Chama

Heron Lake

Tierra Amarilla

Rio Vallecitos

Carson National Forest

Tres Piedras

Rio Grande

64

285

84

El Rito

Ojo Caliente

Abiquiu Lake

Abiquiu

Rio Chama

285

522

Questa

Red River

38

Taos Ski Valley

150

Wheeler Peak 13,161 ft.

Eagle Nest

Angel Fire Ski Area

64

Angel Fire

Taos

Ranchos de Taos

Rio Grande Gorge State Park

68

Pilar

75

Peñasco

518

76

Sipapu Ski Area

Carson National Forest

518

Mora

Pajarito Mt. Ski Area

Española

Chimayó

84

503

Los Alamos

502

Pojoaque

Nambe

4

Santa Fe Ski Area

Morphy Lake State Park

285

Tesuque

475

Santa Fe

Hyde Memorial State Park

Bandelier National Monument

Cochiti Lake

Santa Fe National Forest

Storrie Lake State Park

Las Vegas

Pecos

Glorieta

Rio Grande

25

Cerrillos

Lamy

Madrid

Galisteo

14

41

285

25

Campgrounds with Campsites

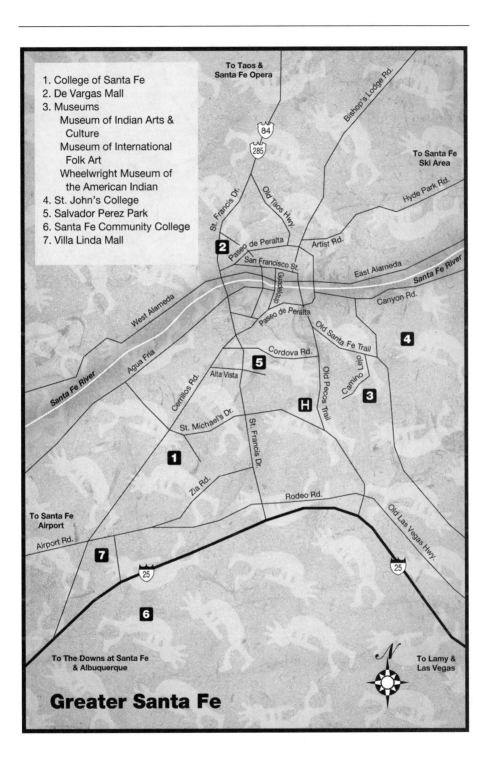

1. College of Santa Fe
2. De Vargas Mall
3. Museums
   Museum of Indian Arts &
   Culture
   Museum of International
   Folk Art
   Wheelwright Museum of
   the American Indian
4. St. John's College
5. Salvador Perez Park
6. Santa Fe Community College
7. Villa Linda Mall

To Taos &
Santa Fe Opera

Bishop's Lodge Rd.

To Santa Fe
Ski Area

Hyde Park Rd.

84

285

St. Francis Dr.

Old Taos Hwy.

Artist Rd.

2

Paseo de Peralta

San Francisco St.

East Alameda

Santa Fe River

Guadaloup

Canyon Rd.

West Alameda

Paseo de Peralta

Old Santa Fe Trail

4

Agua Fria

Cordova Rd.

5

Old Camino

3

Santa Fe River

Cerrillos Rd.

Alta Vista

H

Camino

St. Michael's Dr.

St. Francis Dr.

Old Pecos Trail

1

Zia Rd.

Rodeo Rd.

Old Las Vegas Hwy.

To Santa Fe
Airport

Airport Rd.

7

25

25

6

To The Downs at Santa Fe
& Albuquerque

N

To Lamy &
Las Vegas

Greater Santa Fe

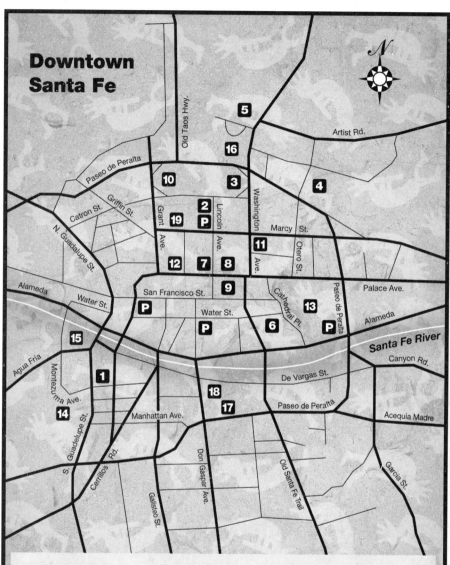

Downtown
Santa Fe

N

Old Taos Hwy.

Artist Rd.

Paseo de Peralta

Griffin St.

Catron St.

N. Guadalupe St.

Grant Ave.

Lincoln Ave.

Washington Ave.

Marcy St.

Otero St.

Alameda

Water St.

San Francisco St.

Water St.

Cathedral Pl.

Palace Ave.

Paseo de Peralta

Alameda

Agua Fria

Montezuma Ave.

S. Guadalupe St.

Cerrillos Rd.

Manhattan Ave.

Galisteo St.

Don Gaspar Ave.

De Vargas St.

Paseo de Peralta

Old Santa Fe Trail

Acequia Madre

Garcia St.

Canyon Rd.

Santa Fe River

1. Chamber of Commerce
2. City Hall
3. Courthouse
4. Cross of the Martyrs
5. Fort Marcy Complex
6. Loretto Chapel
7. Museum of Fine Arts

8. Palace of the Governors
9. The Plaza
10. Post Office
11. Public Library
12. St. Francis Auditorium
13. St. Francis Cathedral

14. Sanbusco Market Center
15. Santuario de Guadalupe
16. Scottish Rite Temple
17. State Capitol
18. State Library
19. Sweeney Center

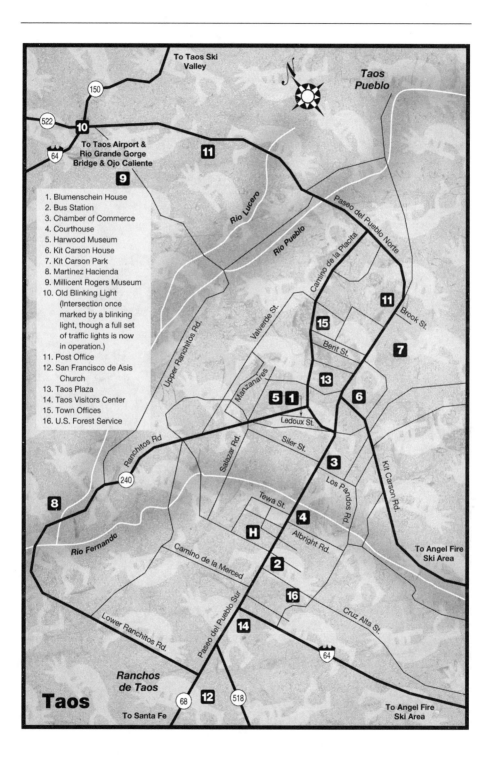

To Taos Ski Valley

Taos Pueblo

150

522

64

To Taos Airport &
Rio Grande Gorge
Bridge & Ojo Caliente

10

11

9

Rio Lucero

Rio Pueblo

Paseo del Pueblo Norte

Camino de la Placita

Brook St.

1. Blumenschein House
2. Bus Station
3. Chamber of Commerce
4. Courthouse
5. Harwood Museum
6. Kit Carson House
7. Kit Carson Park
8. Martinez Hacienda
9. Millicent Rogers Museum
10. Old Blinking Light
    (Intersection once
    marked by a blinking
    light, though a full set
    of traffic lights is now
    in operation.)
11. Post Office
12. San Francisco de Asis
    Church
13. Taos Plaza
14. Taos Visitors Center
15. Town Offices
16. U.S. Forest Service

Valverde St.

Manzanares

11

15

Bent St.

7

13

5 1

6

Ledoux St.

Upper Ranchitos Rd.

Salazar Rd.

Siler St.

3

Kit Carson Rd.

Los Pandos Rd.

Ranchitos Rd

240

Tewa St.

4

8

H

Albright Rd.

2

To Angel Fire
Ski Area

Rio Fernando

Camino de la Merced

16

Cruz Alta St.

Lower Ranchitos Rd.

Paseo del Pueblo Sur

14

64

Ranchos
de Taos

Taos

68

12

518

To Santa Fe

To Angel Fire
Ski Area

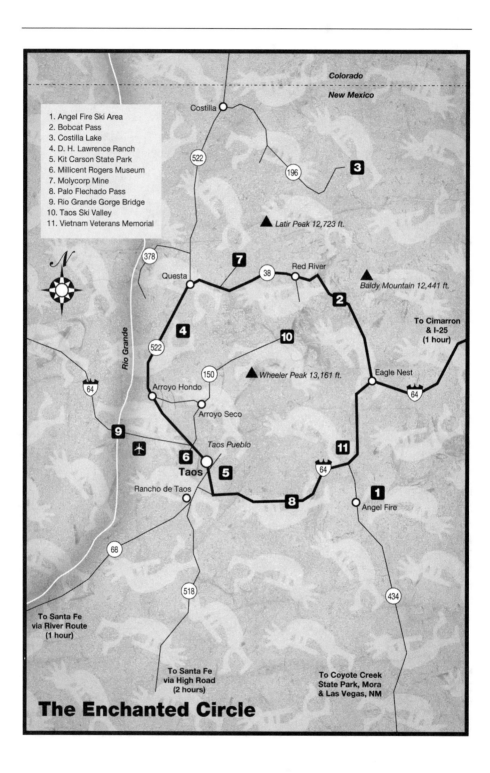

1. Angel Fire Ski Area
2. Bobcat Pass
3. Costilla Lake
4. D. H. Lawrence Ranch
5. Kit Carson State Park
6. Millicent Rogers Museum
7. Molycorp Mine
8. Palo Flechado Pass
9. Rio Grande Gorge Bridge
10. Taos Ski Valley
11. Vietnam Veterans Memorial

Colorado

New Mexico

Costilla

522

196

3

Latir Peak 12,723 ft.

378

Questa

7

38

Red River

Baldy Mountain 12,441 ft.

2

To Cimarron
& I-25
(1 hour)

4

522

10

150

Wheeler Peak 13,161 ft.

Eagle Nest

64

Rio Grande

Arroyo Hondo

Arroyo Seco

9

64

11

Taos Pueblo

6

Taos

5

64

1

Rancho de Taos

8

Angel Fire

68

518

434

To Santa Fe
via River Route
(1 hour)

To Santa Fe
via High Road
(2 hours)

To Coyote Creek
State Park, Mora
& Las Vegas, NM

The Enchanted Circle

About the Author

Photo by Katherine Bomboy; 1938 Dodge courtesy of Mark and Toni Barrow

Author and journalist Sharon Niederman has lived in northern New Mexico since 1980. Former Arts Editor of the *Santa Fe Reporter*, she has written and edited four previous books about the history, culture and cuisine of the region, including *A Quilt of Word: Women's Diaries, Letters & Original Accounts of Life in the Southwest, 1860-1960* (Johnson Books); *Hellish Relish: Sizzling Salsas and Devilish Dips from the Kitchens of New Mexico* (HarperCollins); *New Mexico Poetry Renaissance* (with Miriam Sagan)(Red Crane Books); *Living Treasures: Celebration of the Human Spirit/A Legacy of New Mexico* (with Karen Nilsson Brandt)(Western Edge). She has twice received the Border Regional Library Association Award for literary excellence and enrichment of the cultural heritage of the Southwest. She was the subject of a PBS KNME-TV5 *Colores!* documentary on western women's history. She also wrote the film script for the Pleasant Company's newest American Girl Doll, Josefina Montoya, 1824. Her articles and reviews appear frequently in publications such as *New Mexico Magazine, Cowboys & Indians, El Palacio, New Mexico, Stockman, Albuquerque Journal*, the *New Mexican, Mountain Living*, and *AAA's Journeys Magazine*. Her monthly dining review in *Crosswinds* is widely read. She is a member of Western Writers of America, New Mexico Press Women, Chuck Wagon CowBelles and is the archivist for the New Mexico Jewish Historical Society. She also teaches in the General Honors Program of the University of New Mexico in Albuquerque, where she now lives.